Visual Merchandising and Display

Seventh Edition

Martin M. Pegler

Anne Kong
The Fashion Institute
of Technology

FAIRCHILD BOOKS
NEW YORK · LONDON · OXFORD · NEW DELHI · SYDNEY

This book is dedicated to my sister Professor Mary Costantini, who passed away while I was revising this text.
She was an incredibly supportive sibling who encouraged me to pursue my passion for retail design and
store window display from an early age. I would not be the educator I am today without her guidance and
encouragement throughout the years. She taught beside me for over twenty years as an adjunct assistant
professor, and her students enjoyed her spontaneous nature. She was a gifted sculptor, a mother,
and a friend to many; I will always treasure memories of building spectacular exhibits
together with our students in the D Lobby at FIT.
Anne Kong

FAIRCHILD BOOKS
Bloomsbury Publishing Inc
1385 Broadway, New York, NY 10018, USA
50 Bedford Square, London, WC1B 3DP, UK
29 Earlsfort Terrace, Dublin 2, Ireland

BLOOMSBURY, FAIRCHILD BOOKS and the Fairchild Books logo are trademarks of
Bloomsbury Publishing Plc

Fifth edition published 2006
Sixth edition published 2012
This edition first published 2018
Reprinted 2019 (twice), 2020, 2021

Cover design: Eleanor Rose
Cover image © Bergdorf Goodman Window Display, New York, United States,
2014 © Eugene Gologursky/Stringer/Getty Images

Library of Congress Cataloging-in-Publication Data
Names: Pegler, Martin M., author. | Kong, Anne, author.
Title: Visual merchandising and display / Martin M. Pegler, Anne Kong.
Description: Seventh edition. | New York City : Fairchild Books, 2018. |
    Revised edition of Visual merchandising and display, c2012.
Identifiers: LCCN 2017031472 | ISBN 9781501315299 (paperback) | ISBN
    9781501315329 (PDF)
Subjects: LCSH: Display of merchandise. | BISAC: BUSINESS & ECONOMICS /
    Industries / Fashion & Textile Industry. | BUSINESS & ECONOMICS /
    Industries / Retailing. | DESIGN / Fashion.
Classification: LCC HF5845 .P364 2018 | DDC 659.1/57—dc23
LC record available at https://lccn.loc.gov/2017031472

ISBN: PB: 978-1-5013-1529-9
    ePDF: 978-1-5013-1532-9
    eBook: 978-1-5013-1531-2

Typeset by Lachina
Printed and bound in Great Britain

To find out more about our authors and books visit www.fairchildbooks.com
and sign up for our newsletter.

Contents

Extended Contents

Preface

There have been so many advances and changes in how we perform visual merchandising and create displays, and although I am "old school" and have been out of school for several years now, I have been fortunate to have a co-author who is "new school." She is thoroughly immersed in the ever-changing techniques and approaches to visual merchandising and display, and is actively employed in the industry while also educating the next generation of creative professionals. With much pleasure, I now turn you over to Anne Kong, an associate professor in the Visual Presentation & Exhibit Design Department at the Fashion Institute of Technology in New York City. Professor Kong has served as the chairperson of that department, created much of the BFA, and led all the special projects for the department. Professor Kong is also the recipient of the President's Award for Faculty Excellence. She is an innovative and excellent educator—much loved and admired by her students and greatly respected not only by her academic peers but by many in the Visual Merchandising industry.

We both agree however, that none of these modern wonders, digital devices, and innovative tools that are now available and are a vital part of the industry can take the place of the human mind and the creativity it can conceive. Nothing, as yet, can replace the thinking process, the internal search, and the hand-drawn scribbles, squiggles, and doodles that eventually morph into ideas that can be realized with the assistance of technology. With Anne Kong we welcome the future while holding on to the much valued "good old ways." Meet Anne Kong.

Martin M. Pegler

It is an honor and a privilege to collaborate as co-author with Martin M. Pegler. This book serves as an invaluable resource for anyone interested in learning more about retail design. *Visual Merchandising and Display 7th* focuses on retail design; however, the skills and information offered here are beneficial to those in related industries including architecture, communications, fashion merchandising, fine arts, graphic design, interior design, marketing, and packaging design.

This completely updated book serves as a complement to the original viewpoint. Over 400 new images support the written content as visually inspiring reference. Designed to guide students, designers, and retailers on the fundamentals of retail design, this book examines behind the scenes in a window display—to the morning after the store opening. It defines the practical applications of what few people know or consider in terms of what goes into making windows, stores, events, exhibits, and trade shows. The many former students, now distinguished industry professionals, are a testament that success in any business begins by knowing the applied or "hands-on" approach that begins in the trenches. In fact, merchandising magnates such as Ralph Lauren built their empires just this way.

How the process of show and sell will evolve is a question I pose to my students often. How do we shop? Why do we buy? As technology continues to enhance our lifestyles, the design of the physical store will evolve upwards with the heightened need for us humans to look, touch, and experience beautiful merchandise. The new paradigm of shopping is upon us, inspiring new ideas about store design, store experience, and placemaking. The retail world is ever-changing—new stores, brands, and shopping experiences are become more exciting as they find ways to immerse the shopper in the brand environment, integrate innovative store fixtures, and discover smart wayfinding means to engage the shopper. We hope that the insights you gain from this book serve as valuable reference for the vast opportunities in visual merchandising and display.

Anne Kong

NEW TO THIS EDITION

This new edition of *Visual Merchandising and Display* has been thoroughly updated to include the following:

- Eight new case studies throughout
- Extensively revised and updated images
- Updated content on lighting, fixtures, point-of-purchase displays, and interactive media reflecting the latest technology and practices
- Expanded sections on store planning including more information about CAD programs, floor plans, an planograms
- New section *Tools for Getting a Job* in Chapter 27 includes tips for creating your own website and using platforms like Behance to showcase your portfolio
- Updated and new *Go Green* boxes discuss current topics in sustainability and visual merchandising

INSTRUCTOR'S RESOURCES

Teaching resources include an Instructor's Guide, Test Bank, PowerPoint presentations, and a new Image Bank of key images from the text.

VISUAL MERCHANDISING AND DISPLAY STUDIO

Fairchild Books has a long history of excellence in textbook publishing for fashion education. Our new online STUDIOS are specially developed to complement this book with rich media ancillaries that students can adapt to their visual learning styles. *Visual Merchandising and Display* STUDIO features include online self-quizzes with scored results, personalized study tips and flashcards with terms/definitions, plus videos that bring chapter concepts to life, to help students master concepts and improve grades.

STUDIO access cards are offered free with new book purchases and also sold separately through www.fairchildbooks.com.

Acknowledgments

Martin and I would like to especially thank these architects, designers and store planners who gave so graciously of their time and knowledge to provide us with the quotable quotes that add so much to the case studies scattered throughout the book. We sent them endless "questions" and relied on their patience, good will and erudite statements to provide you, the readers, with first-hand knowledge of how professionals approach design assignments. We thank and applaud—in alphabetical order: Giorgio Borruso of Giorgio Borruso Design, Marina del Ray, California (Carlo Pazolini, London and WithMe, Chicago); Pam Flanagan of Brinkworth, London (All Saints, Glasgow, Scotland); GHA Design of Montreal, QUE. Canada, for Aeropostale, New York; Ken Nisch of JGA, Southfield, Michigan (McCormick World of Flavors, Baltimore Harbor, Maryland and Timberland Exhibit Booth, Salt Lake City, Utah); Roundhouse Portland Oregon, Adidas NBA's All-Star Weekend Concept Store); Bruce E. Teitelbaum, Ellen Friedman, Eric Williams, of RPG, New York City (Burt's Bees, Furminator, Sugarpova, The Glossary); Michelle Alandete, Starbucks Coffee Company, Global Design and Innovation, Janet Wardley of Harvey Nichols, London (Christmas 2015); Steve Weirsema, West Office Exhibition Design for Robert Mondavi and the National Museum of Toys and Miniatures; Jerzy Wodniak and Pawel Garus of Mode:Lina of Poznan, Poland (Clae Pop Up Shop, Poznan, Poland); and the owners of K'OOK in Wormerveer, The Netherlands—Anne van der Spoel and Karen Schoen. And let us not forget to thank profusely the photographers for permitting us to use their artistry to illuminate our stories; Aaron Dougherty, West Office Exhibition Design; Alberto Ferrerro of Milan for Carlo Pazolini; Benny Chan for WithMe; Lazlo Regos Photography, Farmington Hills, Michigan for McCormick World of Flavor; Mark Steele Photography for

Timberland Exhibit; Louise Melchior of Brinkworth for All Saints Richard Caden for RDI; Matt Dutile, Roundhouse Ross J. Morante, Edwin F. Hermoso, Rustan's and Getty Images for Harvey Nichols Christmas windows; and the countless images provided by Windows Wear Pro.

We are also indebted to other architects and designers and design firms and manufacturers for use of the images they provided to illustrate what we hope will clarify for the readers the printed information on these pages. Architectural Systems; Stephan.Anderson, ALU; Michael Katok, Bernstein Display; Blocher Blocher Partners, Stuttgart, Germany; Burdifilek, Toronto, Canada; Caulder Moore, Kew, London, United Kingdom; Dalziel & Pow, London, United Kingdom; Bill Goddu, Fleetwood Fixtures; Wolfgang Gruschwitz GmbH, Munich, Germany; Jared Schiffman, Perch Interactive; JPMA Global Incorporated, Plajer and Franz, Berlin, Germany; Ruscio Studios, Montreal, Canada; Brad Stewart, Hera Lighting; Brian Kampe, Texture Plus. Also, a very special thanks to the, visual merchandisers, display persons and product presenters who add theater to retailing every day all around the world. Thank you for all your efforts and generosity; Dash Nagel, PAVE and Globalshop; Tom Bebee, Hickey Freedman; Elena R. Tantoco, Rustan's: Carlos Aires at Marketing Jazz, Madrid, Spain; Karina Barhumi of Lima, Peru; Lucy Anne Bouman of Sight Geist, New York, New York; Polar Buranasatit of New York, New York; Keith Dillion of Robert Ellis, Josh Tierney, Gradient and Just One LA in Los Angeles, California; Etalage B Display, Montreal, Canada; Ana Fernandes of The Bay, Toronto, Canada; Victor Johnson of White House/Black Market and Ann Taylor, New York, New York; Amy Meadows of Chicago, Illinois; Peter Rank of Deko Rank, Munich, Germany; Potten & Pannen, Stanek Kitchen Aid Concept Store & Gourmet, Czech Republic. Rustan's Department Store, Phillipines; Anna Le, Shoes of Prey; Stacy Suvino of Miss Jackson, Tulsa, Oklahoma; Janet Wardley of Harvey Nichols, London, United Kingdom; and the thousands of display people and "window trimmers" too numerous to mention who make window shopping a delight and a pleasure. If we have omitted your name—we are sorry but please remember that we appreciate your contributions to our particular art form.

My love to all those people who are real and make my life real and fulfilled—to Suzan, my wife, and to my children, Karen, Jess, Lysa, John, Risa, and Adam. And here is to the next generation—Brian, Amanda, Mike, Jake, Sam, Ben, Marley, and Heather.

Martin M. Pegler

Thank you to my faculty colleagues at Fashion Institute of Technology who were incredibly supportive, Professor Marianne Klimchuk, Packaging Design Chair; Professor Craig Berger, VPED Chair; Professor Glenn Sokoli, Creative Director Global Visual Group; and Professor Joshua Benghiat, Lighting Designer. I appreciate the countless emails, proofreading and advice. Thank you to the team at RPG, New York for their time and support of this text, Bruce E. Teitelbaum, Ellen Friedman, Eric Williams, and Samantha Freistat.

Thank you to my parents Victor and Bernice who nurtured me to become a "maker" and create things by hand. To my design partner and husband David, my kids Abby, Hannah and David who supported and encouraged me—each of you inspire me every day.

Anne Kong

Bloomsbury Publishing wishes to thank the reviewers for their insights and suggestions for this edition: J. Baker, London College of Fashion (United Kingdom); Amber M. Chatelain, Art Institute of Tennessee, Nashville; Nancy Lyons, South Dakota State University; Carol J. Salusso, Washington State University; and Emilia Valle, Art Institute of Seattle.

The Publisher also wishes to gratefully acknowledge and thank the editorial team involved in the publication of this book:

Former Senior Acquisitions Editor: Amanda Breccia
Development Editor: Amy Butler
Art Development Editor: Edie Weinberg
Editorial Assistant: Bridget MacAvoy
Production Manager: Claire Cooper
Project Manager: Morgan McClelland, Lachina

PART ONE

Getting Started—Visual Merchandising and Display Basics

Visual merchandising is no longer just a matter of making merchandise look attractive for the customer. It is the actual selling of merchandise through a visual medium. Visual merchandising is a way for stores to say, "This is who we are and what we stand for." An understanding of basic visual merchandising concepts and theory is essential to the effective presentation of a store and its merchandise to the customer. Part One of this text is devoted to those merchandising "basics."

Chapter 1 introduces visual merchandising and display and, for the first of many times throughout the text, discusses the important concept of store image, the retail experience, customer engagement and the challenges of omnichannel shopping. The use of color and texture to add excitement to visual presentations is explored in Chapter 2.

Artistic principles, such as line, balance, contrast, and rhythm, which are central to any visual medium, are applied to visual merchandising and display in Chapter 3. Proper lighting is vital to selling, both inside and outside the store. Light directs customers' eyes to the merchandise and invites them to buy. Chapter 4 discusses the various types of light sources available and how they are used in store merchandising and display.

From the start of writing a design brief to final implementation of a display, Chapter 5 covers the phases of the design process.

Chapter One
Why Do We Display?

A colorful cut-out display at Harvey Nichols, London, United Kingdom. Copyright WindowsWear PRO http://pro.windowswear.com contact@ windowswear.com 1.646.827.2288

AFTER YOU HAVE READED THIS CHAPTER,
YOU WILL BE ABLE TO DISCUSS

- ✦ the definition of visual merchandising
- ✦ the concept of store image and its relationship to visual merchandising and display
- ✦ the purposes of visual merchandising
- ✦ how omnichannel retailing has influenced display
- ✦ new strategies for customer engagement

We show in order to sell. Display or **visual merchandising** is showing merchandise and concepts at their very best, with the end purpose of making a sale. We may not actually sell the object displayed or the idea promoted, but we do attempt to convince the viewer of the value of the object, the store promoting the object, or the organization behind the concept. Although a cash register may not ring because of a particular display, that display should make an impression on the viewer that will affect future sales.

The display person used to be the purveyor of dreams and fantasies, presenting merchandise in settings that stirred the imagination and promoted fantastic flights to unattainable heights. Today's visual merchandiser, however, sells "aspirations." Today's shopper can be whatever he or she wants to be by simply wearing certain lifestyle brands that have a built-in status. The visual merchandiser dresses a mannequin in slim-fitting jeans, flashes the lights, adds the lifestyle graphic depicting the fashionable crowd, and reinforces the image of sexuality and devastating attractiveness that is part of the prominent brand. Wearing Brand X jeans, whether size 8 or 18, makes the wearer feel special. She imagines herself to be that slim, sensuous Kardashian she has seen on social media, surrounded by crowds of admirers. She feels special when she is wearing her slim-fitting jeans.

Today's mannequin represents any shopper on the other side of the glass; it may have a flawless figure, abstract facial features, an egg head, or a branded neck cap, but it still prompts the customer to think, "That mannequin looks great, so why not me?" That's reality; that's selling! The visual merchandiser, therefore, presents more than the merchandise. He or she presents the image of who or what the shopper can be when using the merchandise displayed.

It has been said by presidents and vice presidents of large retail operations, and it has been uttered by experienced shoppers and consumers: There is very little difference between the merchandise sold in one store and that sold in another. Many department and specialty stores carry the same name brands—the same globally advertised lines seen

FIGURE 1.1 *Lights! Color! Line and Action! Theater! Razzle Dazzle!* That is what display is all about—and getting the shoppers' attention and drawing them in to the store. At Christmas time it takes all of the above plus more. *Harvey Nichols, London, United Kingdom. Photo: Heather Berrisford.*

on fashion blogs and in magazines. Often, the real difference is in the price of the merchandise being offered for sale.

Why, then, does an individual shop in Store A and pay more for the same item selling for less in Store B? Why does a shopper tote the shopping bag from Store C rather than an equally attractive bag from Store D? Why do shoppers cover themselves with garments branded with a store's name on pockets, patches, shoulders, and hips? It has to do with the **store image**! If everyone believes that people who shop in Store A are young, smart, sophisticated, clever, trendy, and fun to be with, then a shopper who buys clothes at that store can also be young, smart, sophisticated, and so on. The visual merchandiser reinforces that belief with merchandise displays, the types of mannequins shown, and the manner in which the mannequins are dressed, positioned, and lit. In this way, the visual merchandiser promotes the store's image and fashion trendiness. Often, the visual merchandiser is not selling any one piece of merchandise, but rather the idea that any purchase from that store will guarantee social success and the stamp of the "right" taste level. However, visual merchandising is still *selling*. We will return in later chapters to the concept of image and image projection in merchandise presentation. (See Figure 1.1.)

In addition to selling actual merchandise, displays can be used to introduce a new product, a fashion trend, or a new look or idea. The display may be the first three-dimensional representation of something the consumer has thus far seen only in ads or on the website. Displays can be used to educate the consumer concerning what the new item is, how it can be worn or used, and how it can be accessorized. Displays may also supply pertinent information such as the price, promotion, and other special features.

The visual merchandiser may create a display that stimulates, tantalizes, or arouses the shopper's curiosity to such a degree that he or she is "challenged" to enter the store and wander through it, even though the shopper is not motivated by the displayed product itself. This is still a victory. It gives the visual merchandiser and the merchant many more opportunities to sell that shopper once he or she is inside the store. To make a shopper a stopper and a "walk-in" rather than a "walk-by" is a commercial achievement. And always, as mentioned earlier, the purpose of visual merchandising is to promote the store image—to let people know what the

store is, where it stands on fashion trends, what one can expect inside it, to whom it appeals, its price range, and the caliber of its merchandise and merchandising.

The visual merchandiser always puts the store's best "face" forward. His or her duty is to bring shoppers into the store, while at the same time ensuring that the interior presentation is in keeping with what has been promised on the outside. (See Figure 1.2.)

It is important to remember that visual merchandising and display has always been a hands-on career. Whereas some jobs may be desk- or table-bound, visual display and merchandising has always been out on the floor, in the window, up a ladder, or down in the shop getting ready for the aforementioned activities. It has always been creative and interactive and has involved the person's hands, body, and brain to create something special or memorable. What did the display persons of decades ago do before

FIGURE 1.2 Up close the window is filled with eye-arresting decorative details that help set the look and create the mood for the featured garment. *"The Artist." Stacy Suvino, Director of Visuals for Miss Jackson, Tulsa, Oklahoma. Rachel Everett, visual artist.*

staple guns, Velcro, and hot glue? Pins, tacks, tape, and small nails worked—maybe not as well, but the display person managed. There have been many advances in the tools used today; most visual merchandising departments resemble design labs with the advances in technology. It's not unusual to find a vinyl cutting machine, a large-format printer, and several computers near the worktable and mannequin storage bins. Visual merchandising has progressed way beyond just the display of merchandise in windows and the store interior; it's grown 360 degrees to encompass the "total retail experience."

The Retail Experience

It is an exciting time to be part of the visual merchandising and display industry! More thought, energy, and imagination goes into designing retail spaces than ever before. The consumer no longer comes to the store to shop but rather is on a quest for new experiences, sparking the growth of what is termed "experience design." Shoppers empowered by technology and smartphones have changed the retail landscape. They are making up the rules, and retailers are listening—providing customers with the products they want, when they want it, at the price they are willing to pay.

Technology may have changed the strategy for getting products to consumers, but the job of the visual merchandiser and store designer has remained the same. We continue to innovate new ways to entertain customers and inspire them enough to post, tweet and Instagram about it. The impact of technology on retail has generated the phenomena of **omnichannel** retailing. "Omni," meaning all, and "channel," referencing the many retail mediums, merges an array of shopping experiences to reach consumers. Consumer preferences are reinventing the essence of shopping, as they choose to blend shopping channels either for fun or convenience, or to simplify their busy lives. Smartphones, computers, tablets, social media, email, television, direct mail catalogues, and call centers all afford consumers shopping opportunities. They may visit the retail store to try on the product and then return home to make their purchase online, possibly taking advantage of a value-based offering not found in the brick-and-mortar store.

Omnichannel shopping has increased the need for retailers to stay focused on what customers want, and data analytics are increasingly relied on to aid in this process. The crystal ball, or customer's "click," has presented new ways for retailers to track and learn about consumer behavior. This has spawned a new level of engagement and shifted the approach to visual merchandising and store design. Through observation we know more about consumer habits thanks to social media, websites, or eye-tracking devices within the store environment. Kiosks, digital scanners, and NFC (near field communication) technology allow consumers to find and pay for products more quickly while enabling the retailer to better predict consumer expectations. Retailers are leveraging this information by providing more energetic retail activities including additional space for food services, free Wi-Fi access, and tablets anchored to fixtures to support mobile app purchases during the brick-and-mortar store visit. Omni-retailing and social media have inspired new segments in the marketplace. There are smaller niche shopping environments designed to appeal to a targeted demographic, merchandise offerings that connect luxury goods with value-based items, and online stores establishing temporary or permanent brick-and-mortar store; these are all ways that retailers seek to gain more traction. It is evident that retailers can no longer depend solely on brand loyalty and expect the customer to return—each day is a new day, and satisfying each customer is the first goal on the retail home front.

Consumer Engagement

In the present economic climate, designers, firms, and retailers recognize that forging an emotional bond with consumers—much like a good friendship—is one key strategy in keeping the relationship steady. The following twelve retail strategies are energizing and humanizing the retail landscape:

◆ **Customer-Centric and Service-Oriented** American Girl set a standard by extending its brand, providing personal services for young customers and their dolls. It has partnered with leading NYC hotel brands and offers in-store amenities such as a doll hospital, a hair/nail salon where customers can have their ears pierced, and a café experience to have lunch or a birthday party. These activities not only promote repeat store visits; they forge a heritage and a long-term relationship with consumers.

- **Value Proposition** Provide services and features that are innovative and add value to your brand. Apple was first to inspire retailers to step up in-store customer services and offer educational programs with the "genius bar." The friendly band of Apple associates eased uncertainties about learning new technology and convinced users that the iPhone was as simple as touted in the company's Apple ad campaign. Small niceties go a long way, and add-on services are now "a given" consumer expectation. Retailers need to simplify the checkout process and adopt a friendly payment solution. The checkout experience should be as simple and engaging as the displays in the store; shoppers want to use mobile devices to shorten the wait.

- **Esteem and Aspiration** Promote product quality, transparency, and sustainability. Customers are forming emotional bonds with brands and businesses that align with their beliefs and rewarding them with their loyalty. Retailer Marks & Spencer leads by example through programs that keep employees engaged in social responsibility, sustainable business practices, and customers' health and well-being. Panera Cares stores feed thousands of hungry Americans each day, asking patrons to pay what they can afford. Panera Cares community cafes are designed to help raise awareness about the very serious and pervasive problem of food insecurity in our country. Timberland employees can receive forty annual paid service hours to support local environmental projects.

- **Sense of Community** Build kinship. SoulCycle brings consumers together in an atmosphere that motivates individuals, encourages teamwork, and nurtures community. Capital One Cafés, designed to feel more like a gathering space than a bank, often including public seating, private nooks, coffee bars, and more. Lululemon provides in-store yoga classes that instill a sense of connection to neighbors, friends, and likeminded community members. Comfortable customer-focused spaces are core to humanizing the new retail experience.

- **Personalization** Incorporate selling opportunities that are personalized; engage the consumer along every step of the shopping journey. Nordstrom's partnership with the online retailer Shoes of Prey invites consumers to design a custom pair of shoes in-store. Once seated at the elegant design station, the consumer can explore 170-plus swatches of materials and feel how the different shades and textures work together. A shoe stylist guides the customer through process, from choosing the style, heel height, and materials to deciding which size and special add-ons are perfect for the individual. (See Figure 1.3.) Nike, Converse, and Adidas all offer personalized services that enable consumers to customize their athletic footwear based on their sport, style, comfort, or endurance level.

- **Entertainment** Williams-Sonoma's center-of-the-store "island kitchen" inspires customers to experience and indulge in culinary arts via product demonstrations and hands-on opportunities. Shoppers of all ages can learn how to prepare exotic recipes and use work gadgets purchased in the store. House of Vans, a retail destination located underground in New York and London, entertains visitors with an art gallery, a

FIGURE 1.3 This glossy white table fitted with digital tablets invites customers to design their own shoes at Nordstrom's Shoes of Prey destination. Oversized flowers created from stilettos and flats sprout from the center and hover as shoppers choose their size, fit, and style. An adjacent wall with 170-plus fabric samples offers an opportunity to feel the textures and choose colors with the keen eye of a seasoned stylist on hand. *Shoes of Prey, Nordstrom Stores. Photo: Courtesy of Shoes of Prey.*

VansLab artist incubator space, a cinema, a live music venue, a premium café and bar, and a gifting suite. Their skater-built and -designed concrete bowl, mini ramp, and street course provide a full entertainment experience to customers and community.

◆ **Emphasize the Journey** Warby Parker tells an enchanting brand story. The customer journey emphasizes accessible price points, high style, and a user-friendly store environment. The company's mail order service allows customers to try eyewear on in home, while its showrooms keep consumers engaged with personalized service and experience. IKEA welcomes a world of shoppers to experience home decor with many of the same features. IKEA consumers design their own kitchen in-store using easy to use software tools, eat Swedish meatballs and other delicacies, and entertain the kids in a supervised ball room.

◆ **In-Store Animation** An ever-growing number of fashion retailers such as Urban Outfitters provide a platform for shoppers to take dressing room "selfies" and share them with friends. Eager consumers enjoy the opportunity to taste, listen, smell, and test products boosting the appeal of sensory motivation. Tastings, demonstrations, and classes at Urban's in-store eateries are gatherings to build better relationships with consumers. Notable chefs such as Marc Vetri, Michael Symon, and Ilan Hall have partnered with the store to create a trendy gathering place. Today, making dinner plans with friends could mean meeting them at the local Urban Outfitters. In addition, Urban Outfitters and Marc Vetri support annual philanthropic events like The Chef Event for Alex's Lemonade Stand Foundation (https://www.alexslemonade.org/campaign/great-chefs-eventn).

◆ **Cross-Selling** Customers delight in Anthropologie's "curated" selection of products in the store. This editorial approach to merchandising immerses the consumer in a shopping excursion that feels intoxicating, distinctive and personal. The *treasure hunt* shopping experience of each uniquely designed Anthropologie captures the flavor of an exotic marketplace. Discovery, imagination, and visual stimulation are highlights of the consumer's shopping experience.

◆ **Sweet Spots** Whole Foods transforms endcaps and feature tables into mini destinations as opportunities to engage and educate consumers about its products and ingredients. Every aisle reveals a feast for the senses. The hallmarks include staging colorful products in still-life settings, using unexpected elements such as a bed of soil, hand-painted signage by local artists, and authentic crate and pallet structures.

◆ **The Product Is the Hero** Emphasize the product with dynamic product presentation that is easy to navigate and understand. Nespresso makes it easy and intuitive for consumers to navigate merchandise selections. Groupings by color, style, size, and flavor (depending on the category) keep the products accessible and in the spotlight. Maintaining brand consistency through logo, imagery, color, and other brand assets is essential. The conformity of application of brand elements helps to ensure consumer perceptions are accurate and eliminates brand confusion. Target, Starbucks, Apple, and McDonald's all serve as exemplary models.

◆ **Retail and Technology** As retail and technology continue to merge to provide support and experiences, omnichannel shopping will unify with the brick and mortar store. Virtual reality and augmented reality will present new opportunities for customers to experience products and spaces.

Stores of the future will need to accept and adapt omni-retailing—it is here to stay. The "integration" rather than just the "addition" of technology may be the most significantly beneficial change to future retail models. As social connectivity continues to grow in importance, retailers need to intensify their focus on creativity, authenticity, communication, discovery, and emotion. Any one of these can stimulate the visitor experience in a store setting. Brick-and-mortar stores will eventually evolve from being a place to sell product into a showcase of experiences that can sell lifestyle and entertainment. Stores could rival a museum visit, concert, four-star meal, or sporting event. The successful retail store of the future needs to be all of these bundled into one. The next generation of designers will align these to craft a new store model fusing the physical store, the online store, and the consumer experience.

Go Green 1.1: Sustainable Retail Practices

There are lots of opportunities to "Go Green" and reuse, repurpose, and recycle while enhancing brand identity. Old and maybe seemingly discarded objects can add new life and interest in a retail environment. If the brand is elegant and refined, and real antiques are not within the reach of a limited budget, try making your own "antique" furniture or furniture-as-fixtures by using paint and imagination. A visit to a local secondhand store or a search at garage sales may turn up reproductions of period furniture in imperfect condition. Depending upon your brand and what it stands for and who the customer is, strip off the upholstery fabric; paint the frame a neutral color, a sophisticated shiny black, or a cool, matte white; and reupholster with a fabric that carries through the store's theme—or, if there is one—the signature color of the brand. If the brand is young and trendy and a bit frivolous, the same frames can work in bright, sharp colors or an array of happy pastels.

Always consider the brand first and the clientele you are trying to impress. No matter how contemporary your shop, there may be a spot for a focal fixture that stands out. That fixture may be an armoire that is now a color it was never intended to be or wallpapered over in a striking pattern. A tall chest of drawers with several drawers pulled out to display merchandise can also be a rescued piece from a refuse heap. See Chapter 17: Furniture as Merchandisers and Fixtures.

When it comes to display props, have fun. A shopper who steps into the store with a smile after seeing the window or up-front display is easier to satisfy than one who is glum or frowning. Throughout this book there are references on the use of repurposing everyday objects—especially obsolete ones—in new and enticing ways. Sometimes, you don't even have to refinish the pieces; just dust them off and let the shabby, scaly finish contrast with all the new and bright products. A weather-beaten, age-stained dress form on a cast iron roll-around base can do more than highlight the new arrival. It can suggest tradition or hand tailoring or maybe the vintage quality of the dress design. Whatever the message, that dress will get the shopper's attention in ways a brand new, crisp and clean dress form wouldn't. Relics of the past that perform similar functions as new household products—like coffee makers, steam irons, toasters, and air conditioners—are sure attention getters that may come off the refuse heap and be recycled as decorative props that contrast the items for sale.

It is all about enhancing the brand by making the brand identity more appealing and more memorable while finding a new use for an old disposable device or object.

FIGURE 1.4   In keeping with Robert Redford's feelings about the ecosystem of the world and sustainability and recycling, Redford's Sundance shop in Edina, Minnesota, designed by JGA of Southfield, Michigan, "celebrates the natural characteristics and finishes of the materials" and makes use of rough, hewn, reclaimed wood and the weathered patina. *Photo: Troy Thies Photography, Minneapolis, Minnesota.*

Brand Box 1.1: Brand and Brand Identity

Unless you have been hibernating or totally out of the retail scene, you must have heard the word that is reverberating through the media—the word is *brand*. Everything we do or say seems to refer back to brand and how it is presented. Just exactly what is a brand, and how do we get it? If we have it—how do we show it so that others will recognize and acknowledge that brand?

The other definition of brand—the brand or mark that cowboys burn into the hides of cattle—is not quite the same, but it is close. The brand identifies who you are—what you are or who is the producer of the object or provider of the service. It distinguishes you or your products from same or similar ones. It can be a word (Kleenex), a name (Campbell's Soups), a symbol (the "swoosh" of Nike or Apple's bitten apple), a color (the red-and-white bull's eye of Target), a graphic design that is applied to a product or service (Starbuck's crowned siren), or a combination of any of the above. Companies get graphic artists to render the "look" of the brand, selecting the just-right signature color, a specific (if not original) font, a quirky logo that they hope will be memorable—anything that will make the representation of their brand unique, appealing, and memorable to a specific audience.

What is the brand? In the book *Designing B to B Brands: Lessons from Deloitte and 195,000 Brand Managers* (John Wiley and Sons 2013), Carlos Martinez Onaindia, global brand senior manager, and Brian Resnick, global brand director, both at Deloitte Touche Tohmatsu Ltd., answered that question. In that book, Onaindia said that the brand was more than the logo, tagline, or mission statement—"It's what people say when you leave the room—it's about perception. It's about reputation—why you are different from your competition."

Resnick said, "A brand is a collection of distinguishing intangible assets that is most commonly associated with and shaped by a product, person, or organization, but ultimately defined by the consumer or audience. At the heart of any successful brand is that idea of consistency in communications and consistency in experience." Now, what happens when that company or corporation invites the public into its domain—be it a retail store, a trade show, a café or restaurant, a bank, or even a gone-in-a-minute pop-up shop? How is the corporate brand made evident in that specific site? We now come to *brand identity*.

What is the brand identity? Brian Resnick provides us with this definition in his book. "Brand identity is expressed through the most physically embodied aspects of the organization. It is the manifestation of the brand that can be seen, heard, and immediately experienced. Brand identity encompasses visual identity, aural identity, and other sensory components of a brand"—like walking into a shop and seeing, feeling, and being totally involved in and surrounded by the brand imagery. It is about adding emotions and sensory appeal. This is where the store planners, visual merchandisers, and display persons make their contributions. This is where the creative and talented showpeople step in to create the desired ambience that will define the story that the brand wants to project—with an appeal to all five senses. It is the designers who gives it form and shape—add texture and materials, a color palette, an emotional context and appeal, the sound, or the specific aroma. This is the drama that will create the desired perception of what the brand stands for and adds extra value to the product. And you can be the talent that makes it happen. (See Figure 1.5.)

There is no special formula—no magic word that suddenly provides the ideal brand identity. The presentation of the merchandise and the displays that bring shoppers into the store are vital to creating the brand identity. If the store uses mannequins, are they distinctive? Do they truly represent the retailer's selected shoppers? Do they complement the

FIGURE 1.5 When red is the team color and you are selling merchandise for the team's fans, then you promote the color and all of the items that flaunt the team's brand color. *VFB Fan Club, Stuttgart, Germany. Designed by Blocher Blocher Partners. Photo: Joachim Gropius for Blocher Blocher Partners.*

merchandise? Are they as smart, sophisticated, and stylish as the garments or as amusing, young, and trendy as the retailer would like the wares to appear? What does the display of stock on the wall and floor fixtures—on the display tables and racks—say about the brand and the merchandise? If your brand is elegant and refined, is that evident in the look and texture of the shop interior—the materials and colors used? If it is a fun, funky sort of brand, how much of that feeling does a shopper get as he or she walks into the store? Is the shop fun to be in, and is the presentation of merchandise lighthearted as well? If your brand is represented by a white jungle cat leaping off of a signature red background, how do you make sure that image is woven into the store's decor and its displays? How do you work this familiar logo or trademark into your display calendar so that it is always present but always looking fresh and new? Add a red Santa hat to the puma and maybe a sack overflowing with sports shoes on its back for Christmas or turn the red background into a giant heart through which the puma leaps to greet Valentine's Day. Where the brand features a special or signature color, find clever and surprising ways to use that

color in your visual merchandising and your displays. If "heritage" or "tradition" is an important part of your brand, emphasize it by the use of "antique" or just very old items that refer to the product or the theme you are developing. Reuse and repurposing can be applied here as well.

As you make your way through this edition, be aware and make note of the numerous ways you can enhance the brand you are working with—whether it be the store's brand or the brand of the product you are featuring in your window or interior display or the product line you are highlighting as a shop-within-the-shop in the store. First and foremost is the store's brand, then the product lines that are carried in the store. If you are fortunate enough to work in a designer's boutique, your task is simplified because it is the designer's brand that is the only brand you are presenting.

Today, we are a brand-conscious society and it is important that the brand develop a strong identity that plays well in the chosen marketplace. That "look" can mean continuity and goodwill and enhance the store's reputation, especially if the retailer decides to open up branches of the brand in other locations.

Why Do We Display? Trade Talk

consumer engagement	store image
omnichannel	visual merchandising

Why Do We Display? A Recap

+ Sell by showing and promoting.

+ Encourage the shopper to enter the store.

+ Get the customer to pause and "shop" the selling floor.

+ Establish, promote, and enhance the store's visual image.

+ Entertain customers and enhance their shopping experience.

+ Introduce and explain new products.

+ Educate customers by answering questions on the use and accessorizing of a product or fashion trend.

+ Omnichannel retail practices changing the retail experience.

+ New strategies to promote customer engagement.

Questions for Review and Discussion

1. Describe the role of visual merchandising in retailing today.

2. Compare and contrast the store images of H & M and Urban Outfitters. How does each store promote the individual image through visual merchandising and display? Relate specific examples.

3. List five purposes of visual merchandising and describe a display that would fulfill each of these purposes.

4. How has omnichannel retailing affected retail and display?

5. List three ways to promote customer engagement.

6. What are some of the challenges designers must face when "going green"?

7. Give three examples of branding.

Chapter Two
Color and Texture

The year of the Rooster inspires Christian Louboutin, Hong Kong.
Copyright WindowsWear PRO http://pro.windowswear.com contact@ windowswear.com 1.646.827.2288

**AFTER YOU HAVE READ THIS CHAPTER,
YOU WILL BE ABLE TO DISCUSS**

+ the relationship between color and visual merchandising and display
+ the common associations with, and reactions to, various colors
+ colors in the warm and cool families
+ the concepts of color mixing and of value as it relates to color
+ primary, secondary, intermediate, and tertiary colors
+ the differences between a tint and a shade
+ the relationship of colors to each other on the color wheel
+ how neutral colors are best used in store design
+ the relationship between texture and color

Color is the biggest motivation for shopping. People buy color before they buy size, fit, or price. People also react to the colors around the garment being considered. Some stores, such as Gap, will introduce a whole new palette each season. Although the styling may be similar to or the same as an existing item, it is the new color presentation that brings the shoppers onto the carefully color-schemed and color-coordinated sales floor. Malls, shopping centers, big-box stores, and small specialty stores are all reconsidering the colors they use to attract shoppers and keep them in the store after they have been lured inside. The color of a store's signage sometimes says more than the words on the sign: Is it subtle? Is it sophisticated? Is it daring or demanding? Intrusive? Inviting? Ingratiating? Color says something about the kind of store, the kind of merchandise, and the kind of market the retailer hopes to appeal to. Taste and colors, like everything else in fashion, change, and though some basic conclusions can be drawn about color and how people respond to the various hues, tints, and shades, there is still the "in" fashion or trend that determines when a color is in and when it is out. (See Figure 2.1.)

Many books have been written about color and the psychology of color: which colors expand or go forward, which contract or withdraw, which will "raise the roof" (or the ceiling at least), and which will seem to bring the ceiling down. Some colors make the viewer feel warm, expansive, generous, full of good feelings, all aglow, and responsive enough to buy anything. Other colors make the viewer feel cold, aloof, unresponsive, moody, and impossible to reach.

FIGURE 2.1 The sign says *sale* but the story is about *color*. The panels are painted in an assortment of warm, fashionable colors befitting the Milanese boutique—rather than the sharp red usually used for sales. Note how that complementary turquoise garment pops out of the presentation. *Stefania D'Alessandro/Getty Images.*

To add to the color confusion, not everyone reacts in the same way to the same color. A happy childhood, for example, surrounded by a loving family and associated with a pink and pretty bedroom, pink and frilly dresses—just pink and pampered all the way—can make pink a joyful, loving color. But, if the pink room were forced on the person, the pink-but-not-so-pretty dresses were hand-me-downs, or pink evoked the memory of medicine, hospitals, and sickness, then pink will certainly not be a "turn-on" color. The visual merchandiser/store planner will not be able to provide the ideal setting for each and every customer, but it is possible to satisfy the vast majority while alienating only a few.

Physical and Psychological Reactions to Color

Color psychology is very important in visual merchandising. Many theories have been espoused concerning the effects of color on people and their moods while shopping. Color can immediately create a mood. Most of us have colors that tend to cheer us up when we are feeling down and colors that calm us. Each of us also has colors that can make us physically feel hotter or cooler. The problem for the visual merchandiser is that each person may have a distinct reaction to the same color. In our vast and global marketplace, there are cultural and regional differences in color preference. Also, public taste in color changes, sometimes dramatically, over time. However, in trying to predict the effects of color on the public in general, many visual merchandisers rely on these widely researched color responses.

YELLOW

It is the color that the eye registers first, and therefore it is used for hard hats and safety equipment. It is sunshine and gold; happy, bright, cheerful, vital, fun-filled, and alive; daisies, marigolds, and lemons. It is optimism, expectancy, relaxation, and a wide-open-armed acceptance of the world, suggestive of change, challenge, and innovation. It is spring, summer, and Easter; when it "turns to gold," it is autumn.

ORANGE

A friendly, sociable color, orange is agreeable, overt, glowing, and incandescent. It is exciting, vibrant, and filled with anticipation. It is fire and flame, a rising sun in the tropics or a setting sun in the desert; Halloween and autumn leaves. It signals safety and hazards. It declassifies and indicates an economical product.

RED

Exciting, stimulating, loving, powerful, and sexy—these are some of the words used to describe red. It can be assertive, demanding, and obvious, possibly even cheap or vulgar. Generally, it comes across as warm, stirring, and passionate. Red is Valentine's Day and Christmas. It stands for valor and patriotism—the flag and firecrackers. It conveys "sale," "clearance," a warning, a fire, and a fright. In most cultures, red means stop. It can symbolize luck and has the ability to make you feel hungry.

PINK

It may be regarded as feminine, sweet, lovely, pretty—little girls, rosebuds, and ribbons and lace. Or it may connote something fleshy, raw, undercooked, and underdeveloped. Pink is also flowers for Mother's Day, Easter eggs and bunny ears, intimate apparel, and an elegant approach to Christmas.

GREEN

An alive, cool, and "growing" color, green is springtime and summer—lawns, bushes, vegetables, trees, and rain forests. When lightened it can be sterile and clean and symbolize nature, recycling, and sustainability. It is St. Patrick's Day and the other half of a Christmas color scheme. Some shades of green can also be bilious and stomach turning—or reminiscent of khaki and war. It can also remind people of mold or decay.

BLUE

Blue is always a popular color choice and the favorite of most. Cool, clean, calm, comfortable, and collected, it speaks of soft, soaring skies, serene lakes, gentle horizons, and the security of hearth, home, flag, and patriotic celebrations. It is quiet but can become cold, moody, or even depressing. It is always right for spring and summer skies, shadows on snow, and icy winters.

BLUE-GREEN

This is the happy marriage of blue and green. It is a cool, tasteful color—sensitive and restful, but alive; vital yet quiet. It is water, sky, and grass, peaceful and growing, a great summer color to complement white and glowing tan complexions.

PEACH

Peach suggests the warmth and happy excitement of orange (toned down), with none of its grating qualities. A smiling, glowing color, it is easy to be with and delightful to be in. A new neutral and a pastel earth tone, peach is a friendly color that will go with almost anything.

RUST

The other end of the orange scale, it is deep, rich, and earthy without being earthbound. Rust is a full-bodied color with the warmth of orange, but with none of its obvious, blatant, or irritating qualities. It is the earth color that goes with other colors but is neither invisible nor intruding. It is the personification of autumn.

VIOLET/PURPLE

This traditionally regal color has, in recent years, become a favorite with children. In some shades it is a happy, youthful color, whereas in its deepest and richest form it is a color of taste, distinction, and discretion. It is a high-fashion color that has to be sold. Purple can sometimes come off as overbearing and pompous. Lavender may convey old-fashioned Victorian charm and Easter trim.

GRAY

Gray is the neutral barrier that makes separations, but no statements. Gray exists—and exists well—with other colors that have more to say. Gray may be either a depressing, down-in-the-dumps color or a super-elegant and sophisticated color that suggests fine jewelry, silver, furs, and designer salons.

BROWN

Brown is the earth, hearth, and home; the family and the farm; the simple things: wood, clay, and other natural materials. It steps back to let other colors go forward, but unlike gray, it does not disappear. Brown is warm and can sometimes cast a glow. From the lightest off-white beige to the deepest charcoal brown, it is relaxed, unexciting, and in no way unnerving. It is the deep color for autumn.

WHITE

White is the blankest of the blank, but a strong and able supporting player that makes every other color, by comparison, turn in bigger, bolder, brighter performances. It is innocence and hope, purity, angels and religious celebrations, a wedding gown, and the blinding brilliance of clear light. Cotton white can be a sparkling accent, a sharp highlight, a crisp delineator, or an unpleasant comparison by which other "whites" may come off as dingy or unhappily yellowed. White can also be sterile, antiseptic, bleak, and harsh.

BLACK

This color connotes night, a vacuum, and an absence of light. It is mystery, sex, and death, as well as the color of intrigue and sophistication. Ultrachic or ultra-depressing, it also can be ominous and threatening or downright dull. It can be as sensuous as satin or as deep as velvet. Black is a neutral, but a neutral that requires careful handling.

GOLD, SILVER, AND PLATINUM

Known as metallics, these often suggest premium-priced products and tiers of quality.

Color Families

In the descriptions of reactions to the colors listed in the previous sections, certain adjectives appear over and over again. Some colors are described as warm and glowing, whereas others are cool, calm, or aloof. Still another group of colors could be categorized as neutrals. Thus, most colors are grouped into ambiguous but convenient families.

Red, orange, yellow, pink, rust, brown, and peach can all be classified as **warm colors**, aggressive, spirited, advancing colors. Blue, green, violet, and blue-green are regarded as a group of **cool colors** and receding colors. That leaves white, gray, black, and brown to band together as **neutral colors**. Neutrals can be either warm or cool. Black, white, and all the shades of gray are considered cool, whereas anything from warm off-white through all the shades of beige and to the deepest brown is called a warm neutral.

By personal preference, people of certain age and social groups will respond more readily to one family over another. Young children and nonsophisticates, however, commonly delight in and respond to bright, sharp colors: yellow, red, green, brilliant blue, shocking pink, and clear turquoise. Casual, outgoing, fun-loving, high-spirited people who want fashions and settings to match are drawn to the warm colors. Sophisticated people are supposed to appreciate subtlety: the slightly off-colors, toned down and neutralized without being neutered. Elegant and big-ticket merchandise seems to make a better showing and get a better customer response in a "cool" environment. "Serenity" sells silver, furs, and other choice merchandise.

COLOR MIXING

In working with color, it is wise to have a basic idea about what color is, how it works, and what it can do. If we accept the long-established theory that there are three basic pigment colors from which all other colors can be mixed, we are well on the way to understanding color.

Red, yellow, and blue are called **primary colors**. By mixing red and yellow, we get orange. Blue and yellow combined will produce green. Equal parts of red and blue make violet, or purple. These resulting colors—orange, green, and violet—are **secondary colors**. Furthermore, mixing yellow (a primary color) with green (a secondary)—depending on the quantity of each color used—results in a yellow-green or a green-yellow. These are **intermediate colors**. Mixing two secondary colors (orange plus green or green plus purple) results in **tertiary colors**. All those romantic, exotic names with which fashion and decorating abound, such as shrimp, mango, avocado, chartreuse, pumpkin, plum, and so on, are actually selling names of these tertiary colors. (See Figure 2.2.)

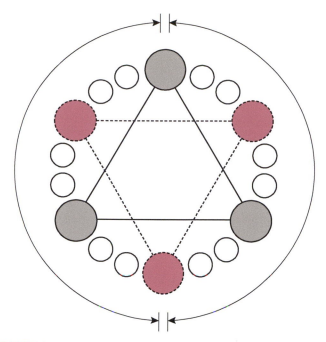

FIGURE 2.2   Mixing color pigments. *Illustration by Rob Carboni.*

Value refers to the amount of light or dark in a color. Add white to any of the full-value colors (primary, secondary, or intermediate) and, depending on the amount of white added, the result will be a **tint**, or **pastel**, of that color—a lighter, more gentle variation of the original color. The addition of black to a color will produce **shades**, or deeper, richer, fuller-bodied versions of the color. Thus, the addition of white to red could result in a pretty, soft, baby-sweet pink, whereas the addition of black to red could produce a masculine, heady garnet, dubonnet, or maroon.

Color Schemes

The color wheel graphically shows the relationship of colors to each other. The location of colors on the wheel is relevant to the following discussion.

ANALOGOUS, OR ADJACENT, COLORS

Colors that exist harmoniously next to each other on the wheel, because of shared characteristics (and pigments), work together in a display area to create specific effects. Yellow, yellow-green, green, and green-blue are examples of neighboring, adjacent, or analogous colors, as are yellow, yellow-orange, orange, and orange-red. Adjacent colors reinforce each other; they are compatible and usually can be counted on to create a close harmony. Thus, when used in close groups or clusters, they create an **analogous color scheme**; for example, blue sky and green grass to make a turquoise outfit appear cooler and crisper.

COMPLEMENTARY COLORS

Complementary colors are found opposite each other on the color wheel. Red is the complement of green (and vice versa); blue and orange are complements, as are yellow and violet. These opposites do not make for close harmony or gentle combinations. Complements bring out the intensity and brilliance of each other. Thus, complementary color schemes are usually strong, demanding, and vibrant. Complementary colors will vibrate against each other (creating kinetic patterns) when placed very close together. They will make "motion" where there actually is none. (See Figure 2.3.)

Complementary schemes are fine in bright, youth-oriented areas, where the creation of a shocking or attention-getting palette is desired. They can be fun, dynamic, exciting, and sometimes irritating. However, it is possible to minimize or even eliminate some of the dynamic or irritating qualities of the complementary scheme.

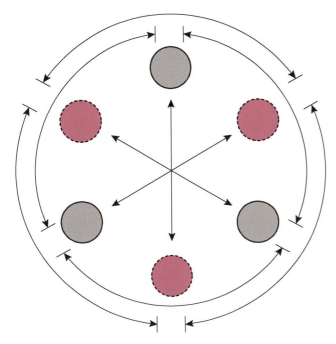

FIGURE 2.3 Complementary and analogous color schemes. *Illustration by Rob Carboni.*

This can be accomplished by reducing the intensity of the colors being used. **Intensity** refers to the purity and strength of the color. The addition of white or black will reduce the intensity, as will the addition of some of the complementary color (e.g., adding a little red to green). A pink-and-apple-green color combination may be basically complementary, but it is easier to live with than a pure, full-strength red and a fully saturated green!

CONTRASTING COLORS

Colors are often selected for the amount of **contrast** they provide. For example, two light colors adjacent to each other provide little contrast, and a light color next to a medium one provides some contrast; however, a light color next to a dark one creates a bold contrast. That is why one rarely, if ever, finds a garment, fabric, or other product designed with black and navy blue. This is an extreme example of minimal contrast.

MONOCHROMATIC COLORS

If you start with one color and develop the full range of that color, from the palest off-white tint to the deepest, darkest shade, you will have a **monochromatic** (one color) **color scheme**. Baby blue and sky blue through the intermediate blues and up to a navy or midnight blue is a monochromatic scheme. A monochromatic color scheme can be restful and easy to accept, and it can provide a controlled setting for merchandise. It generally sits back and takes it easy.

NEUTRAL COLORS

Black, white, gray, beige, and brown make up the neutral color family. Neutrals make good backgrounds for stores because they allow the merchandise itself to have full impact. Neutrals evoke less image and tend to disturb customers less. They do not compete with the merchandise on display, but rather provide a complementary background for the goods.

An all-white scheme can be young, exciting, sparkling, and ultrachic or a perfect foil for brightly colored merchandise. However, all white may also come off as absolutely sterile and bland, draining the color right out of the merchandise.

Beige tones have been used a great deal by store designers in the past few years, and they remain popular, people pleasing, and merchandise complementing. The blending of the casual but warm off-whites and beiges with wood tones (from bleached oak to deepest ebony) has a strong following. Generally, this kind of color scheme is easy to live with; it enhances the merchandise, but hardly ever overwhelms. It probably appeals to the rural instincts hidden inside each urban dweller.

From the past, and continuing strongly into the future, comes the gray color scheme. When elegance, the chic, and ultra-new is desired, it can be found with gray—gray by its aloof, cool self or made even icier with accents of Lucite and chrome. Gray is a foil for bright colors; it tones them down. It is a relief for the whites; it makes white appear whiter. Gray is a buffer for black, relieving the gloom of this noncolor. Neutral gray has long been popular as a setting for silver, furs, and expensive giftware, but it is now reaching into designer areas and even bridal displays.

Black and white may be neutral individually, and most colors will coexist with them, but when used together, they demand and get attention.

Using Color to Promote Color

The visual merchandiser can usually control the color against which merchandise is shown. The background color is important because it can either add to or detract from the color of the merchandise presented. A white dress shown against a white background can be very effective—or a total disaster! Against a stark white background, a dress that is not a pure white, but a soft, lovely ivory color, can look dingy and yellow. If, however, the background were a deep gray or very dark green, the sharp contrast would make the ivory dress appear whiter.

White against white is usually smart, sophisticated, and subtle. White against black is dramatic, sharp, and striking. The price and type of merchandise, the store's image, and the department or area in a store will determine which background is best for the white dress.

FIGURE 2.4 Soft blue tones are complemented and enhanced by the vivid red-orange prints and fabrics shown together in this Parisian shop window. *Antoine Antoniol/Getty Images.*

The white against white will be more dramatic and striking if a red light floods the white background and leaves the dress white, but softly outlined in pink, from the light reflected off the background. The white dress against the black background will seem more elegant if the background is softened with a blue or violet light, to ease the sharp contrast between foreground and background. By using colored panels behind and around merchandise, and assorted colored lights to "paint" those panels, the visual merchandiser can create the best of all possible settings for the merchandise. The use and effect of colored light are discussed in Chapter 4. (See Figures 2.4 and 2.5.)

In many ways, the accessories shown with the merchandise can also affect the color. Imagine the white dress with a navy blue belt, shoes, and handbag and a red-and-blue scarf. The white will appear crisp and sparkling in contrast to the navy. Now, suppose that same dress were completely accessorized in toast beige. The white is softened and warmed by its proximity to the beige. Popularly priced merchandise, however, will often rely on sharper and more contrasting accessories and displays. They help make the garment stand out and look like more for the money.

Visualize a bright red dress with emerald green trimmings. The red appears redder and more intense because

FIGURE 2.5 It is always black and white at White House Black Market—a chain of women's fashion stores that specializes in black-and-white apparel. Even at Christmas, the black contrasts sharply with the white, down to the spots on the dogs. The silvery dark gray abstracts continue the neutral palette. *White House, Black Market, Soho, New York.*

FIGURE 2.6 It is all about blue, as the sign in the window at The Bay, in Toronto, points out. Assorted shades and tints of blue denim are featured in this cool, monochromatic display. Note the blue accent lights that serve to highlight the theme. *The Bay, Queen Street, Toronto, Canada.*

the complementary green intensifies the red. The same red with shocking-pink accessories will seem more red-orange because the "hot pink" of the accessories is bluer by comparison.

Understanding the effect of color on color will enable the visual merchandiser to select the proper settings and accessories for the merchandise and the store's fashion image. (See Figures 2.6 and 2.7.)

FIGURE 2.7 Off-white, beige, toast, and brown—a palette of warm neutrals—come together in this Harvey Nichols Knightsbridge window in London. The framed stained glass windows add to the gentle faded ambiance that extends down to the mannequins' makeup and wigs. *Harvey Nichols Knightsbridge, London, United Kingdom.*

Texture

Another very important aspect of color is **texture**. The texture—surface treatment, or "feel"—can affect the color of the merchandise. Smooth and shiny surfaces reflect light and, therefore, always appear lighter. Satin, chrome, highly lacquered or enameled surfaces, waxed woods, and so on will all pick up and reflect more light than objects that are flat and lusterless. Rough, nubby, and deep-piled surfaces will absorb and hold light and, therefore, appear darker. Velvet, sandpaper, deep carpets, and untreated and natural woods or tree barks will all appear darker. Smooth or shiny reflective finishes around merchandise will add more light to the presentation. The background will reflect more light back onto the product being shown.

Textures are also suggestive. They can suggest familiar symbols by which the visual merchandiser attempts to explain the merchandise, in terms of surrounding materials. Soft silks and satins suggest femininity and sensuousness. Velvet is deep and rich, dark and mysterious, subtle, elegant, and expensive. Rough textures, such as burlap, coarse linens, nubby wools, and tweeds, are masculine, outdoorsy, rugged, natural, earthy, and wholesome. Gravel, sand, stones, brick, and ground-up cork suggest the great open spaces: sportswear, beachwear, camping, and the country.

In creating a setting for a bridal gown, for example, the textures utilized should suggest—and, at the same time, enhance—the softness and loveliness of the gown. A complementary texture to a satin-and-lace gown might even be rough wood planking. The gown would seem even more delicate, fragile, and feminine in comparison to the rough, burly quality of the wood. But what would this do to the bride-to-be and her illusions of romance? In this case, the background should be more of the same: The gown could be enveloped with other soft fabrics and gentle textures—wisps of tulle and net, ribbons and lace. Anything that suggests a fairy-tale setting and a "happily-ever-after" ending should be used with the bridal gown.

The use of opposite textures, however, can work very effectively in promoting other types of merchandise, especially when humor, scale, or shock is the attention-getting device to bring the shopper over to the display. Imagine a pair of natural leather outdoor hiking boots, nail studded and roughly sewn, sitting on a lace-edged, red satin pillow with a sheer, silky fabric draped behind. The copy might read, "It will be love at first sight." The contrast may be silly and out of place, but it is intriguing, unexpected, and attention getting. Or visualize a woman's nightgown—all pink and lace, soft and sheer—hanging from a peg on a wall of rough, split logs. The juxtaposing of two very different textures, the very feminine against the very masculine, makes the feminine seem more feminine and the masculine even more so. With a copy line like "Why rough it when you can go in style?" the visual merchandiser could explain the combination and possibly bring a smile to the viewer's face.

In an ensemble there should be a relationship of textures, a flow and continuity rather than startling change, unless the merchandise is meant to startle and call for attention. A fine wool challis tie, rather than a shiny silk one, is the choice for a tweed jacket, just as an oxford cloth shirt is more appropriate to the texture of nubby wools than a fine broadcloth. Similarly, coarsely textured suits are more compatible with grained leather than patent leather shoes.

Textures have to be balanced in a display arrangement. Rough textures usually seem heavier or suggest more "weight" in a composition or display. A roughly textured cube, for example, appears to take up more space and volume in the display area than a smoothly lacquered cube of the same size and color. Therefore, a visual merchandiser may balance a small, coarsely textured element with a larger smooth or shiny one. A textured floor "sits" better than a smooth or shiny one, whereas a smooth ceiling "floats" better than a roughly textured one. (See Figure 2.8.)

Some materials are especially popular for use in displays because they are texturally neutral (neither very smooth nor very rough) and because they are available in a wide range of colors. Felt, jersey, and suede cloth have neutral textures and can be used with soft or rugged merchandise. Seamless paper is another favorite with visual

merchandisers because it, too, lacks texture. These materials will be discussed more fully in Chapter 18. To learn more about the relationship of brand and color, see Brand Box 2.1: Color and the Brand Identity.

FIGURE 2.8 'Tis the season to warm up, and Macy's women's outerwear is shown against a textured, snowdrift background and accented by a tree of rough cut slices of logs. These "outdoor" textures are complemented by the glossy, slick finish of the stove on the left. *Macy's, Herald Square, New York City. Eugene Gologursky/Getty Images.*

Brand Box 2.1: Color and Brand Identity

If your store or the brand you are featuring has a signature color or color scheme—colors that are associated with your logo or packaging—by all means play them up in your store design or displays. However, be careful not to overdo that usage. If the color is a strong and dynamic one (any full-bodied primary or secondary color) that might intrude on the merchandise or product display, be especially aware of where you use it and how you use it.

The brand's color may be effective on a focal wall or behind a cash wrap in conjunction with the brand name and/or logo. Note how effectively the Joe Fresh's signature red-orange color pops out of the store's façade to stake a claim on Fifth Avenue in New York City. As designed by the Burdifilek design team of Toronto, the occasional focal walls highlight the almost all-white design of the store. On the interior, "a select number of glowing light boxes in Joe Fresh's signature orange contribute to the liveliness of the store and allow the merchandise to glow," said Diego Burdi, the Creative Partner at Burdifilek.

For storewide sales, the brand-colored shopping bags and boxes can be effectively used in displays as well as gift-giving promotions (Christmas, Mother's Day, Father's Day, Valentine's Day), depending on the color. The assorted boxes covered in the color and ribbon-tied to match can be a great way of promoting the brand in a colorful way. Think of Tiffany blue boxes with their white satin ribbon bows. If the sales staff wears store or brand identifying garments or accessories like aprons, T-shirts, scarves, or ties, these could flaunt the store's color without detracting from the merchandise. Examples would be the red aprons that distinguish the sales staff at Ace Hardware stores around the country and the brown uniforms worn by the UPS delivery people.

As previously stated, there is such a thing as "too much"! When enough is enough depends on the brand, the type and appeal of the product, and the anticipated shopper. The more upscale or up-market the brand's appeal, the more subtle the use of the signature color; just whispers or mere suggestions may be sufficient to make the point. Popular-priced operations or more highly competitive fields may require more color emphasis and a bolder display of the company color.

FIGURE 2.9 Through the windows that envelop the Joe Fresh store on Fifth Avenue in New York City, one gets the message: "Bright orange is our signature color." A long and dominant focal wall is painted orange, and the abstract mannequins are wearing their brand-colored jackets to make the branding point even more obvious. *Designed by Burdifilek, Toronto, Canada. Photography: Ben Rahm at A-Frame Studio.*

Color and Texture: Trade Talk

analogous color scheme	intermediate colors	tertiary colors
color	monochromatic color scheme	texture
color psychology	neutral colors	tint
complementary colors	pastels	value
contrast	primary colors	warm colors
cool colors	secondary colors	
intensity	shades	

Color: A Recap

◆ Color is the biggest motivation for shopping.

◆ America's color taste is changing—softening up, warming up, returning to earth tones.

◆ The warm colors are red, yellow, orange, rust, and peach.

◆ The cool colors are blue, green, violet, and blue-green.

◆ The neutral colors are white, black, and all the grays in between as well as warm off-white, brown, and all the beiges in between.

◆ The primary, or basic, colors are red, yellow, and blue.

◆ The secondary colors are orange, green, and violet. They are obtained by mixing two of the primaries.

◆ An intermediate color is obtained by mixing a primary and a secondary color.

◆ A tertiary color is an "in-between" color obtained by mixing two secondary colors.

◆ Intensity is the purity, strength, and brilliance of a color.

◆ A tint, or pastel, is a color with white added.

◆ A shade is a color with black added.

◆ A monochromatic color scheme is one that includes a range of tints and shades of a single color.

◆ An analogous color scheme consists of colors that are adjacent to each other on the color wheel.

◆ A complementary color scheme consists of colors that are opposite each other on the color wheel.

◆ A neutral color scheme is a "no-color" color scheme of whites, blacks, grays, or browns.

Texture: A Recap

◆ Texture is the surface treatment or "feel" of the merchandise.

◆ Smooth surfaces reflect light and appear brighter.

◆ Rough surfaces hold light and appear darker.

◆ Rough textures seem heavier and suggest more "weight," whereas smooth textures seem to take up less size and volume.

Questions for Review and Discussion

1. Provide an example of a current fashion trend that supports the Color Marketing Group's forecast of a return to "earth" colors.

2. Why might two people react differently to the same color? Give an example of two diverse reactions to the same color.

3. For each of the following colors, list some common associations and reactions:
   a. blue
   b. red
   c. yellow
   d. black

4. List some cool colors. What types of customers are most attracted to cool colors?

5. Provide examples of the following:
   a. monochromatic color scheme
   b. contrasting colors
   c. intermediate colors
   d. complementary colors

6. Explain the relationship of the terms value, tint, and shade.

7. What are neutral colors? How are neutrals often used in store design?

8. What is texture? How can textures be suggestive of merchandise and settings?

9. Explain the proper relationship of textures in a display setting. How should textures be "balanced" in a display?

10. How can a signature color be used to support the brand in the overall store design?

Chapter Three
Line and Composition

Like salt and pepper. *Kleinfield, New York City. Copyright WindowsWear PRO http://pro.windowswear.com contact@windowswear.com 1.646.827.2288*

AFTER YOU HAVE READ THIS CHAPTER,
YOU WILL BE ABLE TO DISCUSS

+ the three major types of lines used in display
+ composition and its relationship to visual merchandising
+ the differences between symmetrical and asymmetrical balance
+ how dominance can be achieved in a visual presentation
+ the use of contrasting elements in a display
+ the relationship between proportion and contrast
+ the concept of rhythm as it relates to visual presentation
+ the relationship between repetition and dominance

Line

Line is a direction. It is a major part of composition, and second only to color in creating a response to the merchandise in a display. Lines can be vertical, horizontal, curved, or diagonal. The way in which these lines are utilized and combined determines the effectiveness of the merchandise presentation. Each line suggests something else and, like letters combined to form words, lines are arranged to make selling "pictures."

VERTICAL LINES

What is more inspiring than the soaring spires of a Gothic cathedral? Is there anything more classic or elegant than a tall, fluted Ionic column? How about the power and majesty of a stand of cypress trees? Proud people stand tall and erect. What do the spire, the column, the cypress, and the proud person have in common? They are all straight and vertical. They emphasize and exemplify the **vertical line**. When a display is mainly a vertical one, filled with straight elements that seem to join floor and ceiling, the viewer will get the message: strength, height, pride, majesty, and dignity.

When the vertical elements are not only tall, but also thin, an impression of elegance and refinement is conveyed. For example, a mannequin standing erect with arms at her sides, head uplifted, and shoulders back will look elegant. She will add stature and class to the garment she is modeling. Fur coats, evening gowns, bridal wear, and well-tailored suits are shown to advantage on a vertical figure. The long, straight, falling line of a garment can be enhanced by the "dignified" mannequin, which, in turn, will add a vertical quality to the entire display. A straight line can also be direct and forceful or rigid and precise. (See Figure 3.1.)

HORIZONTAL LINES

Long, low, wide, spreading lines—the bands that run across a window or around perimeter walls—suggest an easygoing, restful quality. All is peaceful and calm in a horizontal presentation. A reclining mannequin, relaxed and at ease, is perfectly compatible with robes, loungewear, or nightwear. The horizon sets the world to rest; lazy ripples and gentle waves are horizontal. As the line stretches out and makes objects look wider, it also tends to make them look shorter.

FIGURE 3.1 The long slivers of mirrored foil board of different lengths and widths create a strong vertical, yet not too formal, pattern in this window. The headless mannequin adds another vertical line to the composition. Dignified—but not stuffy. *Hugo Boss, Milan, Italy. Design: Marketing Jazz.*

A pattern of **horizontal lines** will cut the vertical effect and reduce the "uptight" or dignified feel of a design or setting. A balancing of the horizontal with the vertical can create an easy, restful, but elegant setting. (See Go Green Box 3.1: Sustainable Design Solutions.)

CURVED LINES

The **curved line** personifies grace, charm, and femininity. It is soft and enveloping. The curved line, or arc, can ease the tension that might be produced by too many vertical lines. It is the circle and the sphere, the sun and the moon, the heart, billowing waves, rolling hills, fluffy clouds, the swirl of a seashell, a spiral, an opening rose. Curved lines can also be used for a spotlight or target against which an object is shown or a spiral that leads the eye from object to object. (See Figure 3.2.)

FIGURE 3.2 To bring springtime into the jewelry store, the designer created a soft, graceful frame around the shadow box with a curving garland of flowers and leaves. The gentle, flowing line adds a feminine look to this presentation when compared with the shadow box in Figure 3.11. *Cada, Munich, Germany. Design: Peter Rank of Deko Rank.*

DIAGONAL LINES

The **diagonal line** is a line of action; it is forceful, strong, and dynamic. The diagonal is a bolt of lightning, a firecracker going off, a thrown javelin, rain streaming down, a shove or a push, a seesaw or a playground slide, an arrow, or a pointing finger leading the eye right down to where the action is. The active sportswear mannequin, for example, is often all angles: arms akimbo, knees bent, head thrust back, and shoulders shrugging. That mannequin is a study in diagonals. It is possible to suggest movement and excitement in a static and predominantly vertical or horizontal presentation by adding some forceful diagonals. (See Figures 3.3 and 3.4.)

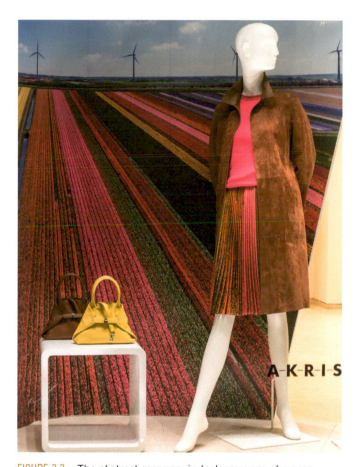

FIGURE 3.3 The abstract mannequin looks away as she poses against the strong diagonal lines in the background, inspired by the texture of the skirt. The strong rows of color compliment the handbags displayed on open cubed fixtures and playfully echo the colors in the printed scene. *Akris, New York City. Copyright WindowsWear PRO http://pro.windowswear.com contact@ windowswear.com 1.646.827.2288*

FIGURE 3.4 Inspired by the shapes and details of the Spring/ Summer fashions, the designers made use of the diagonal lines and triangular and other geometric shapes. "Our aim was to create a moody, almost ethereal scheme. Playing with different textures, shapes, colors, and light allowed us to produce a contemporary flow across the window run," according to Janet Wardley, head of the visual display team at Harvey Nichols. The triangles within triangles add repetition as well as radiation to the design. *Harvey Nichols, London, United Kingdom.*

Composition

Composition may be defined as the organization or grouping of different parts or elements used to achieve a unified whole. In display and visual merchandising, composition is the arrangement of lines, forms, shapes, and colors into a pleasing whole that directs the viewer's eye to the various bits and pieces of the setting and that relays a particular message. The quality of the composition will depend on the elements used and where and how they are used.

BALANCE

A well-designed display should have **balance**. This involves the creation of an easy-to-accept relationship between the parts of the composition. If a design were cut in half by an imaginary line drawn through its center, and one side were an exact replica or mirror image of the other side, that would be a classic example of **symmetrical** or **formal balance**. In reality, however, the objects on each side of the imaginary line are usually of similar weight and prominence, not an actual mirror image. For example, if on one side of a display a mannequin is sitting on a chair, while on the other side a similar mannequin is sitting on a comparable chair, both halves of the composition would be considered the same, equal in weight and importance. This is formal balance and, although staid and traditional, it can be very effective when expensive or quality merchandise is being presented. (See Figure 3.5.)

Asymmetrical balance is more informal and often more interesting. Although the two sides appear to be of equal weight, they are not replicas of each other. The individual units composing the display may differ, but they achieve a dynamic balance of weight and size at each side of the imaginary central line. For example, there may be two mannequins on one side balanced by a mannequin standing next to a draped table. If, on the table, there is a vase filled with flowers and foliage extending to about the same height as the mannequin's head, then visually, the table with the vase and flowers will be equal in weight and shape to the second mannequin on the other side. (See Figures 3.6 and 3.7.)

Sometimes, the creative and experienced designer can do marvelous things by balancing color with form. A strong or hot color may appear heavier than a pastel or cool color, so a mannequin in a vivid red dress might be balanced with an armoire painted antique white. This asymmetrical or informal balance is more casual, more interesting, and certainly more exciting.

FIGURE 3.5 Formal balance figures in this Ann Taylor window, with the composition centered on the central vertical red band, the red bench, and the single suitcase on the floor. Although the outfits on the four headless figures vary, they are set into equally balanced spaces to the right and left of the central band. *Ann Taylor, Madison Avenue, New York. Design by Victor Johnson.*

FIGURE 3.6 A variation of the same Ann Taylor promotion, here the composition features asymmetrical balance. The large graphic serves as the center of the composition, with the two headless forms on the left balanced by the piles of luggage and the column of globes on the right. *Ann Taylor, Madison Avenue, New York.*

FIGURE 3.7 The romantic scene designed for the Robert Ellis boutique in Culver City, California, is an asymmetrically balanced composition, with a dominant curved crescent moon played against a diagonal stream of stars and sparkle dust. The copy on the left adds several horizontal lines while balancing the mannequin on the right. The vertical strings of stars add to the look of the composition and complete it. *Robert Ellis, Culver City, California. Design: Keith Dillion.*

At times, a display presentation can be completely lacking in any sense of balance and still be very good. This is done for a reason. A lack of balance may be used as an element of surprise—as a vehicle to direct the viewer's attention to the merchandise. Or the visual merchandiser may be catering to a particular traffic flow. He or she may find that most shoppers travel north to south on the store's side of the street. It can make for a better presentation if the merchandise is shown in the southern half of the window—angled to face and attract the shopper walking from north to south. The empty or near empty, less weighty northern part of the window gets less attention and, therefore, little, if any, merchandising.

DOMINANCE

In every composition, it is advisable that some element be dominant. There should be some unit or object that, by its color, its size, or its position in the composition, attracts the eye first and possibly directs the viewer to other parts of the composition.

In most displays the dominant element is the merchandise, often with a big assist from a mannequin that is wearing it. In the one-item display, the single unit should dominate—should be the eye-catcher and the eye-filler—and the rest of the design or composition should exist in order to make this one item seem more beautiful and more special. However, some stores with unique images will play games with their viewers. Knowing how very "special" they and their merchandise are, the store designer will casually drop an exquisite single item into a beautifully conceived composition, leaving it up to the shopper to find it. But this can be successfully done only where the store and the visual merchandiser know what they are selling—and to whom—and can afford the luxury of these little games.

A mannequin can be dominant in a display by virtue of its size or the color it is wearing. A small object, like a diamond brooch, can be made dominant in a composition by sharply contrasting it with its background, without any distracting props nearby, and with a strong light on the piece. An object may also be made dominant by the arrangement of lines and shapes, the weights of the various elements of the composition, and gradations of color and light. Through these various techniques, the viewer's eye is directed to the main object or the featured item of the display. (See Figure 3.8.)

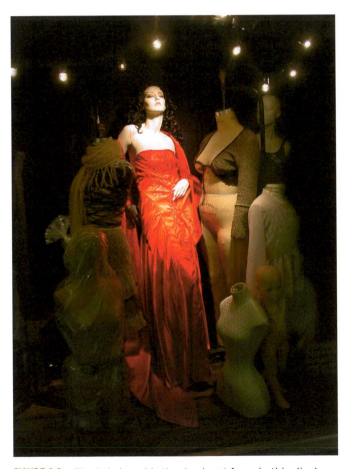

FIGURE 3.8 The lady in red is the dominant force in this display, whereas the assorted dressed and undressed dress forms serve as her ladies in waiting. They also provide a sense of scale and contrast. The swag of bare bulbs adds another interesting touch to the composition. *Design: Polar Buranasatit.*

CONTRAST

Contrast is the composition of elements used to show a sharp difference between them. It consists of a juxtaposition of different forms, lines, or colors in a composition that intensifies each element's properties—for example, a white gown displayed against a midnight background, a diamond bracelet on a black velvet pad, or a pair of red shoes on a green grass mat.

A difference in texture or an incongruity in the objects themselves can also heighten the contrast: a power saw nestling on a fluffy angel-hair cloud. The outrageous difference in the feel and texture between the item or merchandise and its environment will attract attention and maybe even promote the softness, ruggedness, or smoothness of that item. The effective use of contrast makes it possible for the feel, or touch, of an item to be more apparent without actually touching or stroking the object.

PROPORTION

Contrast can also consist of a difference in **proportion**— the relationship of the size, scale, or "weight" of elements and between each element and the entire composition. A pair of baby shoes, for example, will appear more delicate and adorable when placed next to a gigantic teddy bear. A four-foot tennis racket will bring attention to mere human-sized tennis shoes. The visual merchandiser must be careful to consider not only the size of the merchandise and props, but the size of the display area as well.

Experience has taught us to take the size of certain objects for granted. We know, for example, that a mannequin is life-size. Yet, the mannequin, in proportion to a greatly oversized table and chair, would appear to shrink from its actual size. Our mind knows the mannequin is still life-size, but our eyes are not so convinced.

Certain proportions or relationships in a composition or display are easily accepted by the viewer's eye: a ring will fit a mannequin's hand; a hat will sit on a mannequin's head. Put the same feathered hat into a straw "nest" that is three feet in diameter with "eggs" the size of footballs—the hat now appears to be small and fragile. The nest is out of proportion; it is overscaled.

Proportion and contrast are important elements of good composition. Drastically changing the proportions between

FIGURE 3.9   The overwhelming size of the ice cream cones not only attracts the viewer's eye but also serves as a base for the mannequins. This is dominance by size. *Moschino, Meatpacking District, New York. Copyright WindowsWear PRO http://pro .windowswear.com; contact@windowswear.com 1.646.827.2288.*

items and dramatic contrasts of color and texture can work wonders in attracting attention to a display and in helping promote an idea or a look. These attention-getting techniques are discussed in greater detail in Chapter 10. (See Figure 3.9.)

Rhythm

A good display composition should have a **rhythm**, a self-contained movement from element to element, from background to foreground, from side to side. The rhythm should lead the viewer's eye from the dominant object to the subordinate object (or objects), from the major presentation of an ensemble down to the arrangement of accessories or alternate parts of the outfit.

This flow can be created, for example, by the manner in which a mannequin is posed. Her hand may be resting on a chair back that happens to have a coat draped from it; a scarf, which is casually tossed over the coat, is trailing onto the floor over to an arrangement of shoes, handbags, another scarf, a flower, and some fragrances. The eye is led first to the mannequin (dominant in size, color, and weight), down to the chair, and then to the cluster on the ground. That downward sweep may be subtly reinforced by a background design of lines or shapes and by the use of color and lighting, which also lead the eye in the same direction.

The eye will naturally go around in a circular route if the objects are arranged to lead the way—like a snail's shell swirling inward to a central point. The eye will follow a triangular trail, or a pyramidal pattern, that leads from a flat, weighted base to an apex, or point. A successful rhythm or flow is a gentle one, one that guides the viewer in easy movements from one stop to another along the way. In some cases, like sales or hard-sell promotions for which dynamics are demanded, a jumpy and jarring presentation will be more effective. (See Figure 3.10.)

REPETITION

Repetition of a color, a line, a shape, or a form can add to the success of a display composition. By repeating or reiterating an idea or motif, that concept becomes more emphatic, more important, and thus, more dominant.

In this way, even a small object can be made to stand out in a large display area because the eye has been trained to look for it. Try to visualize a dark floor with an appliqué of red footprints "walking" across it. At the very end—in a pool of light—is a pair of red shoes. The pattern, or repetition, of the red footprints will carry the viewer's eye forward to the single pair of shoes, which now dominates the composition and the viewer's eye—and mind. **Radiating** a line, a form, or a product will lead the eye and add a sense of motion to a composition. By graduating the size of shapes, greater depth can be implied even in shallow spaces. Overall, repetition can be used to create larger dynamic shapes by radiating or graduating in size or color. (See Figure 3.11.)

FIGURE 3.10 The stage is set and all eyes are drawn to the star as arrows, angles, dagger points, and lights all converge on the mannequin center stage. Subtle, sophisticated and multipointed, it is sensational. *Bergdorf Goodman, New York. Eugene Gologursky/Getty Images.*

FIGURE 3.11 Caught in the whirlwind of radiating slats, the Cole Haan shoes slide down the ramp in unison. Radiating out from behind the animated figure are more subtle gray-on-gray lines that bring the viewer's eye to the message—Zero Resistance—while the figure's hand directs the eye toward the procession of shoes. *Cole Haan, New York. Copyright WindowsWear PRO http://pro.windowswear.com; contact@windowswear.com 1.646.827.2288.*

Go Green 3.1: Sustainable Design Solutions

To create strong linear patterns in your displays, you might try using easily available, recycled or recyclable materials, such as lengths of bamboo or corrugated paper tubes. They come in assorted lengths and diameters and can easily be hung horizontally, stood up vertically, or even propped at an angle to effect a dynamic angular line. In addition, these materials can be painted and repainted or wrapped in ribbons or tape. Natural bamboo is a perfect fit for beachwear and swimwear as well as cruise-, summer-, and casual wear; however, paint it shiny black, and it becomes quite an elegant thing instead.

Another linear material that can be used effectively and inexpensively and that is also energy efficient is fluorescent tubes. These come in a variety of lengths and can be used when electrically connected—or even when they are dead. Also, there are colored transparent gel sleeves that can slide over the tube to create assorted colored light effects. In that way, you can add not only a linear element to your composition but also color and light. Do not be concerned about the electrical wires that may be providing the current. They can add to the overall display, so use them imaginatively.

Can you think of some other easily obtainable materials that can be used as linear design elements? Props are all over—all it takes is a creative eye to decide how to turn something ordinary into something special. How about clotheslines for horizontal effects? Brooms and mops for verticals? Step ladders? Simple, unadorned workaday ladders can serve as a platform for showcasing merchandise or even as a riser for mannequins or forms. Look around you and imagine—and think recycle, reuse, and repurpose.

Line and Composition: Trade Talk

asymmetrical balance

balance

composition

curved line

diagonal line

horizontal lines

proportion

radiating

repetition

rhythm

symmetrical, or formal, balance

vertical line

Line and Composition: A Recap

+ Line is a direction, and a major part of composition.

+ There are vertical, horizontal, curved, and diagonal lines.

+ Composition is the organization of different elements to create unity.

+ Balance is the creation of an easy-to-accept relationship between the parts of the composition.

+ Balance can be symmetrical or asymmetrical.

+ Dominance refers to the element in the composition that first attracts the eye.

+ Contrast is meant to show differences.

+ Proportion is the relationship of the size, weight, height, or scale of the elements.

+ Rhythm is a self-contained movement that leads the viewer's eye from one element to another.

+ Repetition of an element within a display can make a concept more emphatic.

Questions for Review and Discussion

1. Describe a display using vertical lines. What feelings do vertical lines suggest to the viewers?

2. How can curved lines be introduced into a visual presentation? What type of response do curved lines tend to evoke?

3. Differentiate between symmetrical and asymmetrical balance and explain how each can be achieved in a visual display.

4. Provide a quick sketch illustrating first symmetrical and then asymmetrical balance in a display.

5. What should be the most dominant element in visual presentation? Why?

6. How can contrast be achieved in a display using texture? Color? Line?

7. Describe the concept of proportion and explain why it is important to any visual presentation.

8. How can you tell if a display has rhythm?

9. How does repetition assist in achieving rhythm in a display?

Chapter Four
Light and Lighting

Keep an eye on the accessory display at Dior, Paris, France.
Antoine Antoniol/Getty Images.

**AFTER YOU HAVE READ THIS CHAPTER,
YOU WILL BE ABLE TO DISCUSS**

+ the relationship between color and light

+ the terms of measurement used in lighting: CCT and CRI

+ primary and secondary store lighting

+ techniques for lighting open-backed windows and closed-back windows

+ ways in which lighting can be used to draw shoppers to particular areas within a store

+ new LED lighting technology and retrofits

+ the effective use of light in visual merchandising

Retail Lighting and the Color of Light

Lighting is an important aspect in every area of a retail operation. It begins outside where the customer arrives in the parking lot and stretches into the aisles and perimeters of the retail selling space. It illuminates the window displays, display cases, shelves, fixtures, and dressing rooms, as it functions behind the scenes to light the workplace for employees in stockrooms and warehouses. It affects the mood, safety, brand perception, and the visibility of the merchandise as well as the high electrical cost on the store's operating budget.

Retail lighting is not the same for each store environment; it is an orchestrated blend of color, contrast, control, and energy efficiency. It requires a full understanding of applications and lighting techniques and the latest lamp technology in order to meet the goals of the retailer. When planned by an expert, it has the power to influence decision-making and entice the consumer to purchase merchandise in a striking atmosphere. According to retail statistics, a customer that is excited about his or her shopping experience will stay longer, spend more money, and be more likely to return.

Retail lighting must have great color. Color—as color—means little unless it is considered in relation to the type of light in which the color is seen. It is light that makes things visible. All colors depend on light. There is natural daylight and artificial light, which can be LED, incandescent, fluorescent, or high-intensity discharge (HID) lighting.

It is not quite that simple, however. These four broad classifications of artificial light are further subdivided. There are many different types of LED and fluorescent lamps available, ranging from a warm white deluxe that attempts to create an "incandescent" effect to the cool, bluish "daylight" quality typically associated with fluorescent lighting. HID lamps can cast cool to the warm end of the colored light scale. Traditional incandescent lamps (i.e., bulbs) are warm and glowing, but placing filters over them can change the color and quality of the light. Let us, therefore, consider the color of light, the effect of light on pigment color, and how light can affect the merchandise and the area that surrounds the merchandise. (See Figure 4.1.)

Visible light is actually composed of the whole spectrum of colors, from violet to red. Imagine a beam of light passing through a glass prism or reflecting in a pool of water or oil, and you will see that spectrum broken up into a rainbow of colors—from violet, through the blues and greens, to the yellows and oranges, and finally, red. All light is caused by waves of radiant energy that vary in length. The shortest wavelength of the visible spectrum is violet light; then comes blue light, green light, and so on; and at the other end of the spectrum, with the longest wavelength, is red light. All these wavelengths—the entire spectrum—combine to form visible, or white, light, which is the light we see.

Ultraviolet light, X-rays, and gamma rays have shorter wavelengths than we can see. Infrared and radio waves are too long for us to perceive. For the purpose of understanding light and color in display and store planning, this discussion will be limited to the colors that appear in the visible spectrum. We will find that some light sources reflect the shorter wavelengths and emit cooler, or bluer, light, whereas others have a warmer light and favor the longer wavelengths.

To comprehend the relationship between color and light and why an object is perceived by an observer as a particular color, it is important to understand that light is capable of being reflected and absorbed. The **color of an object** is seen as a result of the object's selective absorption of light rays. Thus, if an object is blue, for example, this means that it absorbs all the wavelengths of light except those of blue light, which are reflected back to the observer. The same occurs with other colors, but with a different wavelength being reflected.

If the object is pure white, the full visible spectrum of light is being reflected back in approximately equal quantities. If it is pure black, then all colors in the spectrum are being absorbed by the object.

Light bounces from one surface to another, and in this movement it is capable of throwing off new

FIGURE 4.1   In the blacked out area of the new Primark store on Oxford Street, a variety of light sources and paints that respond to the lights created this exciting, youthful, casual space. The spotlights, in theatrical barn door fixtures, are hung all over the metal frames that line the ceiling and soffit, while other lamps are focused on the black abstract mannequins and the product presentation in the bright, fluorescent colored wall units. *Design: Dalziel & Pow, London, United Kingdom. Photography: Andrew Townsend.*

colors. For example, a wall or panel is painted pink. A wedgewood-blue carpet is installed. If warm, incandescent lights are used, the carpet may turn slightly lavender from the warm pink reflection cast by the walls. The incandescent light may also play up any reds that are in the warm blue carpet. (A warm blue has some purple in it, i.e., red and blue. Incandescent light reflects most in the red end of the spectrum.) If a daylight fluorescent light were switched on instead, the blue of the carpet might seem more sparkling and cool, and the walls would take on the lavender tone. The overall light will affect the color of the walls, the floor, and the ceiling, and bouncing around as it does, most of all it will affect the color of the merchandise.

Correlated Color Temperature

Choosing light with the right color temperature and color rendering index (CRI) is essential for retail space. CRI and correlated color temperature (CCT) are two units of measurement used to define the properties of light source color.

Correlated color temperature is a measure of a lamp's color appearance when lighted. All lamps are given a color temperature based on the color of the light emitted. All light sources differ. Two white light sources may look the same but can render colors differently or provide a different feel to the space. By using lamps of the same CCT and with the same, or similar, color rendering indexes, the space will have even, consistent illumination throughout.

White light falls into three general categories: warm, neutral, and cool, measured in Kelvin (K). White light with a hint of yellow candlelight is called "warm white" (below 3,000K); it enhances reds and oranges, dulls blues, and adds a yellow tint to whites and greens. Neutral white (3,000K–3,500K) enhances most colors equally and does not emphasize either yellow or blue. Bluish white, like moonlight on snow, is considered "cool white" (above 3,500K); it enhances blues, dulls reds, and imparts a bluish tint to whites and greens. Warm light makes a space feel smaller, more comfortable and familiar, where cooler light make areas appear more spacious. Neutral light improves the feeling of well-being, which may extend the amount of time the customer spends in the store, leading to a purchase. (See Figure 4.2.)

Color Rendering Index

Once you have decided what the color of a lamp is with CCT, you also would want to know how accurate that lamp is in revealing an objects color. Color rendering index is that measurement. **Color rendering index** is a measure of how a light source renders colors of objects compared to how a reference light source renders the same colors. CRI can be used to compare sources of the same type and CCT. A palette of specific colors is used, and the CRI calculation is the difference between each color sample illuminated by the test light source and the reference source. The group of samples is averaged, and a score between 0 and 100 is calculated, with 100 being the best match between light sources.

The higher the CRI of a light source, the better—and more natural—colors appear. For products to be presented in a true-to-life way, which increases a store's credibility, a CRI value of 80–100 is recommended. (See Figure 4.3.)

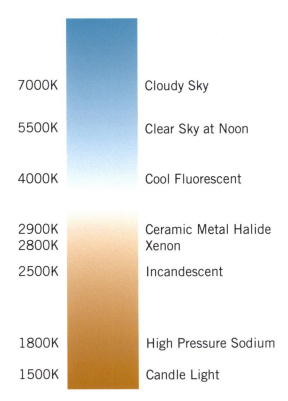

7000K	Cloudy Sky
5500K	Clear Sky at Noon
4000K	Cool Fluorescent
2900K	Ceramic Metal Halide
2800K	Xenon
2500K	Incandescent
1800K	High Pressure Sodium
1500K	Candle Light

FIGURE 4.2   The CCT chart illustrates the color difference between warm white (2,000K–3,000K), cool white (3,100K–4,500K) and daylight (4,600K–6,500K) measured in Kelvins on a scale. Daylight is the most desirable lighting for retail environments and display areas.

Appearance

R1		Light Grayish Red
R2		Dark Grayish Yellow
R3		Strong Yellow Green
R4		Moderate Yellowish Green
R5		Light Bluish Green
R6		Light Blue
R7		Light Violet
R8		Light Reddish Purple
R9		Strong Red
R10		Strong Yellow
R11		Strong Green
R12		Strong Blue
R13		Light Yellowish Pink
R14		Moderate Olive Green

FIGURE 4.3   The CRI color chart reveals the light quality of a particular light source measured against natural light. It can be used to compare sources of the same type to determine better clarity.

New Lighting Trends

ENERGY SAVING RETROFITS

Retailers concerned about economical ways to light stores have been experimenting with LED lighting for some time now. Nearly every day major retailers like Sainsbury's, Tesco, Next, Target, and Walmart are announcing cost-saving new LED lighting rollouts in the news. Completely overhauling a store's existing system with new LED lighting can be extremely expensive, and it can take three to five years for the savings to be realized. This has generated the more affordable trend of upgrading as opposed to complete refurbishments for many stores. The most popular trend in lighting is **energy-saving retrofits**. **Retrofitting** is a term often used when converting older, outdated lighting technologies such as fluorescent, CFL, and HID (metal halide) to a newer, energy-efficient technology, like an **LED** (Light-Emitting Diode) system.

This process has been streamlined with the introduction of a whole new variety of LED light bulbs, allowing stores to reduce consumption without the cost of changing all of their original lighting fixtures.

BRANDING WITH LIGHT

Another ongoing trend is **branding with light**. The competition from online shopping has put more pressure on bricks-and-mortar retailers to distinguish their stores with a brand experience. Lighting is one of the most effective ways to project a distinctive and recognizable brand presence. For stores like Hollister, Sephora, and Primark, lighting has become a part of what makes the brand identifiable in the landscape of competing retailers. Each store's lighting differs in warmth or coolness and the "theatrics," or lighting effects. Note the extreme contrast of lighting used in the Hollister store environment. The brightest amount of light is focused on the merchandise, contrasting against the shadowed store environment. Hollister's exaggerated use of spotlighting makes the products visually pop from the fixtures.

Primark has opted for a bright feel all over, the opposite approach of Hollister, by highlighting its retail space with various strengths of strong, bright light. Hard-goods retailer Crate and Barrel chooses to "paint" its merchandise with light. By using strokes of light on glassware and table-top merchandise, a more subtle contrast of light and dark plays up colors, patterns, and textures. (See Figure 4.4.)

FIGURE 4.4   In a store designed all in black and white and the numerous silvery tones between, the profile silhouette of the designer, Karl Lagerfeld, is outlined and backlit with the cool blue light. The blue is Lagerfeld's brand color. *Karl Lagerfeld, London, UK. Designed by Plajer & Franz.*

SMART LIGHTING

Thanks to digital technology, lighting can guide you around a shop and send you special offer on your phone when you're looking at particular items. This is **smart lighting**. Current market leader GE's LED lighting fixtures use indoor location technology embedded inside to deliver high-value applications to retailers, providing the precise location of shoppers using an opt-in application on their smartphones and tablets. The solution combines Visible Light Communication (VLC), Bluetooth Low Energy (BLE), and inertial device sensors, and supports any Android or iOS application on a smart device equipped with a camera and/or Bluetooth® Smart technology (http://www.gelighting.com). The comprehensive approach enables retailers to reach a broad number of shoppers across the largest area—from the parking lot to anywhere in the store where there is LED light. As a result, retailers can achieve continuous return on investment on their conversion to LED lighting while providing a strategic platform for the connected retail store of the future. To help retailers increase in-store traffic and basket size, leading manufacturers are connecting smart LEDs to digital marketing platforms to deliver relevant content and create social shopping experiences. For example, retailers can use indoor positioning systems to:

◆ Welcome repeat customers with personalized shopping lists as they approach the store front, then provide an easy-to-follow map to optimize their shopping time.

◆ Offer coupons and promotions based on shoppers' position and direction in the aisle combined with shopping history.

◆ Present customer reviews, play product information videos, and connect on-demand with virtual associates to make brand choice easier.

OLED

We are finding new sources for light that are more energy efficient—lamps that burn longer and brighter, with better color rendition—that are revolutionizing lighting as we knew it. The newest and latest lighting is **OLED, organic light-emitting diodes**. OLED comes in the form of large, flat wall or ceiling panels. Without using any bulbs, the panel-shaped fixture allows for a more even distribution of light over a wider space without the need for additional components to distribute the light. Due to its low intensity, there is very little of the glare and harsh shadowing that you might get with single-point lighting.

OLEDs are known for producing the kind of high-quality illumination that closely resembles natural sunlight. Although many high-end LEDs have been able to achieve this, OLED also tends to be superior at bringing out the true colors of the store surroundings, fixtures, and merchandise. Its rating on the color rendering index, a measure of how well a light source performs, is consistently above 90. The maximum score is 100 (sunlight).

Most incandescent lamps are outdated because they deliver too much heat, use too much energy, and need constant maintenance because they burn out too quickly. Fluorescents have long been energy efficient, and now, in a new form, it is possible to screw a fluorescent bulb into a socket meant for an incandescent bulb, and no ballast is needed. LED lamps have finally mastered new color technology. In the past, LED meant compromising on color quality. Halogen has been the benchmark for color quality, but in fact many newer LED products are now outperforming halogen.

Lighting solutions are changing daily. Each new issue of architectural and store design publications brings more news about newer and better lighting techniques, fixtures, bulbs, and such. The only way to know "what's new" and "what's best" for an installation or lighting plan is to work with a professional lighting specialist. It is much too confusing for the layperson to do on his or her own. The following is current for today but may be old news by tomorrow, so consider what is mentioned here as recent, but perhaps no longer "now."

General, or Primary, Lighting

General, or primary, ambient lighting is the foundation or base level of illumination in an area. It is usually the light that fills the selling floor from overhead using a fixed lighting system, such as a pattern of fluorescent troffers or recessed downlighting in the ceiling. Primary lighting promotes good orientation, a sense of comfort for the shopper in the retail environment. It is the first layer of light that subsequent layers of light build upon. It does not include accent lights, wall washers, or display highlighting lamps. (These are forms of secondary lighting.) Also, it does not include "glamour," or decorative, lighting: the sconces, counter or table lamps, indirect lighting, and so on.

Secondary, or Accent, Lighting

Flat, shadowless, overall lighting can create a static and boring selling floor. Glare or overly bright, strong light can be irritating and a detriment to selling. Shadows, highlights, and contrast are necessary; they can delight, intrigue, and pique the imagination. A selling floor, and especially a display, needs changes from light to dark, from highlights to shadows. They need flash and sparkle and should make the viewer's eye travel over an area emphasizing texture, shape, finish, and color. **Secondary, or accent, lighting** should accomplish all this.

Key lighting supplies the hard accents; it is the stronger light that adds "punch" to the selling floor. Using variable strengths of light helps indicate hierarchy or what the shopper should see first. *Fill lighting* provides softer, wider distribution to smooth shadows, and *highlighting* produces wide shadows that reveals the intricacies of products, fabrics, and finishes. *Backlighting* will intensify shapes and size; it makes an object glow and separate from the surrounding space. *Up-lighting* may be used to break up or divide spaces; it causes more dramatic effects. It can also be ghostly if improperly used. Secondary lighting is sometimes referenced as feature and display lighting. It can diffuse a ledge area with a glow or an aura of light. It can be integrated into racks or the light in a case or under a counter.

When lamps are hidden behind valances or recessed under grids or baffles, and warmer colors are not needed, fluorescent lights may work effectively to provide secondary lighting. However, newer LED lights can add highlights, provide shadows, mold and dimensionalize the merchandise, and even flatter the customer's complexion.

Accent or focal lighting not only highlights the product or the group of merchandise but also makes it stand out from its surroundings. Under the accent light, the color of the merchandise appears sharper and more brilliant, the textures are defined, and the details are brought into prominence. The strong, focused light of the accent lamp can make a product stand out in a highly illuminated selling floor or in a sunlit window. It works most effectively when the surrounding area is low-keyed and rather dim so that the accent light seems even more brilliant by contrast. Spotlights are used as accent or highlighting lamps in the showing and selling areas, in display windows, on platform and ledge displays, and on island setups.

Perimeter Lighting

Larger store environments demand stronger perimeter definition that helps contribute to the perception of size and orientation of space. It is common for the shopper to feel weary in a big box store that only uses flat primary or general lighting. Perimeter lighting improves visibility and encourages the shopper to wander out of the main aisle and into the merchandising space.

Perimeter lighting might be a long linear span of fluorescent tubes covered by a baffle that up-lights the perimeter of the store above the sightlines. It can enhance wayfinding by directing attention to department or category signage. Vertical illumination can be achieved in a number of ways depending on the store type, size, and budget. Tubular lighting can be inset into a ceiling drop; other techniques include scalloping the light across the walls or grazing with different light intensities. Wall washing bounces the light back into the store and makes the space seem larger.

Decorative Lighting

Secondary lighting devices can be decorative solutions such as "candlelit" chandeliers, wall sconces, and pendants that

FIGURE 4.5 To affect the desired lush and intimate ambience for the lounge area for the dressing rooms in the Intimate Apparel department of the Galeries Lafayette in Jakarta, the designers at Plajer & Franz of Stuttgart added the crystal chandelier furnished with warm, incandescent flame-shaped bulbs. It helps set the scene in the red velvet surround. Incandescent floods are inserted in the ceiling to provide the deep, sensual mood that inhabits the space. *Galeries Lafayette, Jakarta, Indonesia. Designed by Plajer & Franz of Stuttgart, Germany. Photography © 2012 by diephotodesigner.de.*

suggest warmth and elegance with only a minimum of actual light. Decorative lighting can articulate more about the brand's image by the style of the fixture alone. Imagine a row of dangling Edison bulbs randomly hung above a warm wooden surface in the home design area or a giant pink globe light in tweens; a decorative lighting fixture can be used to accent the space—make it feel homey or trendy or even bring a particular retro style back into mind. (See Figure 4.5.)

LED

LED bulbs are the most efficient and longest-lasting light source, which is why more and more retail stores are moving to LEDs for the majority of their lighting applications. LED technology has made leaps in bounds in the last several years, and is becoming a viable option for nearly all lighting needs.

First introduced as the tiny indicator lights on electronic components, LED is now available in every possible lighting configuration, lending to its versatility. LED puck lights and tape lights were first on the consumer market; screw-based bulbs and a tubular light bar similar to a fluorescent were introduced soon after. LED high and low bays have replaced much of the HID used in larger retail spaces, and the retrofits are available for MR16 and Par lighting.

The newest form of LED lighting is a bendable OLED sheet or panel.

LEDs are solid-state devices that, unlike an incandescent, do not require heating of a filament to create light. The electricity passes through a chemical compound that is excited and then generates light. LED lighting requires a circuit board that allows electricity to pass through it at a specified current and voltage. There are seven distinct colors of visible LED. The blue LED developed in the 1960s is vital for generating white light; scientists who developed the blue LED won the Nobel Prize in 2014. Blue LED mixed with other colors has the ability to generate millions of perceived colors. Since the LED diode only emits light in one direction, it requires the integration of a lens to diffuse the light. The leading manufacturers have innovated LED lighting solutions that simplify directional applications, such as recessed downlights, troffers, tracks, shelf and counter, pendants, and sconces. LED lamps designed to replace traditional lighting are available in hundreds of shapes, sizes, and wattages. (See Figure 4.6.)

The LED's current popularity is due to its broader life expectancy. It also has no toxic elements. LEDs can last 50,000 to 100,000 hours, compared with incandescents and halogens, which last from 2,500 to 5,000 hours. LED

FIGURE 4.6 To break the monotony of straight vertical lines created by the many columns, the designers at Dalziel & Pow came up with these curved arches of LED lighting that soften the overall look while forming illuminated arches. The area enclosed by the illuminated arches is now a shop-within-the-shop. *David Jones, Bourne Street, Australia. Design: Dalziel & Pow, London, United Kingdom. Photography: Andrew Townsend.*

PAR20 floods and spotlights (7 watt) can be used for shop interiors. Color rendition has improved dramatically, and colors in the white and blue spectrum are getting brighter and warmer. With its multiple colored light possibilities, LED is being used for creating color effects in wall washing and signage.

Environmental Lighting Company, a resource for these lighting products, has outlined some of the benefits associated with LED:

◆ Extremely low power consumption
◆ Extremely long life (50,000 to 100,000 hours)
◆ Durable and insensitive to vibration
◆ Dimmable with the use of a driver and programmable
◆ Lightweight and compact
◆ Color without the use of filters or lenses
◆ No reflectors required to direct light
◆ Environmentally friendly
◆ No mercury or other toxic elements
◆ Recyclable

With LED lighting offering so much, and being so new, there will be new advances made daily in the uses and applications of the LED technology for store lighting and point-of-purchase displays and signage. What is important is that LED is cost effective, energy efficient, and "green."

Fluorescent Lighting

Some retail operations are still illuminated by rows of **fluorescent light** fixtures that span the length or width of the store. The fluorescent fixture is usually the least expensive and most efficient fixture to use from the point of initial cost, cost of energy, and length of lamp life. Although it is often the popular choice for the contractor to install and the retailer to maintain, it is not always the best choice for many categories of merchandise. Fluorescent lamps can produce a flat, even, and stultifying blanket of light that offers few shadows and provides little depth or textural interest. There are degrees of "warmth" and "coolness" available in fluorescent lamps, from the rosy quality of "warm white deluxe" to the blue of "cool white deluxe"—with many gradations in between.

The merchandise—or the general type of merchandise to be presented under the lighting—should be tested under the various types of light bulbs. No one type or color will enhance everything, but the one that is generally most flattering should be chosen.

Fluorescents work well for general or primary lighting since they can be shielded, filtered, or softened with grids, baffles, or diffusing panels—all to the good. A **baffle** is any device used to direct, divert, or disseminate light. It can be a louver over a light, an egg crate grid, or even an angled panel that redirects the stream of light. Fluorescent lamps can also be used in showcases or hidden beneath shelves to add the required warmth or coolness that the particular merchandise warrants.

In any area, a ceiling may be regarded as another wall, or the sixth side of a cube, with the walls composing four sides, and the floor the fifth. As much as it might be desirable to use different colors of fluorescent in different areas, to do so would break the ceiling pattern and call attention to the changes of color overhead. It is advisable to test and then select a proper mix of perhaps two different color tubes that can be used in the same fixture and provide the best overall colored light for the store. A grid or diffuser will hide the fact that in a single fixture, daylight and warm white tubes are being used in tandem. According to Green Energy Innovations, fluorescent lamps come in a new variety of sizes and shapes, but tube diameter is the important consideration when it comes to energy efficiency. The lamps are designated by type and their diameters in eighths of an inch. (For example, T12 means tube-type 12/8 inch diameter). The T12 is the oldest, most common version and most inefficient, yet it still enjoys widespread use due to cheap lamps and parts.

The T8 was designed specifically to be compatible with the T12, making retrofits simple. In a given light fixture, four T8 lamps will produce more light than four T12 lamps while consuming the same amount of energy. This makes it possible to de-lamp legacy T12 fixtures and replace four T12 lamps with only two T8 lamps, resulting in energy savings of at least 50 percent while keeping an equal level of illumination. Since fewer bulbs are required, maintenance and bulb replacement costs are reduced.

COMPACT FLUORESCENT LAMPS (CFLS)

With users of electric lights demanding more energy-efficient and longer-lasting bulbs, many companies are now producing compact fluorescent bulbs. These lamps look somewhat like distorted incandescent bulbs and can be screwed into sockets traditionally designed to accept incandescent bulbs. Compact fluorescents bulbs use around 75 percent less energy and last ten times as long as incandescent bulbs. These lamps are mostly used for general, ambient lighting, but some will find the color not as warm or pleasant as the incandescent. When using compact fluorescents, it is important to make sure you are getting the color of light you want. Often, these screw-in fluorescents are used to retrofit existing ceiling light fixtures and can be combined with HID lamps for accenting. Consumers and retailers who quickly transitioned to CFLs for the energy and efficiency were shocked to learn about the potential dangers of mercury poisoning when CFLs are recycled. Mercury from energy production and broken CFL bulbs seeps into soil and water during the recycling process. CFL use is currently being reevaluated.

Incandescent Lighting

This form of illumination is on its way out! With retailers and users of electricity becoming more "green" and looking for more energy-efficient and effective methods of lighting, they have found that the traditional **incandescent light** uses more energy than other lamps; gives off more heat, necessitating the use of additional energy for air cooling; and requires more frequent bulb replacement. Many incandescent bulbs are being phased out of production, and we are looking forward to newer, more efficient, more ecology-favorable lighting devices—some of which are mentioned on the following pages.

Some incandescent spotlights called **Parabolic Aluminized Reflector (PAR) bulbs** are still in use. They can be used as a primary light source but are usually used as secondary lighting. Although these lamps cost more to purchase, they do have a longer lamp life. A PAR bulb can burn for 3,000 hours or longer; however energy-saving LED retrofits are replacing incandescent lighting on a regular basis.

MR16 and MR11

The **MR16** and the **MR11** (miniature reflector) are another form of incandescent; they are used mostly as accent or focal lighting. First introduced as miniature, low-voltage tungsten-halogen lamps, they emit sharp, bright light and produce a color balance that comes close to sunlight (a CRI of 95 to 100). MR16s provide precise center beam intensity and beam control, have excellent color rendering, are available with special lens options for a variety of effects, and they are dimmable. The 75-watt MR16 lamp will provide a more brilliant light than a traditional 150-watt incandescent spotlight and will illuminate merchandise at four or five times the ambient level of other lamps. Colors appear truer under the MR16 and MR11, and, once these low-voltage lamps have been installed, they are efficient, relatively inexpensive to operate, compact, and clean in comparison to traditional incandescents. Also, because they are low voltage, they produce much less heat than the incandescent lamps; they burn cooler and do not harm the merchandise.

The popularity of the MR16 is based, in part, on its compactness, its 2-inch diameter, and the efficient low-voltage tungsten-halogen light source. The MR11 and MR16 are now available in energy-efficient LED retrofits; however, some retailers still prefer the original halogen to the LED retrofit.

HIGH-INTENSITY DISCHARGE (HID) LIGHTING

The **HID** lamp, which is very energy efficient, has been a strong contender in the field of general, overall store lighting. HIDs are relatively small in size (compared with fluorescent lamps) and will, like incandescents, provide shadows and highlights. HID is used for streetlights, stadiums, malls, and large public spaces that require a strong primary light source. The mercury-type HID may be too green, the metal-halide type may appear too blue, and the sodium type is quite yellow, but some manufacturers are producing warmer and more flattering types of light. HID lamps provide so much light that they are best used in areas where the ceiling is at least 15 feet high; otherwise, they will create an excessively bright and sharply lit selling floor. They are often used in big box stores and are referred to as high bay or low bay fixtures.

Ceramic metal halide, or CMH, is another form of HID lighting favored by retailers. This new generation of lamps provides an extra-long life and exceptional color rendition of up to 18,000 hours and over four times the efficiency of halogen lamps. This means significantly improved lumen maintenance and enhanced quality of light. General Electric is producing ceramic metal halide lamps to replace incandescent PAR and halogen, like the new 23-watt GE ConstantColor CMH Integral PAR38. This lamp provides excellent energy savings and can be used for ambient and display lighting in retail settings. The lamps are available as 10-degree spots, 25-degree floods, and 36-degree wide floods with a warm, 3,000K color temperature.

Eye Lighting International of North Carolina produces a line of Cera Arc ceramic metal halide lamps with 39-, 70-, and 150-watt ratings. These feature an R9 value of 90 and a CRI rating of 92—high ratings in the industry. According to the manufacturer, "These values create rich colors, especially red, which is the most important color in retailing." Rated at 3,600K, the Cera Arc blends well with fluorescents and, in addition to the brilliant reds, offers great greens, blues, and white—all essential in showcasing clothing, jewelry, and flowers.

Colored Lights, Filters, and LED Controllers

Just as pigments can be mixed to produce new colors, **colored lights** can be mixed to create new and different color effects. The **primary colors of light** are red, green (not yellow, as with pigments), and blue, or RGB.

White light can be produced by mixing the three primary colors of light. Red and blue light together will produce magenta or a purplish red. Blue and green will combine to form cyan or cyan-blue, which is actually a bright blue-green. Red and green create a yellowish or amber light. Thus, the **secondary colors of light** are magenta, cyan, and amber. The visual merchandiser should be especially concerned with the mixing of colored light on solid, pigmented surfaces. This is usually accomplished with colored filters and gels on incandescent or PAR lighting used in window displays or newer LED lighting systems. A red filter placed over a white light on a white or light neutral surface will turn that surface red. The red filter absorbs all the blue and green light waves present in the white light that is going through the red filter; only the red wavelengths will pass through to the painted surface. A blue filter will absorb the red and green wavelengths, producing a blue light on the white painted area.

LED lights have similar capabilities to change color with the use of a small handheld remote controller. The remote controller allows the visual merchandiser to choose the desired shade or tints of colors and then add to the intensity of a color or gently neutralize some of its intensity, much like colored glass filters and plastic gelatins used in window displays and on the stage in a theater. Advanced lighting systems with color mixing capabilities enable one unit to deliver high color and white light together. Multiple channels of LED light sources combine to produce a full spectrum of precisely controllable light, including millions of saturated colors, pastels, and uniform white light with perfect color accuracy across the entire range of color temperatures. (See Figure 4.7.)

There are, however, many colored glass filters and plastic gelatins on the market, as well as shades and tints of these colors, that subtly can add to the intensity of a color or gently neutralize some of its intensity.

There are all sorts of pinks and blush tones available to warm up skin tones or suggest a sunset. There are ambers that go down to pale straw and strained sunlight. A "daylite" filter is a clear, light blue that will fill in an area with the suggestion of a spring day or will chill shredded Styrofoam with icy blue shadows. The green gels go from the pastel yellow-greens to the deep, atmospheric blue-greens, or cyans.

In most cases, lighter tints are used on displays to enrich the color presentation without appreciably changing the actual color. Strong, deep colors are used to create atmosphere—the dramatic side or back lighting; for example, the mood lighting of a window or ledge display. Deeper-colored lights are mainly reserved for modeling and shaping the merchandise by adding color to the shadows and folds as well as by reflecting color from one surface to another.

Green and cyan light on skin tones should be avoided, although it may work for Halloween or an "out-of-this-world" presentation. Pinks and rose tints are becoming to most skin tones, from the palest white to the darkest browns, and they enhance the warm colors in merchandise.

Planning Window Lighting

You may walk by a store in daylight and catch a glimpse of the window, and it is likely that all you will see is yourself reflected in the window. It may be difficult to determine if the store is open for business. In that glimpse, you can check out what you are wearing, but you haven't a single clue as to what lies beyond the glass. What kind of store is it? What sort of merchandise is sold there? When a store's windows are not illuminated, or are illuminated improperly, they become a giant one-way mirror facing the street or the mall.

This is where good lighting makes a difference. Reflection and glare are both useful and potentially harmful; they can attract the eye to merchandise when used properly, but irritate and annoy when used incorrectly. Using lamps with good glare reduction values avoids direct glare and disturbing reflections on surfaces, such

FIGURE 4.7   By bathing the area in blue light, the designers at Dalziel & Pow of London achieved a remarkable effect and highlighted by low lighting a shop in the Primark store on Oxford Street in London. The blue light is soft, hushed, and mysterious and thus effects a unique feeling for the space and the merchandise. The black abstract mannequins add to the effect, but the clothes on the forms are cleverly lit with clear light. *Design: Dalziel & Pow, London, United Kingdom. Photography: Andrew Townsend.*

as glass windows, glossy surfaces, and digital screens. A very bright window is not the most effective lighting solution. Using contrast to highlight merchandise and different areas of the window draws attention to the featured merchandise. Dramatic lighting is key to attracting customers to a window display, but it is important to utilize several levels of illumination to create contrast. Wall washing fixtures can be used for general illumination; however, they should not compete with the spot lighting on the merchandise. How the shopper perceives color is also very important, and lighting can make red sizzle and shock, make blue appear ethereal or chilly, or allow orange to scream or turn into a rich, earthy shade. Engage the passerby with intense white light using uniform saturated illumination, direct accent lighting to highlight and to define merchandise, and create stopping power that will make consumers want to come inside the store. Different lighting techniques can add interest to props or furniture in the display. Using light underneath will make an object float and create better separation from the floor surface. Lighting from behind or in-between props or pieces of furniture will promote greater separation from the floor.

Lighting the Open-Back Window

If the store has an open-back window, the lighting in the display area up front must be strong enough and bright enough to attract and keep the shopper's eye from going past the featured merchandise in the display directly into the store on view beyond. The window is not the place for strings of fluorescent tubes casting a deadly dull chill over already lifeless mannequins. Fluorescent lighting also casts a flat, dull, and lifeless pall over the colors of the garments. Use only a few sharp spots—incandescent or MR16 miniature low-voltage tungsten LED retrofits or PAR spotlights—and focus the light away from the glass—not into the store, but directly down onto the merchandise.

At all times avoid lighting up the mannequin's face. Chest lighting is the preferred technique; it shows off the color of the garment as well as the detailing of the design while softly illuminating the mannequin's face. If the mannequin's face is viewed in the full glare of the light, it will look less realistic; lifeless. The reflected light enhances the mannequin's mystique and makes it seem more "human." Place the merchandise as far back into the space as possible so the spotlights can be most effective and not have to battle the natural glare associated with daylight—and traffic lights at night—on the plate glass windows. Just as a single match lit in total darkness can become a beacon, a spotlight in a relatively low-lit area becomes a sharp, brilliant point of light. The effect created will all depend upon the contrast. Setting the back panel behind the display as far back as possible and bringing the lights in, away from the window, increases energy efficiency as well.

A simple length of fabric of the right color, texture, or pattern, or a combination of these; a screen; a panel of textured wood; or even a cluster of tall plants can serve as a partial background in the open-back window. The color of the divider can either complement the color of the garments or enhance some value of the color. The divider also effectively separates the display area from the selling floor and the lighting on that sales floor. By cutting out or minimizing the store's light, the window light seems stronger. If a shopper passing by sees the light in the window, he or she will also see the display of merchandise and be aware of the retail space viewed to either side of the partial background. The shopper knows that the store is open; the shopper knows what kind of merchandise is available. (See Figure 4.8.)

If the store has an enclosed display window—three walls, a floor, and a ceiling—the visual merchandiser has greater opportunities for magical lighting effects. Not only can the visual merchandiser highlight the featured merchandise and bring to it the attention it warrants, but he or she can also use light to "paint" the background a complementary or accenting color or dramatize the setting by creating a particular ambience; for example, blue and green lighting to simulate an underwater look or yellows and oranges mixed with reds to create the atmosphere of a setting sun or a rich day in autumn. Colored lights, colored filters, and theatrical gels all work wonderfully well to achieve these effects.

FIGURE 4.8 The landmark modernist building on Fifth Avenue in New York City has become the home of the Joe Fresh clothing company. The interior, as designed by Burdifilek of Toronto, features an all-white ambiance highlighted with areas of the Joe Fresh signature orange color. Combined with the almost all glass façade, the brilliant in-store lighting makes every spot in the store a display area open for viewing from the street. *Photography: Ben Rahn, A-Frame Studio.*

Many theatrical lighting supply stores also carry a variety of inexpensive gobo pattern filters that create images when attached to a special lighting fixture on walls, floors, and even on the merchandise. With these stock gobo pattern filters one can have rain, snow, lightening, or sunshine; light streaming through a Gothic window for a bridal setting; palm trees in the tropics for swimwear; a starlit night for ball gowns; or fireworks for a red, white, and blue promotion—or a spectacular sale event. Lighting suppliers also have the capability to laser cut custom design gobo patterns of brand logos, copy, or even a sales tagline. More expensive but also more effective are the filters that rotate

around the light, causing movement and animation in the window. Projector lamps offer other special effects.

Using these techniques requires great control over the daylight that might, at certain times of the day, overpower the window lighting and the special effects. Awnings drawn down during the sunlight hours can help somewhat, but even better is setting the merchandise and the mannequins as far back as possible in the closed-back window to take full advantage of the lighting effects and to overcome the effects of glare and reflection. Newer LED lamps or retrofits, incandescent lighting, and MR16s (halogen or LED) are the most effective sources for window display lighting. (See Figure 4.9.)

FIGURE 4.9 The all-enclosed display window allows the visual merchandiser more freedom to play with lighting and lights. In the Bergdorf Goodman, New York, display, the back wall is covered with fanciful line drawings overhung with strings of colored bee-lights. The lighting on the abstract mannequins is soft and subtle, as is the general window illumination. *Eugene Gologursky/Getty Images.*

Planning Store Interior Lighting

Light means seeing. Light serves to lead the shopper into and through the store. It directs the shopper's attention from one featured presentation or classification to another, with stops along the way to appreciate the highlighted focal points and displays. It can separate one area from the next, one boutique or vendor's shop from another. The light level and the "color" (the warmth or coldness) of the light in the store create the ambience. Is it warm, welcoming, and inviting? Is it residential, intimate, and comfortable? Is it cool and aloof or just cold and depressing? Is it flat and boring, or does it sparkle with the contrasts of highlights and shadows? A store's lighting is composed of many different light sources and lamps. It is a "palette" of lamps, different color variations, intensities, and wattage, and it can also be affected by natural light that comes in through skylights or windows. Working with a lighting professional is the best way to ensure the proper decision making, especially since color and texture react differently to the quality of light. Since LED and many other light sources have a wide range of warmth and coolness, the selection process begins by actually testing wall surface and material samples under the light to determine what suits the store environment best. After careful examination of how lighting interacts with the color of surfaces, fixtures, and furnishings in the environment a determination can be made.

The **store's lighting plan** has layers or tiers of light, beginning with the general, overall illumination of the retail space and also the accents—the highlighters that point out what is new, unique, or special. It can include atmospheric touches, like chandelier, wall or column sconces, or wall and ceiling washers. Although these may not all show off the merchandise, they do show off the attitude of the store. There are also appraisal lights that allow the shopper to examine things like jewelry, fashion accessories, or cosmetics.

People, like insects, are attracted to light. It is human nature to walk toward the area where the light is brightest. Thus, a store designer can reconfigure a given floor plan using light. If the plan is long and narrow, a strong light on the far wall makes that wall seem closer and encourages shoppers to head toward the rear of the space. If the long perimeter walls are illuminated, the shopper is better able to see the mass display of the wall stock. Bright lights can be added on the displays or fixtures set along the aisle, while the aisle itself can be is kept in slightly lower light. Between the well-lit back wall and the highlighted aisle displays, the middle area of the shop or department can function in medium or general lighting. Using light-colored floor materials on the aisles may also make lights on the aisle unnecessary. (See Figures 4.10–4.12.)

There are definite "moments of truth" that must be considered in the store's lighting plan. One of these moments is when the shopper tries on the garment and stands before the mirror. The light that complements the garment should flatter the shopper. The cash/wrap desk presents another such moment. As the shopper sees the selected garment being boxed or bagged and being paid for, the garment must reach out in the fullness and richness of color to reassure the shopper that he or she has made the right decision.

The department store visit is usually of short duration. The lighting has to get the customers immediately, grab their interest, hold their attention, and show them what they should see. According to Hera lighting specialist Brad Stewart, "There is an 'eye-to-product ratio,' or the percentage of times a customer's eyes lock onto an actual product or brand name, while in your store, versus anything else in the store. Lighting has the ability to physically change a retail environment to increase sales, first by keeping customers there longer and second by getting their eyes to lock onto products more often while they're in the store. Whenever customers look at a product, their brain has an unconscious decision to make—am I interested in that—or not."

Today, designers have so much more opportunity to use lighting in innovative ways within their design of the store; LED requires little maintenance and can integrate into smaller spaces. More and more we see lighting built into walls, shelves, and fixtures on the selling floor—ceiling to floor. With all of the new lighting innovations, there are so many more opportunities to use lighting as a design element in the store environment.

FIGURE 4.10   Long fluorescent tubes are patterned helter-skelter across the dark gray ceiling, adding a cool sense of excitement to the area. Adjustable spotlights, attached to a suspended ceiling grid, add warmth and sparkle and highlight the product display and the dressed mannequins at Primark in Madrid, Spain. *Design: Dalziel & Pow, London, United Kingdom. Photography: Andrew Townsend.*

Suggestions for Using Light Effectively

1. Avoid bright, white lights directly on a mannequin's face, elbows, or shoes. Save the brightest lights for the merchandise, and avoid anything that will detract from the merchandise.

2. Use colored light to create the right setting for the merchandise. Save it for props and backgrounds. If colored light is used on a garment to intensify the color, stay with the pastel filters: pale pinks for the reds and red-violets, pale straw for the yellows and oranges, daylight blue for the cool colors, and Nile green for the greens.

3. It is more effective to light across a display than directly down on it. Direct downlighting can create unpleasant and unattractive shadows. The upper left light can be directed over to the lower right side of the display; the upper right light is then directed over to the lower left. This creates a crossover of light—a more even, more diffused light—and nullifies areas in the display space that are too bright or too dark.

4. The lighting in a window display should be checked at night. Many imperfections, such as wrinkles, are more apparent under the artificial light when the softening influence of daylight does not enter the window. Colored lights will also look different when there is no other source of light with which to contend. What may have seemed perfect during the daylight hours at night may appear harsh or garish. It is also advisable to check that the lights are not "flooding over" into the street—into the eyes of passersby and the road traffic.

5. There is nothing particularly attractive about electric wires unless they are meant to be part of the decorative scheme. Find ways to "lose" them—hide and disguise them.

FIGURE 4.11   Fluorescent tubes encased in the long, frosted-glass-fronted fixtures make a strong pattern against the blacked-out ceiling while providing the general, or primary, lighting for this young people's store. Pencil fluorescent tubes in red plastic sleeves add to the visual excitement and hectic tempo of the shop. *S. Oliver, Berlin. Design: Plajer & Franz Studio, Berlin, Germany.*

FIGURE 4.12   Lords shop in Hampstead, London, stocks a variety of light bulbs. It created this clever dimensional chart to assist its shoppers in selecting the right bulb for their light fixture. An actual electrified lamp bulb hangs down in front of an enlarged line drawing of the bulb shape with a simple description of usage, wattage, etc. *Lords, Hampstead, London, United Kingdom.*

6. Display lights are expensive to use. They use up energy. It is wise to set up a timer device that will automatically turn off all lights sometime during the night after the street traffic has diminished and the store lighting no longer serves any purpose of display or image. Similarly, sensors that turn on the lights of a display setup when they "sense" the presence of a person nearby can be used to save energy—and as a dramatic plus.

Just as you would seek help from a professional health care provider if you had an ailment, so should you consult with a professional lighting designer/planner when it comes to lighting a retail space. The retailer needs help in planning not only the most effective use of energy required by law but also the best way to use the energy to enhance the merchandise presentation and displays and create the desired image for the store.

Let there be light: the best light you can afford. This is not the place to economize.

Brand Box 4.1: Lighting and Brand Identity

Lighting up the store front at night is always a good idea, though it might be an expensive one. If your electric bills are astronomical (or even if they are tolerable), here are some thoughts on reflecting your brand identity—your signature color—at night.

Use LED lamps or energy-saving lamps with the controller set to your brand color—flood the store's front. It doesn't need to be the whole façade: maybe from above the display windows to the roof line or from the roof line downward. If you have display windows on the upper levels of the store, bathe them in the colored light. If your shop is in an older building where windows are arranged on the second and third floors, light the individual windows with the signature colored light. If you are fortunate to be in a newly built store, especially one with a metal grid/screen/lacework effect across the front, the architect will have already designed the lighting effect for night-time splendor as shown here in the hr2 store (Holt Renfrew) in Brossard Quartier Dix 30, Quebec City, Canada. (See Figure 4.13.) As conceived and explained by Mark Janson of the Janson Goldstein architectural design firm, "the hr2 company's signature magenta color lights up the façade at night and makes a strong beckoning call to its target market."

Should your display windows be open-backed with a clear view into the store interior, create a "curtain" of the colored light behind the display area so that the store interior is "hidden" behind the glow of colored light. Light, especially at night, is a great attention getter—so why not use the brand color to gather more interest for the brand?

In this chapter you read about how, psychologically, the shopper may react to the different levels of brightness in the store interior's lighting plan. Soft, subtle lighting—maybe even a bit dim—suggests a more expensive or upscale retailer or restaurant while an overly brightly lit space may bring mass market merchandise to mind. Warm light makes one think of fashion, of beauty, and of luxury items, while cold

FIGURE 4.13 Flaunting the store's signature color and making a big brand statement is how hr2, a new division of Holt Renfrew of Canada, is making itself known to consumers. The store's magenta color literally overwhelms the surrounding area and stakes it as its own. *Design: Burdifilek, Toronto, Canada. Photography: Mikiku Kikuyama.*

light suggests hard goods like hardware, building supplies, and discount operations. Lighting creates the ambience in which the colors, textures, and materials are presented. Designer boutiques usually are low lit, while off-price operations are often blanketed with cold light emanating from a ceiling crisscrossed with fluorescent fixtures. Part of the mystique and draw of Abercrombie & Fitch stores—aside from the provocative photography—is the dramatic lighting: pinpoints of sharp, clear light on highlighted fixtures or product in a surround of almost total darkness. The shopper doesn't need to see the name outside the shop; the dramatic lighting is part of A&F's brand identity.

Light and Lighting: Trade Talk

baffle
branding with light
color of an object
color rendering index (CRI)
colored lights
fluorescent light
general, or primary, ambient lighting
HID

incandescent light
LED
light
MR16 and MR11
Parabolic Aluminized Reflector (PAR)
   bulbs
primary colors of light
secondary colors of light

secondary, or accent, lighting
smart lighting
spotlights
store's lighting plan
visible light

Light and Lighting: A Recap

✦ In an open-back window, the lighting up front must be strong enough to keep the shopper's eye from going past the display, into the interior of the store.

✦ In a closed-back window, the visual merchandiser can use a range of lighting effects, including colored lights and light filters, to create a more theatrical display.

✦ The most effective sources for window display lighting are LED and LED retrofits for PAR and MR16.

✦ When planning a store's interior lighting, a variety of light sources and lamps can be used to create a particular interior lighting "palette" and to draw shoppers to various areas within the store.

✦ General, or primary, lighting is the overall ceiling light of a selling area. It does not include the accent or decorative lighting.

✦ Secondary lighting is the accent and decorative lighting: chandeliers; sconces; wall washers; indirect lighting; spotlights; and lights under shelves, in cases, and in counters.

✦ Fluorescent lighting is efficient and relatively inexpensive to install and maintain. The tubes are available in a wide range of "white" light, from cool bluish to warm white deluxe, which has more of a peach tone. Smaller tubes can be used in showcases, under shelves, and behind baffles as wall washers.

✦ Incandescent bulbs produce warmer and more flattering light than the fluorescent but emit more heat. The lamps do not burn as long or as efficiently as the fluorescents. They are available in a wide range of sizes, shapes, and wattages. The lamps can be decorative as well as useful.

✦ The CMH lamp is an efficient and relatively inexpensive light source that has excellent color rendition for use inside and outside the store.

✦ LEDs are solid-state devices that do not require heating of a filament. They are cost efficient, energy efficient, and green. They are replacing every other light source.

✦ Different light sources can be used on the same selling floor. It is possible to highlight and accent a fluorescent primary lighting scheme with LED or CMH secondary lighting.

✦ White light is composed of a rainbow of colors of different wavelengths, from violet to red.

✦ The primary colors of light are red, blue, and green.

✦ The secondary colors of light are magenta, cyan, and amber.

✦ A colored filter produces a particular color of light by filtering out or absorbing all the other colors in the white light except the color of the filter or gel.

✦ CRI is a measure of how a light source renders colors of objects compared to how a reference light source renders the same colors.

✦ Correlated color temperature, or CCT, is a measure of a lamp's color appearance when lighted.

1. What is the relationship between color and light? Explain your answer by detailing the reason why when looking at a red dress, we see red, rather than some other color.

2. What does CRI mean?

3. Describe three new lighting trends.

4. Define general, or primary, lighting, and provide examples of this category of lighting.

5. Provide examples of the best way to light a mannequin in an open-back window.

6. Highlight the advantages and disadvantages of incandescent lighting.

7. What are the special qualities of LED lighting?

8. What types of light sources would you select for a lingerie department or shop? Why?

9. Why have MR16 and MR11 lamps gained favor in visual merchandising and display?

10. What advice would you give to someone regarding the use of colored lights in display?

11. In selecting the types of lighting and light fixtures for a store, what factors should be taken into consideration?

12. Where should the brightest light be focused within a display?

13. What adjustments, if any, should be made to the lighting within a display window for day and night?

Chapter Five
The Design Process

Disco Era Christmas at Harvey Nichols, London, United Kingdom.
Heather Berrisford/Getty Images.

**AFTER YOU HAVE READ THIS CHAPTER,
YOU WILL BE ABLE TO DISCUSS**

- the four major types of display
- promotional and institutional displays
- five categories of display settings
- the purpose of buildup presentations in display

How does the **creative process** begin? How do the props, backdrops, and sparkle find their way into an eye-catching window? You may walk into a new store environment and wonder: Who chose the vibrant color story, luxurious fixtures, and sleek mannequins? This is the job of visual merchandiser! (See Figure 5.1.)

Today's visual merchandiser has a wide range of skills and typically functions on a collaborative team with store planners, brand marketers, merchants, and store management. They manage a variety of responsibilities as they go through the practice of developing and implementing **design concepts** and creative direction for seasonal and promotional displays and events.

The steps for developing and implementing design concepts are somewhat standard in visual merchandising; however, each store or design firm may have variations in its process. For boutiques and "one of a kind" displays, the designer may simply present a sketch and images to the shop owner for approval of the proposed props or graphics in the display. Large stores set up a yearly display calendar in advance, and in a corporate setting the visual team may take its cues from the creative or marketing department.

Most importantly, the visual merchandiser must have a clear understanding of the store's image/personality, who shops there, and the brand of merchandise to be displayed. These valuable insights are introduced and communicated

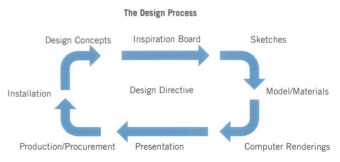

FIGURE 5.2 Diagram illustrating the design process used in visual merchandising and display. *Courtesy of Anne Kong.*

in meetings with an individual client, a design firm, or the store's visual team. Visual merchandisers who work in a department store attend weekly meetings where they interact with product developers, buyers, marketing teams, and fashion offices to better understand the objectives, timeline, and expected deliverables for displays, shops, and the overall store designs. The following steps identify each area and the order of the design process. (See Figure 5.2.)

The steps commonly followed in the design process:

- **Directive or design brief**—sets the goals for the display or project.
- **Inspiration/mood boards**—clearly illustrate the idea, inspiration or story.
- **Sketches**—bring the idea to life, encourage concept development.
- **Model**—reveals any major design flaws or potential problems in production or installation and allows for adjustments.
- **Sourcing and material selection**—brings the design to a higher level and impacts cost and budget.
- **Computer design and renderings**—provide detailed drawings of the design in scale and allow the client/team to understand the designer's intent more clearly.
- **Presentation**—"the pitch" is a formal presentation of analysis and the total design concept; it allows the designer to sell the idea.
- **Procurement, preproduction**—sourcing or finding the appropriate and most economical materials or design elements; preparing and staging the design elements in advance to ensure an efficient installation.
- **Implementation/installation**—arranging for an organized installation; last-minute problem solving and solutions are worked out.

FIGURE 5.1 A reclining mannequin wearing stilettos by Christian Louboutin poses among numerous holiday gifts in a shimmering window environment. Sparkling payette sequins float throughout the space in this Christmas fantasy setting. *Harvey Nichols, London, United Kingdom. Heather Berrisford/Getty Images.*

The Directive and Design Brief

The **design process** typically begins with a document known as a **design directive**, which is also called a **brief** or **deck**. The directive provides a comprehensive review of the proposed initiative. It can originate internally within the company or externally with a contracted design firm working in coordination with the company. Directives can be led by the corporate management or the product development team and evolve with the assistance of the marketing, merchandising, and visual departments. They assure that the initiative is delivered on time and in conjunction with sales and marketing campaigns.

The directive is a document in slide or book format containing a deep and well-researched analysis into every aspect of the initiative. The following documentation may be included in a design brief:

- Company profile
- Capabilities and services
- Goals including deliverables, budget, and timeline
- Process—vision, discover, create, execute, and evaluate
- Research, case studies, and best practices
- Competition comparisons and conclusions
- Project objectives using charts and Venn diagrams
- Visual language, inspiration images, and phrases
- Specifications including square footage of space, fixtures, signage, lighting, and colors to feature
- How long the product will run
- Maps of navigation and customers' journey and touch points
- Sketches and brand identity development
- Working drawings and CAD renderings

An alternate approach, the **one-off**, is suitable for outlining the design direction for a simple singular display and can be derived directly from the merchandise itself without a directive or brief. With the one-off, the physical attributes of the merchandise such as color, texture, or style are the key focus of the design recommendations. Many factors can inspire the design process, including the packaging, geographical origin, or ingredients of the product. To develop design concepts from the directive, the visual merchandiser must engage in regular research while remaining up-to-date on popular culture, current design trends, innovative materials, and the brand's competition. A thorough review of the competition educates the designer on the best approach to take in the design process.

Inspiration Story Board

Once the goals of the project are clear, visual merchandisers embark on assembling their inspiration or ideas for the project. They may begin by focusing on promoting particular attributes of the product, or asking themselves: "What does the brand stand for?" A theme or concept may develop from a current event, trend, or trip to the museum. Inspiration can originate from the imagination of the visual merchandiser; however, it must have a strong connection to the merchandise or brand. Visual designers use many creative tools to develop concepts and ideas. They often create a list of **buzzwords** or a **mind map** that reveals information about the personality of the product or brand and how consumers perceive it. (See Figures 5.3 and 5.4.)

FIGURE 5.3 The initial exploration of the design process begins by defining the brand's DNA. The Burt's Bees mission statement and the attributes of the products inspire the designers to better understand what the brand represents. This step of the design process ensures the client that the designer is knowledgeable about the brand and where it stands in the health and beauty category. *RPG, New York, New York.*

FIGURE 5.4   As part of the creative process, the designer will develop a word list that interprets the meaning of the brand identity color palette to inspire ideas. This exercise would be included in the final presentation or deck to the client. *RPG, New York, New York.*

FIGURE 5.5   This example of an inspiration/mood board suggests a color palette for the Burt's Bees in-store navigation and product line. *RPG, New York, New York.*

FIGURE 5.6   This inspiration/mood board uses compelling imagery to suggest a fresh new style for the Burt's Bees stores. The images could inspire a new store environment or fixture concept. The textured surfaces, materials, and colors articulate the designer's thought process. *RPG, New York, New York.*

Standard creative practice in many design fields includes assembling either a dimensional or digital **inspiration storyboard** that combines compelling imagery, color stories, patterns, textures, and materials that relate to the proposed concept. Although digital storyboards can be shared more easily, many designers prefer to assemble tactile design elements and samples into a dimensional presentation board.

The layout of the inspiration board is as important as its content—it provides the visual designer's style, and approach for the project. The inspiration board communicates the tone or mood of the proposed design while promoting the brand or products. (See Figures 5.5 and 5.6.)

The Sketch

Hand sketching is still considered a vital skill for the visual merchandiser; it remains one of the strongest ways to quickly communicate an idea. Sketching leads to ideation. Ideation is the process of building a series of ideas into a solid concept. The aptitude for illustrating and drawing should not limit the sketching process; skill sets may vary, but the process of hand sketching original concepts is integral to their realization; it unlocks the natural flow of new possibilities that are key to the success of any project. (See Figure 5.7.)

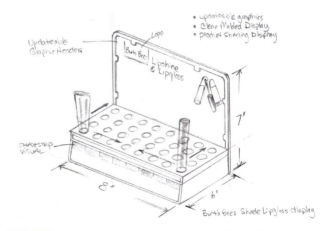

FIGURE 5.7   A hand sketch of a design for a Burt's Bees lip balm fixture. The "napkin," or pencil sketch, allows the designer to ideate and build on his or her ideas before taking the design to the computer. *RPG, New York, New York.*

The Model

Modeling a concept can be done for several purposes. The dimensional model or foamcore **sketch model** activates the visualization process for the visual merchandiser and serves to clearly communicate the design's intent. The dimensional model allows the designer to reconcile with the actual use of space, something a sketch cannot accomplish. The sketch model may or may not be executed in the exact scale; it may be relative to scale to show the placement of objects and the overall concept. The recommended materials for creating dimensional models are ⅛ inch to ¼ inch Foamcore or corrugated board, cut using a number 11 X-Acto knife. Bristol paper or flexible styrene sheets can be used to indicate any curves in the display. Floral T-pins or hot glue help secure the structure together. Mounted images can be inserted to suggest placement of digital assets, mannequins, props, furnishings, or signage into the model. (See Figure 5.8)

Mocking up the design dimensionally also invites interaction between the design team and client that results in a better, clearer understanding between the parties. It fosters the inclusion of stakeholders who may not possess design skills but still have a valuable opinion to share about the portrayal of the product or brand.

Other reasons for modeling a design may relate to the actual production of the display for manufacturing purposes. Here, precision and scale are extremely important and may positively impact how a consumer physically interacts with the merchandise. (See Figure 5.9.) Material choices can be debated, and manufacturers can easily

Model   Actual Installation

FIGURE 5.8   On the left, a small-scale Foamcore model of a window display proposed for a store. On the right is the actual display window installed in the store. *Mary Costantini, Fashion Institute of Technology NYC.*

FIGURE 5.9　A scaled Foamcore model of a Burt's Bees lip balm fixture. The scaled model allows the designer and the client to see how the fixture design functions to promote the sale of the product. The model will help determine the location of branding, copy, and price points. *RPG, New York, New York.*

provide the anticipated costs for quantities of the display to be produced. A scale model can be used to estimate the quantity of the products or **stock keeping units (SKUs)** in the display and be helpful in determining the placement of branding, important product information, and price points if necessary. Some projects require a stronger 3-D model in a rigid material or made by a **rapid prototype** process. Rapid prototypes are printed in plastic using 3-D printing technology, resulting in a model that accurately resembles the final fixture or display. (See Figure 5.10.)

FIGURE 5.10　A rapid prototype model of a Burt's Bees lip balm fixture in production stages. *RPG, New York, New York.*

This helps the client understand what is needed for production. Creating a model can eliminate many of the kinks in the process. **Value engineering** requires the designer to consider the cost of materials and production for the design. A less expensive material with similar characteristics can sometimes substitute to bring the end cost down—for example, styrene may be used replace acrylic. Similarly, an alternative production process can reduce cost as well. Manufacturers, engineers, and controllers will interact with the designer through the stages of mass production, shipping and handling, delivery, and installation. If shipping and handling poses a problem due to the size and weight of a fixture, the designer and engineer will consider manufacturing the piece using a **knock-down (KD)** method. This means the unit is designed to break down into pieces with the ability to be assembled easily once it is delivered to retailer.

Sourcing and Material Selection

Many exciting images and materials that have a connection with the brand or merchandise appear on the inspiration board, but the next stage of the process requires the designer to edit and source the items, objects, or materials most suitable to actually execute the design. The visual merchandiser may request samples and discuss his or her design options with several suppliers before making a decision. By consulting with an array of vendors, the visual merchandiser can learn more about material costs and availability and compare stock items versus custom manufacturing.

Many jobs require the visual merchandiser/store designer to be familiar with a vocabulary of materials and sources. Some designers benefit from working with a professional materials library, such as "Material Connexion," that has showrooms, catalogs, and online resources of a vast range of materials (https://www.materialconnexion.com/). Design institutions such as The University of Texas in Austin host a free open-source materials library for students, alumni, and industry members, and there are many additional resources available on the internet. In larger cities,

Burt's Bees *Acceptable Materials*

Recyclable
✓ Glass
✓ Metal – Aluminum
✓ Metal – Steel
✓ Paper

Sustainable
✓ Paperboard
✓ Corrugated
✓ Plastic – PETE (1) – clear only
✓ Plastic – HDPE (2)
✓ Plastic – LDPE (4)

Natural
✓ Plastic – PP (5)

FIGURE 5.11   This list illustrates the materials that are appropriate for a Burt's Bees store design based on the guiding principles of the brand's core values. *RPG, New York, New York.*

trade shows and professional industry organizations such as RDI Retail Design Institute have chapters composed of designers and vendors that sponsor seminars and events to learn more about materials. (See Figure 5.11.)

The visual merchandiser must have a basic understanding of:

♦ Basic building materials, sono-tubes, plumbing pipe, and electrical conduits.
♦ Wood, MDF, luan, tambour, and Masonite.
♦ Metal, wire, armature, filigree, and extruded aluminum shapes.
♦ Foam products eps, urethane, and rubber.
♦ Acrylics, PVCs, and thermoplastics.
♦ Craft boards and papers.
♦ Fabrics and prints.
♦ Paints and adhesives.

Computer Rendering

After following the traditional methods of design communication, designers turn to their computers for the next steps of the design process. With the assistance of technology they are able to take concepts and sketches to the next level using programs such as SketchUp, V-Ray, Vectorworks, or 3D Studio Max. All of these and many more are known as **CAD** programs, or **computer aided design**. CAD requires formal training, however Google's free SketchUp download is easy enough for most designers to learn independently. Users can access hundreds of You-Tube video tutorials, and many schools and design firms provide online training programs, such as Lynda.com.

Digital modeling empowers the display designer to communicate their vision in a photo realistic dimensional perspective drawing. A 3-D rendering allows for complete visualization with accurate details of the design. It illustrates an actual picture of the proposed project outcome from all views. The greatest advantage of this digital tool is the ability to share the design quickly and electronically. Presentations with renderings include floor plans, detailed elevations, and multiple perspective views of the proposed design. The other standard software used by visual merchandisers is the Adobe Creative Cloud containing Illustrator, Photoshop, and InDesign. These programs support the graphic elements' use of color, branding, and imagery. As technology becomes more accessible via the cloud, everyone in both the creative and marketing fields is expected to have a basic knowledge of one or more of these programs, business people included. Since brand marketers and merchants interface with designers on a daily basis, they can provide useful insights on how the design communicates key strategies. These valuable interactions between designers and business people are closing the gap between design and commerce and encouraging a more collaborative work environment. (See Figures 5.12–5.14.)

FIGURE 5.12   The digital rendering helps the client envision the designer's creative direction for the store. *RPG, New York, New York.*

BURT'S BEES Concept B- Fixture Plan

FIGURE 5.13 The scaled floor plan illustrates a "bird's-eye" view of the store design. This helps the designer determine how the customer will experience the store and assists in the placement of fixtures and furnishings. *RPG, New York, New York.*

Presentation

The presentation of the design concept is one of the most exciting stages of the project—it is the moment to shine! The finished presentation combines all stages of design development into a package that contains a well-thought-out design. A design presentation may be delivered in several formats; often a team will present the final design in a corporate headquarters to the client, or through a videoconference session online, or they may choose to simply share via email. The client will often request **revisions** or additional **iterations** of the design to be made

and presented again. When the final design is agreed upon, the designer is then prepared to procure and implement the display. The final presentation is also used as a tool to communicate the design to other individuals involved in the process, such as a supplier or manufacturer.

Procurement, Production

Procuring supplies and materials in the correct quantities on time is one of the final stages of the design process. It is the moment everything comes together! It requires

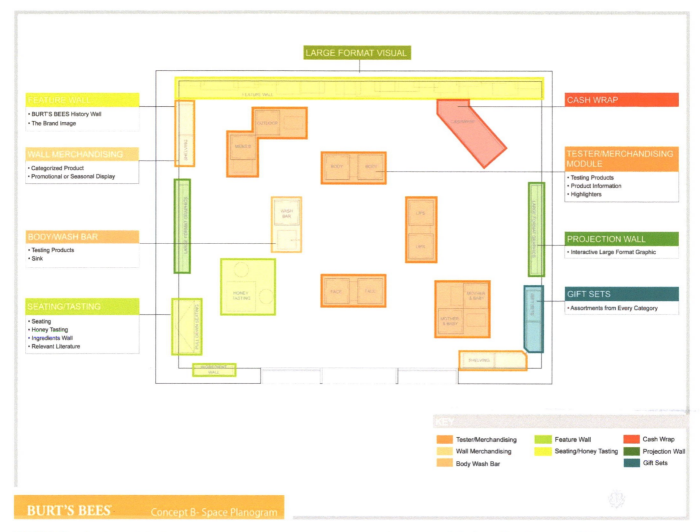

FIGURE 5.14   A color-coded planogram or map assists in space planning and product positioning within the store. *RPG, New York, New York.*

the visual merchandiser to record all the pertinent information in a spreadsheet document. Vendor information, price, colors, quantities, and sizes should be cited in detail; costs and delivery information should be collected here too. Documentation should be detailed and updated, as it could potentially serve as an organizational tool for billing and accounting and a reference for reordering in the future.

In many cases, the visual merchandiser will build, create, or assemble portions of the project in advance of the installation. Background panels or elaborate sets may require **staging** or **prefabrication**, props painted and garlands fluffed and trimmed, ready for delivery

or shipment to a store. This is referred to as **prep** or **preproduction**.

Implementation

The installation of the job is much like opening night of a theater production—it is where all of the parts and pieces fit together to create the finished design. It involves careful timing and orchestration to ensure one phase of the installation does not restrain or hinder the next. Here, the expertise of the visual merchandiser is put to the test.

Only having personal experience or an experienced team of installers can promise an efficient, smooth, and successful installation. The excitement mounts as each phase is completed, and very often there may even be time for unexpected changes to take place. The seasoned visual merchandiser/store designer always keeps the process *fluid* and allows some magic to happen on set. Occasionally, unanticipated circumstances arise, and the visual merchandiser is challenged to problem solve and "think on his or her feet." This is considered normal in the display industry, and installations rarely cease due to problems since displays are public and subject to installation schedules.

In conclusion, it is fair to say that visual merchandisers are artists with an extensive range of skills in both design and business practices. They need to manage a variety of responsibilities while demonstrating flexibility and maintaining a high standard of work while developing design concepts and creative direction for displays, events, and special projects. Visual merchandisers require most of the following skills to excel in today's workplace:

- Standard business organization, working collaboratively, and global vision.
- Knowledge of Google Docs, Microsoft Office Word, PowerPoint, Excel, or Keynote.

- Basic design knowledge and knowledge of art history, furniture design, materials, florals, historic timelines and styles, and photography.
- Graphic design, typography, color theory, and trends.
- Adobe Creative Cloud programs—Illustrator, Photoshop, and InDesign.
- Space planning, furniture elements, custom design, and lighting.
- Google SketchUp, 3D Studiomax, Vectorworks, Rhino, and Revit.
- Signage, wayfinding, and egress for accessibility including building and safety codes.
- Design, materials, process, procurement value, and reverse engineering.

The Harvey Nichols Disco Era Christmas case study demonstrates all of the design processes described in this chapter. Janet Wardley and her visual merchandising team went through each of the design phases beginning with sketches, inspiration boards, and computer renderings. The team mocked up the large faces and staged them in their studio, allowing them time to experiment with the application of decorative elements. This project clearly defines the various roles and responsibilities of today's visual merchandiser.

Case Study 5.1: Disco Era Christmas at Harvey Nichols, London, United Kingdom

Design Objective

Sometime around Thanksgiving in the United States, and in late November in other parts of the world, retailers in stores of all sizes spend a large part of their display budget to bring magic and spectacle out into the street. That is the time when the visual merchandisers are challenged to outdo whatever they did the year or years before and bring more sparkle, more shimmer, more glamour, and more thrilling visual effects to the window-gazers who annually flock about for their feast of holiday good cheer. It is a challenge that often starts each year as the last Christmas ornament in removed

from the window and the last speck of artificial snow is cleared away to make room for the sand that will soon cover a beach scene or cruise setup. When you are a store like Harvey Nichols and your location in Knightsbridge in London is iconic and your neighbor, Harrods, is only two or three streets away and the neighborhood can get pretty spectacular at this time of the year, the pressure is really on.

Janet Wardley, head of visual display for Harvey Nichols, had this to say about the breathtaking Christmas display shown in the images that follow. Discussions and planning began back in April, when Display and Production team leaders held a creative meeting in which ideas and themes were discussed. Also, according to Ms. Wardley, "Our marketing department presented us with the Christmas creative idea of GiftFace in March—actually before our own creative meeting. From this our challenge was to work out how to integrate this concept and campaign line into our Christmas windows. Ultimately, we wanted to capture the playfulness of the season whilst maintaining an instantly recognizable Christmas spirit. We drew our inspiration for our window design from the disco era." The notorious and fabled dance hall in Manhattan in the '70s where the famous and infamous rubbed more than shoulders in the smoke filled space—"Studio 54—had emerged as a key trend during the year's fall fashion shows and was picked up by our buyers, and this contributed to the development of the theme. This ensured a cohesive message from our widows to the products being offered in-store and online."

Design Solution

Ms. Wardley continued, "A number of our team were children of the '70s and, fortunately, had vivid memories of that time to draw inspiration from. Beyond that, there was an abundance of resources available that provided us with inspiration: from archive images, films from that era and—of course—the music. The '70s is such an iconic period which people and, in particular, fashion designers, constantly revisit for inspiration. It was a breeding ground of creativity—from the emerging fashion trends to Studio 54 and Liza Minnelli and Ziggy Stardust. We tapped into this feeling of nostalgia that people have for that time."

According to Ms. Wardley, after creating a series of theme or inspiration boards, came the sketches. "Our initial sketches showed how we wanted to make use of the building and outside glass, and the idea was to draw the scheme out of the windows. Early sketches depicted how the gift boxes could be used to create engaging, oversized props within the windows. We had already settled on the concept of constructing our own versions of GiftFace faces using gift boxes. So, back in

the Harvey Nichols workshop, we began experimenting or 'trialling' with boxes and very soon discovered that it wasn't going to be as easy as we first thought it would be." (See Figures CS5.1 and CS5.2.)

"It became clear," Ms. Wardley continued, "that the hairstyles for each face would be the

FIGURE CS5.1 The original inspiration boards created by the Harvey Nichols display team.

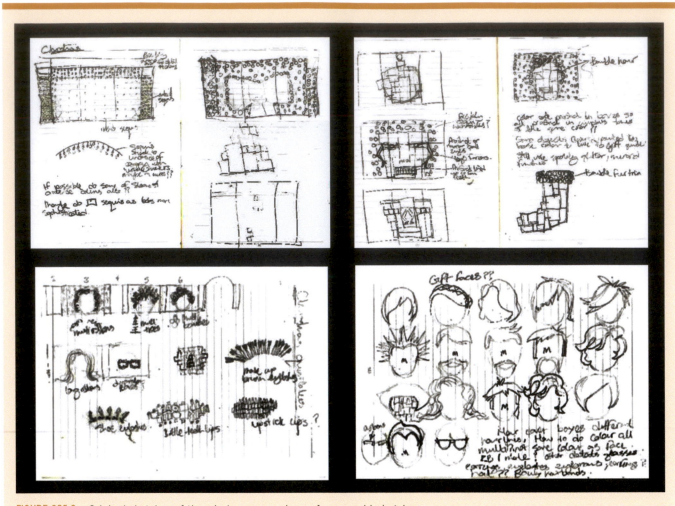

FIGURE CS5.2 Original sketches of the window prosceniums, faces, and hairstyles.

key to creating a run of faces—each one unique and distinctive. Festive materials and decorations would shape the hair and facial features: sparkling lights, glittered and metallic baubles, Christmas tree branches, plastic icicles and snowflakes. We finally made a face that was the turning point in the production of the scheme. It showed how festive materials could be used in interesting ways to produce a striking face—full of character." Thus, going along with the GiftFace theme suggested by marketing, the installation included, as Ms. Wardley said, "a series of giant faces, each one constructed from hundreds of colored gift boxes. Using festive materials and decorations, we created distinctive hairstyles and features for each face. Metallics, sequins, and mirror balls evoking the disco era enriched the design concept. Oversized sequins—each one attached by

hand—adorned the store facade and shimmered across the Knightsbridge run."

In addition to all the time spent planning, plotting, and gathering material, it took a staff of twenty-five a full week to actually install the Knightsbridge windows. Ms. Wardley notes that "a lot of the materials we used for the 'hair' of the giant 'faces' were recycled and reworked elements leftover from previous window schemes." In addition, "Christmas gift products decorated the faces to create a 3-D version of the GiftFace, and accompanying the faces were oversized gift boxes which were featured across the windows. These props were built using the same boxes that shaped the faces and had shelves to display additional Christmas gift products." The mannequins, specially renovated by Global Displays for this trim, were beautifully dressed for their appearance in the windows. (See Figure CS5.3.)

Conclusion

In summing up her achievement, Ms. Wardley added, "The windows captured the energy and excitement of the festive season and allowed us to communicate the Harvey Nichols Christmas message directly to all those passing by and succeeded in drawing people into the store. The windows were hugely popular, and people were enthusiastically engaged with the displays—sharing pictures of themselves in front of the scheme—on all social media channels. These social platforms help enormously to widen the reach of our brand. And increasingly we have found that the Christmas windows draw an international crowd who make a special effort to stop by the store at this time." The displays were also covered and ballyhooed by the British Broadcasting Corporation and the national press. "The press generated achieved 6.8 million opportunities to see, ensuring the Harvey Nichols brand reach was amplified during what is a busy and competitive period for retailers."

It took a week to take down the window display and package up. "We saved the reusable materials [and] lights, and our floorboards were recovered for future uses."

FIGURE CS5.3 "Trialling" or staging of the GiftFace concept in the Harvey Nichol's display studio.

FIGURE CS5.4 Let's Disco!!! Sparkling, glittering, shining, glitzy, and glamorous as well are just a few adjectives that could be used to describe Harvey Nichols holiday windows. Amid swirling mirrored balls and giant Christmas ornaments, the HN design team introduced the GiftFace promotion.

The individual "faces" were created with gift-wrapped boxes and accented with hair-dos of reclaimed Christmas decorations from previous promotions. "We wanted to capture the playfulness of the season whilst maintaining an instantly recognizable Christmas spirit," said Janet Wardley.

FIGURE CS5.6 "Metallic, sequins, and mirror balls evoking the disco era enriched the design concept. Oversized sequins—each one attached by hand—adorned the store's facade and shimmered across the Knightsbridge run." For the total effect, refer to Figure 1.1 on p. 2.

After the glitter and glitz, the shimmer and shine of the last year's Christmas windows were almost all past and this year's holiday plotting and planning had begun—it happened! At the 2016 Global Department Store Summit, Harvey Nichols GiftFace displays won "World's Best Store Window Campaign of a Department Store" award. (See Figures CS5.4–CS5.7.)

CREDITS: *Props, Dressing, and Installation: Harvey Nichols Production Team, 3D Eye. Lighting: ANS Lighting. Photography: Heather Berrisford/Getty Images.*

FIGURE CS5.7 A close-up look at one of the mannequins. Beautiful fashions were worn by these specially renovated and made-up mannequins with disco-era wigs to add to the period feeling.

Design and Process Trade Talk

buzzwords
CAD, or computer aided design
computer design
creative process
deck
design brief
design concepts
design directive
design process
implementation
inspiration storyboard
installation

iterations
knock-down (KD)
materials
mind map
mocking up
model
mood board
one off
prefabrication
prep
preproduction
presentation

procurement
prototype
rapid prototype
rendering
revisions
sketch model
sketches
sourcing
staging
stock keeping units (SKUs)
value design engineering

Design and Process: A Recap

◆ Visual merchandisers collaborative with store planners, brand marketers, merchants, and store management.

◆ A visual merchandiser needs to have both a creative and business skill set.

◆ Steps for developing and implementing design concepts can vary for an individual, store, or design firm.

◆ A directive or design brief sets the goals for the display or project.

◆ Inspiration/mood boards clearly illustrate the idea, inspiration, or story.

◆ Sketches bring the idea to life and encourage concept development.

◆ A model reveals any major design flaws or potential problems in production or installation and allows for adjustments.

◆ Sourcing and material selection can help value engineer and bring the design to a higher level.

◆ Computer design and renderings provide detailed illustrations of the design intent and allow the viewer to understand the design clearly.

◆ Presentation presents the ideas professionally and confidently so the designer can sell the idea.

◆ Procurement and preproduction ensure the appropriate and most economical materials/supplies are used for the job and are prepared for an efficient installation.

◆ Implementation/installation advances a clean, professional installation; last-minute problem solving and solutions are worked out.

Questions for Review and Discussion

1. Describe the visual merchandiser's role in the design process.

2. How can the visual merchandiser communicate his or her ideas to the client? Cite five specific examples.

3. List three CAD programs that can be used in the design process.

4. Explain why building a model may be necessary.

5. Who interacts with visual merchandisers in a corporate setting?

6. Why are materials important in the design process?

7. How does a directive differ from a design brief?

8. What is a rapid prototype?

9. Describe what can be used to create an inspiration board.

PART TWO

Display Locations and Design Methods

For retailers to be successful, they must first entice customers to enter their stores. Even before stepping through the door, customers receive their first impression regarding the retailer's character and image. The store exterior and windows must be inviting, with the intent of bringing the customer into the store to spend money. Chapters 6 and 7 focus on the store exterior and window display types and treatments found in today's malls, strip shopping centers, and downtown areas.

Counters, islands, columns, fascia—all are likely areas for store display. Locations within the store suitable for merchandise presentation are discussed in Chapter 8. From a one-item display to a variety, or assortment, display, Chapter 9 covers the gamut of possible display types and settings.

Most displays must capture the attention of passersby in only a few brief seconds. Chapter 10, to this end, provides some great techniques that are sure to captivate customers. Some of the most popular seasonal themes and schemes in visual merchandising and display are set forth in Chapter 11.

Chapter Six
The Exterior of the Store

The façade of the Dior boutique in Tianjin, China. *WWD/Condé Nast.*

**AFTER YOU HAVE READ THIS CHAPTER,
YOU WILL BE ABLE TO DISCUSS**

- key exterior items that impact store image
- how banners can be tied in with seasons and store promotional events
- advantages and disadvantages of the four major windows used in storefront design
- variations in storefront design often found in malls and shopping centers

How and where we display depends largely on the architecture and **fenestration** (window placement) of the structure, the physical layout of space, and the fixtures inside the building. First, let us consider the façade of the building and the arrangement of the display windows in the storefront design. We will follow with an in-depth survey of the various types of display windows used in retail operations and the advantages and limitations inherent in each type of window.

Signs

The store's **sign**, on the outside of the building, makes the first impression on the shopper. It sets the look and image of the store. How the sign is designed—the materials used, the style of the typography and imagery, and the color—conveys information about the store's brand. The exterior signage should be legible from a distance and illuminated properly for nighttime visibility. Its size and scale, in proportion to the store's façade, the size of the building, and the signs around it, contribute to how the store or brand is perceived by shoppers. The maintenance and upkeep of the storefront is dually important; flickering lights and peeling paint detract from the store image. The sign is the store's "signature"—personal, original, and recognizable. It should make a bold and memorable statement. (See Figure 6.1.)

Marquees

Some older stores, as well as some of the very newest, have **marquees**, or architectural canopies, extending out over

FIGURE 6.1   With lights blazing as the sun goes down, the Primark store in Madrid becomes a beacon that calls out to shoppers. Illuminated 8-foot tall letters spell out the store's name across the façade, while strongly lit display windows at ground level and on upper floors keep the merchandising story strong and far-reaching. *Design: Dalziel & Pow.*

their entrances. The marquee, a permanent awning for protection from the elements, is an integral part of the building façade. It is often cantilevered out over the street, in front of the main entrance to the store. It is similar to the porte cochere (a porch at the door of a building for sheltering persons entering and leaving carriages) of the last century or the big signboards with running lights that used to identify movie houses and theaters in the 1940s and 1950s.

The marquee can be an exciting place to start the display of a storewide event or promotion. A change of seasons can be announced here. When a marquee protrudes from the building line, it offers the advantage of increased visibility and greater prominence compared with all the other store signs from the surrounding operations. A marquee designed to accept changeable announcements (like the change of movie titles) or a rolling digital screen can communicate current promotions more readily. A flat-topped marquee is an excellent place for the grouping of seasonal plants and foliage as well as larger-than-life-sized props. It is a perfect location for a giant Santa or even his sleigh and eight clamoring reindeer.

Outdoor Lighting

There is a whole industry involved in creating and installing **outdoor lighting** displays. The use of hundreds and hundreds of lights on building façades and canopies can be most effective for holidays and store events. The lights can be swagged or draped, or wired to frames to form recognizable symbols or letters. This type of display no longer requires a huge expenditure of electrical energy thanks to the innovations in LED wall washer lighting. LED wall washers are decorative outdoor lights that highlight, with a projection beam of 10 to 90 meters, 1 to 16.7 million colors onto walls of buildings. The LED wall washer lights are programmable in such a way that the user can adjust the colors or light show the way he or she wants it with a remote controller.

The strength and color rendition of exterior LED lighting on storefronts is effective even at twilight. During daylight piette sequins (a shimmering material) attached to panels on the store façade can be used to reflect light and simulate lighting. This provides some degree of decoration

to the store exterior during those hours when the lights are not on or when they are barely visible.

Digital Screens and Billboards

Today, digital screens and billboards are transforming the brand experience with motion graphics on the façades of stores, malls, and cityscapes. These massive, state-of-the-art digital screens that project high-resolution graphics, animated text, and video are made from a sleek, stainless steel mesh fabric interwoven with LED lights. Digital mesh billboards are more environmentally friendly than the digital signage of the past. They require little to no maintenance and are visible twenty-four hours a day. They allow retailers to reach a wider audience about their brands, products, promotions, and services quickly while leaving a lasting impression. Stores can engage consumers for longer periods of time by simulcasting events, integrating mobile and social media platforms that are proven to motivate sales.

Banners

Outdoor fabric **banners** are inexpensive and expendable, but they are colorful, eye-catching, and eye-filling devices that flutter and flap in the wind. They can be and should be changed with the seasons or the store events. A few holes, worked into the design, will allow the wind to sweep through without tearing the fabric. The banners can be hung from flagpoles, projected from the building, or hung flat against it. The same banner design, reduced in size and scale, can be hung from the marquee, between the display windows, or projecting from the columns inside the store.

Digitally printed banners are a popular choice because logos and graphics are so important today. New weather-friendly mesh fabrics are available in various transparencies and can be used to completely wrap the storefront to announce **store promotions**, holiday greetings, or a sales event. The store's window displays can, in color and concept,

FIGURE 6.2 If it is worth saying, then say it loud and larger than life. For the storewide LIVE ART promotion, the display staff at The Bay in Toronto went all out in the windows and on the store's many levels inside and added a giant banner up over the main entrance proclaiming the event. The message was sent—loud, clear, and colorful. *Hudson's Bay, Toronto, Canada.*

reiterate the same graphic theme—but with a difference. If, for example, at Christmas, a store used an irregular gold star on a cerise-and-white peppermint-striped background, the same theme could be carried to the display window, filled with dozens of cascading gold stars of assorted sizes, invisibly suspended. All through this text, we will constantly refer to the advantages of displays that tie in with, and enhance, what is going on inside the store, in the newspaper ads, on television and radio, and in the store mailings. For it to work, display should not only attract and excite; it should also reinforce an idea and present dimensionally what was, until then, a flat representation. (See Figure 6.2.)

Planters

Planters, flower boxes, and landscaping outside a store add to the general ambiance, especially if the store is on

a "concrete-and-glass" Main Street, with neither a leaf nor blade of grass in sight. This is a social amenity, a way the store can show its neighbors and customers a sign of friendship and concern for the beautification of the community. Planters have strong visual impact on storefronts; they slow down pedestrian traffic and attract people who might otherwise keep walking.

Planters can become a part of a display theme, with changes in the varieties and colors of the plants to go with promotions or seasons. Red geraniums could call attention to a "country-casual" display or add color to a "red" promotion—anything from fashion to housewares—or even a spring-into-summer story. White flowers would certainly enhance any bridal setting, and mums and asters speak colorfully for fall and back to school.

Planters, set below and in front of a display window, actually dramatize the window presentation by adding greater depth to the setting. Artificial flowers and plants will do, but the real thing is so much nicer. (See Figure 6.3.)

FIGURE 6.3 On a shopping street in a town filled with charming, retro shops set in century-old buildings—how do you "brand" your space as your own? You add a distinctive awning—maybe in your signature color—to soften the architectural lines and accessorize with planter boxes filled with seasonal plants. *Walton's, Franklin, Tennessee. Photography: MMP/RVC.*

FIGURE 6.4   The battery of individual show windows that stretch across the Harvey Nichols store in London has been converted into a series of old fashioned shop fronts with a display of product in their windows. The overall effect is a "main street" with each shop front representing a category of merchandise sold inside the store. *Visual Merchandising Team at Harvey Nichols.*

Awnings

Awnings add another gracious touch to the exterior of the store. Not only do they supply shelter for the shopper during inclement weather, but they also make viewing a window display more pleasant during the heat of the day. Some visual merchandisers use the awning as a device to cut down on the glare and reflection that turn show windows into giant mirrors. Awnings may also reduce the effects of the sunlight on merchandise, and they provide some shadowed area that allows spotlighting to be more effective. However, many awning users are now relying on them to add color and eye appeal and brand the storefront. The awning can become part of a seasonal display or announce a storewide promotion. The use of awnings is also discussed in Chapter 7. (See Figure 6.4.)

Windows in Storefront Design

STRAIGHT FRONT

Straight front windows run parallel to the street. The entrance to the store may be located between a pair or

a run of windows or to one side of a single window. The windows themselves may be closed back, open back, or elevated. (See Figures 6.5 through 6.8.)

ANGLED FRONT

With the **angled front** design, the store entrance is recessed from the street, and the display windows lead back from the street to the entrance, creating an aisle for the shopper. The windows may go back at an angle to the entrance, thus becoming wider in the back than they are in the front. The back end of the window is actually on the same wall as

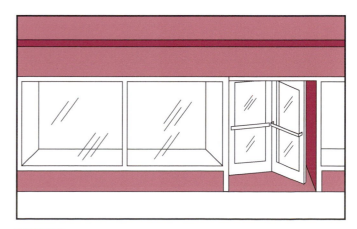

FIGURE 6.5   This straight storefront consists of the entrance and a bank, or series, of display windows. *Illustration by Ron Carboni.*

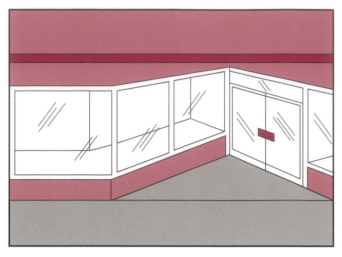

FIGURE 6.6   An angled storefront. *Illustration by Ron Carboni.*

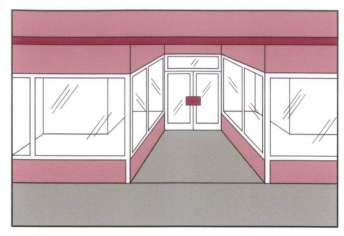

FIGURE 6.7   An arcaded storefront. *Illustration by Ron Carboni.*

the entrance; that wall can be completely closed, partially closed, or open backed. Usually, in an angled front (and the arcade front, which follows), the display windows are under some kind of enclosure, cutting down appreciably on glare. These windows may also be rather shallow to allow an unimpeded entrance into the store and more walk space for shoppers and potential customers. (Refer to Figure 6.6.)

ARCADE FRONT

The **arcade front** consists of a series of windows with backs and three sides of glass, coming forward from the entrance wall, which is set back from the street. The windows are "peninsulas" of glass attached to the store and are usually under some kind of overhead cover. The shopper enters between protruding display windows. (Refer to Figure 6.7.)

FIGURE 6.8   A pair of open-back windows flanks the central entrance to Lords store in Hampstead, London. The white side walls help to reflect the light from the spotlights set in the ceiling over the product displays. Holding the almost all-glass straight front composition together is the soft, deep gray Lords' signature color that was used to accentuate the framework. *Rita Dewan, Brand Director & Founding Sister, Lords at Home.*

CORNER WINDOW

The **corner window** faces two streets that are perpendicular to each other. It is a window with a double exposure and double traffic. The corner window may be the

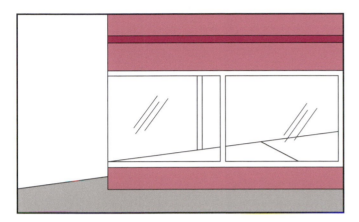

FIGURE 6.9   A corner window. *Illustration by Ron Carboni.*

sole display showcase for a store with an entrance near the corner of a street, or it may be the end of a run of windows.

Usually, this window will have two adjacent panes of glass meeting at right angles. The back may be open or closed. Most stores convert this type of window into a triangular plan. The two glass fronts are the "legs" of the triangle, and the long back wall is the "hypotenuse." The space that is cut off from view becomes valuable storage space. Because the two windows are at right angles to each other, the viewer can almost always see the overhead and side lighting—as well as a view of other stores and signs beyond the display area. Customers can find themselves distracted by viewers looking in from the other side of the window and by mirrored backgrounds that reflect traffic lights and the signs from other stores. (See Figures 6.9 and 6.10.)

FIGURE 6.10   The corner window can be viewed from either of two trafficked streets or from aisles in a mall. In a way, the window is like "theater in the round"—the mannequins and the merchandise have to be viewable from many angles, and there is no real "back," where garments can be bunched and pinned. As shown here, the triangular window has a long back wall (the hypotenuse of the triangle), and the mannequins are arranged to be viewed from either window. *The Bay, Toronto, Canada. Ana Fernandes, window display manager.*

Mall Storefronts

With malls and shopping centers replacing Main Street in many towns and cities, the architecture of the façades, or shop fronts, in some ways is changing as well. The examples shown previously in this chapter are still used, but with variations, and in many cases the mall or shopping center may dictate the type of storefront the retailer may have. Mostly, the fronts are straight fronts—usually with a central opening and windows to either side or an entrance to one side and a window to the right or left of the opening. There can be exceptions, however.

OPEN FAÇADE

Except for the threshold, with the **open façade** there is no visible barrier, or separation, between the shopper on the mall aisle and the store, unless there is a change of flooring material. Security gates, used to close up the shop after hours, are usually invisible, rolled up into a space over the entry and slipped into pockets on either side of the opening. There are no display windows and no door—just a wide open expanse and an invitation to see the whole store. Sometimes, the displays come out to meet the shopper or will appear on a runway that starts up near the entrance. (See Figure 6.11.)

GLASS FAÇADE

A **glass façade** has display windows to one side or both sides of the glass doors that are usually open during business hours. The glass panels of the windows extend from floor to ceiling, and there are usually no raised floors in the windows. Mannequins often stand on the floor—eye to eye with the shoppers or elevated on platforms or risers. These elevations are especially needed to show off smaller products, like shoes, handbags, cosmetics, electronic equipment, and so on. The store interior can be viewed through the glazed façade, and if the mall has an open or glass-enclosed atrium, daylight streams in and can add a decided glare to the windows at certain times of the day.

CLOSED FAÇADE

The **closed façade** is an oxymoron sort of façade development: a closed opening. The windows are completely blocked off, painted out, wallpapered over, or wrapped in graphics, and only the entrance to the store is visible. For certain types of operations, this "secretive," "private club," exclusive feeling might work very well. It appeals to teens and tweens as well as to very upscale boutique shoppers. It suggests something special and a sense of belonging to a certain group of shoppers. (See Figure 6.12.)

FIGURE 6.11 The open façade is like the old-fashioned garage sale that invited people to come in and browse and shop. With no barrier between the mall aisle and the shop, these young, realistic mannequins, casually arranged on platforms and risers, literally come out to greet shoppers as a welcoming display committee. *Kickers, Gateshead, United Kingdom. Design: Dalziel & Pow.*

FIGURE 6.12 The feeling of being special and belonging, or having the "open sesame" to get in, seems to be a new approach for some retail operations. Here, only the entrance is evident, and the tunnel-like, rugged, stony opening suggests a way to a rugby or soccer field or the locker rooms. This closed opening appeals to young shoppers, sports fans, and those looking for exclusivity. *Red Bull, Salzburg, Austria. Design: Gruschwitz GmbH, Munich, Germany.*

Brand Box 6.1: Branding the Store Exteriors

If it is within your job description—or you are free to offer suggestions—here are some thoughts on how to bring the store's brand identity out onto the street where it can interact with the shopping public.

This is where you can introduce the brand name/logo and the company's signature color (the color that is used on the company's website, bags and boxes, and business cards). You may opt to fly banners or pennants that carry the brand design and color over the display windows or introduce them in awnings that extend out over the window displays. The awnings will provide shelter from sun and rain for shoppers while they are "captive" next to the merchandise featured in the windows as well as cut down the sun's glare off the front glass in daylight hours. If planters are in your plan, paint them in the brand's particular color. If the city ordinances allow it and if your clientele warrants it, maybe introduce a canopy that extends from the curb to the store's front door in your company color. If the marquee/canopy is "too much," add a carpet in the entrance foyer in the brand color and accented with the company name or logo.

Whatever you can do and wherever possible—flaunt your brand identity. Show your colors. Make your brand name and logo a visible part of the street scene. Check out the Featuring the Brand Identity recommendations in Chapter 4: Light and Lighting for more ideas on making strong, color-filled statements out front.

The Exterior of the Store: Trade Talk

angled front	corner window	outdoor lighting
arcade front	fenestration	planters
awnings	glass façade	sign
banners	marquees	straight front
closed façade	open façade	

The Exterior of the Store: A Recap

+ Display depends largely on the architecture and fenestration (window placement) of the structure.

+ The store's sign makes the first impression on the shopper.

+ Stores with marquees, or architectural canopies, can use them for announcements. A flat marquee can be used for a prop display.

+ Outdoor displays include lighting, banners, planters, and awnings. Strings of lights can be draped or swagged, or wired to frames to form recognizable symbols or letters.

+ Banners are inexpensive and expendable, but they are colorful and eye-catching and can be changed with the seasons or store events.

+ Planters, flower boxes, or plants add to a store's ambiance. Set below and in front of a display, they dramatize the window setting. If possible, the plants should be part of the display scheme, and the color of the plants can be changed according to the season or the promotion.

+ Awnings add a gracious touch to a store's exterior while providing shelter from inclement weather and shade during the heat of the day. They also cut down glare and reflection.

+ Straight front windows run parallel to the store.

+ An angled front window is recessed from the street, and the display windows may go back from the street to the entrance, creating an "aisle" for the shopper.

+ An arcade window consists of a series of windows with backs and three sides of glass, coming forward from the entrance wall, which is set back from the street.

+ A corner window faces two streets that are perpendicular to each other. Usually it will have two adjacent panes of glass meeting at a right angle.

+ The open façade, glass façade, and closed façade are variations in storefront design that may be found in malls and shopping centers.

Questions for Review and Discussion

1. Describe how window display and the store exterior convey a store's character and image.

2. Comment on the concept of the exterior sign being a store's "signature."

3. What is a marquee, and how can it be used in visual merchandising?

4. Give an example of a theme and explain how that theme could be promoted in the media and reinforced through elements of the store exterior.

5. Explain the difference between awnings and marquees.

6. List the four major types of exterior store windows and provide an advantage and a disadvantage of each type.

Chapter Seven
Display Window Construction

An artist from 9eme Concept decorating a Coach window at Printemps. *Ricard/WWD/Condé Nast.*

AFTER YOU HAVE READ THIS CHAPTER,
YOU WILL BE ABLE TO DISCUSS

- the benefits of closed-back windows for use in display
- methods for reducing glare and reflection in window displays
- three types of floors commonly used in display windows
- the function of ceiling grids in display windows
- methods for turning a large display window into a smaller one
- advantages and disadvantages of open-back windows
- the challenges inherent in displaying in island windows
- merchandise categories best suited to display in shadow box windows

Closed-Back Windows

A **closed-back window** is the typical display window, with a full back wall, sides, and a large plate glass window facing the pedestrian or street traffic. It is also known as an **enclosed window**.

A noted visual merchandiser, discussing trends in display, has stated, "For real drama and excitement in display, there is nothing to compare with what you can do in an enclosed display window." In the familiar and traditional giant, plate glass–fronted "fishbowl," which some merchants and store planners feel is extinct, the visual merchandiser can arrange tableaux and vignettes from life in idealized settings. Here, under perfectly arranged lights, the cast of characters stays where they are placed; remain smiling through sleet, rain, snow, and slush; and wear the garments with nonchalant ease and grace.

The visual merchandiser is the stage designer, the lighting designer, the prop person, the director, and the producer. The only thing the visual merchandiser does not have to produce is the merchandise, although he or she may be responsible for the accessorizing. This is the fun and creative part of the job. The same visual merchandiser who was quoted above predicts that the enclosed window will be brought into the store. These oversized show boxes will become a part of the show and spectacle of interior display.

To grasp what can or cannot be accomplished in a display window, it is necessary to understand the physical construction of the window and the limitations imposed by that construction.

A small store may have a single display window, or a pair of windows, often separated by the entrance into the store. Larger stores, some specialty stores, and downtown department stores will often have a "run" or group of windows (called a **bank of windows**)—maybe two, three, or four windows—and then a physical divider between the windows like a doorway, a wide area of masonry (**pier**), or even a small shadow box. The windows in the group or bank may be separate entities, completely framed and delineated from each other by a heavy molding or pier. (See Figure 7.1.)

The display window may also be one very long, **run-on window** of 20, 30, or more feet. The only visible divider in this run-on window is the thin metal band that retains the plate glass windows. Often, the visual merchandiser will

FIGURE 7.1   The five sides of the closed back window are shown here in La Rinascente in Milan. The sixth side of this cube is the window through which the display can be viewed from the street. Note the entrance to the window on the right side wall. *La Rinascente, Milan, Italy. Stefania D'Alessandro/Getty Images.*

add dividers inside the window to separate the one long stretch of glass into two, three, or four individual areas. In the case of the single long window, the visual merchandiser has greater flexibility and control over the presentations. He or she can, at times, stage a mass scene with five or more mannequins arranged in a realistic grouping in a setting that continues through the length of the long window or, at other times, divide the run into small, separate presentations in which a single mannequin is "starred" in a solo and very concentrated performance.

This flexibility makes a change of pace possible. Some shoppers are so used to seeing the same physical arrangement of window and mannequin that they no longer see the window or the display. A shopper who becomes overly familiar with the same type of display setup week after week will not notice that the merchandise has been changed. But, if one week the mannequin is gone and replaced by a dress form, or the merchandise is draped from a chair, it can be the change itself that will stop the shopper.

Where the architecture of the store is such that the size of each window in a group is predetermined, and the visual merchandiser cannot move dividers to make the windows wider or narrower, there still are options open to the creative window dresser. We will discuss those options shortly, when we consider proscenia and the masking of windows.

One of the greatest challenges the visual merchandiser has with a display window is the glare in the glass that blinds the shopper and cuts down on the visibility of the merchandise presented. Another challenge is reflection. Often, shoppers get a better view of what's going on out in the street and in the shop across the road than in the window into which they are looking.

In some newer stores, architects have experimented with tinted glass, angled sheets of glass, curved glass, and even deeply recessed windows. Tinted glass affects the color of the merchandise and requires more energy to light the window properly. Curved windows can be even more disastrous than flat glass when it comes to reflections. Deeply recessed windows leave costly pockets of space that might otherwise be used for storage or selling. In the past, manufacturers have come up with yellow or green transparent vinyl window shades that look like oversized fly-catching strips. Although they do prevent sun fading, they do not cut down much on glare or reflection, and they also distort the color presentation of the merchandise.

Many stores, in conjunction with their visual merchandisers, have used decorative awnings to shield their windows, thus cutting down on the glare. Reflection is still a challenge, but some visual merchandisers have found that the use of lighter-colored backgrounds in the window creates better balance with the light coming from outside as well as minimizes the reflection somewhat. Decorative awnings are changed seasonally or for holidays or store promotions. This affords the store an opportunity to enhance its exterior appearance, to promote a special event, and to provide a degree of comfort to the prospective customer who would like to "do" the window before entering the store.

Visual merchandisers have also found that placing the merchandise and the lighting further back in the window, away from the glass, makes it possible to see the merchandise in the proper light and setting. The shopper's eye is drawn past the glare and reflection. The major challenge, however, in setting and lighting the merchandise back in the window is that the storefront may appear unlit or dimly lit until the viewer is directly in front of the window. The viewer can only look at the merchandise from 5 or 6 feet away instead of getting a really close-up view. Display manufacturers have been experimenting with optical devices, mirrors, and odd-shaped panels of glass in order to overcome the glare problem. (See Figure 7.2.)

FIGURE 7.2 The closed-back window, in this case, consists of sliding panels that move back and forth on tracks, and the window can be converted to a partial open back as well. With no competition from the light on the selling floor, the spotlights effectively play up the new garments. *Yusty, Madrid, Spain. Design: Marketing Jazz, Madrid, Spain.*

Floor

Once past the plate glass and into the window proper, the floor must be considered. Most display window floors are raised anywhere from 8 or 9 inches to 24 inches from street level. Rarely is the floor of a standard 8- or 9-foot-high window raised more than 2 feet—that would place the mannequin too high above eye level.

A **raised floor** makes it possible to dramatize an object by forcing the viewer to look up to it. The elevated position adds prestige and also allows passersby to see over the heads of window shoppers. Even though the entire window will not be seen over the street traffic, it is possible to glimpse some of the presentation. Hopefully, it will be enough to make the viewer want to come in for a closer look.

Some stores have installed **raked floors**, in which the back of the floor is several inches higher than the front, creating a ramp effect. When merchandise is displayed on this inclined floor, small objects, like shoes, handbags, and cosmetics when placed at the back, are more easily seen. Some visual merchandisers rely on platforms and risers to elevate groups of merchandise or mannequins for greater visibility, separation, or dramatic impact.

A few stores, like Lord & Taylor in New York City, have **elevator-type windows**. The floor is actually an elevator platform that can be lowered to the basement level, where the "window" is prepared and set and then raised to the desired level. Sometimes, the floor is below street level, and the shopper is invited to come in really close and look down into the setting. At other times, it might be raised above the usual floor level for a special effect.

Most display-window floors are finished with parquet wood tiles or carpeted in a neutral and subtly textured broadloom. The visual merchandiser may use floorboards cut out of fiberboard (Homosote and Masonite are two popular trademarks) to cover the existing floor. These floorboards can be painted or covered with fabrics, decorative papers, Scatter Grass, and so on to change the look of the floor without causing damage to the permanent floor. This padded floor also permits the visual merchandiser to use pins and nails without affecting the finished floor. When the floor of the window has been left unfinished (concrete or rough wood), the visual merchandiser may have two sets of

FIGURE 7.3   The bulkhead raises the floor of the window up to 30 inches off of the ground, but to bring the pillows up closer to eye level the designer used the baskets to elevate them as well as the platform with a decorative pattern. Note the strong horizontal line that the platform, along with the artwork on the rear wall, adds to the composition, emphasizing the relaxed, easygoing, and comfortable quality of the pillows. *Plumas, Lima, Peru. Design: Katrina Barhumi.*

floorboards—one in use in the window, and a second set in the display department—where available, should a different floor be required for the next window change. Regular vinyl floor tiles are also frequently used by the visual merchandiser to create color and style changes. They are simply laid down, perhaps with double-faced masking tape, and easily removed and stored for future use. (See Figure 7.3.)

Back of the Window

The back of the traditional display window goes from floor to ceiling and is usually fully constructed. Some stores have removable panels closing their windows so they can, when

Proscenia

Some stores take the theatrical quality of their display windows seriously and enhance the theater-like setting by using **proscenia** (the plural of *proscenium*) around the window glass. The proscenium, from the Greek "before the scenery," is the structural arch, usually rather ornate, often seen in a theater surrounding the curtain.

In the display window, the proscenium consists of a top valance, which masks the lighting across the top of the window, and side valances, which separate one window or display grouping from the next and also hide any side-lighting devices. There are visual merchandisers who use the valance as a decorative frame for the window and will choose different colors, perhaps enhanced with branches, lights, or other decorative motifs, for Christmas or special storewide events. In some instances, the valance or proscenium is structurally fixed, unchangeable, but definitely a part of the store's architecture and its image. (See Figure 7.6.)

Masking

As previously mentioned in this chapter, there are options available to the visual merchandiser with a large plate glass window and a small merchandise presentation. One option is **masking** the window and turning a large area into a small shadow box. The plate glass can be painted out with an opaque paint or partially covered by panels set against the glass inside the window. (See Figure 7.7.)

Stores that do not want to change large windows too often or that are limited in staff find it expedient to mask off these windows and do small shadow-box presentations of accessories and separates. This is especially effective on side streets or in windows facing parking lots or low-traffic areas. Even an occasional change on the main traffic street can have special value. It is the surprise, the jolt, the deviation from the norm or the traditional that can attract attention and bring the shopper closer to the store and, hopefully, into it.

The visual merchandiser may also find it effective, at times, to mask off the window opening of a full-sized window so that, though the window is still dressed and treated as a full window, it can only be viewed through the limited opening in the window mask. It is like the peephole in the construction barrier that always draws the curious. The application of solid or printed adhesive vinyl to mask a plate glass window has simplified this process greatly. The visual merchandiser can install a temporary masking to shrink down the window size and reshape the window opening with a design such as a giant keyhole or a seasonal or brand symbol.

FIGURE 7.6   At Kleinfeld's in New York City, the cutout silhouette figures up against the front glass cut off the shopper's view of the full window while focusing attention on the object of the camera people. The center of attraction is the glamorously clad mannequin bathed in a brilliant yellow "spotlight." *Kleinfield, New York. Copyright WindowsWear PRO http://pro.windowswear .com; contact@windowswear.com 1.646.827.2288.*

FIGURE 7.7   Under the soaring eagle with its widespread wings stands a group of semi-abstract mannequins on a raised platform. The platform is an island in the midst of a heavily trafficked aisle and the merchandise that can be viewed from all sides. *Macy's, Herald Square, New York.*

There is something about looking through a keyhole or a slit that makes the viewer feel as though he or she is onto something special. When used with care and with the appropriate merchandise—but not overused—this "knothole in the fence" technique works particularly well. Both proscenia and masking are discussed at greater length in Chapter 18.

Open-Back Windows

An **open-back window** has no back wall, offering a direct view into the selling area beyond. Much of what has been written about the closed-back window is relevant to the open-back window. The open back creates particular challenges for lighting and background presentations, and extra

FIGURE 7.8 With the exception of the low white platform, nothing separates the window display area from the store beyond. With the clever addition of two levels of clotheslines with garments clothespinned on, an oversized beach umbrella, and effective lighting from above, the two abstract figures become dominant features in the open-back space. *H&M, Bologna, Italy.*

effort is demanded of the visual merchandiser to maintain a sense of excitement in the window while the in-store merchandise and lighting are competing for the viewer's attention. It need not be a losing battle, and neither area has to suffer or take "second place." The open-back window does, however, require special handling. (See Figure 7.8.)

Glare and reflection in the window are ongoing challenges. Approaches to lighting the open back must always be balanced with the effect that the window lighting will have inside the store; lighting the back of the window may also mean lighting up the selling floor. Spotlights that are used to light the window merchandise may be irritating to the customer as he or she approaches the open-back window from inside the store. When possible, the visual merchandiser might use a panel, screen, or ribbon curtain to partially block the view of the store interior and, at the same time, create a positive background for the merchandise featured in the window. The panel or screen can supply the desired color and texture to complement the merchandise and possibly deliver the seasonal or promotional message as well. The visual merchandiser must then divert the attention of the viewer to the area in front of the panel, toward the window foreground. To capitalize on daylight and save energy, the visual merchandiser may use narrower background panels so that more light enters the shop. (See Figure 7.9.)

FIGURE 7.9 The three-part folding screen not only separates the display space from the store itself but introduces and highlights the stylish turquoise-colored home furnishings in the Roberto Cavalli shop in Milan, Italy. *Stefania D'Alessandro/Getty Images.*

Some visual merchandisers will take advantage of the view of the store interior and "dress" the area directly behind the window to enhance the merchandise being presented. This is especially successful in smaller stores and boutiques, where the shop owner has greater control over what is being shown and what is being sold. If the color red is being promoted, and only red garments and accessories are being displayed in the open-back window, it is an effective display and merchandising technique to bring the red merchandise on the selling floor up to the front of the store. Thus, the interior selling story reinforces the window story and, at the same time, provides a compatible backup for the window display. The message becomes stronger and more emphatic. (When we discuss store interior display in Chapter 8, we will again refer to the effectiveness of placing the garment displayed next to the on-floor stock of that garment.)

When a panel, screen, or fabric curtain is used to separate the selling area from the window space, without completely closing it off, the decorative device should be finished on both sides. Whereas the side facing the street is usually decorative, the side facing the selling floor may or may not be. With one panel, it is possible to use one kind of fabric on the front to complement the merchandise in the window, and a different fabric or treatment on the back to blend with the decoration or the merchandise seen inside the store.

Sometimes plants are used as dividers and, depending on the merchandise and the store image, these can be very effective—and very "green." At other times, transparent curtains, fine metal mesh, security grids, or beaded chains have been used as dividers. Most of these will allow some daylight into the store, saving energy; they also permit a view in as well as a look out and, in the case of the smaller store, provide a feeling of greater openness.

Island Windows

An **island, or lobby, window** is a window that has glass on all four sides, allowing the merchandise presentation to be viewed from any angle and any direction. To use theatrical terminology, it is displayed "in the round."

Because there is no back in an island window, the display techniques required for this type of setup are specialized and very different from those used for the standard three-wall display window.

The merchandise must be presentable from all sides. Visual merchandisers must style, tuck, and conceal any pins used to fit the mannequin or form. They may drape a sweater, jacket, or scarf to obscure any unsightly folds. Accessories can be used to draw attention away from any of the styling details. Unless the window is equipped with a turntable floor, there should be something interesting and attention getting from whichever direction the window is approached.

Usually, there is some distinct traffic pattern, and the visual merchandiser will play up one view and play down some other view or approach. For example, if an island window is located directly in front of a store, it would be more important to emphasize the view from the street. It is safe to assume that the side opposite the main entrance is the one seen by the customer as he or she leaves store, whereas the face fronting onto the street should entice the shopper to walk around the island window and come into the selling space proper.

The turntable floor, or a turntable set on the floor, is an excellent device that can be used occasionally to get special action or reaction. The turntable provides motion in the window (animation is an excellent attention-getting device) and makes the entire presentation viewable while the shopper stands in one place.

If a single suit or garment is presented in an island window, it can be accessorized with consideration of the four different views. A three-dimensional, full-round prop (a statue, an urn, or furniture piece), raised up on a platform or riser, can be used to supply a centralized high point or focal point in the window. The merchandise groupings might then be fanned out around that prop so that they blend into each other without losing their individual fashion message. Adhesive vinyl graphics can be used to transform the window into an object or suggest an environment.

Lighting is an important consideration in an island window. The overhead lights may be visible from some direction. They should be positioned to avoid hitting a passerby in the eye. Care should be taken to get the light on the merchandise and off the glass as much as possible. Light on the glass can actually create reflection, preventing the merchandise from being seen! Glare and reflection are part of the challenge in window display, and the all-glass unit can become a store liability, with prospective customers walking into the glass if the island window is left empty or unfinished. (This sometimes happens with unlined or unbanded all-glass doors.)

In older stores the island display window unit is often located under a marquee or in an enclosed foyer, with closed-back display windows on either side of it and the store entrance behind it. By minimizing the overhead lighting in this area and keeping the walk-around space in semidarkness, the lighting in the island window and the other display windows will be more effective and more dramatic. Glare and reflection will be minimized, and the visibility beyond the island window will be greatly reduced.

Special Windows

SHADOW BOXES

A **shadow box** is a small, elevated window used for the close-up presentation of special merchandise or accessories. The size varies, but it is usually about 3 feet by 5 feet, either "portrait" (vertical) or "landscape" (horizontal). Besides having a smaller window surface, the shadow box is often shallower (18 to 24 inches deep) and higher from the street level than the standard display window. All of this tends to bring the merchandise nearer to eye level and the closer scrutiny of the shopper. The shadow box presents a unique opportunity to capture the consumer's eye; the work of the late Gene Moore at Tiffany & Co. is an excellent example. Shadow-box windows can make a short, bold design statement with fewer, more daring elements that tell a story or become a miniature environment like a Broadway stage. Think of the space in layers—glass, foreground, middle ground, and background. The glass window acts as a surface to add vinyl copy or a masking, the middle can support merchandise and prop, and the back wall adds the contrasting color or texture.

Lighting is usually limited to a very few mini-spots or pinpoint spotlights, and the lights are generally directed right at the merchandise. Some stores, selling only small, precious merchandise (jewelry, shoes, belts and ties, cosmetics, or small leather goods), may have more exciting lighting installations, including back and side lighting; atmospheric, or wash, lighting; and highlighting of the merchandise.

Because the glass surface is smaller and the sight line funnels in, dramatic effects and strong color contrasts are required to attract the shopper's eye. Shadow boxes often appear on side streets (they sometimes are full-size windows that have been masked off to create small feature windows) or on either side of an entrance to a store. With a store that has a foyer or some area of separation between the street doors and the doors into the selling floor, shadow-box display cases brighten up the area and "sell" the people waiting to go inside. Shadow boxes may also be incorporated in the interior design of the selling floor; this is discussed in Chapter 8. (See Figure 7.10.)

ELEVATED WINDOWS

An **elevated window** may have its floor raised up to 3 feet above street level. It may be only 5 feet tall, and the display area may be much shallower than is necessary to show certain kinds of merchandise. This higher but shorter and shallower window does present challenges, but none are insurmountable. They do require different treatments and nonstandardized solutions.

A regular, full-size mannequin—be it realistic or abstract—will not be able to stand up in this window, but it can sit, kneel, or lie down. There are many mannequins designed to be used in just those positions. This is fine when a horizontal or diagonal presentation (see Chapter 3) will work with the merchandise and the store's fashion attitude. If the informal and rather relaxed mannequin will not do justice to the garments, then a dressmaker form or suit form might do the job. A shorter, headless, and possibly legless form may also fit in the low-ceilinged window.

Another technique for showing merchandise in these shallower, elevated windows, without the use of a three-dimensional form, is called **flying**, in which the garments

FIGURE 7.10   The shadow box is a small, self-illuminated display window usually raised higher off the ground than a traditional display window. Mostly designed to showcase small and specialty items, like jewelry, cosmetics, fashion accessories, and eyewear, the shadow-box window serves to raise these pieces up closer to the viewer's eye level. *Cada, Munich, Germany. Design: Deko Rank.*

seem to be in motion, soaring through a display window, controlled by invisible wires, pins, and tissue-paper padding. Many boutiques also make an "art" of shaping, draping, and adding dimension to clothes against walls, on panels, and cascading from furniture. (See Chapter 12.)

In an elevated window, the floor is higher and thus closer to the average viewer's eye level. It is a good window in which to do a lay-down presentation of the merchandise and the accessory groupings with an occasional buildup for special interest. Some stores prefer this type of display setup because it creates a boutique-like atmosphere and gives the store the opportunity to show more merchandise, especially if the merchandise is separates and related fashion accessories. (These techniques will be discussed more fully in Chapter 20.)

DEEP WINDOWS

A very **deep window**, even if it is of standard height and width, presents other types of challenges. It may require too much merchandise, too many mannequins, and too much electrical energy to light the back of the cavernous window. Also, the back may be so far from the front glass that showing merchandise in the rear is worthless. The viewer cannot really see that far back and misses the details of the merchandise and nuances of the display.

If the deep window has an open back, a screen or drapery with a finished back can reduce some of the depth of the window as well as provide a setting for another display, this one viewable from the inside of the store. Thus, by cutting the depth, the visual merchandiser can create two display areas, tell two different merchandising stories, and provide shopping interest inside and outside the store.

If the deep window has a closed back, the visual merchandiser may build a new back wall, closer to the glass line, and utilize the space between the existing back wall and the new back wall for the storage of props, fixtures, and mannequins.

TALL WINDOWS

With the window glass that soars well above the usual 9 or 10 feet in height, the visual merchandiser has several challenges with which to contend. The simplest solution, it would seem, would be to add a valance or top proscenium. Either of these devices will visually cut down the window size but may be at odds with the architectural look of the building. They may destroy the sweep of the line or the repetition of shape and pattern intended by the store's architect.

In a very **tall window** the overhead lighting, which is usually attached to the ceiling above the front glass line, is so far away from the merchandise or mannequin on the floor that it ineffective as a strong accent light. The visual merchandiser will either have to rely more on side lighting for the emphasis and use the overhead lamps for atmospheric wall and floor washes. Most stores try to keep the lighting fixtures out of sight since they can be distracting. Some stores feel the lighting fixtures add a theatrical quality to the setup. They recognize that display lighting is an honest and integral part of the display; they see nothing wrong with showing the lighting equipment as part of window construction.

In such a window the visual merchandiser can elect to take full advantage of the extra height and raise the mannequins onto pedestals, piers, or columns. The merchandise can soar, if the architecture and style permit, to create new and startling effects. Instead of a horizontal lineup of mannequins, they can be staggered on different levels. The assorted heights tend to separate the mannequins from each other and, though part of the same composition, each will be individualized and highlighted. If it is right for the store's fashions, or if a bit of whimsy is desired, a mannequin can be made to float, fly, or just be suspended in midair à la Mary Poppins—umbrella and all! The magic of suspended forms or gravity-defying feats is certain to gain window attention. (See Figure 7.11.)

A self-standing screen or drapery hung from a ceiling track will also work to cut down the depth of the window.

FIGURE 7.11   A tall window can be a problem, and in a run-on, or overly long, window, it can make creating a suitable display a nightmare. By using overscaled letters to spell out the company name and designing a multilevel composition with the headless mannequins in animated poses standing, sitting, reclining, and leaping throughout the expansive space, the designer may create an eye-catching spectacle filled with light and action. *Ann Taylor Loft, Broadway & 42nd Street, New York City. Design: Victor Johnson.*

Make-Your-Own-Display Windows

A relatively new shop front has become very popular and is now appearing in major shopping areas as well as in malls and shopping centers, where the concept originated. It takes place within the all-glass facade, and it does away with the display window as we know it. Sheets of glass now go from floor to ceiling, either flanking glass doors or off to either side of the glass entry. There is no traditional back or partial wall. There is no raised floor. There is nothing that marks off this space as the display area except its location up close to the front glass and facing the street or the mall's aisle.

For this architectural design the visual merchandiser must create his or her own "window." The visual merchandiser needs to add platforms, elevations, or risers to raise the product display up closer to the viewer's eye level. Screens, moveable panels, or hanging drapes can be introduced to set off this display space partially from the store behind it. The installation of a ceiling grid over this front area will make it simpler to hang drapes, panels of fabric or paper, ribbon streamers, or even framed graphics. A lighting track also needs to be installed to light the featured merchandise.

Often in these makeshift display areas the mannequins stand on the floor and on a level with the shoppers, and the accessories are shown atop chairs, tables, or pieces of furniture that also serve as atmospheric props. To highlight this area as the display area, rugs, grass mats, felt-covered floor pads, wood chip scatter, gravel, or even floor tiles may be laid down to delineate the area while adding to the ambiance. Better still, a 1-foot platform set down in the space will make the presentation more emphatic and raise the mannequins up over the passersby outside the store, thus making the mannequins more visible.

For shoe and handbag displays, a table may be added up front as the primary elevation and then additional risers used to create different viewing levels. Jewelry may

FIGURE 7.12   There is no doubt that there is a party going on in the Hickey Freeman store, and it is formal. As the shopper enters into the store, he is engulfed in and surrounded by "musicians" in tuxedos and loads of black and white sheets of music. Who can resist or pass up the music-sheet clad mannequin on the piano? This is a celebration, and everyone is invited. *Tom Beebe, Hickey Freeman and students at the Fashion Institute of Technology.*

require a suspended platform to raise items even higher for appraisal (Figure 7.12).

Runways, Catwalks, and Up-Front Displays

With mall stores being more and more open, and without true display windows, these devices serve to bring the new and featured items out to the shoppers on the shopping center aisles. When the store has an open front—all opening and no windows—bring the runway right up to the store line and start the excitement there. Or, use a platform or a series of risers, up in the opening, to create an island display, with the mannequins showing off the newest styles. Thus, with the addition of some attractive and attracting props that create interest and suggest a lifestyle, the island display becomes a real up-front "window" display.

Display Window Construction: Trade Talk

bank of windows	fins	raised floor
ceiling grid	flying	raked floor
closed-back window	island, or lobby, window	run-on window
deep window	masking	shadow box
elevated window	open-back window	side walls
elevator-type windows	pier	tall window
enclosed window	proscenia (proscenium, singular)	teasers

Display Window Construction: A Recap

+ A closed-back window is the typical display window. It has a full back wall, sides, and a large plate glass window facing pedestrians on the street. It is also called an enclosed window.

+ Glare and reflection are two of the greatest challenges with display windows.

+ Decorative awnings help shield windows and cut down glare.

+ Light-colored backgrounds help minimize reflection.

+ Most display window floors are raised anywhere from 8 or 9 inches to 2 feet above street level.

+ In a raked floor, the back of the floor is several inches higher than the front, making it easier to see small objects such as shoes and cosmetics.

+ An elevator-type window is actually an elevator platform that can be lowered to the basement and prepared.

+ Most display-type window floors are finished with parquet wood tiles or a neutral, subtly textured carpet.

+ Some stores have removable panels closing the backs of their windows, allowing the window to be used as a closed-back or open-back window or the display space to be converted into selling space.

+ A ceiling grid enables the visual merchandiser to attach lighting fixtures or other devices when the window ceiling is concrete or another dense, impenetrable material.

+ A proscenium is the structural arch, usually rather ornate, often seen in a theater surrounding the curtain. In the display window the proscenium consists of a top valance and side panels.

+ Masking a window is accomplished by painting out part of the window with opaque paint or partially covering the window with panels set inside the glass, thus creating a shadow box. Masking is helpful when working with a large window and a small merchandise presentation.

+ An open-back window has no back wall, offering a direct view into the selling area beyond.

+ An island, or lobby, window has glass on all four sides.

+ A turntable floor allows an entire presentation to be viewable while the shopper stands in one spot.

+ A shadow box is a small, elevated window used for close-up presentation of specific merchandise.

+ "Flying" is a technique by which garments seem to be in motion, controlled by invisible wires, pins, and tissue-paper padding.

+ A deep window presents challenges because it is difficult to light and requires too many mannequins and too much merchandise.

+ Tall windows can be difficult to light but offer opportunities for striking, elevated displays.

+ Makeshift display areas in which the designer creates his or her own window are becoming increasingly popular.

+ Runways, catwalks, and up-front displays bring the display to the shopper in open-front shopping areas.

Questions for Review and Discussion

1. Explain the challenges of glare and reflection in window displays and identify possible solutions to these challenges.

2. Are there advantages in the use of ramped windows? If so, describe them.

3. Describe the benefits of an elevator window.

4. What are proscenia and masking, and what purpose do they serve in display windows?

5. Compare and contrast open-back and closed-back windows. What are the advantages and disadvantages of each type?

6. Explain the challenges inherent to displaying in an island window.

7. What advantages are gained by the use of elevated windows?

8. What type of merchandise is best displayed using shadow-box windows? Give specific examples.

9. What is the difference between an elevator window and elevated window?

10. Describe a display that could be very effective in an elevated window, in a deep window, and in a tall window.

Chapter Eight
Store Interiors

Interior view of the new Villa Moda store in Bahrain.
Teuten/WWD/© Condé Nast.

**AFTER YOU HAVE READ THIS CHAPTER,
YOU WILL BE ABLE TO DISCUSS**

- how landing areas affect shoppers
- how wayfinding assists in navigating the store
- how a focal point directs consumers
- the unique characteristics of island displays
- the use of counters and display cases for merchandise presentations
- the differences and similarities between museum cases and demonstration cubes

- displays appropriate for ledges within the store
- how structural columns can be used for interior display
- the term *fascia*
- uses of fascia
- the use of T-walls in the store interior
- 100 percent traffic areas within the store

After a shopper has passed through the entrance area or foyer, he or she is on the selling floor. This is the store's opportunity to meet and greet the shopper with a strong first impression. Consider the different methods (or strategies) the store might use to welcome shoppers at the entranceway or give them a reason to pause. A smiling greeter might call out and welcome the shopper to the store, or the visual merchandiser may have created a spectacular display of mannequins to awe. A store planner might design a captivating traffic pattern or informational kiosk. In some big box stores a mini food or beverage service may offer some relief before the shopping trip commences. The idea here is to engage or capture shoppers for a few brief moments before they begin their descent into the depths of the store. We identify this space as a **landing area**. A landing area is an area at the entrance of the store specifically designed to slow down shoppers, possibly targeting them with a curated merchandise offering and elevating the overall store experience. Big box stores favor food services and value-based offerings to interrupt the pace, whereas department and specialty stores entertain with stunning displays. Both of these are successful solutions.

Much like visiting the home page of a website, the shopper requires direction to navigate the store interior. This is better known as **wayfinding**. Wayfinding is informational and directional store signage that stimulates and enhances a customer's journey throughout the store environment. Store directories and maps are typically positioned in high-traffic areas such as entranceways and escalator landings. Many store directories utilize a digital touch screen on a kiosk for increased navigation. A digital directory empowers the store to offer even more portals: a gateway to information about products, services, events, current weather conditions, and even news or sport feeds.

The development and placement of in-store signage is the job of the visual merchandiser or store planner. It often requires collaborating with a signage vendor or a graphic design team. Today, in-store signage is fully integrated with the look and architecture of the store and is part of the overall store design. Signage should not only identify an area but also encourage and enhance the customer's movement around the store through all forms of environmental graphics. Floor graphics, ceiling danglers, and the surfaces of walls and columns assist in directing shoppers throughout the store environment. As the signage directs the shopper to the merchandise on display, the display in turn entertains the shopper, hopefully resulting in a sale.

Focal Points

In planning traffic patterns and store layout, architects, store planners, and visual merchandisers will often speak of

FIGURE 8.1   In the large, open space, the bright orange panel highlighted with the store name logo becomes not only the draw and attraction but the unifying element for a free-standing shop-within-the-shop. *TopShop, New York City. Design: Dalziel & Pow.*

locating feature areas, hotspots, or focal points. The **focal point** is a generic term that refers to any place in the retail setting where emphasis has been placed to attract the shopper. Focal points are strategically positioned to pull the shopper further into the selling floor. This can be an area on a rear wall that has been painted a strong color and against which a well-lit armoire or fixture or furniture arrangement has been placed and then arrayed with featured merchandise. The focal point can be a mannequin or form on an elevated platform with a dynamic prop, in a pool of light, or a series of product displays on high shelves set above wall fixtures.

The focal point is the exclamation point in the design—and it is always well lit! It is the accented area on the floor where the newest merchandise is usually featured. Sometimes, the focal point can be a large image, a graphic, or a huge seasonal floral arrangement. Even if merchandise is not featured at the focal point, the focal point serves to reinforce the store's sense of style. It also serves as a beacon that attracts the shopper and then as a directional force that points him or her toward other products displayed in the space. (See Figure 8.1.)

Island Displays

In newer mall stores, where the windows are played down and the interior is played up, the shopper will be greeted immediately on entering the store by an **island display**, a featured display space viewable from all sides. This is an important area, well-lit and clearly identified by a raised platform, a change of flooring material, or an area rug. An abstract construction may highlight the area.

In an island display, the store presents an editorial style merchandising story—inspired by color, a trend, an event, or a storewide promotion. Sometimes this display is intended to support the exterior window display. If a color trend is highlighted in the island display, the visual merchandiser can coordinate the surrounding area of the selling floor with the same color in related products (accessories) or even nonrelated items (throw pillows, luggage, china and glass, and so on). An island display that is on a slightly raised platform can be more effective and get more attention than an on-the-floor display, but whatever the "structural design," it should be changed regularly, as the merchandise and the promotions evolve.

When an island display is laid out on the store's floor plan, effective lighting for that area should be anticipated. The visual merchandiser may still find it necessary to supplement the lighting in this area for more drama and emphasis. As in the window setup, some kind of ceiling system will be needed for the suspension of props or lights, or both. Although the presentation is thought of as a 360-degree presentation, the view from the entrance is the most important aspect of the "show." (See Figure 8.2.)

FIGURE 8.2 Set where two major aisles cross, the central build-up and display with floating chairs is meant to be viewed from all around. It is further accentuated by the domed lighting canopy over the major display area. *Galeries Lafayette, Jakarta, Plajer & Franz Galeries 6.*

Risers, Platforms, Pedestals, and Feature Tables

A **riser**, or **platform**, set just off the aisle and spotlighted from above will also serve to identify a specific merchandise area or category and promote a particular piece of merchandise. If a shopper sees a mannequin wearing athletic wear raised up on a platform for better visibility over the traffic on the floor, he or she will logically assume that athletic wear is stocked next to or behind that figure. A series of risers in varied heights may also be used for the same purpose or to supplement the raised platform. (See Figure 8.3.)

FIGURE 8.3   A round, two-tiered merchandise table acts as a riser for the trendily dressed, semi-realistic white mannequins in this unisex fashion store. The doughnut-shaped dropped light fixture not only illuminates the mannequins but also serves as a strong attractor. *MisterLady. Design: Gruschwitz GmbH, Munich, Germany.*

In Chapter 14 we discuss this concept of selling and also go into more detail on the many freestanding floor fixtures that are available not only to hold and sort garments but also to present a display of that merchandise to the prospective customer. We explain the use of kiosks, easels, drapers and costumers, outposts, and so on.

The Runway Platform

A fashion show staple has become a popular showplace in retail settings. The wide, spacious drive or central aisle of a store that may have previously featured a small mannequin arrangement on an island platform may now have given way to a longer platform—a long runway such as those used in fashion shows.

When window display space is either too shallow or too scarce to do a real presentation—or does not exist at all—the runway becomes the focal display element inside the store. The raised platform—often no more than 12 to 18 inches in height and under-lit so that it seems to float off the ground—starts near the shop entrance. This up-front location makes it visible through the open entranceway and serves to guide the shopper to the rear of the store. Shoppers follow the runway as it goes back into the heart of the retail setting.

A line of mannequins or forms on this platform can show off the newest or most exciting fashions available. The presentation has even more impact if it is accentuated by a line of spots directly over the long platform. The accenting lights turn the lineup into an eye-arresting spectacle.

As in all good visual merchandising, the runway presentation is enhanced if all the garments have a common denominator: a color, pattern, look, or theme. If that single concept is carried through, the effect can be dynamic. Propping can be a nice touch but is not necessary. This is all about merchandising. (See Figure 8.4.)

The Catwalk

If a store has an extra-high ceiling—anything from 15 to 20 feet—the designer may add overhead catwalks, or walkways, that cross over the sales floor.

Counters, Cash Wraps, and Display Cases

FIGURE 8.4 It is a new look at New Look, a swinging young people's store. The runway starts at the entrance and ends at the escalator that takes shoppers to the upper level of the shop. The runway is peopled with fun-loving, active, realistic mannequins dressed for the moment, and they are probably a reflection of the shoppers in the store. *New Look, Liverpool, United Kingdom. Design: Caulder Moore.*

These are used to show off mannequins in featured garments. The figures may be positioned in lifelike clusters or in lineups on these metal-framed units that have wire mesh or clear Lucite floors. These transparent truss systems allow the shopper a clear view of what is on show and are less likely to interfere with the ceiling lighting needed to illuminate the floor fixtures on the selling floor. Adding to the interest and spectacle is the use of seated figures on the floor of the catwalk, which look down onto the shoppers below. The term *catwalk* is from theater and refers to the bridge that usually goes across the stage, way up above the theatergoers' sight line.

There are many places on the selling floor where the visual merchandiser can use his or her own special blend of fashion know-how to affect the selling environment. **Counters** and **display cases** are two such areas. (See Figure 8.5.)

A counter is a major area for merchandise presentation. It is truly the point of purchase—the place where the merchandise is presented and the sale is concluded, where the money or credit card is taken and the bagged or boxed purchase is delivered to the shopper. It must be staffed, and it does take up a specific amount of floor space. More often than not, it requires additional space or drawers beneath or behind to hold the merchandise or the stock being sold. There are many variations of counter fixtures available, and many are custom designed for specific merchandise categories or services. A cash wrap may be incorporated into a counter with merchandise or freestanding on its own. Some luxury brand stores are relocating cash wrap counters behind the scenes in an effort to "purify" the look of the store. Cash wraps require less space as stores transition to smaller digital operating solutions; many stores use a tablet and a small cash drawer beneath the counter for transactions.

FIGURE 8.5 The clustered collection of soft, white-washed wooden cabinets, consoles, and tables serves as a basis for the glass-sided museum cases in which the jewelry is displayed. Note the clever use of uprights that support mirrors for the shopper's comfort and convenience when trying on pieces. *Sundance, Edina.*

The counter itself may be no more than a tabletop or ledge on which a sampling of the merchandise can be displayed or presented to a potential customer. The counter may be the top surface of a piece of furniture that stocks merchandise on shelves or in drawers below, or it can be an all-glass or partially glass case for a below-eye-level display. The most common, basic display case design has a glass or transparent plastic top and at least three sides of glass. This enables the shopper to see the merchandise displayed for sale, while at the same time protecting the setup from "touch, feel, and steal." The unit is usually raised off the ground on a pedestal and seems to float, in keeping with the trend for lighter, more open, and less nailed-down-looking interiors. The bottom, or floor, of the display case can coordinate with the store's interior design (made of marble or bronze or fine wood), or it can be equipped with Upson fiberboard pads and covered with various fabrics that can be changed with the seasons or the color of featured merchandise. Many designer brands customize their counters and display cases to complement their products by using materials that reflect the character or "DNA" of the brand. In turn, the store will afford enough square footage for this brand to have its own "vendor shop" within the store landscape.

Because display cases are often about 2 feet deep, it is advisable to use risers and saddles (see "Assorted Counter Fixtures" in Chapter 12) in the case to raise some of the merchandise closer to the shopper's eye level or to make interesting setups of assorted merchandise at different levels. Small groupings can also be shown as individual collections by varying the viewing levels. For example, watch or jewelry brands will distinguish themselves by using risers in special colors, fabrics, or leathers to win equity in a shared display case or for a particular gift-giving time.

The all-glass-fronted case/counter is becoming scarcer on the selling floor as stores adopt the "open sell" method of merchandising. Open sell merchandising requires less sales assistance and empowers the shoppers to help themselves and explore the product offerings more readily. Sephora's open sell environment encourages shoppers to play and experiment with more products in a single visit; however, it demands more increased security measures such as magnetic labels or gravity feed tracking devices.

Museum Cases

The **museum case** is primarily a display case that can, on occasion, serve as a counter or demonstration area. As the name implies, the case is similar to those found in museums and consists of a column or pedestal (square, rectangular)

FIGURE 8.6   With all that excitement going on in the main aisle, how do you tell shoppers that the real action is on the sides? It helps to raise up the mannequins on ledges, atop merchandising fixtures, and on platforms to reveal what is available where, as they did in TopShop in Soho in New York City. *Design: Dalziel & Pow.*

with a five-sided glass case on top. It is often taller than a counter, and the merchandise, precious and special, is raised up closer to the viewer's eye level. Again, the base of the case or floor pad should be coordinated with the merchandise presented or the seasonal theme. The museum case is approached and viewed from all sides, and small platforms or risers can be used to enhance the presentation and to help delineate the assorted pieces of merchandise in the same case. (See Figure 8.6.)

Pedestal or Display Cubes

Pedestals, or **display cubes**, are laminate-covered, acrylic, or wood-finished cubes found on the selling floor. These pedestals are prepared in standard heights such as 12-inch, 18-inch, 24-inch, 30-inch, 36-inch, or 42-inch. The footprint depends on the merchandise that will be displayed on top of the cube. Standard footprints include 11.5-inch × 11.5-inch, 15-inch × 15-inch, 18-inch × 18-inch, 20-inch × 20-inch, and 23-inch × 23-inch, and they can be grouped and clustered or used individually. The pedestal can serve as a mannequin platform, as a display surface for a "lay-down" of a single item, or to support a line of products in a formation. A salesperson may use pedestals for demonstrations

to show, to explain, and to sell an item. These cubes are particularly popular as mid-traffic islands to gain attention for a special product, or used right off the aisle as a "draw-into-the-department" device. Shoe departments will often use them in clusters or in an echelon configuration, along an aisle or as a low divider, to feature samples of shoes. Low cubes—17 or 18 inches tall—also double as seats or benches. (See Figure 8.7.)

Ledges

The traditional **ledge** is raised about 5 feet from the floor and is often an "island," that is, a freestanding structure on the selling floor. The ledge is usually the top surface of a backup storage unit behind a selling counter. Department store ledges were standard sizes at one time; however, store architecture and custom cabinet design have changed the traditional size and shapes of ledges in stores. A ledge can also be the top surface of a storage unit that is set flat against a perimeter wall with a counter set in front of it. This type of ledge would be viewed only from the front.

In the department and large specialty stores built before the mid-1970s, it was not unusual to have 18- to 25-foot ceilings on the main floor. With this great openness above the

FIGURE 8.7 The big, blocky cubes standing out in mid-floor serve as demonstration cubes. A complete outfit can be displayed on top of them, they can be used to hold stacked merchandise, or they can be left bare so the shopper can use them to assemble his own assorted pieces. In some areas of a store, the demo cube can be used as a work surface on which a product can actually be demonstrated. *Tommy Hilfiger, London, United Kingdom. Design: Caulder Moore.*

level of merchandise and customers, the ledge displays were the major focal display areas inside the store. It was here that fantasies grew to unprecedented heights. Each new season or promotion was greeted with fully dressed and accessorized mannequins, often in groupings, in settings complete with budding trees or towering flower and foliage arrangements. In this elevated location, above the traffic of the floor, the ledge display was an eye-filling spectacle.

The lowering of store ceilings and budgets and the rising of energy costs, as well as concern over energy expenditure, have simplified the type of ledge displays in use today. The newer selling floors and stores that are actively renovating their selling areas are bringing the ceilings—and thus the lights—closer to the merchandise. Some of the mall stores being currently designed use a dropped ceiling for emphasis as well as for economy in heating, air-conditioning, and illuminating the floor. The lower ceiling focuses the shopper's attention onto a particular spot. It also creates a more intimate feeling. Shops within shops, or boutiques, use this technique to separate the special area from the rest of the floor or department. Although some ledges will still accommodate standing mannequins, more stores are using kneeling, sitting, or reclining figures on their ledges; the scale, in relation to the lower ceiling, is better.

Customers cannot and should not be able to handle merchandise displayed on ledges, but because it is space that is very visible, the visual merchandiser should not lose any opportunity to use the ledge for seasonal or promotional displays that may include merchandise and props.

A ledge that backs up onto a wall may have panel backgrounds behind the merchandise presentation. Headless forms or torsos, as well, may work well in these areas to show the garments dimensionally.

By the nature of their location, ledges are usually lit from overhead by wall washes or by fluorescent lights hidden behind fascia boards. The displays will probably need more definition and brightness, and a few well-aimed spots from overhead can achieve that. (See Figure 8.8.)

Shadow Boxes

As previously discussed in Chapter 7, **shadow boxes** are miniature display windows—or elevated display cases. Very often,

FIGURE 8.8 Since the Tegernsee shop offers a variety of packaged foods and beverages, the designers created several small, decorative display areas to feature the products. The natural textured pebble walls contrast the wooden units, and accents of LED light help to highlight the products showcased in the shadow boxes. *Gruschwitz GmbH, Tegernsee, Germany.*

however, they are worked into the design of the selling floor. They may appear above and behind counters, when the counters are situated in front of floor-to-ceiling walls or partitions. They are usually at eye level, are shallow, and offer possibilities for limited lighting effects. Small merchandise and fashion accessories are commonly shown in shadow boxes.

Every effort should be made by the visual merchandiser to keep the shadow-box displays fresh and current, in line with the store's promotions and seasonal changes. They should be changed frequently. The colors and textures of the floor, background, and riser should be varied. Arrangements should be altered. Props should be used to complement the merchandise and the department. If the interior design of a shop or area dictates a monochromatic color scheme, the clever visual merchandiser can still work wonders with patterns, textures, and unusual materials within the restrictions set by the store architect or designer.

If the lighting inside the shadow box is limited to a thin-line fluorescent tube, the visual merchandiser may attempt to introduce an LED ribbon of lights in the shadow box. There are many compact and attractive highlighting fixtures available on the market today; if the lamp fits the decor, it can be integrated into the shadow-box presentation. It might even become an attention-getting device and add to the interest of the presentation. Small, high-intensity lamps also fit into the scale of small shadow boxes and, at the same time, do a big accent lighting job. (See Figure 8.9.)

FIGURE 8.9   Eye entertainment is provided for shoppers strolling down the aisle of the fashion floor devoted to top designers. The series of self-enclosed glass "windows" have structural columns to back up the mannequins dressed in the designer outfits and raised platforms to elevate them. *Bloomingdale's, Chevy Chase, Maryland. Designer: Mancini Duffy, New York City.*

Enclosed Displays

Larger than a shadow box, an **enclosed display** is usually a fully glassed-in platform that can hold a mannequin or two. It may be located at the entrance to a department, line an aisle, or be part of a perimeter wall. In size and construction, an enclosed display may be very similar to a closed-back display window found in the front of a store. The purpose is the same: to show the merchandise in a protected area.

High-priced luxury merchandise made from buttery leathers or fragile silks can decrease in value when handled too often. Inside the glass display window, on a mannequin or form, the garment can be shown at its best and can get a boost from some well-chosen and expensive accessories. The merchandise can be properly lit and come out a week or two later as crisp, fresh, and saleable as it was when it went in. And all the accessories will still be there—as well as the mannequin's hands! This is one way to add drama and excitement inside the store, especially when there are no display windows out front.

Columns are an integral part of a store's construction. They hold up ceilings, support the weight of the roof, and are an excellent place to hang decorative props. Columns often delineate a department's beginning and end. They

may be lined up on either side of a major aisle, adding vertical highlights on a horizontal floor. That is where the column shines in the display scheme of things: Banners can hang from them, wreaths can adorn them, garland can entwine them or be swagged from them. Arches can spring from them and cross over aisles and ledges for dramatic effects. Storewide event posters can illuminate them and, if need be, a column can be a directory or signboard for a shop or area. The column can be a background panel for a mannequin on a platform. It can be a four-sided mirror, which adds the illusion of space to a department or supplies the necessary reflective surfaces into which most customers want to look.

Columns not only hold merchandise; they can also be used to show merchandise decoratively. Some ledges are adjacent to columns, and the combination of ledge and column can offer interesting display possibilities. Columns can be covered with panels, painted, or camouflaged, but the wise visual merchandiser will take advantage of the rhythm and repetition of columns in the floor plan of the store—and their obvious verticality—and of their visibility above the traffic, and use them creatively whenever possible (Figure 8.10).

FIGURE 8.10   Almost daring you not to see and admire them and what they are wearing, the abstract mannequins are perched atop the simple fixtures—along with alternate selections—that are lined up along the aisle. The mannequins are at the shoppers' eye level, while pants forms extend up over the figures. *Galeries Lafayette, Jakarta, Plajer & Franz Galeries.*

Fascia

A **fascia** is a band—a horizontal board or panel. In stores the fascia is often found 6½ to 7 feet off the ground, above the bins, shelves, or vertical hang rods that are attached to a wall or partition. It can be used to conceal lights and as a background for merchandise displays.

Any ceiling lights that are directed down to the merchandise on the selling floor will lose intensity because of the distance; therefore, it is a common practice and good merchandising to bring a light source closer to merchandise that is to be sold. These lights are often placed 7 feet above the ground and are extended out from the wall or partition. The fascia covers the light fixture from the shopper's view and also helps focus the light down onto the merchandise.

In the past, a broad expanse of fascia (starting at 7 feet off the ground and often reaching up to the ceiling) was the area that carried department identification either in permanently attached letters or graphic symbols. Today, with departments in flux, expanding and contracting as merchandise and seasons dictate, vinyl transfer signage and temporary adhesive wall decorations have the ability to change out quickly as a part of the store design.

The fascia is about 4 plus feet wide. It is close to the ceiling lights and is usually visible from across the floor and certainly from the aisle. It has become a popular place to pin up merchandise and seasonal displays: jeans, shirts, sweaters, accessory groupings, and so on. The display on the fascia is used as both a merchandising and a decorating technique. The fascia still functions to identify the merchandise in the department and, at the same time, calls the customer to come over.

As the type of merchandise sold in a specific area changes (for example, from skiwear to swimwear), the display can change the identity and ambiance of the area. Environmental graphics or images from ad campaigns can be imaginatively arranged in geometric patterns. The seasonal or promotional events that take place in the store can be tied in with the fascia trim. A spotlight should be directed at the above-eye-level display to attract more attention to the display and to the area below.

If properly used, the fascia will tell what is being sold below, suggest the variety, and specify the time of the year or the look that is in vogue. (See Figure 8.11.)

FIGURE 8.11 If you have the space to spare, then really put on a *show* as they did in the Primark department store in Madrid. The two-tier presentation of mannequins in a variety of outfits and looks is a spectacular way to get attention and set a special look for the store's brand. *Primark, Madrid, Spain. Design: Dalziel & Pow.*

FIGURE 8.12 A composite drawing of some of the architectural, lighting, and fixturing details that might be found in a real operation. The selling floor has been trimmed for an Americana promotion. Note the many ways and places in which the theme was used for a storewide impact. *Illustration by Ron Carboni.*

T-Walls

Often one area or department will be separated from another by bins or double-sided, open-faced "closets" hung with merchandise. These two-sided walls or partitions—called **T-walls**—will extend from the back or perimeter wall out to the aisle. The flat end of this unit, on the aisle, can be converted into a valuable display space. A panel to cover the end of the unit makes the top stroke of the T. The merchandising wall is the upright of the T.

A platform can be placed on the aisle, in front of the panel, to highlight the merchandise stocked behind the display. A fully dressed and accessorized mannequin, a prop, a piece of furniture to hold another garment or complementary outfit, a plant, a colored panel to emphasize the outfit on display, a seasonal device—all can add to the importance of this wall, which is often only 4 to 6 feet wide and 8 feet tall.

High-Traffic Areas

There are locations throughout the store that get very heavy traffic, and they are referred to as **high-traffic areas**. These areas are in front of and around escalators or elevators, at entrances or exits, and near major featured spots like restaurants, atriums, and central meeting areas. Displays in these areas are, and should be, changed frequently, and they are often combined with a salesperson or demonstrator plus a certain amount of stock for quick, "impulse" shopping. Low-priced, easy-to-sell merchandise is promoted in these locations, and the displays serve as flags to catch the attention of and slow down shoppers long enough to get them involved in what is being offered. Color, motion, and even sound can be effective here.

Figure 8.12 shows some of the architectural, lighting, and fixturing details that might be used by a visual merchandiser inside the store.

Store Interiors: Trade Talk

columns	enclosed display	island display	pedestals
counters	fascia	landing area	platform
display cases	focal point	ledge	riser
display cubes	high-traffic areas	museum case	T-walls

Store Interiors: A Recap

+ A focal point refers to any place in the retail setting where emphasis is placed to attract the shopper. It is used to reinforce the store's image and to lead the shopper to particular products in the space.

+ An island display, which is viewable from all sides, is usually found immediately upon entering the store.

+ The counter is a major area for merchandise presentation because it is the point where the sale is concluded and the merchandise is packaged.

+ The display case usually has a transparent glass or plastic top and at least three sides of glass. It enables the shopper to see the merchandise, while protecting it from being touched or stolen.

+ A museum case is primarily a display case that can be used as a counter or demonstration area. It consists of a column or pedestal with a five-sided glass case.

+ Demonstration cubes are rug-upholstered, laminate-covered, or wood-finished blocks found on the selling floor. They vary in size and can be used alone or clustered, or can serve as mannequin platforms or display surfaces for lay-down displays.

+ In large department and specialty stores built before the mid-1970s, ledges were major focal display areas. The 18- to 25-foot ceilings in these older stores provide space for dressed mannequins or groupings of mannequins as well as promotional settings.

+ In newer stores the ceilings are lower and focus the shopper's attention on a particular spot, creating a more intimate feeling. The scale of the display, in relation to the lower ceiling, must be considered. Newer stores, therefore, are using kneeling, sitting, or reclining mannequins.

+ Structural columns can be used to hold decorative props, delineate a department's beginning and end, or add vertical highlights. They can be used to hold banners, garland, arches, posters, signboards, or directories or can be used as background panels for a mannequin. A column can also be a four-sided mirror, which adds the illusion of space and necessary reflective surfaces.

+ A fascia is a band—a horizontal board or panel 4 or more feet wide and about 6 1/2 to 7 feet off the ground—above the bin, shelves, or clothing rods that are attached to a wall or partition.

+ The T-wall is a two-sided wall or partition extending from the back or perimeter wall out to the aisle. A panel to cover the end of this unit makes the top stroke of the T. The merchandising wall is the upright of the T.

+ Locations throughout a store that get very heavy traffic are called high-traffic areas. These areas are in front of and around escalators or elevators; at entrances or exits; and near major features, such as restaurants, atriums, and central meeting areas.

Questions for Review and Discussion

1. Identify the specific functions of counters and display types.

2. What types of merchandise are best suited for presentation in display cases?

3. What is a ledge? What types of displays are best suited for ledges?

4. What are some of the advantages of enclosed interior display areas?

5. How can structural columns be used creatively as display areas within the store? How might you use a column for display in a children's department? A lingerie department?

6. What is fascia? Explain how fascia is used with lighting, with signage, and with merchandise display.

7. How should displays in high-traffic areas be handled?

Chapter Nine
Types of Displays and Display Settings

A BHV Marais Christmas window is seen as part of the World Fashion Window Displays.
Antoine Antoniol/Getty Images.

**AFTER YOU HAVE READ THIS CHAPTER,
YOU WILL BE ABLE TO DISCUSS**

+ the four major types of display
+ promotional and institutional displays
+ five categories of display settings
+ the purpose of buildup presentations in display

Fashions change, and so do the ways in which fashion is presented. During the "golden age" of display—back in the 1950s and 1960s—window displays were events or happenings, and shoppers were treated to spectacular trims that are now only seen at Christmas. Shoppers couldn't wait to walk down Main Street to see the newest extravaganza in the department store and specialty store windows. Mannequins were stately, glamourous, and beautiful beyond belief. They were models of perfection, fashioned after the movie stars of the day.

In the 1970s and early 1980s such spectaculars gave way to "street theater." Shocking displays were meant to disturb or provoke the viewer. Mannequins developed human-like imperfections, personalities, bumpy noses, eyes too close together, squints—and they took on more animated poses to complement the fashions of the day.

In the 1980s and 1990s, displays became static, minimalistic, and industrial. Hanging, draping, or laying garments down on the ground was common. Mannequins with heads made a rare guest appearance; more often we'd see hangers, drapers, forms, and torsos and a sameness of presentation as we walked down Main Streets or covered the aisles inside malls and shopping centers. Closed-back windows gave way to open-back windows, and "propping" was sometimes limited to a plant.

But display is not dead today, nor is it dying. It is simply evolving with our lifestyles, and visual merchandisers are learning to accept and even triumph over budget cuts and staff cuts and even over the loss of display windows, production facilities, and the magical lighting systems that once turned a display space into a theater. What has not changed is that shoppers, now more than ever, are looking for entertainment in the retail store and that the entertainment is often to be found in the displays. The displays have, in some stores, disappeared from the windows only to revive and thrive inside the store on platforms, on ledges, on T-walls, or around the fascias over the stocked merchandise. Although it is only one of the techniques used to bring attention to the new and featured merchandise, "humor" is more and more frequently being used to deliver the store's fashion image statement. It has become a significant element in visual language.

A humorous or amusing display says something up front about the store and about its customers; it humanizes the process of shopping. The humor can be broad and obvious or subtle and clever. It can be a "belly laugh," a giggle, a titter, or even a knowing smirk. It is entertaining and establishes an emotional bond. With humor, we reach out to our particular customer and say, "You'll love this one!" Americans have a long history of appreciating humor—we are a fun-loving nation that would rather smile than sigh, laugh than cry—and it is a great approach to effective displays, especially because improvisation is what display is all about.

Types of Displays

The primary purposes of displays are to present and to promote. A display is at its best when it simply shows a color, an item, a collection, or just an idea. Types of displays include the following:

- One-item display
- Line-of-goods display
- Related merchandise display
- Variety, or assortment, display

ONE-ITEM DISPLAY

A **one-item display** is just that—the showing and advancement of a single garment or any single item. It might be a gown designed by a top designer, a one-of-a-kind piece of ceramic or jewelry, or a Saarinen Tulip chair. Using one item can suggest exclusivity, simplicity, or minimalist style. (See Figure 9.1.)

LINE-OF-GOODS DISPLAY

A **line-of-goods display** is one that shows only one type of merchandise (all blouses, all shoes, or all pots and pans), although they may be in a variety of designs or colors. A window display showing three or four mannequins wearing daytime dresses of assorted colors, styles, and prints would be an example of a line-of-goods display. However, for a more effective presentation, and for better comprehension and acceptance by the shopper, there should be some connection or relevance indicated as to why these three or four articles are being shown together. They could all be

FIGURE 9.1 The finely dressed abstract mannequin is set in an environmental or lifestyle setting that reeks of class, elegance, and "money." The miniature red-coated soldiers are tying the figure up as a humorous and "What's that all about?" moment. *Stacy Suvino at Miss Jackson, Tulsa, Oklahoma.*

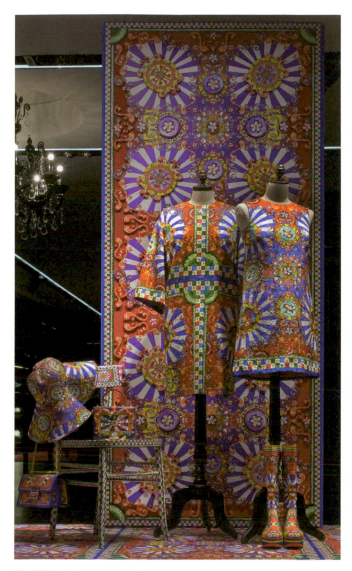

FIGURE 9.2 When Dolce & Gabbana creates a new fabric design, the designers let their imaginations flow. The result, shown here in the open-back window, is a variety of outfits, accessories, and home furnishing elements presented before a panel of the fabric that serves to set the window area apart from the store beyond. *Stefania D'Alessandro/Getty Images.*

designed by the same designer or created with the same fabric or print, or they could all feature a common theme. (See Figure 9.2.)

RELATED MERCHANDISE DISPLAY

In a **related merchandise display**, separates, accessories, or other items that "go together" are displayed because they are meant to be used together, because they are the same color, or because they share an idea or theme. It could be an "import" window, in which all the items are from the same country (from clothes, to handicrafts, to kitchen utensils to furniture, and so on). It might be a color promotion, in which all the clothing in one window is red, and the next display setup consists of all-red household supplies and hard goods. That presentation may be followed by a room setting in which red is the dominant color. Or it could be a display of lizard shoes, bags, and belts—all related because they are made of lizard skin. Red, white, and blue striped hats, sweaters, scarves, and leggings would be a related merchandise display. The items go together and reinforce each other. (See Figure 9.3.)

FIGURE 9.3 The quartet of white abstract figures is all set to mix and match their coordinated separates in this Parisian interior setting. The variety of yellow and white striped and solid yellow, white and pale gray tops and bottoms offer numerous possible combinations. *Stefania D'Alessandro/Getty Images.*

VARIETY OR ASSORTMENT DISPLAY

A **variety, or assortment, display** is a potpourri of anything and everything. It is a collection of unrelated items that happen to be sold in the same store. It can be work shoes, eyewear, tea kettles, Hawaiian print shirts, wicker chairs, flannel nightgowns, and cowboy boots. It is a mélange of odds and ends, a sampling of the merchandise contained within. With the popularity of vintage style, eclectic mixes, and the social media platform Pinterest, variety displays like those found in Anthropologie are trending. (See Figure 9.4.)

PROMOTIONAL VERSUS INSTITUTIONAL DISPLAYS

A **promotional display** can be a one-item, a line-of-goods, related merchandise, and even, for storewide sales, a variety type of display. The display advances or emphasizes a particular concept, trend, or item. It promotes! For example: Father's Day is coming up and is to be promoted by the store. A theme has been developed for advertising the event. That theme will be carried out in direct mail offers, email blasts, websites, and television, and the displays (windows and interiors) will tie in with, and advance, that theme. If the store's promotion is "Dad—Our Kind of Man," then the displays will be related. In one window there may be a display for "Dad, the Athlete," with everything from active sportswear to sporting equipment, sports magazines, and even spectator sports items. Another window may have gifts for "Dad, the Connoisseur," consisting of a collection of formal clothes, classical records, wine, gourmet foods, and exotic cooking equipment. Each different "Dad" would

FIGURE 9.4 For a worldwide promotion, The Bay department store, in Toronto, took samplings from its many departments and gathered them in a series of variety windows featuring particular countries. Here in the French window, men's and women's apparel and accessories are shown amid pieces from home goods. *The Bay, Toronto, Canada.*

be gifted with a variety of merchandise based on a particular type of man. (See Figure 9.5.)

A sale can also be the basis for a promotional display. It might be a storewide sale, an anniversary sale, a pre- or post-holiday sale, or an end-of-season sale. As another example, if turquoise is the trending spring color, and the store is investing heavily in turquoise merchandise, then turquoise should be promoted inside and outside the store.

Often, a one-item type of display is used to promote the store's fashion image. The presentation is designed to tell the shopper where the store stands on the current fashion trends, what it thinks its customers want to look like, and to whom it is trying to appeal. So, the particular outfit may not promote a designer or department within the store but rather the latest fashion look seen on the runway. In some cases, the visual merchandiser takes merchandise from various departments, interprets the look, and styles the mannequins to promote the trend.

An **institutional display**, on the other hand, promotes an idea rather than an item or a product. The display presents the store as a worthwhile and interested member of the community. If a national hero dies, a window may be set aside to honor his or her memory, and no saleable merchandise will be included in that display. If the community food pantry has a drive, or any other worthwhile charity is in need of

support, and the store promotes the organization and all the good it does, without including store merchandise, that would be considered an institutional display.

The local opera company or symphony orchestra may be starting its new season and need more subscribers. The store might promote this cause in a small window or shadow box. Remember, this is not the same as using posters and paraphernalia of a visiting ballet company to provide a background for a window filled with ruffled ballerina-like dance dresses. That is a good example of the use of a current event or what is new in town to set the scene for store merchandise, but it is not purely an institutional display.

An institutional display helps further the store's image in efforts to support an **NFP, or not-for-profit** organization. It is a sign of goodwill toward its neighbors and the neighborhood. It shows the store as a concerned party interested in the welfare of the community or the nation. An intuitional window may recognize breast cancer awareness, a local scout troop, or a museum. (See Figure 9.6.) The big Christmas extravaganza, full of animation, fantasy, and the delight of children 8 to 80, may not sell any special merchandise, but it certainly sells the store. People may travel from all over to see a store's institutional Christmas windows and, often, the "tourists" end up inside after having seen the "free show" outside.

FIGURE 9.5 It is quite obvious from the signage, the flowers, and the gift-wrapped boxes that Valentine's Day is almost here and that it is time to think of gift giving. For this promotional display, The Bay, in Toronto, dedicated several windows—each in a different color theme—to the upcoming date. *The Bay, Toronto, Canada.*

FIGURE 9.6 To celebrate Christmas and the festive season, Isetan, the Indonesian department store, tells its customers that "Life is a Gift" and we are all part of one world. To emphasize its message of goodwill, no product is shown. *Ayumi Kakamu/Getty Images.*

Types of Display Settings

In presenting any display, there are some basic approaches the visual merchandiser can take to set the scene for the merchandise or the concept to be sold. These approaches include the following:

- Realistic setting
- Environmental setting
- Semirealistic setting
- Fantasy setting
- Abstract setting

REALISTIC SETTING

A **realistic setting** is essentially the depiction of a room, area, or otherwise recognizable locale, reinterpreted in the allotted display area, either in the windows or inside the store. The realistic setting is best controlled and most effective in a fully enclosed display window. Here, the visual merchandiser can do a miniature stage setting. He or she can simulate depth and dimension and use color and light with great effect—all viewed, as planned, from the front, through a large plate glass window. The scene can be the theater, the office, or a restaurant environment. It may incorporate wallpapered walls, carpeted floors, matching tables and chairs, flowers, ferns and potted palms, china and crystal, candles, and chandeliers. It seems so real, so complete, so recognizable that the viewer can relate to it. Showing formal or semiformal clothing, for example, in this setting would be very appropriate.

Sometimes the cleverness and meticulousness given to the details of the setting can work against the presentation of the merchandise. The viewer might get so involved in the settings and the background that the merchandise, the "star," is upstaged by the "set."

At certain times and in certain stores, however, a realistic setting can be most effective. Some holidays are just right for a true-to-life presentation. On Christmas morning, for example, mannequins wearing assorted robes and loungewear might be busily engaged in unwrapping more of the same merchandise. On New Year's Eve, a gala party is the perfect setting for gala clothes. Thanksgiving is a time to show tableware, while the family is "dressed" for dinner. Import promotions can be attention-getting displays when the settings are realistic, though foreign. The display humanizes the experience because people do want to see how other people live.

When realism is the thing, scale is of the utmost importance. The display area should not be weighted down with props or elements so large that the scale of the setting shrinks by comparison. A realistic setting requires the careful blending of color, textures, shapes, and the proper lighting to keep the background at a proper distance. It must be powerful enough to lure the viewer to the merchandise presentation. (See Figure 9.7.)

ENVIRONMENTAL SETTING

This is a merchandise presentation that shows an assortment of various related items in a setting depicting how and where they may eventually be used. In this form of realistic setting, the "background" is actually the "foreground" because the details that make up the realistic set are actually the merchandise being promoted in the display.

An example of an **environmental setting** is a display showing a corner of a room with a bed, made up with matching sheets, pillowcases, and a comforter; a window with coordinated curtains and drapes; and an area rug of the appropriate color and design. A chair near the bed has a robe casually tossed over it, and there is a pair of slippers on the floor. The setting also includes a bedside table, on which is an arrangement of frames, boxes, a lamp, and a clock. Everything on display in this setting is for sale in the store. (See Figure 9.8.)

SEMI-REALISTIC SETTING

When space and budget do not allow the time or effort for a fully realistic presentation, the visual merchandiser may opt for the very popular **semi-realistic, or "vignette," setting**. (See Figure 9.9.) The visual merchandiser presents the essence, the tip of the iceberg, and leaves the rest to the active imagination of the shopper. In many ways, this is a simpler but more effective approach to merchandise settings; this way, the merchandise and mannequins do not have to compete with the details in the setting.

Other examples of semi-realistic displays: In a predominantly black or dark gray window (walls, floors, and side walls), imagine a small table covered with an indigo tablecloth, two wooden café chairs, a candle in a wine bottle

FIGURE 9.7 In a rather small and narrow window a fall forest has been realistically rendered, with real tree trunks and branches and boughs of autumn foliage. The floor is covered with fallen leaves and wood chips. The artwork on the rear panel gives the suggestion of more trees, while adding depth to the window. *Robert Ellis, Culver City, California. Design: Keith Dillion.*

FIGURE 9.8   A complete environment has been suggested in the home area at The Bay through the use of a bed frame, an open armoire, a trunk, some lamps, and a carpet. Although not an actual live-in room, the display does suggest a time, a place, and a period, and the merchandise that makes it all possible is shown on the shelves around the bed and in the armoire. *The Bay, Toronto, Canada.*

FIGURE 9.9   Priape, a men's store, shows off its newest swimwear/ underwear in a window divided into "shower stalls." The vignettes are suggested by the showerheads, the simulated tile enclosures, and the color-coordinated plastic shower curtains. Note the color-keyed towels that dry off the stylized forms. *Priape, Montreal. Design: Étalage B Display, Montreal, Canada.*

FIGURE 9.10   When knights were bold and damsels were fair, winged horses were a reality—or so it seems in the Bergdorf window featuring a dreamlike fantasy setting for the designer gown. *Bergdorf Goodman, New York City. Copyright WindowsWear PRO http://pro.windowswear.com; contact@windowswear.com 1.646.827.2288.*

already heavy with rivulets of melted wax, a cheeseboard next to a San Pellegrino bottle, and a terracotta potted lemon tree. Couldn't this be any romantic neighborhood Tuscan restaurant? Or, think of simply a palm tree dripping heavy with green leaves; a mound of sand; an open, boldly striped beach umbrella—anybody would know it was some tropical island in the sun. The dark nebulous, no-color, no-detail background functions as blank canvas for the consumer to imagine his or her own scene.

On ledges, in island displays, and in store windows with open backs, a semi-realistic setting works most effectively. It is theater-in-the-round, but the viewer does not go beyond the fragment being shown. The visual merchandiser must choreograph the convincing design elements and merchandise to tell the story without overstyling the setting. A park bench, a tree, some pigeons or a squirrel, the hint of sky, some grass and gravel—it's a park! An awning swagged off the dark back wall; a small metal table for two; two ironwork chairs, a bottle of wine and two glasses, a suggestion of a kiosk, over to the side, bedecked with French posters—it's April in Paris!

FANTASY SETTING

A **fantasy setting** can be as detailed or as suggestive as the visual merchandiser, budget, and time permit. It is creative, and it does require thought, energy, and lots of planning, but it can be very rewarding.

It may be surrealistic or just a "touch of the poet"; it is a strange Never Neverland, a fairyland, Oz, an enchanted forest, Alice's Wonderland. A fantasy setting can be tables on the ceiling and chairs on the wall. It can be 6-foot toadstools or a mannequin drifting, in midair, on a magic carpet. It can be a world frozen in ice and icicles or a trip in a spaceship to visit a faraway planet. A fantasy setting can be a stairway going nowhere, with a crystal chandelier to light the way, or an underwater spectacular of swimsuit-wearing mermaids and giant seashells.

These are just some examples of the touches of whimsy that can be a delightful change of pace after several realistic or semi-realistic installations. A good imagination is the most important requirement. (See Figure 9.10.)

ABSTRACT SETTING

An **abstract setting** might seem as if it would be the easiest to do, but it is often the most difficult. The least amount of display often makes the biggest statement. In an abstract setting the merchandise is the dominant feature, and the setting supports and reinforces the message, often subliminally. For example, a viewer may look at some white abstract shapes protruding from the back wall and know that the classic gown posed in front of the shapes is elegant.

The abstract setting is predominantly an arrangement of lines and shapes, panels, cubes, cylinders, triangles, curves, arcs, and circles. It is like a nonrepresentational painting done in three dimensions, in various planes. The design does not really represent or look like anything in particular, but it does evoke certain responses from the viewer. An abstract setting is like a skeletal stage set, in that there is form that functions. It divides the space, and the lines, shapes, and forms give a graphic message. (See Figure 9.11.)

Buildup Display

There is a vast difference between creating a one-item or line-of-goods display and a mass display of a variety of items related only in use, material, color, or place of origin. To display different dinnerware place settings, one is dealing with a group of objects that are similar in material, construction, and use, but that are decidedly different in appearance. It is the difference in pattern, color, shape, and size that will make one design of dinnerware more attractive to a customer than another.

In doing a display of five, six, or more place settings or groupings of different china patterns (or pots and pans, luggage, toiletries and cosmetics, or other related types of merchandise), certain methods of presentation are more effective than others. The overall display must be balanced and easy to look at. There has to be a movement from grouping to grouping or item to item. Each group or item should be able to be viewed as a separate entity, somehow set apart from the others.

FIGURE 9.11 For the Hugo Boss store in Milan, Carlos Aires of Marketing Jazz created a simple abstract window setting of assorted size mirror circles that seem to rise and float off into the white ambience of the window. The steps, on the left, serve as elevations for the Boss-designed accessories. *Hugo Boss, Milan, Italy.*

If, as in the case of the china, the visual merchandiser is working with objects of the same general size or weight, he or she might use assorted-size cubes or cylinders clustered together to create a **buildup display**. It is easy for the viewer's eye to travel upward, making a stop at each level to absorb what is being shown before moving on to the next level and the next showing. Thus, each group is separate and apart in space. Each group can be dominant as the viewer's eye climbs the setup. The topmost group, by its position, could be assumed to be the best or the most attractive—the most desirable. Therefore, if the visual merchandiser wants to make all the items equally "best" or "beautiful," the top step could be reserved for a plant, a vase filled with flowers, or any decorative or related item or prop.

The buildup itself can be a series of forms of different sizes arranged in a straight line with each cube or cylinder butting up to the next tallest one, but all flush in front. For the sake of interest and effect, there can be a combination of bigger steps and smaller steps. In a formal or traditional arrangement, however, each step would be exactly the same increment of height (for instance, 6 inches or 9 inches) until the next plateau is reached.

When there is sufficient depth in which to set up the display, the buildups can go from front to back as well as from side to side. It would be like creating a pyramid with risers or cubes building up from either end while, at the same time, building from a low point out in front to the high point in the center.

When displaying merchandise that is related, but of different sizes and shapes (such as handcrafted ceramics, which includes boxes, plates, bowls, decorative figures, and maybe even urns and vases), the step or pyramid buildup will work, but it requires a very deft feel for balance—especially asymmetrical balance. It is now a matter of building up one riser (or platform) with an object on it while balancing it with another riser that has a different-sized object displayed on it. The overall height and look of the riser plus the merchandise must be visually weighted against the other riser and merchandise. It might, therefore, require a lower platform or elevation to hold a tall vase, for example, if it is to balance with a low, squat bowl on a taller riser. This asymmetrical buildup must be arranged so that the viewer's eye will still move

FIGURE 9.12 The open-back boxes that are stacked throughout the window hold a selection of small electronic devices that many men would love to possess. With the buildup of the boxes in this display, the products get featured in their own framed environments, and the viewer's eye moves from one group up to the next. *The Bay, Toronto, Canada.*

comfortably, through the various levels, to the top. This is called visual follow through. **Visual follow-through** is how the eye is directed or forced to view the display due to its arrangement or composition. The visual merchandiser may use variations in height, color, and lighting to guide the viewer's eye. (See Figure 9.12.)

Types of Displays and Display Settings: Trade Talk

abstract setting	line-of-goods display	related merchandise display
buildup display	NFP, or not-for-profit	semi-realistic, or "vignette," setting
environmental setting	one-item display	variety, or assortment, display
fantasy setting	promotional display	visual follow-through
institutional display	realistic setting	

Types of Displays and Display Settings: A Recap

◆ The purpose of a display is to present and promote.

◆ A one-item display shows only a single item.

◆ A line-of-goods display shows one type of merchandise, though the merchandise might vary in size or color.

◆ A related merchandise display shows items that are meant to be used together.

◆ A variety, or assortment, display is a combination of unrelated items.

◆ A promotional display emphasizes a particular theme, for example, Father's Day.

◆ An institutional display promotes an idea, rather than an item or a product. For example, a national hero or a community drive might be promoted in a window display. This presents the store as being a part of the community.

◆ Display settings can be realistic, environmental, semi-realistic, fantasy, or abstract.

◆ A realistic setting display is a recognizable display, such as a room.

◆ An environmental display shows how and where various related or coordinated items can be used.

◆ A semi-realistic setting presents the essence of a setting and leaves the rest to the imagination.

◆ A fantasy setting is usually suggestive, creative, and unusual.

◆ An abstract setting is an arrangement of lines and shapes, with the merchandise as the dominant feature.

◆ A buildup carries the viewer's eye from grouping to grouping by means of a combination of steps, such as a series of forms of different sizes arranged in a straight line, but all leading the eye to one point.

Questions for Review and Discussion

1. Classify the following display examples as one-item, line-of-goods, related merchandise, or variety displays.
   a. Three mannequins wearing ensembles from Liz Claiborne's new spring collection.
   b. An evening gown by Armani.
   c. A window filled with leather items including bags, jackets, caps, briefcases, and skirts.
   d. A display of small appliances from Black & Decker.
   e. A pawnshop window filled with samples of its latest wares.

2. Explain the difference between a promotional and an institutional display and provide an example of each.

3. When is it appropriate to display an abundance of a single item in a display?

4. How does a realistic display setting differ from a semi-realistic display setting?

5. Describe how a fantasy setting might be achieved. What props would you use to help set the stage?

6. What is usually the most dominant feature in an abstract display? What elements can be used in the creation of abstract displays?

7. What is a buildup presentation, and under what circumstances are buildups most effective?

Chapter Ten
Techniques Commonly Used in Visual Merchandising

A perfect point of view, Kleinfeld, New York. *Copyright WindowsWear PRO http://pro.windowswear.com; contact@windowswear.com 1.646.827.2288.*

AFTER YOU HAVE READ THIS CHAPTER, YOU WILL BE ABLE TO DISCUSS

+ the purpose of using concepts and techniques to attract consumers
+ design techniques to support a design solution
+ how a store can use humor to attract customers
+ the ways in which motion can be created in a display
+ how surrealism can play a role in displays
+ the careful use of shock as an attention-getting device
+ sources of props for visual displays

The design and creation of window displays have attracted many notable artists and designers. Many people are unaware that Salvador Dali, Jasper Johns, Robert Rauschenberg, James Rosenquist, and Andy Warhol experimented with this temporary medium behind glass at some point in their careers. Throughout time, window display has been proclaimed an art form, street theater, and one of the most compelling methods for stores to communicate to the public. With little formal training available for the art and craft of creating displays, self-made designers jumped into the process. All they needed was an eye for composition, endless creativity, incredible resourcefulness, and the skill to snap it all together in a short period of time. Photographers, painters, sculptors, interior designers, furniture makers, and more were lured to the glamorous art form of window display—expressing themselves through the arrangement of props, the mannequin, and the merchandise.

As art and commerce flourished over the years, display or visual merchandising became a recognized career. Even though the approach to designing displays has transitioned greatly over time, the show window still remains an important "calling card" for the retail store. Much like the cover of a magazine or a landing page for a website, it beckons 24/7. Window display has been coined as "the silent salesperson" and the store's "first impression." It is relatively cost-free advertising space embedded in the store's architecture—and each year, this temporary showcase inspires millions of people in small towns and large cities around the world as it heralds the opening of the holiday season.

As discussed in Chapter 5, the initial concept for a display should be derived directly from the merchandise or design brief; however, there are tried and tested techniques for designing displays known as "attention-getting devices." These techniques are the designer's toolbox or secret weapons. Some display designers develop a style or signature by using one or more of these formulas repeatedly.

There are many devices that can be used to attract the shopper's attention. They include:

◆ Color and texture
◆ Lighting
◆ Line and composition
◆ Scale and proportion
◆ Contrast
◆ Repetition and harmony
◆ Humor
◆ Nostalgia
◆ Motion
◆ Surprise and shock
◆ Fantasy and surrealism
◆ Props

Color, line, and composition were discussed in greater detail in Chapters 2 and 3; and lighting was discussed in Chapter 4. Additional information dealing with props can be found in Chapter 17.

Color

Color is the biggest motivator for shoppers. It is what we see first, what attracts us to an object. Consumers buy because of color, before size, fit, or price, and they make this decision in less than ninety seconds. Color tells a story, sways our emotion, and causes us to react. Color has meaning and can be used to suggest environments, historic time periods, and styles. Color combined with texture evokes more insight related to the overall theme. For example the color green combined with a leaf texture/pattern may translate to "rainforest."

Color can contrast with the merchandise or blend in a monochromatic color story. Muted colors may indicate a vintage look, and bright colors may appeal to younger shoppers. Using a particular group of colors in groups such as those found on a beach ball can signal a summer theme. Color can create the story for a concept or be the concept itself. (See Figure 10.1.)

Lighting

Lighting is another device used to draw shoppers to both window and interior displays. Effective display lighting can be the jolt that catches the eye and carries it to the product. A forceful spotlight in a subtly lit display area can grab the consumer's attention.

FIGURE 10.1　Rather than detract from the assorted small, colored fashion accessories, the bright red background enhances and clarifies the multi-hued story being told in this Christmas window at Macy's, New York City. *Eugene Gologursky/Getty Images.*

A display bathed in fiery red or eerie green or dramatic blue light can effectively intrude into the gray environment of concrete sidewalks and building facades. Brilliantly colored lights can command instant eye contact. By casting shadows or using a theatrical scrim, the visual merchandiser can use the window space as a stage for merchandise. Rows of dangling Edison bulbs or configurations of sleek bare fluorescent tubes in a row are examples of how lighting can lead a concept. (See Figures 10.2 and 10.3.)

FIGURE 10.2　Thin fluorescent tubes radiate out from behind the entwined pair to focus the viewer's eyes on the action in the foreground of the Selfridges' holiday gift idea display. The strong light pattern also serves as a means of attracting attention. *Heather Berrisford/Getty Images.*

FIGURE 10.3　The formal, almost rigid vertical line of the mannequins is complemented and "relaxed" by the soft curves created by the clusters of colored Christmas ornaments in the Dior window shown here. *Antoine Antoniol/Getty Images.*

Line and Composition

Line and composition can be valuable techniques after color and lighting have done their part. The use of vertical, horizontal, curved, and diagonal lines can help determine the effectiveness of a merchandise presentation. Each type of line suggests something different (for example, vertical lines: height, dignity, strength; horizontal lines: width, elegance, tranquility; curved lines: softness, grace; diagonal lines: action, force, excitement). Each can be used in different ways to arrest the attention of the passerby to the display.

Composition is the arrangement of different visual elements in order to achieve a unity and wholeness. When brought together effectively, line and composition lead the eye around the design of the display, through the patterns created by the mannequins and the merchandise, around props and platforms, graphics and signage—we call this "visual follow through." In this way, the attention of the shopper is brought to the entire display as well as to each of its parts. Visual merchandisers use the composition of merchandise and props in basic shapes such as a triangle, circle, and square to direct the consumer's eye through the composition.

Scale

A change of proportion, an abnormal size relationship, is an attention getter. Something overly large makes an average-size object appear tiny, whereas something tiny (such as miniatures or models) makes something average in size (like a mannequin) appear to swell and soar to superhuman size. These are examples of playing with scale and proportion.

Our eye accepts objects in relation to other objects. We know approximately how tall a door is because we know about where an average human being would stand in relation to that door. As the relationship between a known object and a known figure (such as a mannequin) changes, and slight differences are replaced with glaring differences, the look or size of the object to the figure, and vice versa, appears to change as well. Next to a door scaled up 12 feet, a 6-foot mannequin seems to shrink to about 4 feet. The human figure is dwarfed by comparison.

Place a full-size mannequin in a setting of child-scaled furniture, and the figure grows in stature and in appearance. The change from the traditional or usual proportion is the attention-getting technique. It promotes the double take: the viewer knows that the mannequin is not shrinking and that the door is overscaled, but the unexpected sight of a normal figure "growing" or "shrinking" will draw attention. (See Figure 10.4.)

FIGURE 10.4 These mighty little men are showing their strength, and eye appeal, as they yank and pull the twine that holds some of Cada's rings. Sometimes, scale refers to miniature objects, like these boys who make the rings look bigger by comparison. See Figure 3.9 for an overscaled object that makes a human-sized figure look smaller. *Cada, Munich, Germany. Design: Deko Rank.*

Contrast

Contrast accomplishes with light and color what a change of scale or proportion accomplishes with line and form. A white gown against a black background or a white spotlight on an otherwise dark display—these are the types of jolts that cause the eye to react and to relay a message to the mind that says something different is going on here, something special.

A beachwear or resort wear display, glowing with sunshine, blue skies, and palm trees, is particularly effective when the street outside is mired in slush and dismal winter gloom. That is an example of contrast, too.

Repetition

Repetition is an idea used over and over again to make a strong visual impact. It may be apply to mannequins, merchandise, props, and decorative objects. Imagine the same three mannequins, each in the same pose but wearing different merchandise or a lineup of props of the same size and color, strung across a display and ending at a single piece of merchandise; both are effective examples. Mounting palm leaves in a linear grid pattern on the back wall of a window display is another example. Repetition builds visual intensity with use of numbers of an object that share a common likeness. The repeated objects can be the same but in different colors or different objects in the same color. The pattern or repeated lineup is up to the designer's imagination—it may be linear, a grid, or in a shape that is symbolic, such as the brand's initials or a logo. Seasonal or abstract icons can also function as a basis for the design layout.

Repeating the same object along the back wall of a window or interior space can make a powerful statement using very little budget and resources. The designer can use products, brand labels, shopping bags, or props—the design method of repetition makes a strong visual impact on the viewer.

Three windows in a bank, or group, reiterating the same color or promotional theme have more impact than a single, isolated window. They are also much more emphatic than three windows, each different, with different merchandise, each in competition for the shopper's attention. Seven coats (odd numbers work better than even numbers) hung on hangers, all at the same height, will dramatize a coat story, especially if the different coats are all in the same color family or are presented in a dramatic, light-to-dark grouping of color.

Repetition emphasizes. If something is worth repeating, repeat it several times over. It is a fact that seeing objects used in greater numbers takes more time to visually process; therefore, the visual merchandiser is holding the viewer's attention longer to peruse the display. (See Figures 10.5 and 10.6.)

FIGURE 10.5 Three panels, composed of what looks like luggage, set the look for the wearable and travel-able suits at The Bay in Toronto. What keeps the setting from being boring is how the luggage is artfully up-ended or turned about and yet maintains the desired repetitive pattern of the design concept. *Ana Fernandes, director of display, Hudson Bay.*

FIGURE 10.6 The reverberating figures behind the mannequins at Chanel create the illusion of movement and excitement during Paris Fashion week. The repetition of the white figures adds depth to the window environment and highlights the fall merchandise. *Chanel, Paris, France. Antoine Antoniol/ Getty Images.*

Humor

A smiling shopper can be converted into a customer much sooner, and with much less effort, than a frowning shopper, so humor is a great strategy. People will laugh at themselves and human foibles, much like a good cartoon in *The New Yorker* magazine. Show the human and humorous side of life in display; show the "happily-ever-after" type of display. Freeze a moment out of the "reality show"—an embarrassing situation or an awkward scene. Most people love to laugh at the harmless discomfort of others. Display is theater.

Examples of uses of **humor** include a holiday window with a mannequin in an evening dress, escorted by a giant white polar bear sporting a black satin bow tie, a couple dancing with lampshades as heads, or a bank safe revealing a beautiful satin shoe encrusted with faux diamonds. Humor embodies the element of surprise—the unexpected. Humor and satire were the success of many Barneys' window displays under the direction of display director Simon Doonan. Humor should never offend; it should be quick and easy to ascertain. Copy or text can sometimes make a humorous display more effective. The humorous display only needs to inspire a smile and a relaxation of the tense feelings for shoppers to be successful. (See Figures 10.7–10.10.)

FIGURE 10.7 A life-sized "Ken" (or Kevin) doll is prepackaged and ready to go. The "package" idea is reinforced by the other "dad-doll" display windows, but the idea is fun and familiar and puts a smile on the shopper's face, especially if the shopper is a grown up "Barbie." *Bloomingdales, New York City. Eugene Gologursky/Getty Images.*

FIGURE 10.8 To set the scene for cruise/resort wear, Victor Johnson, director of visual merchandising for Ann Taylor stores, went "south of the border—down Mexico way." The idealized sketch of a local street in Mexico is reproduced on a semi-sheer fabric and serves as a separation from the store beyond, and the cactus plants in terra cotta pots and rustic chairs prop the scene. *Ann Taylor, 42nd Street, New York City.*

FIGURE 10.9 Getting a good night's sleep is a serious matter but Karina Barhumi, the designer of the Plumas windows, takes a light-hearted approach. There is the promise of a smile that goes with a cartoon so the cartoon character—simply drawn and cut out of board—is complemented by the frieze of cartoons drawn along the top of the display that shows the humorous aspects in selecting the right pillow. *Plumas, Lima, Peru. Design: Karina Barhumi.*

FIGURE 10.10 Mirrors can be great gimmicks, but they are also tricky. Sometimes, the reflections become more important than the object being reflected, or the shopper gets more involved with how he or she looks than with the merchandise on display. Here, the various mirror panels are set at different angles to create a dazzling, but dizzying, fun house look for urban fashions. The controlled color palette of red, white, and black helps keep things from getting completely out of hand. *Marshall Field's, State Street, Chicago, Illinois.*

Nostalgia

Many people dream of the "good old days," when life was simpler. They find a backward glance to the settings of the 1940s, 1950s, and 1960s as special as looking back to those of the 1880s and 1890s. They are referred to as the "golden days," days of charm and romance, when everything was simpler. Movies, theater, and television shows can spark the popularity or trend of a time period much like the shows *Mad Men*, *Friends*, or *Downton Abbey*.

Antiques and antique reproductions can add character to garments, hard goods, and environment. People also love to see elements of "before and after." Show an old-time chemise, bustle, or crinoline in relation to today's intimate apparel. A sepia scroll containing a line drawing of Da Vinci's Vitruvian man can inspire us to think about Renaissance history, architecture, and design when displayed alongside beautiful Italian leather accessories.

Nostalgia is the dramatic black-and-white imagery of photographer Lewis Hine depicting a group of men eating lunch, perched on a beam above the Chrysler building in the 1931 New York skyline paired with a group of well-styled male mannequins. The success of using nostalgia as a technique lies in the visual merchandiser's ability to creatively pair the right merchandise with the nostalgic image or prop. (See Figure 10.11.)

Motion

Motion or **movement** within a display area will get attention. A shopper is made suddenly aware, out of the corner

FIGURE 10.11 Christmastime is a time for looking back and recalling "the good old days." Nostalgia doesn't mean going back a century or more—"retro" will also do. At Le Chateau in Toronto, familiar but no-longer-used 78 record holders line the back wall and mannequins in dressy black dresses loll about at various levels on music-producing pieces of mid-century and the disco-days eras. "Do you hear what I hear?" *Shawn Schmidt, Director of Visual Merchandising, Le Chateau.*

of his or her eye, that something moved in an otherwise static setup. People of all ages will line up just to walk by and savor, for a few minutes, the delights of an animated Christmas display.

Motion can be created by a using a line of electric fans across a window, whirring and stirring up a small breeze to emphasize the cool, cool wonder of the flowing clothes on the mannequin. A single, old-fashioned ceiling fan, right out of the film *Casablanca*, lazily spinning above a tropical setting, can move a palm frond or two below. (This display would be a combination of movement and nostalgia.) A fan, way off to the side and out of the shopper's view, can send a soft wind wafting through a window display just enough to play gently with the grace and lightness of a chiffon gown or to set a scarf in motion.

Just as it can be attractive, motion can also be disturbing, irritating, and distracting. Blinking light and strobes have the impact of motion but can be unpleasant and may do nothing positive for the presentation of the merchandise. The motion is intended to draw the curious over to the window for a better view of the merchandise. It is generally not intended to be the whole show, except in those animated displays in which no merchandise is being shown (such as Christmas institutional displays).

A turntable will make a garment visible full round. It can show a variety of items as they come into view, each in its own space and each getting its moment in the spotlight. A turntable is relatively inexpensive to buy, easy to use, and versatile enough to use over and over again, in and out of the windows. Inside the store it can add excitement to a gift display or tabletop feature table.

Some stores, usually those with open-back windows, have found that a live mannequin, walking into, around, and out of the display window—like a miniature fashion show—will draw crowds to the window. Any live action in a window—a mime, a juggler, a disc jockey, a demonstrator, or even the display person setting up a window—is a great attention getter. All the store is a stage, and everything that moves—or looks as though it might move—becomes a player, attracting the attention of an audience of shoppers. (See Figure 10.12.)

Surprise and Shock

Much of what has been described in the various techniques outlined above will succeed in attracting attention because the elements of surprise or shock are involved. A smashed window with a brick flying through it will stop a viewer in his or her tracks. Windows, floors, and props splashed with paints of all colors can be shocking and cause the shopper to take a second glance.

FIGURE 10.12 It is not the wind—or even a fan. It is the art of curling paper and a clever, painstaking installation. For the "Blown Away" promotion, reams of curled and unfurled sheets of paper fly, flutter, and sweep through the series of windows as though propelled by a mild hurricane. This is motion! *Harvey Nichols, Knightsbridge, London, United Kingdom.*

A **surprise** can be fun. It can be a pleasant or amusing, unexpected moment frozen in time. A surprising display can be an inverted room setting, a stack of teetering chairs, a 7-foot take-out food container from a Chinese restaurant (a combination of surprise and scale), or an elegantly dressed mannequin conversing with a giant dinosaur.

A surprise can also be surrealistic or a bit of fantasy—the juxtaposing of people or objects out of a proper place or time sequence. For example, mannequins made into marionettes or "flying" off the ground like Mary Poppins or Peter Pan will also get a second look from a passerby. The sign or copy would clarify the scene.

Shock goes beyond surprise. It must be used sparingly and carefully. It is a shakeup that can work against the store and its merchandise even though it does attract attention. If not handled properly, a display aimed to shock can be upsetting or in bad taste. Shock value presents an unexpected or intriguing display that requires the viewer to give time and thought to evaluate the scene. A massive object or the informal use of space can be shocking. A giant bobblehead on a mannequin can shock or surprise the consumer. For many years, Visual Merchandising Director Simon Doonan used shock value consistently in Barney's windows as a signature for the store's window displays. Simon used shocking and controversial art pieces to make a statement and in turn gained notoriety for him and the store. In his book *Confessions of a Window Dresser*, Simon reveals his success using these tactics and illustrates many of the past windows at Barney's on Madison Avenue. Shock value can also employ the use of nontraditional materials and objects of beauty, or a scene of mannequins engaged in an activity.

Surprises can be delightful and ingratiating, capable of charming and amusing their audiences. They can become topics of conversation: "Did you see what they did in X's window?" sparking a whirlwind of social media. They can and will be remembered, and if the display is done well, the merchandise will be remembered, too. (See Figures 10.13 and 10.14.)

Fantasy and Surrealism

Fantasy is a technique that can temporarily transport the viewer, much like reading a good book. Fantasy concepts can be abstract or absurd or tell a story; they often take inspiration from an iconic reference in film, theater, or literature and are most effective for holiday displays. This type

FIGURE 10.13 Imagine coming across this surreal scene! The surprise of the unexpected, and the shock of the semi-undressed duo looking back at you through the suspended window frame, are enough to make one stop and say, "What's happening?" The elephant in the jungle of hanging greenery and garments does not provide an answer. *Harvey Nichols, Edinburgh, Scotland.*

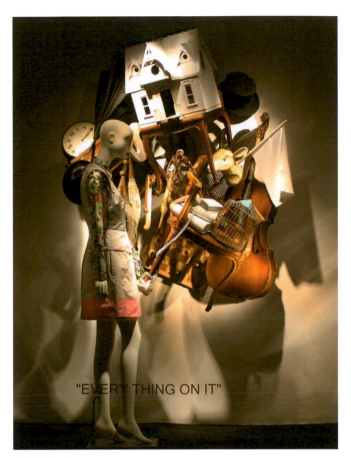

"EVERY THING ON IT"

FIGURE 10.14 What's it all about? What is going on and what does it mean? It means that Stacy Suvino "Gotcha." She got your attention with a little shock and awe and a surprise in the Miss Jackson windows she designed in Tulsa, Oklahoma. But—where is the kitchen sink? *MMP Stacey Suvino.*

enjoy using snippets of visual elements from this art period to create surrealistic displays. Magritte's signature blue sky has served as a backbone for many seasonal and surrealist themed displays. This art movement is a favorite because surrealist artists shared a fascination with mannequin parts and prop popularly used in displays.

Props

Props and decoratives are the elements that breathe life into display and visual merchandising. They are used as seasonal or lifestyle accents that add depth to the storyline of a display. The chemistry that happens between the product and the prop ignites the theme of the display, defines the style of the brand, and elevates the store's image in the shopper's eyes. A bentwood chair from a particular era can articulate many feelings about the brand to the shopper while appealing to his or her personal senses. The design of the chair may be used to capture the shopper's attention or to physically support the merchandise.

Visual merchandisers realize by combining objects with products, the product is empowered.

Objects such as Venetian masks, stacks of baskets, worn leather books, and a wooden steamer trunk are all considered viable props for visual merchandising. There is an entire industry dedicated to the design, production, and sourcing of props and decoratives. Prop companies can specialize in one type of decorative, such as foliage, or offer a wide variety of products and services. These design components include foliage, architectural elements, furniture, statuary, and other oddities.

Each type of store utilizes different methods for procuring props based on their needs, annual budget, storage, or allocation to other locations. Department stores have the ability to share props in numerous locations, unlike boutiques and specialty stores. Stores generally have prop budgets dedicated to holidays, events, and year-round installations. A store may choose to buy, rent, or borrow props.

Each year manufacturers who specialize in props, decoratives, mannequins, dress forms, and fixtures showcase

of display can play on the viewer's senses through the use of a theatrically exaggerated setting using the right choice of visual elements. Some display designers use fantasy and surrealism as a signature style for store windows. Linda Fargo of Bergdorf Goodman, author of the book *Dreams: Through the Glass* illustrates beautifully executed fantasy displays orchestrated by David Hoey and the Bergdorf Goodman team. These illusive displays draw from many iconic storybook moments with luxury merchandise to match. They are the pinnacle of fantasy appeal. Consumers who lead busy lives can appreciate these enchanting displays; it only takes a few minutes to take their minds away from the daily stress of life.

Surrealism has similar design qualities but utilizes some of the trappings of artists Dali, Magritte, Man Ray, Miro, Duchamp, and many others. Visual merchandisers their products at large trade shows or "market week" show-room events. Professional organizations that sponsor these events such as Shop!, Design: Retail, and VMSD provide directories and galleries for these products and manufacturers on their websites, easily allowing visual merchandisers to find them. The industry is composed of many types of manufacturers and design services that are constantly evolving, so websites are the best way to keep updated and informed.

Prop and decorative houses often have their own distinctive style, specializing in only vintage items or imported artifacts from all over the world. Some manufacturers stock items; others create custom-designed props in local studios and offshore factories. Many vendors have in-house designers ready to work with the store's design team on the development of customized props for their store. Each season, exciting new props and materials are launched, and visual merchandisers are tasked with staying on top of the current design and manufacturing trends. Innovative sustainable solutions, laser cut and custom routed materials are introduced each season. Maintaining good vendor partnerships is crucial to the success of the store design and the creativity of the visual merchandising team.

When props are needed on a temporary basis, they may be rented or borrowed. Many large cities have prop rental warehouses that are used by the television, event, and the photo industries. These larger facilities amass thousands of iconic artifacts from an array of time periods for the sole purpose of renting to stylists, interior designers, and visual merchandisers. The prop is usually rented for a percentage of its tag price or bundled into a large rental agreement for a quantity of items.

Antique dealers are another valuable resource for window display props. Antique dealers will usually forgo a rental fee in exchange for a legible credit sign in the window display. The window display guarantees much more exposure for the item, and the antique dealer is more likely to sell the rented prop this way. Boutiques in small communities can also benefit by featuring each other's goods in window displays.

Visual merchandisers are often the purveyors of their own props. For example, Anthropologie has a procurement team that purchases "found objects" that are incorporated into the overall store design and store displays. Notable flea markets and tag and estate sales are all part of the visual merchandisers' repertoire of resources. Tight budgets test the display person's ability to improvise, be clever, be creative, and see "splendor in the trash."

The visual merchandiser can also utilize unconventional objects like old wooden ladders and drop cloths with mannequins to promote a story. Stores will occasionally purchase less expensive goods as props from arts and crafts stores, dollar stores, or even the local thrift store. It is truly up to the discretion of the visual

FIGURE 10.15 What is more everyday and mundane than plain brown shopping bags? However, when dozens of them are clustered together and accessorized with poufs of white tissue, they can say "sale" in a smart and stylish way. The logos and brand names splattered across the back wall and floor represent the many famous brands on sale. *The Bay, Toronto, Ontario, Canada.*

FIGURE 10.16 Like in Figure 10.14, all kinds of props—related to each other or completely unrelated—can make the display attention getting. At Anthropologie in New York, the collage of "things" plus some sprays of foliage create a semi-wall in an otherwise open-back window that is full of interesting items that are almost as interesting to study as the outfit on the dress form. *Copyright WindowsWear PRO http://pro.windowswear.com; contact@windowswear.com 1.646.827.2288.*

team, and very often when budgets are tight, innovation kicks in. With the popularity of repurposing materials, visual merchandisers can take advantage of wooden pallets, reclaimed wood, cartons, and crates if they fit the theme.

The visual merchandiser must possess the skills of a stylist, set designer, interior decorator, museum curator, and graphic designer rolled into one. Display and merchandising requires a high level of initiative, creativity, and imagination. (See Figures 10.15–10.17.)

FIGURE 10.17 The closest outdoor sporting goods store provided the props for this seaside display. The fully inflated yellow raft closes off some of the open-back window, while also setting the scene. The red life vests are more than fashion accessories; they bring the assorted headless mannequins into the composition, while the oars, ropes, and such tie the various levels of the display together. *Henri Bendel, Fifth Avenue, New York City.*

Techniques Commonly Used in Visual Merchandising: Trade Talk

composition	line	nostalgia	scale
humor	motion	proportion	shock
lighting	movement	props	surprise

Techniques Commonly Used in Visual Merchandising: A Recap

+ The basic concept of a display is to show and to have seen what is shown.

+ Some important eye-catching devices include color, lighting, line and composition, scale, contrast, repetition, humor, mirrors, nostalgia, motion, surprise and shock, and props.

+ Color is what the eye sees first.

+ Effective lighting can catch the eye and lead it to the product.

+ Different types of lines, such as vertical, horizontal, and diagonal, can arrest attention.

+ Composition is the arrangement of visual elements to achieve unity.

+ Scale, as in an abnormal size relationship or a change in proportion, is an attention getter.

+ Contrast uses light and color to attract the eye.

+ Repeating an idea over and over makes an impact.

+ Although the use of mirrors can add depth to or show new angles in a display, they must be used carefully, so as not to show anything at a disadvantage. Poor placement of mirrors can show pinned-in clothing, unfinished backs, light cords, debris, and so on.

+ Nostalgic props are a pleasant reminder to the viewer of the "good old days."

+ Surrealism presents abstract concepts and can utilize cloud imagery, mannequin parts and other household objects.

+ Motion, something moving in an otherwise static setup, will always catch the eye, but too much motion can distract the viewer from the merchandise.

+ The element of surprise in a display can be fun or surreal. Shock goes beyond surprise and must be used carefully, so as not to upset or irritate the viewer.

+ Props for display is an entire industry unto itself. Props can be bought, rented, borrowed, or improvised from whatever is on hand.

+ Many props can be found in local stores, such as appliance centers, hardware and paint stores, antique shops, travel offices, and toy stores.

Questions for Review and Discussion

1. Explain the importance of using the techniques in the creation of visual presentations.

2. Describe a display that effectively combines any three of the techniques commonly used in visual merchandising discussed in this chapter. Include in your descriptions the display location within the store, the merchandise, and the props that you would select.

3. How can a nostalgic feeling be introduced into a visual presentation? For what types of displays would nostalgia be most appropriate?

4. Where can a visual merchandiser acquire display props that are both interesting and cost-effective?

5. What technique successfully employs the use of mannequin parts such as arms and hands?

6. List three household items that could be creatively used as props in a jewelry display. Explain how you would utilize these items to support your display theme.

Chapter Eleven
Seasonal Displays and Familiar Symbols

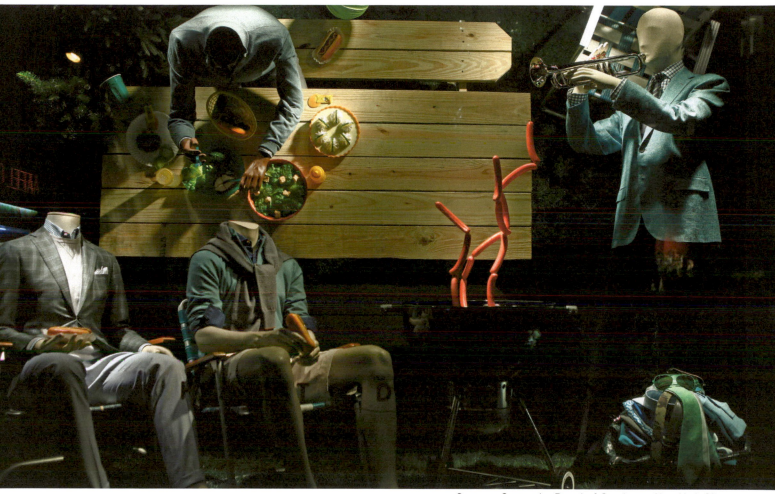

Summer Serenade, Bergdorf Goodman, New York City. Copyright WindowsWear PRO http://pro.windowswear .com; contact@windowswear.com 1.646.827.2288.

AFTER YOU HAVE READ THIS CHAPTER, YOU WILL BE ABLE TO DISCUSS

- ◆ the major seasons, holidays, promotions, and store events for which visual merchandisers must prepare
- ◆ appropriate settings, props, and display themes for major seasons, holidays, and store events

Because they are used over and over again, certain symbols used in display presentations are so familiar that they have become **formulas**. These formulas are familiar symbols, images, and materials that telegraph the message, sometimes more readily than signage copy. One has to read to understand signage copy, but these symbols are iconic; they speak for themselves. We have previously mentioned how certain colors or color combinations are recognizable as representing holidays or events; for example, red and green for Christmas; red and pink for Valentine's Day; red, white, and blue for presidential sales or the Fourth of July; and so on.

The following are everyday—and not so everyday—things that can be used to set a display scene, trim a case, accompany a mannequin on a ledge or platform, accent a column or fascia trim, illustrate a copy line, or illuminate an event or promotion. They are simply ideas and "word pictures" that hopefully will stimulate the display person's imagination.

FIGURE 11.1   When you make it to 150 years, you are entitled to brag, blow your own horn, and turn back the pages of the company's history. Blowups of vintage pictures from the store's archives are used to create a "times gone by" experience, with reproductions of catalog ads from the 1920s, pictures of the delivery service from even before that, and rotogravure images of the store's famous atrium of a century ago. *Marshall Field's, State Street, Chicago, Illinois. Amy Meadows, display director.*

Back to School and College

It happens every fall, starting with alphabet blocks and advancing to busts of Caesar and Shakespeare. Symbols of **back to school** can attract the consumer and inspire memories from the past. Consider using a simple facade of a quaint little red schoolhouse, stacks of colorfully covered books, or a grid of backpacks on a wall surface. A current favorite is black or green chalkboard paint. A chalkboard-painted backdrop with playful graphic illustrations of class rules or mathematical equations can pay homage to the local school district. This is a relatively budget-friendly idea. A mounted graphic of a yellow school bus could feature an assortment of products in the lineup of windows; maybe each window becomes a dimensional shadow box by using Foamcore. The symbolic apple for the teacher can repeat in rows, barrels, or graphically on the glass or wall surface with an inexpensive vinyl cut-out. Giant crayons and pencils can be easily fabricated from carpet tubes and wrapped with a printed paper graphic to replicate the authentic Crayola or #2 pencil. An oversized ruler can be made from a simple plank of wood shelving material with the addition of vinyl cut numbers. Pink Pearl erasers cut from inexpensive insulation foam available at your local home improvement center can be painted with a flat pink paint to resemble the original; with a steady hand and a Sharpie, add the recognizable Pink Pearl branding. Oversized props are tremendously popular with children and certainly command a second look. A hundred flying paper airplanes darting above the merchandise display will cost no more than a ream of paper. Scan and print vintage bookplates found at flea markets in encyclopedias. They may depict literary scrolls with famous quotes' entomology or early engineering devices adding a historical touch to a back-to-school display. Replicating vintage picture books or rounding up a collection of old brass school bells will imply a sense of tradition and heritage. The graphic found on the popular black-and-white marbleized notebooks can effectively work with bright primary color merchandise. Period desks and chairs, and the inkwells that are now no longer used are all still great symbols of school.

FIGURE 11.2 If the color and the setting don't grab you, the details will. Janet Wardley, head of display at Harvey Nichols, London, and her team filled the space with traditional back-to-school sights and symbols in new and untraditional ways—like the oversized, caricature heads on regular mannequins. *Harvey Nichols, London, United Kingdom.*

And then the student grows up: halls of faux ivy and vacuum-formed walls of red brick can line the window or display wall. This can be the time to show a giant spiral pad, date books, or an iPad containing an inspirational message. A nod to clubs sports and school pride conjures up props like banners, pennants, pom-poms, and megaphones. Transform old mannequins into trophies on pedestals and add vinyl to indicate, the engraving. Sports gear or a graphic cut-out of the local team mascot can preside. For setting the scene in the classrooms, default to the classics: dictionaries and enlarged graphics of definitions that illustrate pronunciation and word usage are particularly novel. If you can find an old leather book collection or wooden library-style bookcases, the display will have a nostalgic ivy league style. (See Figure 11.2.)

Bridal

Today's **bridal** symbols are far less traditional and reflect a less formal approach then the past. Weddings displays may include the hint of the bridal aisle lined with a selection of antique chairs, strewn carnival lights, floral crowns, tulle drapes, and wildflower bouquets. Vintage and natural items seem to rival using cherubs, rhinestones, and roses. You are more likely to see an archway constructed of repurposed wood, wound with florals or a row of antique medicine bottle vases and tea lights glistening on long narrow tables. Bridal décor has succumbed to the taste and lifestyles of newlyweds as opposed to the wedding planner in a world where tiers of cupcakes have replaced the traditional wedding cake. Today's wedding themes symbolize the lives, traditions, and experiences of the aspiring bride and groom. Barn, farm, and destination weddings are extremely popular, and the do-it-yourself (DIY) and maker movements have influenced a wide variety of wedding styles. The social media platform Pinterest commands much of the design for today's weddings, and the visual merchandiser should actively use it as a resource. Other classic symbols such as top hats, canes give way to the popularity of the Gatsby era, while stained-glass windows, arches, or a column can suggest church architecture. Bridal and wedding displays can embrace fantasy settings and humor and may resemble a moment frozen in time. (See Figure 11.3.)

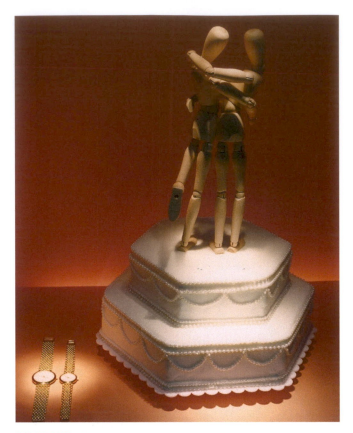

FIGURE 11.3　The wedding cake looks familiar and sets the bridal theme, but the miniature wooden artist's mannequins, in a warm embrace, have replaced the formal, stilted bride and groom figurines. The matching gold his-and-hers watches are the wedding gift being featured. *Birks, Montreal, Canada. Design: Lucy Anne Bouwman*

Holiday

The diversity of our population is constantly changing in culture and religious worship, influencing the approach to the traditional celebration of Christmas in stores and window displays. Many international brands such as Gucci, LVMH, and Prada have migrated away from traditional symbols to the holiday celebration approach in window displays and store décor. This design method is intended to communicate inclusion of cultures that do not celebrate the traditions of the Christmas holiday. The nondenominational approach to the holiday may include themes such as circus elements, literature, astrology, or the winter solstice. Frosty scenes that depict winter weather with woodland creatures, or the suggestion of giving both suit this technique too. Some stores incorporate marketing and advertising concepts as illustrated in the Harvey Nichols case study where Studio 54 and the infamous style of disco inspired the holiday windows. (See Figure CS5.1–CS5.7 on pp. 64–67.) Lighting and digital effects have become increasingly popular as a way for stores to attract and entertain shoppers.

Christmas

The **Christmas** list is endless. It starts with Santa Claus, a sleigh, elves, and reindeer, and then continues with trees, garlands, swags, and drops of evergreens sprinkled with snow and "diamond dust" or glittering with ornaments and paper chains or strings of cranberries and popcorn. It is a "sweet" time: peppermint canes, bonbons, and candies gay with stripes and swirls. It is cakes and cookies, gingerbread boys and girls and little houses, all iced and sugarcoated. This holiday can shimmer with snow and snowflakes; ice and icicles; stars and comets; the fireplace and the hearth; families and friends; and gifts and gift boxes, opened or ribbon tied.

Christmas is the poem "A Visit from St. Nicholas," by Clement Clarke Moore; 100 children's fairy tales; and the sweetest dreams come true. Christmas can be "sung" with songs such as carols by characters out of Dickens's England, "Silent Night," or "Rudolph the Red-Nosed Reindeer." Musical instruments, music boxes, dancing ballerinas, nutcrackers, and toy soldiers all suggest Christmas. It is a time for stuffed animals falling out of overstuffed stockings, model trains and planes, old-fashioned baby dolls, and chrome-plated computerized robots. Set the scene with chimneys or rooftops on which red-suited strangers can prance about.

For the religious emphasis of this holiday, try stained-glass windows or a crèche, organ pipes, oversized candles, and a choir of angels or angelic choirboys holding sheets of music dotted with familiar songs. Santa is Père Noël and Father Christmas. It is also time for piñata parties, Mrs. Claus, signs directing the viewer to the North Pole, letters to Santa, and endless lists of gifts. It is a party time as well as a time for "peace on Earth" and "goodwill to all." (See Figure 11.4.)

FIGURE 11.4 It is still green trees and shiny ornaments that say "Christmas," but here they have been given a smart and sophisticated look to match the dress-up outfits on display. The twisted topiary trees are enough like the traditional evergreens, and the fantasy collection of ornaments in burnished gold adds to the upscale look. *Ann Taylor, New York City.*

Clearance Sales

Clearance and sales events are less influenced by the calendar and instead are dependent on the need to reduce stock. The cleanup of a **clearance sale** can be represented by iconic or ordinary props such as brooms, pails, shovels, corrugated cartons, oversized shipping crates, wrapping paper, and twine. It also could be shopping bags and store boxes "walking," "riding," or "flying" out of the display area loaded with the sale goodies. A window filled with assorted mannequins and forms, stripped down to fig leafs or palmetto fans for modesty's sake or dressed in big oversized shopping bags because everything is gone, can be fun.

A few pipe rack fixtures festooned with a few forlorn and naked hangers—some already lying on the floor—says, "Going, going, gone!" Giant scissors cry out that "prices have been cut—or slashed," as does a setting of shelves or bins, denuded of merchandise, with boxes scattered helter-skelter. The big iron ball used to demolish buildings could be "breaking" into the plate glass window—with "cracks" beginning to appear—and announcing, "We're making way for the new season." Clearance sales demand dynamics—action and movement, diagonals, and direction. It's the only way to go.

Cruise Wear, Resort Wear, and Swimwear

Summer is a time to transport the great outdoors inside the store or window display. Crystal blue skies can appear on the back wall surface, or transform the window into a giant postcard using vinyl on the glass with the concept "wish you were here." Large-scale scenery and green grass convey the resort season. Cover floors with grass mats or sandy stretches (the dunes can be painted on the background), and add some sea grass, seaweed, and seascapes. Palm trees and palmetto leaves, rain capes, thatch, tatami mats, and tapa cloths are the textures of summer, **cruise and resort** wear. It is the South of France and the South Seas. Get playful with beach umbrellas, beach blankets, beach balls, and beach chairs; yacht chairs and canvas sling chairs; outdoor furniture; and fishnets and tennis nets. Try travel posters, steamer trunks, steamboats, sailboats, model boats, and boating supplies; or anchors, oars, lifesavers, rubber rafts and inflatable toys, gangplanks, and boardwalk planks.

Summertime is also sports time and spectator time—baseball innings and outings, golf and golf carts, bleachers and poolside sitting, tennis matches, lemonade and coolers, picnic benches, barbecues, and grills. Electric fans and ceiling fans are part of the message too. (See Figure 11.5.)

FIGURE 11.5 Bamboo, straw hats, and a deck chair all proclaim that it is "fun-in-the-sun" time—time to go cruising or just lounge in some tropical clime. The bamboo panels also serve to close off the open-back window from the store beyond. *Ann Taylor, New York City.*

Easter

What would **Easter** be without plush pastel bunnies; decorated eggs in a rainbow of colors; or stately, elegant, and pristine white lilies on slender stalks? What would this holiday season be without daffodils, tulips, and gift wrappings in yellow, pink, and lavender? What about Irving Berlin's "Easter Parade" and the "Easter bonnet with all the frills upon it"?

Easter is also fluffy yellow chicks, ducklings, and other baby denizens of the farm and forest. It is the time of rebirth and renewal.

There is also the spiritual side of Easter: sunrise services, pipe organs, stained-glass windows, architectural vignettes of a church or cathedral, choirboys, and the essence of the Renaissance. Easter may have its origins in pagan lore, but today it is a Christian holiday that sometimes shares the calendar with the Jewish Passover holiday. It is a time for dressing up and getting out, a time for families to gather and dine together.

Often Easter gets absorbed into the general spring trim, but it could rate an institutional window—in memory of what the holiday is all about. The window can be "religious" without using religious symbols. Show the beauty of nature and the natural growth of plants and flowers, which is spiritual, yet nondenominational. (See Figure 11.6.)

Fall

Fall is the "ripest" season of the year, the time for harvesting fruits and vegetables of rich, warm, earthy colors; vines and vineyards, grapes and wine. Fall leaves are painted red, gold, and glowing. The season is a bouquet of asters, mums, marigolds, and other flowers of amber and rust.

People expect to see pumpkins, gourds, jack-o'-lanterns, scarecrows, and owls. It is the time for rakes and brooms, bushels and baskets, and all sorts of earthy materials and textures. Fall is a medley of music: "September

FIGURE 11.6 Bunnies and chicks are the usual heralds for Easter. Priape takes the bunny situation seriously as it fills its window with the floppy-eared denizens. Adding a touch of humor—and eye appeal—are the bunny ears attached to the semi-realistic men in the newest underwear designs. *Priape, Montreal. Étalage Display B, Montreal, Canada.*

FIGURE 11.7 The suggestions of the colors and textures of fall foliage is all it takes—plus creative talent—to turn the Anthropologie, New York City, open-back window into a forest glen for the headless mannequins. *Copyright WindowsWear PRO http://pro .windowswear.com; contact@windowswear.com 1.646.827.2288.*

Song," "Autumn Leaves," and "Autumn Serenade"—and everybody is "Falling in Love." It also happens to be the time for going back to school and when career fashions make their seasonal statements. (See igure 11.7.)

Father's Day

Make a celebration for that "Great Guy," dad, pop, papa, pater, or father. Dad is everything: masculine, sentimental, playful, and amusing. The sentiment should not be contrived, but touched with humor. Familiar symbols associated with **Father's Day** are cars, tools, sports, games, and apparel. Accessories like ties, watches, and small leather goods also sum up Dad. Whether Dad is the adventurist or the bookworm, he can be portrayed as superman, the sportsman, the breadwinner, the careerist, and also a cartoonist's delight.

Father's Day can be remembered using a giant calendar or an appointment book. Retro dads dressed in suits and Stetsons who take inspiration from the TV show *Mad Men* bring back memories of the "good old days. Bicycles built for two, Model T's, and barbershop chairs are meaningful and iconic, even though Dad's father probably was not even a father back then! (See Figure 11.8.)

FIGURE 11.8 It doesn't matter from which angle you view Bergdorf Goodman's Father's Day window; you will get the message. Whether you are looking at the headless mannequins seated and being entertained by the "magic" of the trumpeter making hot dogs rise up from the grill, or at the one seated at the upended table with picnic treats laid out, the "story" is clear—"This is what Dad could or should look like and we have the 'fixin's' here." *Bergdorf Goodman, New York City. Copyright WindowsWear PRO http://pro .windowswear.com; contact@windowswear.com 1.646.827.2288.*

Formals

Dressing up can be classic or fun and funky. It can be an elegant, smart, and sophisticated dinner party, complete with crystal, silver, linen tablecloth, prismed chandeliers, candlelight, orchid centerpieces, and potted palms in the background. It can be a realistic setting with fine boiserie panels or flocked damask wallpaper and Persian rugs or a vignette setting that suggests as much but does not include all the details.

Formals could mean a night at the opera or ballet, a charity concert, or a fund-raising celebration. A few well-selected graphics and props could set the scene: railings, balustrades, columns, arches, stairways with red velvet runners, brass stanchions swinging velvet-covered ropes, marquees or canopies, photomurals of famous opera houses or concert halls, or some gold opera chairs set to simulate a box at the opera, with the addition of some velvet swags and drapes and a program or two.

A formal setting is a view of a skyline at night, a midnight sky scattered with diamond-like sequins, a garden with ghostly pale sculpture, a fountain, or clipped and shaped plants. Furniture can be formal Louis XV, Louis XVI, or mid-century modern Eames, Saarinen, Corbusier, or reasonable reproductions. The scene can be Versailles, Monte Carlo, or contemporary New York, Shanghai, or Amsterdam.

Antiques may also suggest formal wear. Coromandel screens, oriental lacquerware, and fine porcelain vases sparingly and artfully filled with branches and blossoms can bespeak formal wear. A man's top hat and cane resting on a small velvet chair says it, and so do opera glasses, theater programs, dance cards, and oversized menus. A nice bucket and two champagne glasses on a long skirted table can imply the start of something big.

Formal can also be disco, jazz concerts, or jet-setting to "in" places. Dress-up clothes also belong at a New Year's Eve gala with balloons, confetti and colorful streamers, champagne, party hats, party favors, a clock and a countdown to midnight, "Auld Lang Syne," "Cocktails for Two," and more. Father Time and Baby New Year appear together—for one night only! It can also be a gambling casino, dice, and chips galore. Formal wear is synonymous with "going out," gala, grand, gracious, the arts—how the "other half" lives. Formal is fantasy and dreams. (See Figure 11.9.)

Halloween

The fall season climaxes with **Halloween**. Traditionally recognized as a children's holiday, it produces great revenues in the home décor merchandise category. It is a time for entertaining, parties, masquerades, and the celebration of

FIGURE 11.9 The realistic mannequin in the elegantly furnished surroundings of a powder room in a manor house shows off the beautiful back of her gown while affording us glimpses of the frontal bodice details in the console mirror. *Le Château, Toronto, Canada.*

the fall season. Times and costumes have changed, but what hasn't changed is that retailers take the opportunity at this time of year to flood their windows and shelves with festive merchandise. It is also a time when stores show an array of black apparel with orange accents. What says "Halloween" more than black and orange?

Witches, owls, black crows, ghosts, and goblins—add a skeleton or two to the holiday brew, and stir briskly with scenes from old or new horror films. Whether you dig up Frankenstein's monster or Dracula from a 1930s black-and-white movie or bring in Freddie from Elm Street or white walkers from *Game of Thrones*—or have Harry Potter make a guest appearance—will depend upon what you are selling and to whom. If the target shopper is young and trendy,

go with *Game of Thrones*. If you are appealing to a more sophisticated clientele, you might want to back up your svelte outfits with the threesome from Macbeth. Whatever you do for Halloween, keep it light, even when going dark and gloomy. (See Figure 11.10.)

imagery or a modern twist of interests that range from cooking and crafting to world travel. Today's mom is a superhero, a juggler, and very often the breadwinner. (See Figures 11.11 and 11.12.)

Mother's Day

Florals and fragrance may say it all, but it can also be said with soft feminine symbols like ribbons, ruffles, laces, lavender, and lilacs. Today **Mother's Day** is about celebrity mothers and all the other famous mothers of history. It is represented by cameos, lockets, black-and-white imagery in beautiful frames. A bell jar protecting a fragile floral arrangement on a moiré skirted table or a pink-and-white boudoir setting can say "mother." Tiny creatures nesting can be reaching out to a providing mother for nature-based theme.

Mother's Day is traditionally the time to bring out the Victoriana and turn-of-the-century elements that portray the historic journey of women's history from lady to the working mother of the present day. Even though Mother may be smart, sophisticated, and ultrachic, on Mother's Day she can become all "lavender and lace," fragile and feminine, and froufrou. However, more often we see Mother's Day celebrate women in the workplace, or the mom who "does it all," raising the kids while working 9–5. Mother's Day display settings may feature nostalgic black-and-white

FIGURE 11.11 Oversized baby portraits in black and white suggest a nostalgic vibe for Mother's Day to contrast the contemporary fashion at Bergdorf Goodman. *Bergdorf Goodman, New York City. Copyright WindowsWear PRO http://pro.windowswear.com; contact@windowswear.com 1.646.827.2288.*

Patriotic

Presidents' Day, Fourth of July, Election Day—these are times when flags are unfurled. It is hooray for the red, white, and blue and "Stars and Stripes Forever." Now is the time to show pictures of George Washington and Honest Abe, hatchets and cherry trees, log cabins and log fences. Bring out the eagles, the White House, the Capitol, victory wreaths, Columbia, and the Statue of Liberty. Add fireworks, firecrackers, and the light of "the rockets' red glare." Show Betsy Ross sewing away at a star-studded flag, Washington crossing the Delaware, or the three weary Revolutionary fife and drum players in a cloud of dust.

The setting can be a map of the United States, the Declaration of Independence, the Bill of Rights, or the Constitution. Musically, it is any song by George M. Cohan, from "You're a Grand Old Flag" to "Yankee Doodle Dandy"—or Irving Berlin's tribute, "God Bless America."

The Fourth of July or any **patriotic** promotion could stress brotherhood, liberty, and equality—the "melting pot" concept that is America and its citizenry. Surround the promotion with striped bunting, white stars spattered on a blue field, and gold fringe; shields and frames;

campaign buttons, banners, and election-type placards and posters; and red, white, and blue balloons, confetti, and streamers. The viewer will get the message and salute your efforts.

Spring

Green is busting out all over, and the early bloomers are daffodils, jonquils, crocuses, tulips, and hyacinths. Trees are budding and ready to bloom. Grass and shrubs are sprouting, and birds are on the wing. **Spring** is the time for seeds, rakes, hoes, and lawn equipment; April showers and May flowers; and maypoles. It is a period of renaissance and rebirth. Baby birds appear in nests, and bunnies hop onto the scene. All kinds of soft, adorable animals announce spring is here.

Spring can be represented by a clock made of branches, flowers, and ribbons that say "springtime"; by butterflies, dragonflies, and flying kites; or by flowers and flowerpots, vegetable gardens, latticework, and garden hoses. Spring can be a woodland nymph, a forest fantasy, or an enchanting setting for a fairy tale. It is a state of mind, a reawakening, and a return to nature. (See Figure 11.13.)

FIGURE 11.13 Oversized, overscaled, and definitely blue-ribbon worthy are the green leaf veggies loaded into the extra-large wheelbarrow. It is spring, and everything is coming up green at Anthropologie, New York City. *Copyright WindowsWear PRO http://pro.windowswear.com; contact@windowswear.com 1.646.827.2288.*

Valentine's Day

After red hearts, pink hearts, and cerise hearts, it is "sweet-hearts" all the way: Romeo and Juliet, Tristan and Isolde, Scarlett and Rhett. This is the time for cherubs in pink, white, and gold. Make a hero of Cupid with bow and arrow, or simply show the bows and arrows dripping with ribbons, rosebuds, and lover's knots, with heart-shaped targets as a lovely reminder. (See Figure 11.14.)

An oversized deck of playing cards will win a lover's heart, if the display shows a suit of hearts—all kings and

FIGURE 11.14 Hearts and flowers in red and pink means Valentine's Day. From the target of concentric hearts, to the flowers being offered by the male figures, to the floor covered with a scatter of red and pink petals, everything says, "Give a little." *The Bay, Toronto, Canada.*

queens. Deliver the message with Valentine's cards, both sentimental and humorous, trimmed with ruffles and scrolls, flourishes, and furbelows. For a sure reminder, use stuffed animals with arms entwined, and red, red roses on extra-long stems. There are love songs and serenades; madrigals to be accompanied by lutes, lyres, harps, and flutes; and minstrels to sing them.

Tell a fairy tale with a happy ending, or show love poems, love stories, and love letters tied in red ribbons. **Valentine's Day** is a date on the calendar circled with a red heart and surrounded with lipstick kisses, chocolate kisses, and lovebirds. It is a day lovers remember, and a ribbon tied around an elegantly gloved finger will serve as a lovely reminder.

Seasonal Displays and Familiar Symbols: Trade Talk

back to school	Easter	Halloween
bridal	fall	Mother's Day
Christmas	Father's Day	patriotic
clearance sale	formals	spring
cruise and resort	formulas	Valentine's Day

Seasonal Displays and Familiar Symbols: A Recap

✦ A familiar symbol or image is used constantly and telegraphs a message. The image is so recognizable that it explains itself even without copy.

✦ Back-to-school displays are enhanced by alphabet blocks, owls, blackboards, pens and pencils, notebooks, dictionaries, books and bookcases, and dunce caps.

✦ Bridal displays are promoted by use of wedding music, antique chairs, carnival lights, floral crowns, wreaths, top hats, Gatsby elements, stained-glass windows, and tulle or net materials.

✦ Christmas symbols are almost endless and include Santa Claus, garlands, Christmas trees, snow ornaments, snowmen, candy canes, reindeer, sleighs, bells, music boxes, Christmas music, and stuffed stockings. For a religious emphasis, a crèche, stained-glass windows, organ pipes, angels, or a choir can be used.

✦ Clearance sales can be promoted by cleanup symbols such as mops, brooms, pails, crates, plastic bags, and cartons. Mannequins stripped down or in paper coverings can mean "everything is going." Empty hangers or

shelves, or a giant scissors "slashing" prices can be used. Clearance sales demand dynamics—action and movement—and direction.

✦ Cruise wear, resort wear, sun wear, and swimwear are enhanced by blue skies, green grass, blue water, and bright yellow sunshine. Seascapes, beach and picnic scenery, fans and air conditioners, pool and barbecue equipment, and travel posters are good backgrounds and props for displaying this type of merchandise.

✦ Easter is perfect for soft bunnies and chicks, decorated eggs, Easter bonnets, white lilies, daffodils, and tulips. The spiritual side of an Easter display can involve church scenes, stained-glass windows, sunrise services, and pipe organs. Because Easter sometimes shares the calendar with the Jewish Passover holiday, this can be a good time for a store to make use of an institutional window, to commemorate what these holidays are all about.

✦ Fall is the perfect time for using fruits and vegetables; red and gold fall leaves; asters, mums, and marigolds; and pumpkins, gourds, and jack-o'-lanterns. Baskets, leaves, rakes, and any sort of earthy materials are good for display at this season.

+ Witches, owls, black crows, ghosts and goblins, skeletons, and horror films are all just right for Halloween.

+ Father's Day displays should be sentimental, but also touched with humor. Familiar symbols are sports equipment, chess pieces, playing cards (with Dad as "king"), and trophies and awards for years of giving. Old-fashioned props, such as a Model T or a barbershop chair, can bring memories of the "good old days," even if Dad wasn't born yet.

+ Formal display settings can be elegant and classy or fun and funky. They can be realistic, as in a finely decorated room, or merely suggestive of a scene. Or the display can be New Year's Eve and champagne or jet-setting to "in" places. A top hat and cane or champagne glasses on a table can also indicate a formal setting. Formal is fantasy and dreams and synonymous with "going out."

+ Mother's Day displays are usually pink carnations or roses, ribbons, ruffles, laces, lavender, and lilacs. Mother's Day can be represented by cameos, lockets, ornate frames, Victorian settings, or anything fragile and feminine. Delicate floral arrangements; velvet-covered albums; a white boudoir setting; chicks in a nest reaching out to a mother bird; a giant, lace-edged sentimental

card; and various gift items usually associated with Mother's Day will also serve to promote this display.

+ Patriotic holiday sales, such as those taking place around Presidents' Day, the Fourth of July, and Election Day, are best served by using flags, eagles, fireworks, the White House, the Statue of Liberty, George Washington, and Honest Abe. A map of the United States or reproductions of the Declaration of Independence or the Constitution are good props. A promotion stressing brotherhood, patriotism, or the melting pot would make a good display. Any red, white, and blue color theme will get the message across.

+ Spring is best represented by early-blooming flowers, such as daffodils, crocuses, hyacinths, and jonquils. Baby animals will emphasize the season of rebirth. Garden equipment, vegetable patches, flower pots, latticework, butterflies, a flying kite, spring music, or a forest fantasy can also make good displays for spring.

+ Valentine's Day is perfect for hearts and for well-known sweethearts, such as Romeo and Juliet, Tristan and Isolde, and Scarlett and Rhett. Any props signifying romance can be used: Cupid, cherubs, a bow and arrow, heart-shaped targets, lover's knots, playing cards showing the king and queen of hearts, and so on. Red and pink are the usual colors for a Valentine's display.

Questions for Review and Discussion

1. How do props relate to visual merchandising?

2. What are the color stories for Valentine's Day? Easter? Fourth of July? Halloween?

3. List three holiday periods for which a visual merchandiser must prepare. Describe the types of displays that might be produced for each.

4. Create a theme and describe supporting props that would successfully portray the following store events:
   a. Swimsuit sale
   b. White sale
   c. End-of-summer clearance
   d. Italian import fair

PART THREE

What to Use for Successful Displays

As *"silent* salespeople," mannequins speak a clear message to customers regarding the store image. Chapters 12 explores the vast range of mannequins, alternatives, and the variety of forms used in displaying apparel items, with emphasis on their proper use. Chapter 13 examines the use of the mannequin and provides detailed instructions for proper assembly and dressing.

Chapters 14, 15, and 16 explore fixtures and systems used for merchandise presentation. Instructions for assembling, positioning, dressing, and stocking of fixtures and systems are also discussed.

Since the beginning of theater more than 3,000 years ago, props have been used to help set the scene. As in theater, props are being used today in visual merchandising to tell a story about the merchandise. Furniture props, such as chairs, tables, and armoires, can quickly establish the mood or theme in a visual presentation. Chapter 17 details the creative use of furniture as both props and selling fixtures. Chapter 18 introduces a variety of materials for manufacturing and creating dynamic displays and closes with ideas on graphics and production.

Chapter Twelve
Mannequins and Alternatives

Double Take, Dior, Paris, France. *Antoine Antoniol/Getty Images.*

**AFTER YOU HAVE READ THIS CHAPTER,
YOU WILL BE ABLE TO DISCUSS**

- ✦ the diverse physical characteristics available in today's mannequins
- ✦ appropriate measures for proper care of mannequins
- ✦ the different types of mannequins available
- ✦ situations in which headless mannequins would be appropriate

A mannequin may be a store's most valuable asset: it is a "silent salesperson," speaking the clearest fashion message. The selection of a mannequin is probably one of the most important professional decisions a visual merchandiser is called upon to make. There are so many mannequins available: various sizes and age groupings, racial and ethnic types, makeup and hairstyles, and poses and attitudes. In addition to the many "images" to select from, there is also the serious consideration of quality and cost. Mannequins are manufactured from fiberglass (a strong material commonly used to make automobile bumpers) or an unbreakable hybrid that contains a small percentage of rubber. They are made by hand in factories using a traditional casting and molding processes similar to sculpture; however, less detailed mannequins and forms can be manufactured through a rotational mold machine process. (See Figure 12.1.)

Traditionally, an experienced sculptor initiates the original mannequin figure in clay taking inspiration from a live model or a design inspiration before the final production mold is produced. Each mannequin is hand poured into the mold that contains metal fittings. The metal fittings allow the arms, torso, and legs to later separate for assembly and dressing. The raw fiberglass figures fresh out of the mold will require several hours of sanding before applying the undercoating and final painted finish. If the mannequin requires realistic makeup or painted eyes, a skilled artist will follow up using oil base paint to blend the soft complexion, brows, and eyes.

The visual merchandiser may share images of makeup styles with the artist as inspiration for the makeup and keep a painted mask of the desired makeup on file for future reference. Stores will choose the most appropriate style of makeup for the mannequins based on the category of apparel they plan to use on the mannequin. More dramatic makeup, longer lashes, and defined brows are best suited for eveningwear, while basic or neutral makeup is preferred for career. Athletic wear, swimwear, and intimate apparel require a softer approach. Eyelashes, a wig, and metal ankle or butt rod with a floor stand come with most mannequins for the price. The cost of purchasing a good quality mannequin can be anywhere between $600 and $2,000 USD, a considerable investment for larger stores that require large

FIGURE 12.1   Wet modeling clay is attached to a wire and wood armature structure to create the human form using modeling tools. The sculptor, Michael Katoh must measure and sculpt the mannequin to the proportions of the model. *Bernstein Display Courtesy of Anne Kong.*

inventories of mannequins. The gap in cost may reflect how the mannequin is produced, who designed it, and royalties. The material used to cast or mold it will also affect price. Refurbishing the mannequin's painted finish, adding a new makeup, and repairing cracks is considered routine yearly maintenance.

The mannequin must represent the brand and the lifestyle of the brand's consumers by size, style, pose, color, and attitude. It is a long-term investment for a store, and the mannequin may transition to different departments within the store or be interchanged with regional stores. Mannequins are purchased in groups or collections (not singularly), and careful consideration is used in the selection of poses. When visual merchandisers are selecting poses for a collection of mannequins, they may choose a variety of stances and head and arm positions so the mannequins' body language works cohesively as a group. Grouping mannequins to interact naturally is a skill learned through experience. Nesting mannequins in angular configurations similar to the letterform "W" is a great way to start a grouping of mannequins. Mannequins are typically grouped in a pair or threes. It works well to balance the composition by positioning another a few feet away. Consider the body language, and the interaction between them. Are they facing away from one another, with attitude, or do they appear to be communicating by exchanging glances?

Even though mannequins are expensive, stores will purchase collections or varieties of mannequins including those classified as specialty mannequins. There are many mannequin companies that design collections for specific merchandise categories such as yoga poses for activewear, dramatic poses for evening, or mannequins with both legs molded onto the torso without seams to display swim or undergarments. An effective collection of mannequins should accommodate a wide category of merchandise to be displayed, including pants, skirts, jackets, coats, and dresses. If the mannequin collection will be used in more than one location of the store, it should be composed of poses to showcase both pants and dresses, with arm positions that accept jackets and a layered coat. There are specific mannequin poses that enhance the look of certain apparel. For example, if the pant leg is wide, a walking pose with a wider leg separation will accentuate the layer of the pants. Skirts and dresses appear more natural on a mannequin with her weight shifted on one hip, allowing for a natural break in the fabric. Arms posed on the waist can beautifully reveal the shirt under a jacket with a layered coat. Utilizing a range of styling techniques, wigs, and arm positions, enables the mannequin's look to be reinvented regularly, and the visual merchandiser can avoid having the display looking mundane or repetitive. Alternating different mannequin styles in high-traffic areas ensures the display will have a fresh new look for the customer. The visual merchandiser must also try to anticipate the mannequin's present and future placement in the store; all of these are factors that influence the mannequin purchasing process.

The measurements and sizes of mannequins vary for each manufacturer. The visual merchandiser may have

FIGURE 12.2 As a tribute to the famous runway and fashion magazine models and personalities who have contributed their faces and figures to be immortalized as display mannequins, the design team at Le Château assembled a collection of these look-alike celebrities to feature in a window presentation called Model Behaviour. The list of famous models realistically rendered range from Twiggy, from the early 1970s, through to other, more recent notables, including Tina Chow, Sayoko Yamaguchi, Tyra Banks, and Dianne Brill. These are as "real" as realistic gets! *Le Château, Toronto. Clinton Ridgeway, senior vice president, and Shawn Schmidt, director of visual presentation. Photo: James Dorion.*

to try the same garment in three different sizes—from 4 to 8—to get one best suited to the particular mannequin. Mannequin manufacturers assign a "dress size" for their mannequins because many are sculpted "from life"—based on the body proportions of a noted model or celebrity— and thus not a "perfect 6" or an "ideal 8," as mannequins have been in the past. One "Miss" mannequin may have a 34-inch bust, whereas another may have a 35-inch bust or even larger. Waist measurement will vary from 23 to 25 inches. (See Figure 12.2.)

Mannequin Trends

There are some exciting new trends taking place in the mannequin industry. Manufacturers are consulting with visual merchandisers about their needs, and their response has influenced the design and customization of mannequins. Some companies are offering mannequins with arms that detach magnetically instead of using the traditional interlocking hardware.

The introduction of interchangeable heads allows a mannequin with a head to transition into a headless mannequin that can wear a custom-branded neck cap. Additional detachable heads in various styles offer the store and the visual merchandiser the opportunity to change the look of the mannequin quickly, on location in the store window or interior. Customization of mannequins has always been appealing to store brands, and by simply changing a realistic head to a semi-realistic, the display can appear fresh and new. The interchangeable heads may be produced in different materials such as fabric, wood, or a metal framework. (See Figure 12.3.)

FIGURE 12.3 These hybrid mannequins offer the flexibility to change the look of a display on-site immediately. The mannequin can transform into a form with a neck cap, an abstract, a semi-realistic, or a realistic mannequin by simply changing out the head and arms. The fabric-covered torsos offer another option to the visual merchandiser. *Almax Mannequins, Courtesy of Glenn Sokoli, creative director, Global Visual Group, New York City.*

Types of Mannequins

REALISTIC MANNEQUINS

The **realistic mannequin** of the past looked like a famous model or a classically beautiful movie star. Today's realistic mannequin, more often than not, looks like the face *outside* the display window, the one looking in.

Mannequins are more natural, more true to life, more animated, and more identifiable as the people who shop the stores. The mannequin may be young, wholesome, and homebred, or it may appear worldly and sophisticated. Whatever the mannequin is, it will be well made up, proportioned to wear a particular size, and well positioned to show off a certain group or style of merchandise.

The realistic female mannequin can be a tween with freckles, a sassy teenager, a student at college, a junior who is petite, or even a mature petite. It can be a svelte size 4, an exquisite size 6, or a fuller size 14–16. Mannequins depicting the fuller woman are being seen more and more frequently. A greater number of manufacturers are sculpting plus-size mannequins that are attractive and proportioned.

When using realistic mannequins, the visual merchandiser needs to consider the region and consumer demographic where the mannequin is going to be displayed. Ethnicities and skin tones should reflect locality and the population of the area at all times. Realistic mannequins used in resort areas may have a golden bronze tan finish. Fashion bibles and the runway can also influence the design and popularity and choice of realistic mannequins. Makeup and wig styles can target a specific type of customer, and the mannequin's pose can also help suggest the type and class of merchandise being presented. The erect mannequin with only a slight bend to an arm or a subtle weight shift to a hip is ideal for showing formal clothes, fur coats, suits, or elegant lingerie. Tailored clothes are best shown on an unanimated mannequin. The vertical line promotes the unbroken flow of the garment—the sweep of a gown—and as discussed in Chapter 3, it suggests elegance and refinement.

When action clothes are shown, they look even sportier when the mannequin is all angles and diagonals: arms akimbo, head thrown back, hip thrust out, legs spread, or seemingly in motion. Diagonals suggest the dynamics of movement and add to the excitement of the merchandise presentation. Bent arms and legs, however, are difficult to dress and may cut the line of the garment, causing creases in pants and sleeves. If the fabric of the garment is heavy or bulky, the resulting wrinkles at the bent joints may resemble a "washboard" of bunched-up fabric without any regard to the flow or design of the garment.

Using seated mannequins makes for a change of pace. They add variety and interest to an arrangement of two or three mannequins. When the display areas have ceilings too low to allow the use of a standing mannequin, sitting, kneeling, or bending mannequins can work effectively to show separates, casual wear, lingerie, and active sportswear.

There are also horizontal mannequins available (lying down flat on the back or stretched out on one hip). These work best for merchandise such as intimate apparel, swimwear, and some sportswear. An elegant evening gown may work well too. Although the relaxed and easy horizontal line can enhance the presentation, it does not always show the merchandise to its best advantage. The visual merchandiser must style the mannequin appropriately to limit wrinkles and sagging of the merchandise. Some American manufacturers tend to make their mannequins bigger, more athletic, and more muscular than European manufacturers do. Also, some mannequins will be less muscular, softer, and better suited physically for evening wear rather than casual outfits or swimsuits, for which "stronger" bodies would be preferable. This is true for male mannequins as well. European manufacturers may offer bodies that are slighter, more slender, and less muscular than American mannequins, which tend to be more muscular, "buffer," and "hunkier" when stripped down to outfits that show off the body.

The sizing of the garments is always a strong consideration. European-styled, -cut, and -manufactured garments are often smaller than their American equivalents. It does become a matter of "trial by trying on" or just knowing the cut of the garments most often used on the mannequins the visual merchandiser or display person has selected.

When choosing a mannequin—realistic or otherwise—it comes back to considering the following points:

♦ Does this form and its proportions represent your target market?
♦ Will your customer relate to her or him?
♦ Is she or he shaped and proportioned to wear the type of garments you show? Tall enough? Short enough? Soft or muscular?
♦ Does her or his pose and body language reflect the consumer demographic?
♦ Does she or he communicate the kind of fashion statement your store wants to make?

Many mannequin manufacturers sculpt figures that will relate to or interact with other mannequins of the same collection. Two or three mannequins can be used together in a natural and realistic arrangement or grouping. A mannequin couple may pose in an embrace or lock hands. Some groupings are designed to include both males and females. By using alternate arms that are available for the same mannequin, it is possible to create different positions, and by adding, subtracting, or replacing one of the mannequins in a group, it is possible to form a whole new tableau or scene from life.

Types of Realistic Mannequins

Most female mannequins manufactured today are a **misses, or missy-size, mannequin**. They wear size 4 to 8, depending upon the cut and the mannequin's proportions. The manufacturer and the pose determine the height of the mannequin, which can stand anywhere from 5 feet, 8 inches tall to almost 6 feet tall. The measurements are typically: bust, 35 inches; waist, 24 to 25 inches; and hips, 35 inches. The shoe size will run from 6½ to 7B up to 8 and 8½B. (These measurements vary with the manufacturer.)

The **junior mannequin** is a size 5, with all the proportions to match (32-22-32). (Bust, waist, and hip measurements may vary slightly, depending on the manufacturer.) The figure averages about 5 feet, 7 inches to 5 feet, 9 inches in height and is a bit shorter in the waist than the missy mannequin. Many juniors are positioned and made up as young and active figures, but with the proper pose, makeup,

FIGURE 12.4 A group of Greneker junior mannequins poses for a "selfie" at the entrance to the Globalshop trade show. The attitude and poses reflect the current trends in junior mannequins. *Courtesy of Shop! Association.*

and wig, this figure can be representative of a young executive or sophisticate. (See Figure 12.4.)

Smaller in all proportions, the **petite mannequin** has a 32-inch bust, a 21- to 22-inch waist, and 32-inch hips. It is only about 5 feet to 5 feet, 4 inches tall. This figure wears a size 4 or 6. The shoe size is about 6 to 6½B.

A store catering to certain ethnic groups, especially Pacific Rim clientele, may need a mannequin that is shorter than usual to show off garments to women who may be smaller in size and proportions.

The **full-figured mannequin** is the size 14–16 woman, with a larger bust, waist, and hip measurements but still well proportioned. It is fairly tall as well. This mannequin represents a woman who wears plus sizes but embodies today's fashionista or professional with a sensuous vibe. The popularity of plus-size mannequins has grown enormously over the past decade to represent more body types, since a size 14 customer may not respond to a mannequin wearing a size 6. Today's sizing norm is changing with the changing population, and mannequin companies are responding to produce a wider range of options for store displays. (See Figure 12.5.)

The **preteen, or "tween," mannequin** is designed to wear the young girl's dress, sizes 8 to 10, which is proportioned for the 10- to 12-year-old. The sculpting suggests

FIGURE 12.5 The seventeenth century Dutch artist, Peter Paul Rubens, loved using fuller-figured women as his models. The "Rubenesque" mannequin as shown here is scaled to wear size 14½ and is gaining in popularity as retailers recognize the importance of featuring a diverse range of body types to better reflect their customers. *Plus-size mannequin courtesy of Manex USA Display, New York City.*

the beginnings of a woman's body, but the figure is still relatively flat, uncurved, and childlike.

The **male mannequin** is about 6 feet tall and wears a size 39 or 40 jacket and size 32 trousers (with an inseam measurement of 31½ inches). The chest measurement is about 32 to 40 inches, and the shoe size is anywhere from 12 to 10. Without clothing, many male forms seem "skinny" and not virile enough for shorts, swimsuits, and active sportswear. However, active-sports figures are appearing on the market that, in addition to their animated poses, have better muscular definition.

Some manufacturers also produce a **young man mannequin** that wears "preppie" sizes; that is, size 16, 18, or 20.

Child mannequins range from tiny tots to the preteens and teens in a variety of ethnic groups, facial expressions, poses, and makeup styles. The various types include "the kid next door"—freckle-faced, eyeglasses barely poised on a snub nose, and maybe even braces capping the teeth—and a porcelain, Victorian-like doll with no sculptured features, but an artfully painted face and hairstyle. Depending on the child's size and the target market (appealing to the young mother, the sports-conscious father, the affectionate grandmother), the choices are many. (See Figure 12.6.)

Accessories for Realistic Mannequins

Most of the realistic mannequins manufactured today come with removable wigs. It is usual to purchase several wigs for a mannequin, especially if the display person or retailer is buying several mannequins from the same group. The different wigs add variety to the presentation and change the mannequin's appearance. There are two major types of wigs used for mannequins: **hard wigs** and **soft wigs**. A hard wig is highly lacquered or plasticized—never to be restyled. At one time, this type of wig was virtually the only kind used. The hard wig usually features coarser "hair," less subtle colors, and more elaborate and decorative styles and is generally better suited to the semi-realistic or highly stylized mannequin.

Soft wigs emulate the softness of natural hair and usually can be combed and brushed. Some synthetic hair fibers can be reset with hot rollers. The texture is more natural; the wig looks and feels more like real hair. Most realistic wigs have a skullcap for a base, and hairs are woven into it. Some of the better and more natural wigs have the hairs at the forehead set in by hand in a slightly irregular pattern to simulate a natural hairline. The hairs are then feathered and blended back, giving the hairline an indistinct rather than a sharp, artificial look. (See Figure 12.7.)

FIGURE 12.6 Semi-realistic child mannequins or almost abstract; these neutral white finished child figures span the divide in age and attitude. *Almax Mannequins, Courtesy of Glenn Sokoli, creative director, Global Visual Group, New York City.*

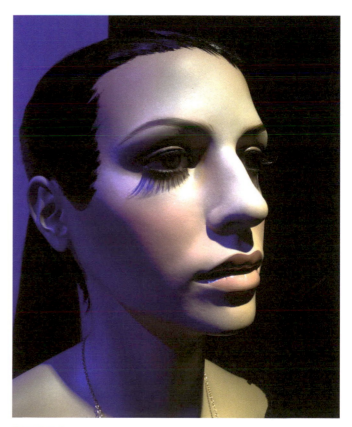

FIGURE 12.7 A hard lacquer wig simulates a natural hairline on a realistic mannequin. The soft makeup illustrates a painted brow, real eyelashes, and a subtle lip shade and blush. *Makeup by Barbara Graff of Rootstein Mannequins. Courtesy of Anne Kong.*

Semi-realistic mannequins are proportioned and sculpted like realistic mannequins, with makeup that is neither natural nor realistic, but more decorative or stylized. They may also possess a completely realistic face with sculpted features but without any makeup at all. The entire figure may be all white or all black, or a color to match a particular department or area. The "hair" may be part of the sculpture—it may not be changed, replaced, or restyled. Although the viewer knows the mannequin simulates a real "type," the lack of makeup definition keeps it from being categorized as a realistic mannequin. (See Figure 12.8.)

SEMI-ABSTRACT MANNEQUINS

The **semi-abstract mannequin** is even more stylized and decorative than the semi-realistic mannequin. Its features,

FIGURE 12.9   Three semi-abstract mannequins with only suggested features are artfully arranged to asymmetrically balance the novel flag in the Memorial Day window at Macy's Herald Square, New York City. *Copyright WindowsWear PRO http://pro.windowswear .com; contact@windowswear.com 1.646.827.2288.*

FIGURE 12.8   Not quite realistic—but close! With no makeup and no variations in skin tone, these semi-realistic male and female mannequins are finished monochromatically. The sculpted features, hair styling, and poses make them adaptable for showing anything from jeans to formal wear. *Almax Mannequins, Courtesy of Glenn Sokoli, creative director, Global Visual Group, New York City.*

such as a stylized nose or a hint of a lip, may be painted on or merely suggested. The semi-abstract mannequin will often have a hairstyle painted onto its otherwise smooth, egg-shaped head. (See Figure 12.9.)

ABSTRACT MANNEQUINS

The **abstract mannequin** represents the ultimate in style and decoration. It is more concerned with creating an overall effect than with reproducing natural lines and proportions. The arms and legs may be overly long or slender. Rarely is there an attempt made by the sculptor to indicate features or specific details: fingernails, elbows, musculature, and so on. The abstract figure is frequently finished in white or black or sprayed in a color to match an interior design scheme or a specific color promotion. Some manufacturers will supply abstracts in chrome, copper, gold, metallic, or pearlized finishes.

The abstract mannequin is a quite sophisticated and versatile figure. Depending on the pose, it can wear a wide range of clothing: fur coats, gowns, lingerie, and sportswear. In small retail operations, where the display budget and the number of mannequins available are limited, the abstract mannequin may prove to be especially satisfactory. There are no wigs to style or change; the "shoes" are often sculpted right onto the figure. Because it has no ethnic qualities and is so nebulous and indefinite, the abstract mannequin

FIGURE 12.10   In the striking architectural setting in Joseph's window in London, the two stylized abstract mannequins wear the featured outfits. Their "look" says refined elegance, and their poses are casual yet elegant. *Heather Berrisford/Getty Images.*

can be whatever the visual merchandiser cares to make of it with color, accessories, or the surrounding trim. The abstract mannequin can wear the clothes of the future or of the historic past and look more comfortable in these fashions than a realistic figure will. It crosses color and ethnic lines and knows no age limits. (See Figure 12.10.)

CARTOON/CARICATURE MANNEQUINS

Mannequins can easily be transformed by creating an oversized caricature, or cartoon head, that is set atop a normal-sized mannequin. In the past, Barney's commissioned artists for special promotions and used the head caricatures to satirize noted and recognizable celebrities during the holiday season. The heads are overblown for effect, and the exaggerations are carried over to the features, the coloration, and the artworked hairstyles. Occasionally, mannequin companies will produce a caricature mannequin that imitates an iconic movie star, a retro figure, or a hero. (See Figure 12.11.)

HEADLESS MANNEQUINS

The **headless mannequin** has a full-size, realistic, or semiabstract body with arms and legs, but no head. It may stand, sit, or recline, but because it is headless, it offers no age, no ethnicity, and it can appeal to anyone. A headless mannequin is thought to put more emphasis on the merchandise.

FIGURE 12.11   Sure attention-getters! Mannequins topped with giant exotic animal heads make a colorful statement in the window display at Coach. *Coach, Hong Kong. Copyright WindowsWear PRO http://pro.windowswear.com; contact@windowswear.com 1.646.827.2288.*

Because there is no head, makeup, or wig, this type of form is considerably cheaper than a realistic mannequin.

Mannequin Alternatives

THREE-QUARTER FORMS

A **form** is a three-dimensional representation of a part of the human anatomy, such as the torso, the bust, or the area from shoulder to waist or from hips to ankles. The **three-quarter form** has a body extending to the mid-thigh or just below the knees and can have an adjustable rod (located

FIGURE 12.12 A dozen or so of leg forms are stepping out atop the fixtures in the denim department in Levis Regent Street store designed by Checkland Kindleysides. The repetitive use of the forms in the same position creates an impactful selling statement. *Design by Checkland Kindleysides.*

beneath the form or in the butt) and a weighted base. It is usually headless and commonly called a **torso form**. The legs are usually parted. It may or may not have arms. The **dress form** is an armless version of the three-quarter form. The lack of detailing means that this neutral, three-dimensional body form does not make a strong fashion "statement."

The three-quarter form can wear a wide variety of apparel. There may be a degree of swing and movement to the torso. The form can be raised or lowered on the rod to accommodate it to the height of the area in which it is being used and to the merchandise it is required to wear. The torso can be lowered almost to the cut-off knees in order to model swimsuits, shorts, or intimate apparel, or

FIGURE 12.13 A variety of fabric-covered forms on display at Victoria's Secret store in Shanghai. Note how the forms come together to highlight the details and textures of the merchandise. The varied heights complement the look of the overall display. *Victoria's Secret, Shanghai, China. VCG/VCG via Getty Images.*

FIGURE 12.14 A three-quarter form with head by Universal Display serves as a dramatic change from the usual headless form. Men's underwear is featured in the shower-like setting. The same figure can be used as a decorative prop to "wear" shoulder strap bags, crisscrossed belts, neckties, and other male or female fashion accessories. *Priape, Montreal, Canada. Design: Étalage B Display.*

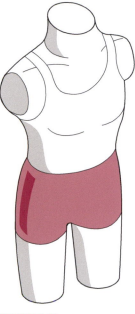

FIGURE 12.15 A three-quarter form. *Illustration by Ron Carboni.*

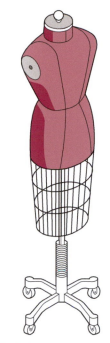

FIGURE 12.16 A dress form. *Illustration by Ron Carboni.*

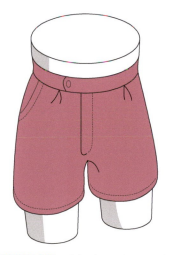

FIGURE 12.17 A body trunk or trunk form. *Illustration by Ron Carboni.*

it can be raised way up to show off a long gown, a robe, a full-length skirt, or even trousers.

These forms are not as expensive as mannequins, but they do very little to promote a fashion image. In experiments conducted on the selling floor, it has been found that the partial form or torso is more effective than a hanger or draper, but less effective than a mannequin. (See Figures 12.12–12.14.)

OTHER FORMS

Most of the following forms are made of PVC and are vacuum formed or, in some cases, made of rubber-mâché and cast in a mold. (See Figures 12.15 and 12.16.)

Body trunk or trunk form—A male form that starts at the diaphragm (above the waistline) and continues to just below the knees. Shorter forms, however, will be cut at mid-thigh. It is used to show shorts, underwear, swimwear, and so on. (See Figure 12.17.)

Bra form—A headless, armless form that ends just below a defined bustline, with or without shoulders. The forms are usually scaled to wear a size 34B. Junior bra forms are proportioned for a size 32A bust. (See Figure 12.18.)

Bust, blouse, or sweater form—An armless, headless form that ends just below the waistline. It has a defined bust and is used to show ladies' blouses and sweaters. (See Figure 12.19.)

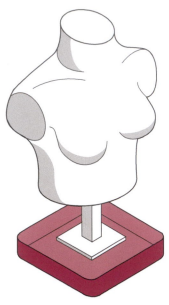

FIGURE 12.18 A bra form. *Illustration by Ron Carboni.*

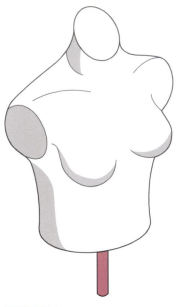

FIGURE 12.19 A bust, blouse, or sweater form. *Illustration by Ron Carboni.*

FIGURE 12.20 A pants or slacks form. *Illustration by Ron Carboni.*

Coat, or suit, form—A headless, usually armless male form that starts at the neck and ends around the hips. It is used to present suits, jackets, and sweaters. Arm pads or bendable rod arms may be used with this form. It also comes with an adjustable rod and base. (See Chapter 11.)

Pants, or slacks, form—A male or female form that goes from the waistline down to, and including, the feet. Men's forms will usually wear size 30 trousers with a 32-inch inseam. Female pants forms are designed to wear a size 8. If the legs are crossed, one leg will be removable to facilitate dressing the form. It is often provided with a foot spike that will hold the form in a standing position. (See Figure 12.20.)

Panty form—A waist-to-knees form for showing panties or bikini bottoms. These forms are about 2 feet tall and are usually used for counter and ledge displays. (See Figure 12.21.)

Shell form—A half-round, lightweight partial torso form similar to a bra, blouse, or sweater form. The front is fully sculpted, but the back is scooped out. (See Figure 12.22.)

Shirt form—The male version of the bust form.

Stocking, or leg, form—A form in the shape of a leg, used for merchandising hosiery. It has a hollow top into which

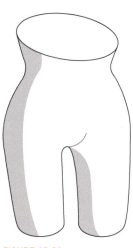

FIGURE 12.21 A panty form. *Illustration by Ron Carboni.*

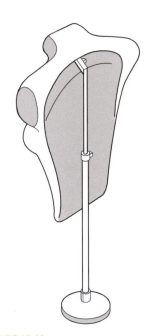

FIGURE 12.22 A shell form. *Illustration by Ron Carboni.*

the waistband of the hose can be inserted. The form is available in assorted lengths, depending on the merchandise to be displayed, such as thigh high, knee high, or calf high.

SOFT-SCULPTED FIGURES

The **soft-sculpted figure** is a life-size doll—male, female, or children of all ages—and is available covered in black, dark brown, or off-white jersey like fabric with little or no facial detail. The skeleton is a bendable wire armature that can be shaped and positioned. The armature is imbedded in a soft, spongy foam filler that holds its shape inside the jersey "skin."

The figures are abstract, not realistic, and, if well-handled, they completely disappear in the display setting. They hold and give shape to the merchandise, but the dark body becomes invisible when seen against a dark background. The lighting will pick up the merchandise but will disregard the body wearing it. The floppy figure needs to be positioned properly in order to look real; it has to be

propped, pinned, and secured in place, or wired in order to stand. The soft sculpture may require extra padding or primping. (See Figure 12.23.)

ARTICULATED ARTIST'S FIGURES

These life-size figures are based on the wooden miniatures used by artists and designers to get correct anatomical proportions and poses for figure drawing when a live model is not available. Movable joints can be swiveled or turned into new positions. The figures are usually made of wood or white plastic.

The abstractness of the full-sized **articulated artist's figure** lends itself to decorative and undressed applications as well as fully dressed and accessorized setups. These figures can be made to stand and can interact with other

FIGURE 12.23 The soft sculptured pair sitting beneath and surrounded by gifts is as relaxed as a pair can be. Easily manipulated into almost any human position, these life-size "dolls" are adaptable and fun to use. *Marais, Paris, France. Antoine Antoniol/Getty Images.*

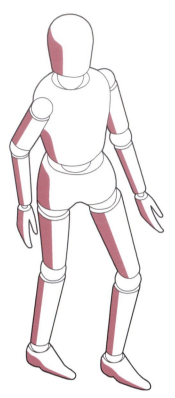

FIGURE 12.24 An articulated artist's figure. *Illustration by Ron Carboni.*

abstract, articulated forms. They can wear only accessories (belts, ties, scarves, or hats) and still not look underdressed. The figures—male or female—have no age, no personality, and no ethnic quality. In addition, they are fun to work with—in windows, on ledges, or anywhere in the store. (See Figure 12.24.)

CUTOUT FIGURES

The **cutout figure** can be trendy, high style, and avant-garde. True to human proportions, this figure is a silhouette cut out of wood or heavy board. Clothes are pinned or draped over it for a frontal or elevated view of the merchandise. Because the figures are flat cutouts and virtually two-dimensional, they provide very little form to the merchandise. The garments can be made to sag on the figure,

or the visual merchandiser can stuff and fill the garments with pads and tissue in order to provide greater form and roundness.

HANGERS

A simple **hanger** can be an alternative to the mannequin, but without taste or talent it can also look like something that was just pulled out of stock or off the rack without fuss, bother, or presentation. Ideally, dimensionalized, or padded, hangers that are variations on bust forms should be used to ensure that the garment drapes better.

As with the draper, in dressing the hanger—if a complete outfit is to be shown—the blouse or shirt goes on first. The pants or skirt is pinned onto the blouse or shirt where the waistline would be. The jacket or coat is then put on top to finish off the presentation. Scarves or ties can be knotted around the neck, or jewelry, such as necklaces, chains, or brooches, can be added. A shoulder bag can be secured over the shoulder; it must be pinned so that it doesn't slide off. If trousers are shown, the excess material is folded back inside the leg, and a pair of appropriate shoes can be set beneath the trousers. Even a dress can be accessorized, with the right shoes, bag, and gloves arranged on the floor beneath the dressed hanger.

The hanger can be hung by either invisible wire from a ceiling grid or from a hook that extends from a wall or panel. With some imagination, the visual merchandiser can create more seasonal or promotional ways of suspending the hanger, such as from a bare tree branch pushing through a back wall or tied from above with festive ribbon streamers or ticker tape or streamers and confetti. It takes some ingenuity, but it can be done. A little judicious padding doesn't hurt, and some animation can be achieved by bending a sleeve, crossing a leg, and so forth. A soft roll of tissue paper or a bendable tube can be inserted inside the sleeve to make the arm seem more believable. (See Figure 12.25.)

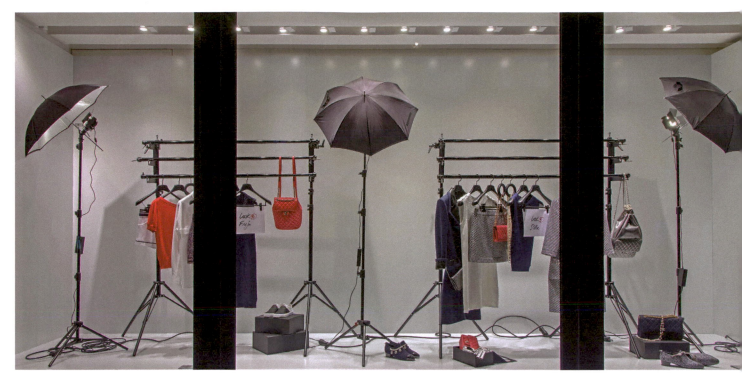

FIGURE 12.25 The scene is a fashion shoot, and all that is missing is the model and the photographer. But we *can* see the assorted coordinated pieces the photographer will be able to mix or match—now displayed on hangers—and even the accessories that help tell the "story." *Chanel, Paris, France. Antoine Antoniol/Getty Images.*

Go Green 12.1: Repurposing Mannequins

Old mannequins need not die, though they may fade away! When a mannequin becomes dated, scarred, scratched, and generally in need of a full-body resurrection, it may be time to go green and turn it into a semi-abstract mannequin.

Lose the wig, clean the body surfaces, and spray the figure all white or black—or a metallic color or a high-fashion color—being sure to use a low-VOC spray paint. Or, turn the mannequin into a fanciful display prop for seasonal promotions, appliquéing it with autumn leaves for fall, wrapping it in ivy and flowers for spring so it resembles a topiary, or coating it with diamond dust accented with snowflakes and icicles for winter. Be imaginative.

When you have used it, reused it, and repurposed it, and are really finished with it, either offer the mannequin to a fashion or art school for its students to have a go at dressing or decorating it, or have fun with the assorted parts yourself. Use the arms, legs, torso, and head as elements in a surreal or fantasy display; float them throughout the window suspended from a ceiling grid by colorful ropes, twine, or ribbons. The mannequin's "last stand" can be a bravura performance. Also, think of what props you can make from these leftover parts. The legs can be made into supports for a tabletop. The arms can be electrified and made into lamp bases topped with lamp shades or used as wall sconces or torchères. The torso can be wallpapered over or textured with sand and white glue and used as a decorative "statue" to show off shoulder bags, belts, scarves, and so on.

Don't be in a rush to discard a worn-out mannequin. With imagination, there is still display life in the old girl (or guy) yet!

Mannequins and Alternatives: Trade Talk

abstract mannequin
articulated artist's figure
body trunk or trunk form
bra form
bust, blouse, or sweater form
child mannequins
coat, or suit, form
cutout figure
dress form
form
full-figured mannequin

hanger
hard wigs
headless mannequin
junior mannequin
male mannequin
mannequin
misses, or missy size, mannequin
pants, or slacks, form
panty form
petite mannequin
preteen, or "tween," mannequin

realistic mannequin
semi-abstract mannequin
semi-realistic mannequins
shell form
shirt form
soft-sculpted figure
soft wigs
stocking, or leg, form
three-quarter form
torso form
young man mannequin

Mannequins and Alternatives: A Recap

◆ A mannequin may be a store's most valuable asset, and its selection is one of the most important decisions a display person can make.

◆ Every mannequin should be given a "rest period" so as not to become too familiar to the customer.

◆ Types of mannequins include realistic, semi-realistic, abstract, semi-abstract, and headless.

◆ Today's realistic mannequin resembles the everyday person rather than a movie star.

◆ Formal clothes should be displayed on an unanimated mannequin.

◆ Action clothes should be shown on a mannequin seemingly in motion.

◆ Seated mannequins add variety and interest to a group of mannequins and can work to show separates, casual wear, lingerie, and active sportswear.

◆ Horizontal mannequins should only be used for specific merchandise such as nightwear, lingerie, swimwear, and some sportswear.

◆ Types of realistic mannequins include misses or missy, junior, petite, full-figured, preteen, male, young man, and child.

◆ There are two major types of wigs used for mannequins: hard wigs and soft wigs.

◆ A hard wig is highly lacquered or plasticized and cannot be restyled.

◆ A soft wig emulates the softness of natural hair and can usually be combed and brushed. Some synthetic hair fibers can be reset with hot rollers.

◆ A semi-realistic mannequin is made like a realistic mannequin, but its makeup is more decorative and stylized.

◆ The semi-abstract mannequin is more stylized than the semi-realistic mannequin, and its features may be painted or suggested rather than defined.

◆ The abstract mannequin is concerned with creating an overall effect rather than reproducing natural lines and proportions. Features such as elbows, musculature, and fingernails are rarely indicated.

◆ A headless mannequin has a full-size or semi-realistic body with arms and legs but no head. It offers no personality or image.

Questions for Review and Discussion

1. Detail the criteria used to select a mannequin for a store.

2. What is the average fashion life expectancy of a mannequin?

3. Explain how a mannequin can be a store's "silent salesperson."

4. What is the relationship between mannequins and store image?

5. Make a list of the types of realistic mannequins and indicate measurements and sizes for each type.

5. How should wigs be selected for store mannequins?

6. Briefly describe each of the five major types of mannequins: realistic, semi-realistic, semi-abstract, abstract, and headless.

Chapter Thirteen
Dressing the Three-Dimensional Form

Entranceway to Aéropostale, Roosevelt Field, New York.
GH+A Designs www.ghadesign.com/portfolio/.

AFTER YOU HAVE READ THIS CHAPTER,
YOU WILL BE ABLE TO DISCUSS

- ✦ the steps to be taken in dressing a mannequin
- ✦ the methods in which mannequins may be attached to a base for standing
- ✦ the method for striking a mannequin with wire
- ✦ the edges of rigging a suit form
- ✦ the process of dressing a shirt form

Dressing a Mannequin

To dress a mannequin, it must first be taken apart and then carefully reassembled as the various items or merchandise are put on the figure. After dressing a mannequin for some time, the visual merchandiser will develop his or her own technique for handling the mannequin and assembling the parts. For the beginner, the following steps will serve as a convenient way to start.

If a mannequin has a removable wig, it should be carefully taken off the head and set aside so that it will not be crushed when garments are being pulled over the figure's head. If the wig on the mannequin cannot be removed, or if the visual merchandiser does not choose to remove it, a plastic bag, slipped over the head before the dressing starts, will help protect the wig.

The head and neck are part of the bust or torso, and this upper half is usually removable at the waist or hips from the legs below. To remove the top from the bottom, one simply holds the torso securely, gently rotates it to the right, and then lifts it up. The fitting that connects the parts consists of a peg extending up from the lower half and

another element, similar to a keyhole, buried in the base of the upper half.

If the hands are removable, hold the arm securely with one hand and rotate the mannequin's wrist to the right in order to disconnect the hand from the arm. The hand has a peg or extension that locks into the keyhole slot in the base of the arm. To avoid confusion when reassembling, it is important that the dresser keep track of which side the various parts came from (for instance, right hand replaced on right arm).

The arms are hooked into keyhole slots in the shoulders of the mannequins. Holding the torso securely, move the arm a bit to free it from the socket in which it is hooked, and then raise the arm up and out of the socket.

If the mannequin is to wear shorts, pants, or pantyhose, one leg will probably need to be removed. The legs are hooked into the torso and are usually removed from it in the same manner as the hands.

The assorted parts should now be lying before the dresser, on a clean surface, and, of course, the dresser's hands should also be clean. Even though most mannequins do have washable finishes, they should be handled very carefully. Some visual merchandisers cover their hands with cotton gloves during the dismantling and reassembling of the mannequin.

FIGURE 13.1 The casually dressed semi-abstract mannequins are combined with assorted draped jeans on the attention-getting background of fluorescent tubes to promote "Fade to White" wear. Note the ankle rods on the mannequins that keep them erect. *The Gap. Design: Wonderwall, Japan and GreenbergFarrow, New York City. Eugene Gologursky/ Getty Images.*

The lower half of the mannequin is usually dressed first. The pantyhose or hosiery (of the proper shade to go with the outfit) or trousers are put on first. Invert the lower half of the form, and remove one leg, if possible. With this lower half in the inverted position, pull the hose or trouser leg over the leg still attached to the torso. Insert the free leg into the other leg of the hose or trousers. Secure the detached leg, and pull the hose and trousers up to the waist. (See Figure 13.1.)

If the mannequin has a **butt-rod fitting** (an attachment on the buttocks into which the floor rod is inserted so that the mannequin can stand), an opening has to be provided in the crotch or the seam in the back of the pantyhose (or trousers or shorts) to permit the butt rod to slide into the fitting. (If the shorts or pants have wide enough legs, it might be possible to have the rod go up through the garment leg into the fitting without opening the seam.) (See Figure 13.2.)

Many new mannequins, particularly those designed primarily to wear pants or active sportswear, are equipped with **ankle-rod fittings**. In this case, the fitting for the supporting rod is inserted into a piece of hardware attached to the back of the mannequin's leg, above the ankle. (See Figure 13.3.)

Another alternative for positioning a mannequin is referred to as **striking**. The mannequin is rigged with two wires that thread through the butt hardware where the set-screw for the butt-rod has been removed. The ends of the wires are nailed in to the floor using common two-inch nails and a hammer. The tension of the wires keeps the mannequin standing. In order for the mannequin to remain balanced and secure, it must wear a shoe with the correct heel height. If the heel height is incorrect, a shim or spacer must compensate for the difference to obtain stability. For safety reasons, it is a technique reserved for closed-back windows or a place where a customer can't access the mannequin.

Mannequins can also be purchased with a removable **foot rod** that inserts into the foot of the non-removable leg. The 4-inch foot rod comes attached to the baseplate, and the mannequin's foot with the opening slides on to the 4-inch foot rod, keeping it upright. Occasionally visual merchandisers remove the base flange from the baseplate and reposition it by drilling it into the floor or interior platform with screws. This method is used mainly for mannequins that do not require shoes—such as boutique mannequins that have a sculpted shoe and abstract style mannequins.

A skirt, if the mannequin will be wearing one, is put on next. If the outfit includes a top that will be tucked into the waistband, the skirt opening is not closed at this time.

The mannequin is now ready for shoes. When a mannequin is purchased, the manufacturer will supply information concerning the appropriate shoe size and heel height. If the store does not carry shoes in stock, the visual merchandiser or management can try to make arrangements

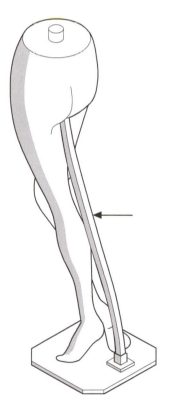

FIGURE 13.2   A butt rod. *Illustration by Ron Carboni.*

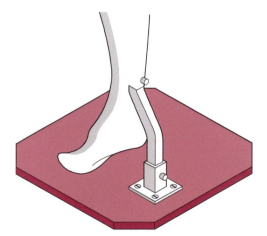

FIGURE 13.3   An ankle rod. *Illustration by Ron Carboni.*

with a local shoe store to have it supply the right type and color of shoes in the right size to go with the ensemble being presented. Often, this can be done in exchange for a credit in the window stating, "Shoes courtesy of . . . ." If such an arrangement is not possible, the display department should invest in purchasing several pairs of basic shoes in basic colors—but in the current season's style—to use on the mannequins. A mannequin's feet are no longer bound in ribbons, and it is not proper for a dressed and accessorized mannequin to appear in public without shoes.

With the shoes securely on, the dressed lower portion of the mannequin can be set into the butt or ankle rod, which is attached to a floor plate. If the mannequin will eventually be wired in place, lean the dressed lower half against a soft, clean, nonabrasive surface until the upper portion of the mannequin is ready.

To attach the top half to the bottom, place the two parts together so that the projecting peg, on the top of the lower part, fits into the keyhole slot at the base of the upper torso. Turn the torso gently to lock it in place. The two parts will now make a smooth, even line.

If a sweater or over-the-head blouse or top is to be displayed, pull it on and slide the detached arms up through the sleeves. Fit the peg on the end of the arm into the keyhole slot at the shoulder. Do not force it. Be sure to insert the right arm into the right slot and the left arm into the left slot.

If the garment is a button-up-the-front (or back) type, put it on over the shoulders. Next, fit the "action arm" (the one with the most bend or twist) in through the proper sleeve and into its slot. Follow with the other arm. Lock the second arm into place and then button up the garment.

If the ensemble includes a jacket, cardigan, or coat over the sweater or shirt, the outer garments should be slipped on over the shirt or sweater before the arms are inserted into the sleeves and locked into the shoulder joints. In this case, it is simpler to slip the sleeves through each other and then introduce the arm through the armhole opening with the wrist end down. The arm is then ready to fit into the shoulder slot. When the arms are positioned, and the shirt cuffs are buttoned down or turned back, the hands are then joined to the slot in the wrist and turned into place. The cuff is then pulled down. (If a bangle bracelet is part of the accessory setup, it is slipped on before the hand is set in place.)

Smooth down the front of the blouse, shirt, or jacket, and gently tuck any excess fabric around to the sides (preferably under the arms, as the back may also be viewed). If the costume requires it, pull the skirt or slacks up over the bottom of the shirt, close the top of the skirt or pants, and smooth down the seams. If a scarf or ascot is to be worn under the shirt, blouse, or sweater, it should be put

FIGURE 13.4 The supporting cast of assorted types and shapes and sizes of dress forms makes for an eye-arresting background for the dressed abstract. The contrast between the new and the old method of showing clothes also points up the fresh, new look of the featured garment. *Barneys, Ginza, Tokyo, Japan. Copyright WindowsWear PRO http://pro.windowswear.com; contact@windowswear.com 1.646.827.2288.*

FIGURE 13.5 Suit forms on roll-around metal bases are fully dressed and accessorized and stand welcoming customers into the men's store. *Hickey Freeman, Chicago, Illinois. Design: JGA, Southfield, Michigan.*

on before the shirt is buttoned—and it should be smoothed down to avoid any unsightly lumps.

Any necklaces, chains, or over-the-head jewelry is added before the mannequin's wig is set back in place. The other accessories (handbags, gloves, pins, sunglasses, and so on) may be added after the wig is replaced.

A mannequin that is to wear a dress, gown, or all-in-one garment may have the garment dropped over its shoulders after the pantyhose have been put on and the mannequin is standing erect. Other garments, such as skirts, will be easier to put on by "stepping" the mannequin into them and pulling them up from the bottom, before the removable leg has been secured. This will depend on the top opening of the garment.

Some garments will require a slip or a crinoline to fill out the dress properly. Others may require some padding or puffing with tissue paper or soft pads.

A mannequin that is dressed in one area and then transported to the display space or window should not be moved with the butt or ankle rod attached to the mannequin and the floor base. After the mannequin is located where it will be set up, the supporting rod should be set into the proper attachment on the mannequin and then on the floor or platform. The mannequin, up to this point, is treated just like one that will be wired or nailed into place. (See Figures 13.4 and 13.5.)

Rigging a Suit Form

The man's suit form is traditionally a fabric-covered torso made of papier-mâché or rigid urethane foam. It is headless, legless, and often armless. The unit is supported by a rod that is attached to a base. The neck is a straight cut, sometimes capped with a neck plate of chrome or brass or covered with fabric. Some coat or suit forms are equipped with ball-jointed arms that can be bent into realistic positions. More often than not, the visual merchandiser who rigs, or dresses, a suit form will have to rely on padded sleeve inserts to give substance to the loose, limp, hanging jacket sleeves.

Start with the shirt by putting it over the bare suit form. The collar button is left open until the tie is placed under the shirt collar; the collar is then closed. The tie should be tied neatly and securely and "dimpled" to sit perfectly in the inverted V of the collar and to hang straight down over the shirtfront. Many visual merchandisers still prefer the very neat and symmetrical Windsor knot; others use more casual or more fashionable ways of knotting a tie.

For a classic approach, tuck the sleeves back, out of sight, and then carefully pin, in the back, all the extra shirt fabric in two equal folds or pleats. This will create a smooth, wrinkle-free shirtfront. If a vest is to be shown, it is now put on the form and then buttoned. Allow the shirt sleeve to go through the sleeve jacket and then extend about one-half inch below the cuff of the jacket.

A jacket will hang below the usual hipline of the suit form. To make the jacket lie just right and not flap in the open space below the elevated form, the rigger will sometimes cut out cardboard shields to pin onto the "hips" of the form. These will conform to the line of the bottom of the jacket. The jacket is now placed over the well-smoothed-out shirt and the cardboard cutouts.

If arm pads, or sleeve pads, are used, they are pinned to the inside of the jacket at the shoulder and then brought down through the sleeve. If the cuff of the shirtsleeve is seen below the jacket cuff, the shirtsleeve will be behind the padding. The sleeve pad can then be pinned to the form for a smooth, close-fitting line with the suit form. Some visual merchandisers prefer a more casual or relaxed kind of rigging. They will not pin the sleeve or sleeve pad to the form. Instead, they may prefer to fold the sleeve, bend it, or suggest some form of animation. Shaped rolls or wads of tissue can also be used in place of sleeve pads.

After the jacket is centered and set perfectly and squarely on the form, the dresser will often anchor the jacket in place by means of some pins placed in back, under the collar, and in front, under the lapels. If the suit has been properly pressed or steamed, and is wrinkle-free, the visual merchandiser should not have too much trouble smoothing down the jacket fabric so that it will mold itself to the shape of the form beneath it. This might require an assist from a handheld steamer. Pins may be used along the way to hold the jacket in place, but they should be hidden and employed only when necessary.

If pants are to be displayed with the jacket, they can be pinned underneath the form and then draped over the surface on which the suit form has been placed. They can then be rolled, cascaded, rippled, or just sharply folded over the table, riser, or ledge or allowed to stop just above the floor.

Instead of cutting off the excess fabric of the trouser legs or sewing an invisible hem—or anything else, such as taping, that would permanently shorten the pant legs—the visual merchandiser can turn the excess fabric back inside the trouser leg, simulating a finished pants leg. This

is called a **quick cuff**. The proper pair of shoes, set below, could meet the turned back cuff, or the pants may be shown with the waistline at the bottom, using that opportunity to show a belt worked through the belt loops. Depending on the space, the store's stock, and the availability of alternate accessories, the visual merchandiser can do many things, in many ways, with the space below and around the form.

SHIRT BOARD

Displaying a shirt with a jacket presents other problems. Some visual merchandisers will opt for a **shirt board** (a flat board about 10 inches by 14 inches), onto which a shirt can be folded with only the shirtfront and perhaps a folded-over sleeve cuff visible. The board can then be pinned onto a wall or panel. An easel, slightly angled and set behind the shirt, makes it possible to show the shirt on the floor, counter, ledge, or inside a showcase. (See Figure 13.6.)

SHIRT FORMS

When a shirt form is used, the shirt is carefully pressed to get out all the fold lines before it is placed on the form. If a tie is to be included, it is slipped under the collar, and the shirt is then buttoned. The first pin is inserted into the form at the top button to keep the shirt in place. The shirtfront is then pulled taut and another pin is placed near the bottom button. The shirt is then smoothed out over and around the

FIGURE 13.6 This shirt and tie are pinned and shaped for display over a shirt board. *Illustration by Ron Carboni.*

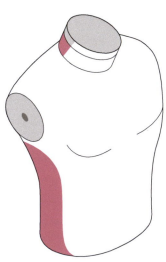

FIGURE 13.7 This shirt form is capped with a neck block. *Illustration by Ron Carboni.*

shoulders. Two more pins are inserted in the back yoke of the shirt to keep it from sliding. The excess fabric is gathered around in the back and arranged into two symmetrical folds or pleats, which are then pinned. The pins should be as invisible as possible and worked underneath. The shirttail and any excess hanging from the bottom of the shirt is then folded up and, in small, neat, tight pleats, pinned to the underside of the form. Long-sleeved shirts can either have the sleeves pinned at the cuff, close to the body of the form, or be treated more casually with pleats or ripples or even "postured" to give some semblance of reality. (See Figures 13.7 and 13.8.)

Forms and Customer Attitude

The more sophisticated and expensive the merchandise, and the more educated and selective the customer, the more abstract and nonrealistic the mannequin and the merchandise presentation can be. The visual merchandiser may not have to define the shape or fit of the garment, but instead may have to spend more time showing the fabric, the details, and the accessories.

The more popular or moderately priced the merchandise, the more realistic and literal the merchandise display must be. The customers of the popularly priced store want to see it all—all the variations and combinations. They will not necessarily be impressed with clever tricks of folding, pinning, or placing clothes on the floor, on panels, or on flat cutouts. They want to see the form, the fit, what goes where, and who is wearing it.

Whichever mannequin, form, or dimensional device is used, its selection must be determined by what it will do for the merchandise and how it will affect the customer's attitude toward the merchandise and the store that is selling the goods. It always comes back to the store image.

FIGURE 13.8 In the Children's Area of Stoeker's Department store in Eferding, Austria, the headless soft sculpture figures appear on the right and a steel-gray child abstract mannequin stars above a lay-down display on the display fixture on the left. *Designed by Gruschwitz GmbH.*

Dressing the Three-Dimensional Form: Trade Talk

ankle-rod fittings	foot rod	shirt board
butt-rod fittings	quick cuff	striking

Dressing the Three-Dimensional Form: A Recap

+ A mannequin must first be taken apart and then carefully reassembled as items of merchandise are put on the figure.

+ The lower half of the mannequin is usually dressed first.

+ To dress the mannequin, first remove the wig and the upper half of the mannequin. Remove arms from the upper half. If the mannequin is to wear shorts, pants, or pantyhose, one leg will need to be removed. Pantyhose or hosiery should go on first, then trousers or a skirt. If the mannequin has a butt-rod fitting, an opening needs to be provided in the crotch or seam of the shorts or pants. Shoes are put on next, and then the dressed lower portion can be set into the butt or ankle rod, which is attached to a floor plate. The top half of the mannequin is attached and dressed, and then arms may be slid up through sleeves and attached to the torso. Outer garments, such as coats or jackets, should be slipped over the inner garments before arms are attached. Accessories and jewelry are added and the wig is set in place.

+ In rigging a suit form, the shirt is put on first, and the collar button is left open until the tie is placed under the shirt collar. The sleeves may be tucked back, and extra shirt fabric is pinned back in two equal folds, to create a smooth shirtfront. The vest is put on next and then the jacket. If sleeve pads are used, they can be pinned to the inside of the jacket at the shoulder and brought through the sleeve. If pants are to be displayed, they can be pinned underneath the form and then draped over the surface on which the suit form has been placed. Excess fabric is tucked inside the trouser leg to simulate a finished pants leg.

+ A shirt board is a flat board about 10 inches by 14 inches onto which a shirt can be folded, leaving only the shirtfront, and possibly a folded-over sleeve cuff, visible.

+ In dressing a shirt form, the shirt must be pressed to get out all the wrinkles. If a tie is included, it is slipped under the collar and the shirt is then buttoned. The first pin is inserted at the top button. The shirtfront is then pulled taut and another pin is placed near the bottom. The shirt is smoothed out over and around the shoulders and pinned in the back, at the yoke. Excess fabric is gathered in the back and arranged in two symmetrical folds, which are pinned. Any excess fabric hanging from the bottom is folded up and pinned to the underside of the form in small, neat pleats. All pins should be invisible. Long sleeves can be pinned at the cuffs close to the body form or may be pleated or "postured" to simulate reality.

Questions for Review and Discussion

1. How might a pair of pants be displayed with a jacket on a suit form? Provide at least two creative methods.

2. How might a suit form be rigged to achieve a casual look?

3. Explain the relationship between mannequins or other three-dimensional forms and customer sophistication.

Chapter Fourteen
Fixtures

David Jones, Bourke Street Mall, Melbourne, Australia.
Courtesy of David Jones.

**AFTER YOU HAVE READ THIS CHAPTER,
YOU WILL BE ABLE TO DISCUSS**

+ the fixtures often used in window displays, on counters, and as floor fixtures
+ the common materials and finishes used in the manufacture of display fixtures
+ how stands are assembled and used for displays
+ the differences among costumers, valets, and drapers
+ criteria for the selection of fixtures

As retail continues to evolve and stores rival the online shopping experience, store fixtures have become increasingly important in their role of presenting merchandise and establishing good store design. Store **fixtures** must project the brand image, solve marketing and merchandising challenges, and go beyond basic functions of simply hanging and displaying the merchandise. Just as furniture complements a residential interior, the fixtures add excitement and personality to the store environment. Fixturing can be compared to interior designing. It is the selection of the "furniture" for the selling area of a retail establishment. It is the selection of the right "accessories" and details that creates the personality or the image of a selling space. A sofa, which might dominate a living room, might be compared to the larger racks, gondolas, or perimeter wall hang-rods. Just as a sofa ordinarily will seat the most guests and disappear under the load, so will these larger fixtures carry the most stock and become invisible under and behind the merchandise they carry. As we compare fixturing to furniture in function, it is interesting to learn that today's store design and fixture trends are taking cues from the hospitality industry. As retail continues to focus on environments that support experiences combined with more intimate and exclusive services,

they recognize the important role fixturing has in establishing the customer's journey and perceptions. Hence, we see more customization in fixture design and finishes than ever.

The fixture industry is a global industry that serves both prestige and mass merchants for permanent, temporary, and promotional fixture solutions. Smart fixture design should invite consumers into the world of the brand visually through appearance, kindling an emotional engagement with the consumer while differentiating the brand from its competition. The materials and finishes used to fabricate fixtures and cabinetry must echo the brand's personality and character in every way possible. Wood, veneers, laminates, and metal finishes offer the consumer more insight about the brand. The highly polished gleaming wood surface will certainly appeal to a different consumer than the dark rough reclaimed surface. A dress form with a satin nickel base will distinguish the brand more readily than a basic black iron stand. These small details elevate the brand's originality, contribute to the authenticity, and reinforce the brand heritage. Manufacturers are continuously exploring new forms of customization and manufacturing techniques that allow custom fixtures to be produced faster, making it easier for retailers to refresh, transition, and open new doors.

FIGURE 14.1 The swirling overhead ceiling panels, combined with the sleek metallic column enclosures and textured wall finishes, set the very contemporary atmosphere for this active sportswear retailer's flagship store. Add to this the unusual, softly rounded and organic white molded fixtures and furniture, and the overall effect is one of speed, action, and NOW! *Fila, Madison Avenue, New York, New York. Design: Giorgio Borruso, Marina del Rey, California.*

Fixtures are divided into categories to best suit the merchandise to be displayed. There are floor fixtures, wall fixtures, and fixtures that float from the ceiling. Counter fixtures are designed to display specific categories of merchandise or a line of goods. Basic fixtures can be wood, metal, or plastic fabrications specifically designed to hold or elevate a pair of shoes, a shirt, or a skirt, or they can be props or decorative elements that can work effectively as drapers or costumers. These fixtures elevate merchandise; they hold it up and give it form. (See Figures 14.1 and 14.2.)

Stands

The **stand** is a very widely used, basic fixture. It comes with an assortment of tops that may be slipped interchangeably into an adjustable rod set on a weighted base. The base sits securely on the floor (or on a platform, elevation, counter, or ledge), and the rod may be adjusted to the desired height for presenting the merchandise.

The top element can be a straight rod, like the top stroke of a T, and can hold an assortment of scarves; ties; towels; or any soft, drapable merchandise. The **hanger top** consists of a gentle curve (like the arc of a coat or dress hanger) and serves to show a dress, sweater, jacket, and so on. This fixture is also called a draper. Another kind of hanger top ends with two reverse curves (like a handlebar moustache). It serves to display lingerie and other sleeveless garments that hang from straps and that do not have sleeves or shoulders to keep the garment from slipping off a regular hanger top. There are also special attachments for hosiery, shirts, shoes, hats, and so forth.

Stands are usually used in a variety, or assortment, window as a means of building up—from the glass line to the back of the display window—a variety of merchandise. The smaller items are set low and up front. As they get larger, the merchandise gets higher and set farther back. A truly elegant and beautifully designed base can provide a drape-away point for a lovely piece of lingerie in a one-item or a related merchandise window presentation. (See Chapter 9.)

Platforms and Elevations

Platforms and **elevations** are small buildups used to provide interest and to help separate merchandise in

FIGURE 14.2 The choice of materials used for the fixtures in an area not only helps identify the merchandise shown but can also inspire and motivate the shopper to spend more time perusing the merchandise. The cyclone fencing and the industrial metal racks on oversized wheels, plus the dynamic display of yellow lighting fixtures overhead, say that this is a trendy, urban, sports-minded department. *Zen, Bangkok, Thailand. Design: Blocher Blocher Partners, Stuttgart, Germany.*

FIGURE 14.3 The fixtures shown here merchandise the products at various levels on the round racks and multi-level tables. Square or round metal tubing can be crafted into a variety of forms and, with assorted attachments, become multifunctioning fixtures. Whether finished in bright chrome or dulled down, rubbed, or antiqued—or even sprayed a color—the metal fixtures are long lasting and serviceable. They can exist in almost any retail setting. *Adessa, Oberhausen, Germany. Design: Plajer & Franz Studio, Berlin, Germany.*

mass displays. They can be cubes, cylinders, or saddles of any size or shape. Elevations can be tables and chairs and other pieces of furniture that can be used to raise up a mannequin, a form, a stand, or an arrangement of merchandise. An elevation can also be a platform that covers a large portion of a display floor.

Platforms and elevations are used to separate mannequins in a window or on a traffic aisle inside a store, so that each figure can be seen in its own space, at its own level. The use of elevations is also discussed in Chapter 9. (See Figure 14.3.)

Costumers, Valets, and Drapers

Costumers, valets, and drapers are important fixtures that show coordinates or complete costumes on a single stand.

The **costumer** is a freestanding fixturing unit used on a floor, ledge, or counter, depending on its size. It has a hanger set onto the top of an adjustable upright, which is set into a weighted base. The unit usually has a skirt bar, which makes it possible to display a pair of pants or a skirt under a blouse or jacket. (See Figure 14.4.)

The **valet**, very similar to the costumer, has a heavier and wider hanger along with a slacks bar, which makes this fixture especially useful for menswear. As with most fixtures designed today, the hanger and the slacks or skirt bar attachment are adjustable, riding up and down on the vertical rod. Sometimes it includes a shoe platform raised off the floor, but still attached to the same vertical rod on which all the other pieces are assembled. When using either fixture, a scarf, jewelry, a handbag, a tie, and maybe even a hat can be draped over the various parts of the collected costume. In a specialty store, a boutique, a one-item-type window, or even a related merchandise presentation in a limited space, the costumer and valet are excellent and reliable fixtures. (See Figure 14.5.)

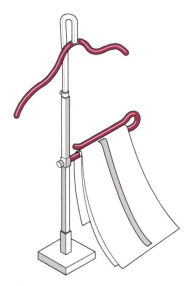

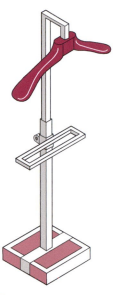

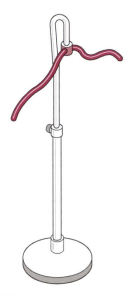

FIGURE 14.4   A costumer with a skirt/slacks bar attachment. *Illustration by Ron Carboni.*

FIGURE 14.5   A valet fixture is especially useful for menswear. *Illustration by Ron Carboni.*

FIGURE 14.6   A hanger top, or draper. *Illustration by Ron Carboni.*

The draper is also a hanger on a stand, adjustable in height, but without a skirt or slacks bar. It is usually smaller than the costumer and the valet—a compact unit meant to be used on a counter or on a buildup. It may be produced with a bendable armature that allows the sleeves of the garment to be positioned after the jacket, blouse, or sweater is hung or buttoned over the top hanger. Coordinating skirts or slacks can be laid out at the base of the draper. (See Figure 14.6.)

Pipe Racks

A **pipe rack** is a utilitarian fixture with wheels, made of round tubing and resembling an inverted U. It may have a flat wooden or metal base to which the wheels are attached, or it may be made completely from pipes. Recently, industrial style pipe racks have regained popularity due to the trend of repurposing raw materials in retail design. (See Figures 14.7 and 14.8.)

FIGURE 14.7   The old-fashioned, utilitarian pipe rack has been transformed into a sleek, contemporary unit that complements this upscale women's fashion shop. The concept remains the same: garments are lined up at eye level for the shopper's perusal. As shown here, the fixture lacks the mobility usually provided by the rollers on the base but makes up for it with style and elegance of line. *Breuninger, Stuttgart, Germany. Design: Blocher Blocher Partners.*

FIGURE 14.8 Traditional stacking tables have been updated and given style and polish. These square, U-shaped tables, designed at assorted heights, can nest within one another or be pulled out to show products at various levels. Here, they are finished in white and chocolate brown to become part of the furniture setup as well as to provide eye interest up front in the shop. *Högl, Bratislava, Slovakia. Design: Gruschwitz GmbH, Munich, Germany.*

Cash Wrap Sales Counter

Cash wrap counters are points-of-purchase, where sales are actually made. It is here that the customer makes the final decision to purchase an item, possibly adds an impulse item, determines the method of payment, and watches his or her purchase get wrapped or placed in a shopping bag. The counter needs to effectively stage the merchandise during the sale, driving volume into sales with add-ons as it blurs the lines between shopping and transaction.

The cash wrap counter can stand on its own or be integrated into the floor fixturing. It may combine a staging area with a merchandising area below or on either side. It may include a glass front or top—for showing, holding, and selling merchandise—combining the storage capacities of a cabinet, the selling surface of a table, and the display

potential of a shadow box. The unit may be made entirely of glass, with everything under it on view. It can be all wood or laminated or combined with metal to look like a closed cabinet.

In the past, the cash wrap counter was rooted to the floor of the selling area—large, immovable, set to stay in one place. With stores in need of greater mobility, flexibility, and the ability to rearrange their layout as merchandise changes, counters have become lighter—residential looking and, in some instances, almost table-like. The feeling of "floating" furniture has taken over on many of the main floors of department and specialty stores. To reinforce the light, airy look, some units have indirect lights located below the counters in order to light the floor beneath. New technology has enabled the bulky cash register to transition into a smaller digital POS system with a drawer. This new technology has also inspired the use of mobile cash wraps and shifted cash wraps locations throughout the selling floor, easing up the waiting times for busy shoppers to make purchases.

Ideally, a fixture is no more than 24 inches tall and rarely runs more than 36 inches when adjusted to its greatest height, maintaining Americans with Disabilities Act (ADA) compliancy. ADA guidelines ensure that people with disabilities can interact within store environments. A taller one would be an insurmountable barrier to the give-and-take between customer and salesperson. (See Figure 14.9.)

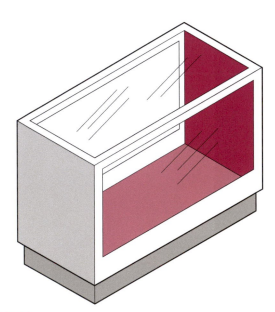

FIGURE 14.9 A typical showcase with glass top and front. *Illustration by Ron Carboni.*

Assorted Counter Fixtures

Counter fixtures are designed to sell, display, and stock merchandise. Many are designed to showcase one particular category of merchandise, such as jewelry or cosmetics. A counter fixture may have a surface for displaying merchandise, shelving for stacking, drawers for storage, and/or a locking glass enclosure on top. Some counters mix many of these features. The goal of the counter fixture is to make the merchandise accessible, feature and highlight items, protect against shrinkage (theft), and provide ample space to stock merchandise. Jewelry and cosmetics counters often require mirrors, allowing customers to test or try on the product. A **mirror** may be attached or weighted, with the ability to tilt or adjust to meet the customer's needs. Lighting inside the case can vary in type and is dependent on the merchandise; LED tube lights or small miniature LED spots focus light differently. Today, lighting is used beneath shelves and under the fixture if it has legs or a kick plate. By illuminating from beneath, the counter seems to float on the selling floor. Backlit translucent panels or recesses may add a glow for better recognition. Figures 14.10 through 14.15 show some of the usual counter fixtures required to furnish counters in various departments adequately.

Trays or **bins** may be useful adjuncts to counter selling. Risers or small elevations will add interest to a display of small items (such as fragrance, cosmetics, or small leather goods). More and more often, a bowl of fresh flowers or greenery is becoming a counter "fixture." It enhances the merchandise, relaxes the customer, adds to the ambiance, and effects the eventual sale. (See Figure 14.16.)

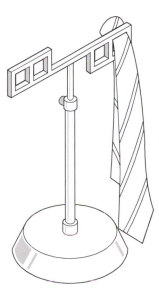

FIGURE 14.10   A tie displayer. *Illustration by Ron Carboni.*

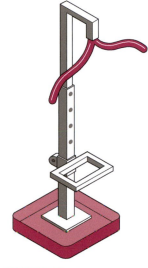

FIGURE 14.11   A costumer with a hanger set on the top of an adjustable upright. *Illustration by Ron Carboni.*

FIGURE 14.12   A flex arm displayer. The hanger continues down into flexible cable "arms" that can be bent into animated positions. *Illustration by Ron Carboni.*

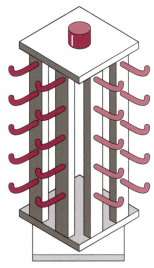

FIGURE 14.13   A hook stand. A counter unit that can hold bagged or carded merchandise, chains, and so on. *Illustration by Ron Carboni.*

FIGURE 14.14   A rope displayer. A counter unit designed to show necklaces, chains, and so on. *Illustration by Ron Carboni.*

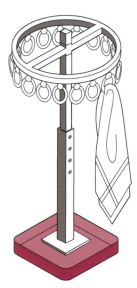

FIGURE 14.15   A circular, spinning scarf wheel. *Illustration by Ron Carboni.*

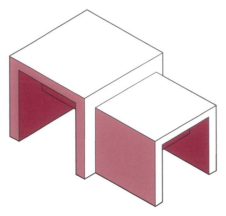

FIGURE 14.16 Risers and saddles are buildups, groupings of geometric shapes and forms to create multi-levels for the display of small associate merchandise, such as cosmetics, toiletries, leather goods, and shoes. *Illustration by Ron Carboni.*

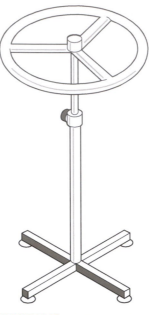

FIGURE 14.17 A round rack. *Illustration by Ron Carboni.*

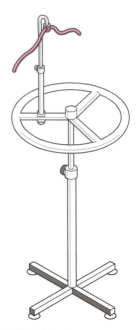

FIGURE 14.18 The superstructure on top of this round rack is used to display one of the garments stocked below. *Illustration by Ron Carboni.*

Floor and Freestanding Fixtures

Floor fixtures and **freestanding fixtures** are units designed to hold and show merchandise out on the floor—where the traffic is. The major types of fixtures include round racks; T-stands; and quad racks, or four-way face-outs. (The dressing and stocking of fixtures is discussed in Chapter 15.)

ROUND RACKS

The most commonly used fixture is the **round rack**. This unit usually consists of a circular hang-rod, 3 feet in diameter, raised anywhere from 45 inches to more than 6 feet off the ground. It is set on an adjustable upright that is securely attached to a wide, weighted base, which is stable and holds the floor, even when fully weighted down with merchandise.

The round rack, when fully stocked, carries almost 115 inches of shoulder-out merchandise in an area less than 5 feet by 5 feet. (See Figure 14.17.) This is, at the same time, the big advantage as well as being the big disadvantage. It is good to be able to show a great deal of merchandise in a small area of selling space, but all with shoulders out? The disadvantage of not being able to see more than the sleeve of a garment can be remedied by setting a draper on top of the round rack, as a superstructure, and displaying fully one of the garments from the collection sandwiched in below. (See Figure 14.18.)

For some classifications of merchandise—for example, children's wear, bras and panties, bikini swimsuits, and pre-packaged goods—the round rack may be ordered with two or even three tiers of hang-rods. Merchandise should not be indiscriminately loaded onto the round rack just because it is a mass unit. It should be carefully arranged by color and style.

T-STANDS

At the other end of floor fixturing from the round rack is the **T-stand**. It is a specialty unit—a highlighter or accent piece. It is small, light, carries a minimal amount of merchandise, and makes big fashion statements. Originally, the T-stand was simply an upright rod attached to a heavy base with a cross bar (like the top of a T) on top of which about a dozen garments could be hung. These "lightweights" were set out on the selling floor to show what was new and what was being featured. They were, and still are, used along an aisle to introduce the merchandise being housed in the area beyond.

There have been many improvements and sophisticated changes in T-stand construction. They are adjustable and may have two or more arms to show merchandise in two or more directions as well as at different levels. The arms can be **waterfalled** (i.e., merchandise can be presented on hangers in descending order on a sloping arm; evenly spaced hooks, knobs, or notches keep the hangers from sliding down). A T-stand can even incorporate a dress form, a draper, or a costumer with an arm bracket or a waterfall. In this way, a sample of the garment can be shown dimensionally on a form, and a supply of the same garment—in a range of sizes and/or colors—can be stocked in back. The T-stand is versatile and most effective when used for emphasis. (See Figure 14.19.)

QUAD RACKS, OR FOUR-WAY FACE-OUTS

A **quad rack, or four-way face-out**, stands somewhere between the T-stand and the round rack, in use and in size, on the selling floor. Basically, it is a four-armed fixture with each arm extending out from a central core. Most often, each arm is turned out at right angles from the center or upright; in a floor plan this configuration will look like a pinwheel. The idea behind this design is that, from certain angles or approaches, the customer sees a shoulder-out arrangement of the collected merchandise, but when coming at the unit straight on, the facing arm will present a "face-out" or "front-forward" view. The potential customer will be able to see the front of the first garment on that particular arm. The arms that extend out in the four directions are often individually adjustable, up and down, so that the merchandise can be seen at four different levels. Some manufacturers are making quad racks in which

some or all of the arms are waterfalled. The viewer sees not only the entire front of the first garment but also the upper part of the following garments in ascending order.

Because the quad-rack unit is designed with four separate views, it is ideal for showing separates or coordinate fashions. On one fixture it is possible to show skirts, pants, jackets, and blouses that go together. The pants should be hung from the highest arm to accommodate the extra hang space necessary, and the blouses (or vests or sweaters) will probably be hung on the lowest level. The four arms can also be used to tell coordinated color stories. (See Figure 14.20.)

OTHER FLOOR FIXTURES

A **gondola** is a long, flat-bottomed merchandiser usually with straight, upright sides. This fixture is sometimes designed with adjustable shelves combined with a table surface and storage cabinet or drawer space below. Because it has a central dividing panel (perpendicular to, and equidistant from, the end uprights), the gondola is two-sided. The unit is frequently used in groups on the selling floor and oriented perpendicular to the traffic aisles. The ends of the gondolas are valuable feature areas known as **endcaps**. Endcaps can offer product trials, tasting, or testing. They are key areas facing main aisles that highlight and promote products. Gondolas are found in linen, housewares, china, and glassware departments, and, most commonly, in big-box and grocery stores. The shelves of the gondola are particularly adaptable to stackable and prepackaged merchandise. (See Figure 14.21.)

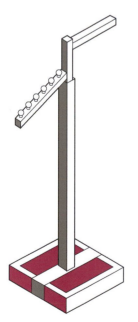

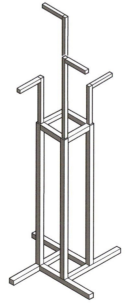

FIGURE 14.19   A T-stand with one straight arm and one waterfall. *Illustration by Ron Carboni.*

FIGURE 14.20   A quad rack, or four-way face-out. *Illustration by Ron Carboni.*

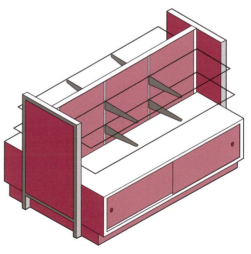

FIGURE 14.21   A typical gondola, with adjustable shelves and storage space below. *Illustration by Ron Carboni.*

A French term for a displayer shelf unit, an **étagère** is an open, multi-shelf display fixture. It is most often used to show china, glass, home furnishings accessories, and small gifts. (See Figure 14.22.)

A **kiosk** is a self-standing booth or structure on the selling floor that may accommodate a salesperson as well as merchandise. It can be used as a mini-boutique, an outpost, or an enclosed information or special-events desk. Today a kiosk may also be defined as a digital fixture that houses a directory using a touch screen; these are common at the entrance to a store, mall, or exhibit hall.

An **outpost** is a freestanding, self-contained selling unit that contains a stock of a given type of merchandise, along with display and signing relevant to that merchandise. The outpost features merchandise not ordinarily sold in the department in which it is set up (such as a cosmetics outpost in a teen department or handbags in a shoe department).

A **three-part rack** is a round rack composed of three separate but equal arcs. Usually, the height of each arc is individually adjustable. It is effective for showing separates, coordinates, or assorted colors and styles of a particular item. (See Figure 14.23.)

A **C-rack** is basically one-half of a round rack. (It is also called a **semicircular rack** or a **half-circle rack**.) It consists of an arc-shaped base with a similarly arc-shaped hang-rod above it. The two arcs are connected by two adjustable uprights. A pair of C-racks can be combined to form a two-part round rack. If each arc of the two-part round rack is set at a different height, it is possible to get greater variety in the merchandise presentation. Two C-racks, placed end to opposing end, make an **S-rack**, which also has a greater potential for variety of merchandise presentation. The C-rack can be used for dresses, coats, suits, and coordinates. (See Figure 14.24.)

A **vitrine** is a glass-enclosed, shelved cabinet or **showcase**. It often has glass shelves and partitions. A vitrine is usually a decorative piece, sometimes made to look antique. Like the étagère, it is used to display small, "precious" items or accessories.

A **spiral costumer** is a corkscrewing or descending waterfall extended out from a central upright or post. The merchandise is visible from all around (360 degrees), but the presentation is essentially shoulders out, with an occasional glimpse of the front of some of the merchandise. (See Figure 14.25.)

FIGURE 14.22 An étagère. *Illustration by Ron Carboni.*

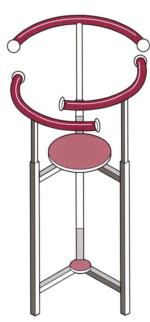

FIGURE 14.23 A three-part rack. *Illustration by Ron Carboni.*

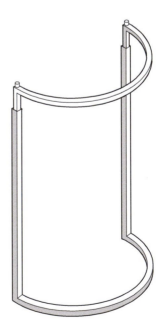

FIGURE 14.24 A C-rack. *Illustration by Ron Carboni.*

FIGURE 14.25 A spiral costumer. *Illustration by Ron Carboni.*

Selecting a Fixture

In selecting a fixture to use on the selling floor, there are certain criteria the visual merchandiser may have. The criteria include appearance, construction, end use, upkeep, and finish.

APPEARANCE

How does the fixture look on the floor? Does it go with the architecture and interior design of the area, the style? Does it go with the other fixtures and furniture already selected or in use? If the interior of the shop attempts to be Bohemian (e.g., Boho in style) and charming, a shiny, slick chrome fixture would be shockingly out of place and out of character. A weathered wood unit or some other natural or antique-type piece would be more fitting, more in keeping with the established image. The new fixture would also have to be in scale and in proportion to the area.

CONSTRUCTION

Is the unit flexible? Is it adjustable? Can the arms that hold the display or stocked merchandise be raised or lowered as hemlines and fashions dictate? Can the fixture be adapted for use with different types of merchandise if the shop is a seasonal one and sells anything from swimsuits to full-length raincoats—and everything in between? Are the elements of the fixture rearrangeable and adaptable? It is not absolutely necessary that one fixture do everything, but in a small shop with a limited fixture budget, the more versatile the fixture, the better.

END USE

Ask yourself the following questions to determine if the fixture meets the intended end use: Does the unit make full use of the valuable area of the selling floor that it will occupy? Does it hold as much merchandise as necessary and show it in the most desirable manner? Can the unit be adjusted to double or triple hang, if the merchandise is small (e.g., children's wear) or short (e.g., shorts, miniskirts), or can the hang levels be varied to add interest? Is there a way of displaying in all the unused "air space" above the unit, an area that can be seen from many parts of the shop but often goes unused? (See Figure 14.26.)

FIGURE 14.26   A special fixture may also be a focal element in a store interior. In the Marni boutique, in London, these unique units not only carry an array of garments but are designed with shelves to hold the "go with" accessories. *Marni, London, United Kingdom.* Copyright WindowsWear PRO http://pro.windowswear.com; contact@windowswear.com 1.646.827.2288.

What is the display value of the fixture? Does it have maximum merchandise exposure? Is there some "front-out" viewing of the collected stock? Can the featured garment be dressed and accessorized? Does the fixture lend itself to creating color and style excitement? Does it allow for the coordination and combination of merchandise? Does it "show and sell"?

Is the unit a self-selector, one that the customer can "shop" by himself or herself and still find what is being looked for? Is it self-explanatory? Can the merchandise be removed and replaced on the fixture without too much difficulty for the customer? Does the fixture contain and hold the merchandise—safely and securely—with few ill effects to the merchandise, or does it create "as is" merchandise by increasing wear and tear?

UPKEEP

Is the fixture serviceable, dependable, reliable, and safe? Will it stand and not topple when loaded with merchandise or used as a swing by a customer's child? Does it require constant care, repair, polishing, and housekeeping? Are the parts replaceable and easy to get? How good, how reliable, and how dependable is the manufacturer/supplier? Will it stand behind its product with some sort of warranty?

FINISHES

What the fixture is constructed of and how it is finished will affect not only its "floor life" but also its appearance on the floor.

Chrome is one of the most popular finishes for fixtures used for counters, floors, and walls. It is made by electroplating chromium onto another metal. Stronger and often superior fixtures have a base of steel with an electrolytic deposit of chromium on it. Fixtures can also be made of brass or nickel and then given the bright, silvery, chrome finish. **Polished chrome** and **mirror chrome** are only two of the standard names for this shiny finish. The more care given to the preparation of the welded steel, nickel, or brass—the polishing and cleaning of the raw metal framework—the better the chrome finish will be.

Generally, chrome fixtures can be moderate in cost and are usually quite durable. A good finish is uniform, smooth, unblemished, and without the pinkish or coppery discolorations that may occur in welded corners. Chrome plating does not require an outer lacquer coating to prevent discoloration or tarnishing from oxidation as other finishes may require. A chrome finish will resist scratching and scarring from normal use, such as stacking and moving metal hangers along chrome hang-rods. It is a popular look in department store fixturing.

A variety of finishes in chrome are available: antique, rubbed, satin, and brushed. The surface to be chrome-plated is first treated with an abrasive material to roughen it. This will tend to dull the shine on the final chrome-plated surface but will still maintain the silvery quality. These duller and more satiny looks can be quite elegant and are considered more for luxury goods. With the addition of some color rubs, the resulting toned-down and deeper silver-gray surfaces are referred to as either a stainless-steel finish or a pewter finish.

Nickel-plated surfaces are similar in appearance to chrome-plated surfaces; however, in a satin finish it has a soft, luxurious cast perfect for lingerie.

Brass fixture finishes are second in popularity to chrome, but this finish does need extra protection and care. The bright, golden gleam of a brass finish can be applied over steel or nickel, or even on soft brass itself. Brass metal, not the finish, is rarely used to make large floor fixtures, though it is used in counter fixture construction. Brass is also available in satin finishes—soft, low-luster finishes that can be very smart, elegant, and particularly attractive in wood-filled men's departments. Deep walnut and mahogany tones are enhanced by rubbed, antiqued, darker brass finishes. Creamy whites and very light neutral tones look even more refined with the soft gleam of satin-finished brass—very feminine and very expensive looking.

Copper and **bronze** finishes also need special care, special handling, and special lighting on the selling floor if they are to resemble copper or brass closely. A copper finish tends to be a pink or rusty-gold color; the bronze is often brown and dark with just a mere metallic glint. A copper finish goes well with natural, light woods and could create an earthy, vintage, or country setting. It works well with menswear.

Painted finishes include baked enamel, lacquered, and epoxy paint finishes. All these methods are used to create fixtures with color. The metal or wood that is to be colored has to be cleaned, sealed, primed, and prepared before being given the particular color coating and allowed to dry in special heat-maintained ovens or kilns.

More and more colored units are appearing in children's, tween, and active sportswear shops and departments. They are also becoming increasingly popular in hardware, gourmet, and kitchen supply areas. For many years, painted fixtures were white, black, or metallic gold, but today there is no limit to the range of colors available. The use of colored fixtures adds to the ambiance of a shop or area, cuts down on the sharp and sometimes shrill quality of chrome, and creates a bold fashion statement. How and where one uses color on fixtures

will depend largely on the type of merchandise involved. Most painted finishes will eventually scar, scratch, or scrape off. Enamel painting is the cheapest and least durable finish, but even enamel can be made more efficient if it is applied electrostatically. (See Figures 14.27 and 14.28.)

Wood Fixtures and Store Fittings

After a decade or two of living with the shimmer and shine of chrome and the sparkle of smooth, clear plastics, today's

FIGURE 14.27   In the Kitchen Aid Concept Store Potten & Pannen the curved enamel cash wrap invites the shopper into a kitchen lover's paradise. The red enamel finish is used to detail the walls, fixtures adding a pop of color and contrast with the wood. *Potten & Pannen— Stanek Kitchen Aid Concept Store & Gourmet, Czech Republic.*

FIGURE 14.28 The bold red pedestals merchandised with kitchenware complement the red enamel wall fixtures, creating a rich contrast against the wooden back wall of the shop. *Potten & Pannen—Stanek Kitchen Aid Concept Store & Gourmet, Czech Republic.*

stores see a continued emphasis on richness and refinement. This return to a classic, or reclaimed style finds store designers specifying the most luxurious and versatile of materials endowed by nature—wood. With an infinite variety of patterns and grains available in an expansive palette of tints and shades of neutral brown, wood can complement almost any design.

Today, store designers and visual merchandisers have many excellent, adaptable systems available to them with a wide choice of woods, finishes, and accessories.

Industry manufacturers and importers are showing **wood fixtures** and furniture. Many manufacturers are fashioning elaborate furniture/fixturing memorabilia. Items reflecting the 1930s and 1940s are designed for use as props and fixtures. Trade shows feature manufacturers of country-style or upcycled furniture specifically designed to function as primary fixtures. There are units that can be strategically placed to add interest, character, and visual exclamation points to spaces otherwise functional and "undecorated."

In addition, there are furniture-like fixtures that can easily blend with residential store design. Iconic panels with embossed designs routed into surfaces, wall units as well as modular elements can be used to span an entire wall or to highlight a part of it, serving as a visual break.

Wood is natural—it's real—and it fosters an aura of warmth and comfort. Wood can suggest the now popular Southwest look, with natural timbers accented against pastel-tinted stucco surfaces, or it can create the handsome, country-casual atmosphere of a Ralph Lauren Polo shop. Likewise, a West Elm shop is characterized by the use of weathered bespoke finishes on built-in fixtures and well-placed furnishings. When it comes to elegant designer settings, it's the smooth, rubbed wax sheen on wood moldings and floors that reinforces the designer's message.

Some specialty retailers will continue to opt for a rustic or log cabin look because of the customers they appeal to and the merchandise they sell.

Just as homes are furnished, not fixtured, actual furniture is being used more and more as permanent fixtures in department stores' shops within shops and specialty stores. Large pieces of furniture such as cupboards, hutches, tables, and chests are juxtaposed with fixtures to create homelike vignettes.

At one time, the most popular fixture stationed off a main aisle in a large store was a gleaming chrome T-stand. Today, it's more likely that shoppers are greeted by nesting tables—albeit ones that are longer and taller than those found in one's home—displaying folded and stacked merchandise. These fixtures, more often than not, are made of solid wood and are finished like actual furniture, making them appear more substantial, less mass-produced, and less high-tech. Rounding out the setting might be a pair of chairs, not there for the weary shopper, but artfully draped with featured garments.

Wood's natural timelessness says home, hearth, and security. Humanizing the store through the use of wood in construction, finishing, or furnishings provides the means for achieving a warm and inviting ambiance. (See Figures 14.29 and 14.30.)

FIGURE 14.29   In keeping with the Sundance theme of natural and nature, the designers at JGA made effective use of wood and other "natural" materials in furnishing the new store. The hand hewn timber and reclaimed and "found" objects offer a feeling of warmth as well as a real sense of the rugged outdoors, which is, in a way, the individual spirit and soul of Robert Redford's Sundance concept. *Sundance, Edina, Minnesota. Photograph: Troy Thies Photography.*

FIGURE 14.30 Old and new complement each other in the use of reclaimed lumber and antique chair to set the stage for the newest in fashionable footwear. The company's theme of "Tradition & Modernity" is also apparent in the reuse of materials throughout the store's design. The old, weather-textured timber creates a decorative background for the wall system as well as a pedestal for the elegant black lacquered chair that serves as a riser for the featured shoe. *Garhammer, Waldenkirchen/Stuttgart, Germany. Designed by Blocher Partners.*

Today's Fixtures

The design and look of today's fixtures are different from what they were just a few years ago. Everything moves! Retail is all about change—*fashion* is about change—and the retail setting must be able to change. It should be possible to alter the look and layout to complement what is going on with the merchandise.

In the spring a store may feature swimwear, whereas in the fall that same store does a large part of its business in sweaters. Retailers do not always have the luxury of having specialized fixtures, stored somewhere in the back, to pull out as needed. Fixtures must be versatile and adaptable, and with various attachments and add-ons it is possible to switch from swimwear to sweaters with just a few turns of an Allen wrench. Also, a store's fixture layout needs to be changeable, which means fixtures should be moveable. Many new fixtures, including tables, counters, and cabinets, come equipped with wheels or casters. Sometimes, these are oversized and are a definitive part of the design. With brake pedals on the wheels, they can be securely anchored to a spot and then moved when desired.

Interactive Fixtures

Interactive fixtures let shoppers participate in the store's action. The shopper is actually touching, tasting, pressing, and pulling—physically moving or manipulating a fixture or something on it. Digital touch screens invite us to look, listen, and learn—or browse the web. An interactive dressing room allows shoppers to change the lighting, share their choices on social media with friends, or request that the store associate bring them another size. Whether it is swinging a golf club on a mini-green or just using a touch screen to bring up alternate selections, these are part of today's shopping experiences and the reason why fixtures need to be more hands-on and accessible.

The **interactive fixture** invites shoppers to be involved with the product. It can be an electronic device that shoppers can experiment with or the ability to design their own custom sneakers. *Interaction* means an action between the shopper, and the store environment to create an experience. Thus, whether it is trying, tasting, or even just "playing" with a new product, or browsing the web for additional colors and sizes available or other options, that is interacting. The fixtures may be no more than a touch screen contained in a unique cabinet, or on a stand or table, whatever or wherever—it is the future, and it is now! (See Figure 14.31.)

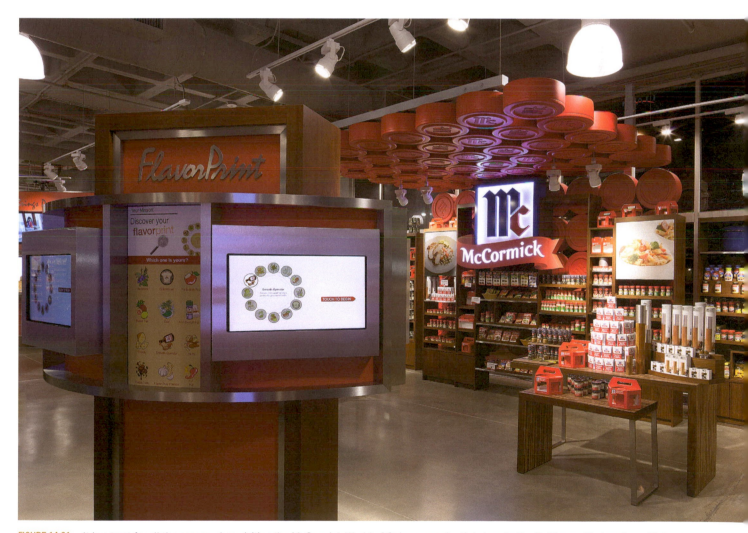

FIGURE 14.31   It is a treat for all the senses when visiting the McCormick World of Spices experiential shop in the Baltimore Harborplace. Fixtures abound that beg to be tried and tested. Tastes are tested, smells are questioned, and answers are provided. It is all fun and games with hidden nuggets of information always provided. Giant screens show oversized images so groups can enjoy the experiments and the experiences. *McCormick World of Spices designed by JGA. Photograph: Laszlo Regos Photography.*

Go Green 14.1: Reused and Reclaimed Fixtures and Furniture

This is where reused, repurposed, and reclaimed all come together. This is an open invitation to take fixtures or furniture or other things that have outlived their first time around and give them a chance at a new existence. It can all be possible with imagination and a can of low-VOC paint or some wallpaper or fabric—and, of course, low-VOC adhesives. Not only is it economical to refinish and refurbish a tired armoire into a focal element in a shop or to turn an old, beat-up and nonworking refrigerator into a curio cabinet for small fashion accessories, but it is gratifying as well. These reused and reclaimed items add new interest and a unique quality to the retail setting. Recycled lumber makes wood fixtures look different and special. Worn-out and leaky plumbing pipes and joints can be combined to create simple yet cutting-edge fixtures. Look for objects that nobody seems to want anymore, and with effort, imagination, and lots of "sweat equity," a really great focal or feature fixture may evolve. And it will be one of a kind! Your local Anthropologie store is a great destination to begin your research.

Fixtures: Trade Talk

bins	gondola	round rack
brass	half-circle rack	S-rack
bronze	hanger top	semicircular rack
chrome	interactive fixture	showcase
copper	kiosk	spiral costumer
costumer	mirror	stand
C-rack	mirror chrome	three-part rack
elevations	nickel-plated	trays
end caps	outpost	T-stand
étagère	painted finishes	valet
fixtures	pipe rack	vitrine
floor fixtures	polished chrome	waterfalled
freestanding fixtures	quad rack, or four-way face-out	wood fixtures

Fixtures: A Recap

+ The major functions of store fixtures are to accept, hold, stock, and show merchandise.

+ Basic fixtures used in window displays include stands; platforms and elevators; costumers, drapers, and valets; and pipe racks.

+ Common materials used in the manufacture of basic fixtures are metal and plastic.

+ A stand comes with an assortment of tops that may be slipped interchangeably into an adjustable rod set on a weighted base. The base sits securely on a floor, platform, counter, or ledge, and the rod may be adjusted to the desired height for presentation of merchandise.

- The valet, although similar to the costumer, has a heavier and wider hanger and a slacks bar, which makes it especially useful for men's wear.

- The draper is also a hanger on a stand, adjustable in height, but without a shirt or slacks bar. It is usually smaller than the costumer and the valet and is meant to be used on a counter or buildup.

- Counter fixtures are important because they are at points of purchase, and this is where a customer can be influenced to buy. The counter fixture is also small and does not interfere with the give-and-take between the customer and the salesperson. However, a counter fixture much higher than the salesperson's eye level is an invitation to shoplifters to take items without being seen.

- Fixtures with enclosed glass cases protect or lock in the merchandise.

- The major types of floor fixtures include the counter or showcase, round rack, T-stand, and quad rack or four-way face-out.

- A round rack consists of a circular hang-rod, 3 feet in diameter, raised anywhere from 45 inches to more than 6 feet above the ground, set on an adjustable upright and securely attached to a weighted base.

- A three-part rack is a round rack composed of separate but equal arcs. The height of each arc is usually adjustable individually.

- A C-rack is basically one-half of a round rack. A pair of C-racks can be combined to form a two-part round rack that can be set at different heights.

- Criteria for selecting a fixture include appearance, construction, end use, upkeep, and finish.

- Finishes available for fixtures include chrome, nickel plate, brass, copper, bronze, paint, and wood.

- Interactive fixtures that invite shoppers to be involved with the product are a part of the increasingly hands-on experience that shopping has become.

Questions for Review and Discussion

1. Explain the correlation of fixturing to interior design, with fixtures being the furniture for the store.

2. List the types of top elements available for stand fixtures. Explain the use for each type.

3. Give three examples of how interactive fixtures can engage a consumer.

4. What is a counter fixture? Why is proper height so vital in the selection of counter fixtures?

5. List fixtures suitable for use on ledges. Explain how each could be used in a merchandise presentation.

6. How do the showcases of today differ from those of the past?

7. Describe the use of each of the following floor fixtures, then identify its advantages and disadvantages:
   a. round rack
   b. T-stand
   c. quad rack
   d. gondola

8. List and explain the criteria visual merchandisers should use for selecting fixtures.

9. Discuss the strengths and weaknesses of the various fixture finishes mentioned in the chapter. Which is currently the most popular type of fixture finish? Why?

10. Why are wooden fixtures gaining popularity?

Chapter Fifteen
Visual Merchandising and Dressing Fixtures

White House/Black Market, Yorkdale, Toronto, Ontario, Canada.
Designed by Victor Johnson, Visual Merchandising Director.
Photography: Jeffrey Totaro.

AFTER YOU HAVE READ THIS CHAPTER, YOU WILL BE ABLE TO DISCUSS

+ seven objectives of visual merchandising
+ six factors that can be used to provide a dominant emphasis in visual display
+ techniques for stocking merchandise that reflect the dominance factor
+ seven benefits of visual merchandising for the retailer
+ the various ways in which clothing may be dressed on T-stands, stock holders, front-to-back racks, and hang-rods

Visual Merchandising

Visual merchandising takes place where the shopper and the product come together in a real, hands-on situation: It is the presentation of the stock on the selling floor. Visual merchandising is not quite a science, nor is it solely an art. Although it is possible to draw up plans, draft diagrams, make schedules, and turn the merchandising techniques into a series of graphs and charts, visual merchandising is more than these elements. It takes a feeling for color and mass, for adapting volume to space, for arrangement and balance. It takes everything that goes into making a good composition. Taste and talent are required if the result is to be more than just neatly stacked shelves. It takes a sense of knowing when to be daring, when to be different, and when to surprise if the presentation is to be different from the competition's look—especially if they are following the same "graphs and charts."

To produce good visual merchandising, the visual merchandiser must understand what good visual merchandising is and must know both the product and the shopper to whom the retailer hopes to appeal. Often a store's visual merchandising is only as good as the fixtures and fittings the visual merchandiser has to use. Good visual merchandising produces a neat, easy-to-see, easy-to-follow, easy-to-shop sales floor. It involves arranging merchandise in a manner that will not only make fashion sense to the shopper but also help the shopper buy quickly, efficiently, and comfortably—and, hopefully, more than he or she planned to. Simply stated, visual merchandising seeks to achieve the following objectives:

- To inspire and engage the shopper with a strong merchandising story.
- To make it easier for the shopper to locate the desired merchandise.
- To make it easier for the shopper to self-select.
- To make it possible for the shopper to coordinate and accessorize on his or her own.
- To provide information on sizes, colors, prices, and such.
- To take the stress out of shopping.
- To save the shopper time.

- To make the shopping experience more comfortable, convenient, and customer friendly.

CUSTOMER-ORIENTED VISUAL MERCHANDISING

Visual merchandising works best when it is customer oriented! One can only sell when one knows to whom one is selling and when the merchandise is explained clearly and visually to that targeted market. The product must be shown in a way that makes it relate to that shopper's needs, preferences, and aspirations—his or her lifestyle and fashion attitude. Only then are the wares being properly marketed.

Make the shopping experience an adventure! Provide the shopper with a sense of discovery and not one of confusion or frustration. Visual merchandising is effective when it brings together the shopper and the product in a comfortable and convenient manner that also contains an element of surprise or wonderment—a uniqueness that may startle or delight the shopper with its novelty. It is even better when the visual merchandiser can include the coordinates, the alternatives, and the accessories in the same space or setting. The number of items that can actually be seen, studied, and appreciated is often more important than the actual number of items stocked on the sales floor. Several dozen folded and stacked shirts arranged in rising tiers of shelves will read as so many ribbons of a color to the shopper's eye. The number of garments that stretch across a wall in a shoulder-out lineup are just so many slivers of sleeves. A single garment brought forward on a draper/hanger or form, given depth and dimension, well lit, and maybe even accessorized, can do more to sell the product than the staggering piles and endless sleeves that surround it. Sometimes, depending on the store's image, seeing too many of the same product or garment can actually devalue the item or make it less attractive, especially when the merchandise is upscaled, expensive, or designer labeled. Volume may be fine for popular-priced stores and for promotional events, but too many of the same item can be a disaster for some fashion images.

When preparing a visual merchandising layout, it is desirable that the visual merchandiser give emphasis to some special aspect of the product. It can be the color, the coordinates, the brand name, the size, the price, or the end use. This emphasis is the **dominance factor**.

DOMINANCE BY COLOR

Color dominance is the simplest, the most direct, and usually the most effective way to present products visually. People see *color*! People buy *color*! *Color is what sells*! Effective visual merchandising means, first and foremost, folding, stacking, and hanging products by color. Color takes precedence over style and size. Thus, in a display of variously colored items, all the red items are shown in a cluster or group. Within that cluster, items are arranged by size or style, or both—for example, all the red-colored "smalls" are grouped together followed by the red "mediums" and the red "larges." If red short-sleeved shirts as well as red long-sleeved shirts are to be displayed, line up all the short-sleeved red shirts by size—from small to extra-large—and then repeat the procedure with the long-sleeved garments. In this way, the shopper can immediately locate the color he or she wants, can then differentiate between the styles, and, finally, can find the desired size within the presentation. When stacking folded garments, arrange them from small to large, usually with the larger sizes on the bottom and the smaller on top. Because smaller garments seem to be more attractive in proportion, they are usually placed at eye level or just above eye level. However, logically, the people who wear the smaller sizes are often too short to reach up comfortably for their selections. If the signage clearly identifies which size is on which shelf, then it doesn't really matter if the small goes on top or on the bottom.

If separates are being shown, and there are skirts and pants that go with the red shirts in the previous example, the logical and customer-friendly way to show them is the same. Arrange the red skirts together—from the smallest to the largest sizes—followed by the red pants in the same size order. If the garments are hung on the wall, use two hang-rods. Show the shirts on the upper rod and the coordinated skirts and pants below on the lower rod. The more orderly the arrangement of merchandise on the wall, the easier it is for the shopper to see the whole range of products and then focus on what he or she really is interested in.

When stocking and presenting by color, the visual merchandiser can show a single color either horizontally—on a **hang-rod** or on a long shelf—or vertically, on boxes, cubes, or a series of descending shelves. When there is a range of colors to promote, try to follow the color wheel—or the spectrum of colors—by showing colors with their traditional neighboring colors. This provides a natural and gentle progression from white, to cream, to beige to yellow, orange, red, and so on. Within each color, items would thus progress from the palest tint to the deepest shade; for example, in the orange family, colors would move from the pastel peaches to the dominant oranges to the subdued and subtle terra-cotta and deep earth tones. In the red family, items would be arranged from pink to red to dubonnet and maroon. The subtler the show of the total range of colors, the more upscale and sophisticated the fashion look.

For more popular and promotional effects (e.g., casual wear, sportswear, or trend apparel) the colors might be blocked—especially in the vertical arrangements—so that red is seen next to its complement, green. By putting the clashing colors together, the reds appear redder, and the greens are greener; the sharp contrast also creates an animated pattern on the wall or fixture. Yellow complements violet, orange is the complement of blue, and, of course, black and white are the perfect contrasts. The use of conflicting colors next to one another will make a stronger, more exciting and colorful visual merchandising story—so use it only when that is what you really want. When colors may clash, and a tamer effect is desired, place neutrals between the fighting colors.

For certain seasons or holidays, consider altering the color arrangement on the floor so that the overall ambiance is more festive or more in keeping with an overall color scheme. If the merchandise is mainly white, gray, and black, perhaps intersperse some red garments to enliven the space and also tie in this area with the rest of the color-filled floor. By using accents and accessories, the visual merchandiser can add sparkle to what would otherwise be an uninteresting space. (See Figure 15.1.)

DOMINANCE BY COORDINATION

Merchandise can also be presented with the emphasis on **coordination**. In any visual program it is always effective to coordinate merchandise. The shopper sees how pieces can be matched or mixed—coordinated to go together to create

FIGURE 15.1 When red is the team color and this shop is entirely devoted to promoting and selling team-related merchandise, as expected the merchandise is mainly red. In addition, the walls are lined with assorted, coordinated products—in red. The interactive fixture in the foreground provides information on the team's history and achievements. *VFB Showroom designed by Blocher Blocher Shops, Stuttgart, Germany.*

a wardrobe of alternative outfits. In this case, instead of a single color being dominant, it can be a team or a group of colors or patterns or prints, plus solids that are organized for easy shopping.

Dominance by coordination can be achieved using a wall system on which garments are hung to show how the various pieces can be arranged or rearranged in a variety of ways. Rather than hanging all the garments in a long, continuous, eye-wearying row, the hang-rods can be staggered in height—set at different levels—and even interrupted occasionally to show off a fully accessorized, coordinated outfit.

A single quad rack, or four-way floor unit, can also carry the components of several different coordinated outfits. A single fixture can carry the pants, skirts, blouses, and jackets—dressed in a color-coordinated way (red/white/blue; yellow/black/black and yellow print on white; red/pink/green floral print plus solids in red, pink, or green). A combination of prints, patterns, or plaids can be presented with the solid-colored coordinates that were designed to go with the prints. When prints and patterns need to be separated for the overall look of the area—or to make it easier for the shopper to see what he or she is looking for—the solid garments should be used as "spacers," or separators, between the conflicting prints.

Whether the merchandise is presented on a wall unit or floor fixture, it is desirable that there be a **dressed leader** on the fixture. The dressed leader can be either the first face-out hanger on a four-way fixture or the first garment shown on a face-out or waterfall of a wall system. That first hanger can be the visual explanation of how the assorted parts come together and how the prints and solids can be combined to create a variety of looks. Skirts or pants can be attached to the bar of the hanger, and a shirt or blouse added, topped by the jacket. The coordinated outfit, depending on where it is located and what type of store it is in, may even be accessorized with a piece of costume jewelry, a handbag, or shoe.

(See Figure 15.2.) If a draper is set atop the floor fixture, it can carry the coordinated ensemble, and the display can be enhanced with folded alternatives and accessories like hats, bags, and shoes around it.

FIGURE 15.2 Assembled—face out—on the wall on a unique wall system of poles are coordinated parts of outfits for young women. Set between the face-out displays is a shoulder-out group of garments. Note the shoes, on the low shelf, that complete the leading outfit and the graphic above that shows some of the coordinates in use. *Springfield, Fuencarral, Spain. Design by Caulder Moore, London, United Kingdom.*

Dominance by coordination works with apparel, accessories and is easily adapted and applied to home furnishings and fashions, such as bed and bath linens and kitchen requisites. Bring the merchandise together by color or pattern with compatible solids and highlight the presentation with a display vignette showing all the pieces together. Even though the merchandise is coordinated, the display is still promoting color because color is what sells.

DOMINANCE BY BRAND NAME

All of us are aware of how important **brand names** and designer labels are in the competitive retail field. In the vendor shops or shop-in-shops (see Chapter 24) the manufacturer often provides not only the fixtures and promotional graphics but also the visual merchandising and display directives as well. Other stores may want to feature or merchandise products by brand name dominance—perhaps highlighting the company's own brands. The visual merchandiser may want to create a "boutique," or shop within a shop, in which such brand-name products are visually presented to help promote and sell the name, the product line, and the compatible accessories. (See Figures 15.3 and 15.4.)

FIGURE 15.3 Denim is not a brand, and most stores that carry denims carry them in a variety of manufacturers' brands. At the Eastlands David Jones store, as designed by Dalziel & Pow of London, the brands are indicated on the red-orange acylic panel that introduces and separates the denim area in the store. Note the lay-down up-front followed by the half forms and the carefully arranged cubicled back wall. *David Jones. Design by Dalziel & Pow, London, United Kingdom.*

FIGURE 15.4   In the autumn shop-in-shop in the Primark store on Oxford Street in London, the replication of the underground or subway sets the look and place for the shop and the garments. From the rods—that travelers grasp for dear life—hang the featured garments while the bags take up some of the seats below. The white abstract mannequin appears before the graffiti wall of the underground station with its familiar white ceramic tiled surfaces on the right. Note the band of graphic images—like subway ads—above the hang rod and over the graffiti. *Primark, Oxford Street, London, United Kingdom. Design by Dalziel & Pow.*

DOMINANCE BY SIZE

In some stores, especially specialty stores, **size** is the determining factor when a purchase is planned. This is particularly so in the larger-size women's wear, the "big and tall" men's shops, and, of course, in children's clothing stores. Here, size can be dominant in the visual merchandising program. But it can be more difficult to create a harmonious and easy-to-shop space out of what can look like visual chaos. One effective technique is to use—as previously outlined—solid- or almost-solid-colored garments as separators. If, for example, the merchandise consists of printed or patterned dresses—whether they are sizes 14W to 22W or children's sizes 3 to 6X—arrange the garments first by size, with the smallest sizes up front. Then—within the same size group—arrange the garments by color, using the dominant color or color family in the print as the criterion. A red/pink floral print on a white background accented with assorted greens would be placed in a red or pink cluster, and then, wherever possible, red, pink, or white dresses would be used to separate this floral from—let us say—a red/pink-and-green plaid dress. The solid or almost-solid colored garments allow the shopper's eye to rest before attacking or being assaulted by the next pattern or print. Here, as in color dominance, the dresses should be grouped from lightest to darkest within a single size and, whenever possible, the color clusters should follow the spectrum of colors.

DOMINANCE BY PRICE

If this translates into inexpensive, bargain, or sale merchandise, with the discounted or slashed **price** first and foremost, then maybe this is the time to turn the area into a "bazaar," or open marketplace. Let the volume of the product and the savings be dominant, and support the concept with banners, awnings, kiosks, and colorfully skirted tables that support the load of merchandise "tossed" upon it. Make it a treasure hunt in which bargain hunters can rummage through the merchandise in hopes of finding a noted designer's label or famous brand name somewhere in the midst of the visual mayhem. In an upscale shop this technique will only work on rare occasion and for very special promotions. If you do it, do it with flair—with fun and imagination—and with the customer's sense of taste always in the forefront.

DOMINANCE BY END USE

This kind of merchandising is very much like dominance by coordination, but here the term is mainly applied to white goods and hard goods. Just as the merchandiser may group fashion separates and apparel together with accessories for multiple sales, so may the visual merchandiser or merchant show and stock items that go together or complement each other, but that are not clothing items.

Sheets, pillowcases, throw cushions, quilts, blankets, duvets, floor mats, and even bed trays could be shown in color- or pattern-coordinated clusters, because their **end use** will be in the bedroom. Assorted towels, shower curtains, mats, scales, cups, toothbrush holders, tissue boxes, and soaps will eventually have their end use in the bathroom; thus, they could logically be shown arranged by colors or patterns that go together. The basic concept is simple: If the products will end up being used together or will appear near each other, then it is effective merchandising to show how they fit together. The concept of end use dominance explains why it is usual to show table settings of china, glassware, tablecloths, place mats, napkins and napkin rings, serving pieces, and even cutlery, and then stock those items together to make it simpler for the shopper to purchase what he or she sees, knowing that they all are coordinated. (See Figure 15.5.)

Front-to-Back Visual Merchandising

No matter what the dominance factor, when creating a visual merchandising pattern in any area of the store, it is best to show the stock in a **front-to-back display**, from the main aisle to the rear wall of the space. A few of the garments or products should be featured up front, facing the main traffic aisle on a table, an aisle liner, a T-stand, or even a mannequin or a mannequin alternative. This is where the item is "introduced," and it should be coordinated, accessorized, and well illuminated. If a mannequin or form is used, the outfit should be presented as a totality, and alternatives or coordinates should be shown close by on T-stands or as lay-downs on a table or any other light-looking piece of furniture.

As the shopper steps into the area—past the introduction—the garments or products should be displayed in a range of sizes and colors on floor fixtures that

FIGURE 15.5 Putting it all together for add-on sales: products that go together—that complement or enhance each other—can and should be shown together. At Karaka, the Turkish home fashion store, products for the bed and bath are collected on the back wall while the bed features the bed linens and the chest, up front, introduces more choices that "go with." The color palette is determined by the bed linens. *Ayse Demirtepe, Director of Visual Display, Karaka.*

are not too densely or heavily merchandised. Here, the total concept of coordination and the mix and matchability of the items can be shown. The lighting doesn't need to accentuate the items as strongly as on the aisle display, nor should it be as bright as that on the rear wall, which is usually heavily stocked. This is where the dominance factor is most important. The well-lit rear wall brings the shoppers into the area or department, and it is where the final selection of what will go with what is made.

At the start of a season, when there is the most stock in the store, merchandise may be shown shoulder out or side out, with some face-out garments featured to show what the garment looks like and also to break up the run of sleeves or sides. As the stock starts to dwindle, a good visual

FIGURE 15.6 At Rich & Royal, designed by Blocher Blocher Shops of Stuttgart, the shallow area starts at the aisle with a metallic cube with a lay-down of product, followed by a feature table where a selection of accessories are presented. The rear wall consists of coordinated garments hung shoulder out and topped, in recessed shadow boxes, with alternate pieces neatly folded and stacked. Other garments that go with those featured here are shown on the rack on the left. *Design by Blocher Blocher Shops of Stuttgart, Germany.*

merchandiser—before completely compressing the space—will display more face-out merchandise, using waterfalls, and fewer shoulder-out garments on the rear wall. It takes fewer garments to fill the space—and it makes the area look as though the stock is still viable and in style. The shop doesn't look empty, and the stock doesn't look like "leftovers." (See Figure 15.6.)

Visual Presentation

Visual merchandising is the orderly, systematic, logical, and intelligent placement of stock on the sales floor. So, if the visual merchandiser can logically chart what to do and what not to do—how to organize the perimeter walls, arrange the floor fixtures and dress them, stock the tables and aisle liners—where is the difference? How can Brand X products be shown in a way that appears more fashionable, enticing, and desirable than the same Brand X products being shown down the street in a competitor's store? How does one store get that special look, that unique fashion image, that one-of-a-kind ambiance that the shopper remembers and returns to? Where is the difference—and how is it created?

Display is the difference! Display is the imaginative, the unexpected, the fun and the flash, the panache that turns good visual merchandising into exciting and stimulating **visual presentation**. We are more than showing—we are presenting! We are adding color as well as lights that flatter and highlight and that bring the shopper back into the space. These are the lights that bring the shopper off of the aisle and closer to the actual merchandise assortment.

Visual merchandising goes beyond putting out stacks of product when we add display. We animate the stock—we activate it. We add form and figures, depth and dimension, and, sometimes, atmospheric lifestyle decor. We add a personality, a fashion image, a lifestyle feeling, and wish fulfillment. We humanize the product and breathe life and excitement into it. The accessories, like the props we use, can be unusual and unexpected or subtly elegant and understated. The color combinations can be outrageous and avant-garde or stylish and classic. It is how we present and display the product that makes the difference. Here, there are no rules, no charts, no guidelines. Here, the visual merchandiser relies on knowledge of the brand, customer's tastes, lifestyles, and attitudes as well as the store's fashion image. What can be on target for one store in one particular location may be all wrong for the same store in a different location, with a

FIGURE 15.7   The rear and focal wall of this teen-tween shop has been divided into "show-and-sell" shadow boxes. Some contain stock, some are filled with draped garments, and one large cube has been reserved as an in-store display case for a pair of dressed abstract mannequins. The reflective mirrored ceiling in front of this focal wall plays back the action on that wall as well as that of the realistic young male mannequins sitting about on the billiard tables, which add to the atmosphere and also serve as laydown tabletops. *New Look, Liverpool, United Kingdom. Design: Caulder Moore.*

different market makeup, even though both stores are selling the exact same items. There must always be some criteria for **taste**: what is right for the store, for the product, for the customer, and for the location. (See Figure 15.7.)

Visual Merchandising and the Retailer

We have discussed what visual merchandising can do for the shopper, but how does it benefit the retailer? Why should the retailer invest in the talents of a visual merchandiser, buy special fixtures, pay for additional lighting, and perhaps even keep some of the stock off the sales floor? Visual merchandising can benefit the retailer in the following ways:

1. By increasing sales, especially in add-ons.
2. By promoting operational efficiency in the store.
3. By motivating and activating the sales force and making it easier for them to satisfy the customer's needs in the least amount of time.

4. By saving both the salesperson's and the shopper's time.
5. By making the salesperson more effective and more efficient.
6. By providing a "silent salesperson" that can give shoppers all sorts of information and suggest ways in which the product can be worn or used until the salesperson is available.
7. By simplifying the inventory process.

Dressing Fixtures

Stores and even departments in the same store may vary in format and image, but there are certain methods that are generally followed for dressing fixtures with the merchandise they are to hold and display. Some stores will display their merchandise by size and in that size arrangement will show a variety of styles, patterns, and colors. Other stores or departments will show by color or by pattern and style. In the latter situations it is simpler to get a good, sharp merchandise presentation as well as a pleasant, overall ambiance in the selling space. It is not quite as simple when the merchandise is varied and multicolored, multi-patterned, long and short, and in between.

T-STANDS

The **T-stand** is an aisle facer. It is a feature presentation unit that should be trimmed lightly and emphasize a look, a color, or a special style. It is even more effective if it is located near a mannequin on which the garment is shown dimensionally. If there are spacers on the arms, only one hanger per hook should be used, and all the hangers should be the same.

Whether the T-stand has a simple, straight arm at the top or an angled waterfall, the garment that faces out toward the approaching shopper should be dressed; this lead garment should be completely trimmed. If the T-stand is showing navy suits, and the skirt is clipped onto the jacket hanger, a coordinating blouse should be shown under the jacket of the first suit. There could be a scarf tied on, a piece of costume jewelry, and maybe even a shoulder bag added. The first garment can almost be treated as if it were a costumer, and a special hanger might be used on the lead garment to allow more of the skirt (or pants) to show below the jacket. Some T-stands are fashioned with a draper or dress form as part of the unit.

If this navy suit is also available in gray and red, then all three colors might be shown on the single T-stand—the lead garment making the most effective statement for the design as well as the area. The red garment might have the most attention-getting color, but if navy is the color being presented in this area, the front outfit should be navy, followed by the gray, with the red garment bringing up the rear. If a descending waterfall arm is used on the T-stand, the lower garments should be navy, followed by gray, and ending with the red on top. The navy garment would get the full, front-dressed treatment.

If blouses or sportswear—all of the same design, but in assorted colors—were to be shown on a T-stand with a waterfall, the usual technique would be to follow the spectrum of colors and go from the neutral off-whites to cream and ivory to beige-tan and brown into the warm colors—yellow, gold, orange, peach, rust, pink, red, cerise, lavender, and violet—and then into the cool colors, ending up with blues, greens, grays, and black.

Now, that is a lot of color for a little T-stand to hold, so limit the amount of merchandise and the colors on each T-stand, but follow the basic scheme. Again, if the area is featuring a lot of red, the lead garment should be red; then go on to the red-violets, into the violets, blues, greens; then yellow, orange, and so forth. It is a logical use of the rainbow or spectrum of colors—adapted to the promotion. People think of and see colors in that pattern and, as mentioned in Chapter 2, the analogous color scheme is an easy one to live with; neighboring colors coexist and lend each other character and color.

A final reminder: merchandise on T-stands should be changed frequently; there should always be a new "show."

STOCK HOLDERS

Stock holders are "bread-and-butter" fixtures, the workhorses that actually hold the selling stock. They may display—and they should display—but primarily they are "stockers." Two examples are the quad rack and the round rack.

Almost all stock holders are used in the following manner: Merchandise is hung from left to right—the way most people read or scan—from the lightest colors to the deepest, from the warmest to the coolest, from the smallest sizes to the largest. Color is the big "come-on," the single most important attention getter. When a variety of styles are shown, the assorted styles are grouped by color. If there are six styles of blouses available in red, then style A, in red, will be hung from the smallest to the largest size available; followed by style B (also in red), sized from smallest to largest; and so on, until all six styles are shown in red. The procedure will begin anew with the next color available that follows red; a red-violet, a lavender, a purple, or whatever. Remember, this is not a rule! This is a technique that works in stores involved with mass merchandising and with a popular appeal. It works where there is a great deal of merchandise to get out on the selling floor and a minimum of sales help to fetch, carry, and answer questions.

QUAD RACKS

The quad rack, or four-way face-out fixture, is usually placed just past the T-stand, in the front of the selling area. Though the quad rack is a "mass merchandiser"—when and where the merchandise and stock permit—it is used to show coordinates or special promotional merchandise. The design of the quad rack allows four frontal views of the displayed garments. From whatever angle the customer approaches, one arm should basically be facing in that direction. (See Chapter 14, Figure 14.20.)

The main idea of showing coordinates on the single fixture, with each arm holding another component of the outfit, is that from this single fixture a customer can put together a complete ensemble of three or four parts. All the parts that are displayed go together and are grouped by color and by size, and unless a particular piece is not available on the rack in the customer's size, the customer can make his or her selection and bring it to the cash/wrap desk without any sales assistance. Again, the lead garment—a jacket, for example—could be "dressed" with all the component parts of the outfit.

A draper set in the middle of the quad rack and elevated over the stocked arm could also effectively display the total look. The use of some elevated points in a merchandise presentation is good, when they attract attention and help lead the viewer from area to area. However, a landscape of peaks, with hardly a "valley" in view can be quite demanding—and deadly—as a selling ambiance. The use of too many high points means nothing is really highlighted. It can also cause an obstructed view of the back of the selling space.

ROUND RACKS

Round racks are the real, no-nonsense, all-shoulder-out, mass-merchandising fixtures. (See Chapter 14, Figure 14.17.) When the quantity of stock decreases, the merchandise can be consolidated, and some of these fixtures can be removed from the central area. It is better to have fewer fully stocked fixtures than many partially filled ones. Psychologically, when the fixtures are sparsely stocked, it looks as though what remains are "leftovers" and, therefore, less desirable or saleable.

Although round racks may be used for sale merchandise or clearance items as much as possible, the following setup is probably best for the customer's convenience and comprehension and for the general look of the area. When a single "rounder" carries assorted coordinates, they can be presented in the following order: pants, being the longest, are first, followed by skirts. Next come long-sleeved jackets, then short-sleeved jackets, and vests. Sweaters, solid-colored blouses, and printed blouses finish the round rack and, thus, bring the viewer and the merchandise full circle.

It goes from long to short, from solid to print, and from the smallest to the largest. If a single classification of merchandise is being shown, color again is uppermost: warm, to cool, to neutral. The strongest, most attention-getting, or most saleable color faces the front of the area or the store.

When color-coordinated groupings are arranged on the round rack, they go, within the single color, from the viewer's left to right: tops, jackets, vests, and bottoms (skirts, slacks). This is followed by another color grouping in the same order. Between the two color groupings, print blouses that can be used with either of the color coordinates may be shown. For example, a red color-coordinated group followed by blouses printed in red, white, and blue on a gray ground may be followed by a coordinated group of gray merchandise. This, in turn, may be followed by more print blouses, this time, gray, white, and blue printed on a red ground. Either of the groups of blouses will work with the red ensemble or the gray one. This arrangement informs the customer that an extra gray skirt with the red-coordinated group will greatly increase the outfit's use and versatility. The trimmed rack is doing what a salesperson would ordinarily do: it is making suggestions and assisting the customer in putting together the right colors and parts.

Some round racks, called three-part racks, are made up of three equal arcs or segments. (See Chapter 14, Figure 14.24.) The height of each arc may be individually adjustable. These units can conveniently show three separate groups of color coordinates on a single unit. They can also show pants on one level (the highest), jackets on another, and shirts or vests on the third arc. Each arc should be treated by color—light to dark, warm to cool to neutral—and by size—small to large. The treatment all depends on the type of merchandise, the amount of stock, and the kind of department.

When the merchandise that is to be presented is small or short, it is possible to use a two- or three-tier rounder. If two levels of shorts are being shown, for example, the color range should still go from left to right, with the shorts grouped by color and by size within each color. But—and this is an emphatic "but"—the smaller sizes of a color should be hung on the top tier and the larger sizes of the same color should be hung directly below, on the bottom tier. This is called **vertical presentation**. Should the merchandise consist of separates, such as color-coordinated bras and panties, the mauve bras would be on top, and the matching mauve panties would be placed directly below—always from small size to large within a given color.

Sale merchandise is usually located between the aisle and the perimeter or back wall of a selling area. Advertised sale or promotional merchandise should be prominently located and properly signed for quick identification. Clearance merchandise is usually set further back in the area and signed. When the merchandise for clearance or sale consists of odd pieces and broken-size lots, it might be better merchandising to arrange the offerings by size rather than color. However, if color groupings can also be done, do it; it looks so much better.

BACK WALL

There is a psychology in the presentation and buildup of stock in an area of a shop or a department. The lowest fixtures are up front; the next area, or midsection, is next in fixture height; and the **back wall** is the highest merchandising area.

The basic idea is to make the back wall visible from the aisle or the front of the shop or area. The stocking of the back wall should not be minimized or disregarded. Store planners will wash the back walls with light or add perimeter lighting effects for emphasis. They will use light under the fascia for attention and attraction, even spotlighting some of the superwall (the area over the stocked merchandise).

The back wall is best used for coordinates, with top over bottom, or to create an impact for the classification of the merchandise contained within this area. The walls, whether they are used for hanging, shelving, binning, or a combination of these, are also treated in the light-to-dark, small-to-large, left-to-right manner of merchandising. Because the lowest hang-rods, shelves, or bins will not be visible from up front, a vertical presentation is used. Ordinarily, the lower part of the back wall is all but hidden by fixtures, sales help, and customers collected in front of it. The merchandise that is to be hung on the two levels of the vertical presentation will be shown red over red, yellow over yellow, and so on; the larger sizes on the bottom, smaller sizes on top; blouses on top, skirts and trousers on the bottom.

Ideally, the back wall should be broken into coordinated groupings or color patterns to stimulate, please the eye, and alleviate the curse of uniformity and boredom. Endless rows of sweaters or jackets hung at the same level or binned without a break tend to be boring. (See Figure 15.8.)

FIGURE 15.8 The various classifications of blue and white merchandise featured on the back wall makes a strong statement in both color and silhouette at Joe Fresh Fifth Avenue. The T-stand fixtures and aisle table offer coordinating merchandise selections that complement the back wall offerings. Mannequins create a perimeter by framing the area, while the green palm leaves add a lively pop of contrast. *Design by Burdifilek Toronto, Ontario, Canada. Photography by Ben Rahn A Frame Inc.*

By using slotted standards set into the wall, and the wide variety of brackets available to secure into the slotted uprights, the visual merchandiser can raise or lower hang-rods, occasionally setting in a waterfall or face-out rod to break up the all-shoulder look. Displays can be set up on a shelf or pinned directly onto the wall in order to explain the merchandise around and below the display. Even row after row of binning on the perimeter wall can be broken up by devoting one of the bins to a dimensional presentation of some of the merchandise that is neatly folded or bagged around it.

Sometimes, merchandise will be presented on the wall at a level that is too high to be reached comfortably by the customer. This top level may be reserved for the display of color-coordinated accessories that go with the merchandise below, or it may be used for reserve stock. These visual focal points, or displays, on the heavily stocked back wall area are absolutely necessary to stress the "new" and the "special" contained within and below.

GONDOLAS

When there are **gondolas** on the selling floor and they are shelved or binned (see Chapter 14, Figure 14.21), it is advisable to carry through the same aforementioned "color-size" procedure. A gondola, carrying a complete color and size range of women's socks, for example, could show a spectrum of the colors across the unit, while each color would be vertically presented according to length. The vertical lineup of a single color presented in a horizontal spectrum of color is effective. It is easy to look at, and more important, it is easy to shop.

Because the merchandise that is usually stocked on the gondola is either folded or bagged, display is desirable. A draper set on top of the gondola can be used or a displayer specifically designed for the type of merchandise (e.g., a towel displayer, a bust form for sweaters or blouses).

The visual merchandiser can also emphasize products on the endcap of the gondola. **Endcap displays** are especially effective when the gondolas are set perpendicular to the aisle; this is what the customer sees as he or she approaches the area. The endcap display can be merchandised to highlight product in a lifestyle or mini-environmental setting that shows towels, for example, with a pedestal sink and all sorts of decorative go-togethers displayed in a semi-realistic scene: a draped shower curtain

as a background, a wastepaper basket, a drinking glass and matching soap dish, a makeup mirror, and maybe, if space and material permit, a laundry hamper with more towels neatly tied and stacked on top. A softly draped towel will always "sell" better than a folded one, but it is the neatly folded one that the customer wants to take home.

AISLE TABLES

Aisle tables are **feature tables** or hot spots set in an aisle for impact selling. They may be an elegant antique table—maybe skirted and covered with a branded color cloth, or a variation of a fixture perhaps highlighted with a prop; they may even be beautifully arranged with a form and platforms or risers to form a cascading display. (See Figure 15.9.)

FIGURE 15.9 Beneath two stunning black chandeliers, a feature table in the aisle of Galeries Lafayette in Jarkarta, Indonesia, calls out to shoppers with a promotional offer for the fragrance Alien by Thierry Mugler. A floral arrangement adds height to the table, and the cascading orchids bring your eye down to the products. *Plajer & Franz Studio, United Kingdom. Design by Burdifilek Toronto, Ontario, Canada. Photography by Ben Rahn A Frame Inc.*

FIGURE 15.10 The Adidas wall fixture clearly illustrates several variations of hang-rods and face-outs. The first tier of fixturing uses shadow boxes to display footwear and caps. The two additional tiers show merchandise faced out and shoulder-hanging. The merchandising technique allows the shopper to entertain all of the coordinating merchandise. The pendant lights that come together in the form of a chandelier are glass basketballs. *Round-house, Portland, Oregon. Photographer: Matt Dutile.*

Occasionally, during a sale period, they may simply be **dump tables**, a term that sounds just about as awful as the end result may be. They can be arranged to form a **bargain square**, or an **economy square**, conveying the message of "come and get it," "what you see is what you get," "there isn't any more." The dump table may be piled with merchandise that is organized or jumbled and plopped down on the table. To the aesthete this is a very inferior display, one that certainly does not add to the store's image. But is it really so bad?

Many people, and that includes those with money, love a bargain. There is adventure, excitement, and a sense of discovery in shopping in bazaars, flea markets, and garage sales. Occasionally—and only occasionally—a dump table can be an effective merchandising device, but it takes a good and talented visual merchandiser to make it aesthetically pleasing, exciting, and an adventure in scavenging rather than a demeaning, rag-picking task. If the concept is used as a "special sale" technique and then "displayed," it will work and can even enhance the store's image.

Stores that pride themselves on their "better," or more expensive, images should tuck away the final clearance, or "as is," tables toward the rear of the department. In popular price and discount operations, however, they are expected right out in the open, in the middle of things.

Clothing on Hang-Rods

SHOULDER-OUT HANGING

The hang-rod should be about 12–15 inches away from the wall when **shoulder-out hanging**. Allow approximately 2 inches for the width per garment, 1 inch to either side of the hang-rod.

FACE-OUT HANGING

In **face-out hanging** the hang-rod should be 4 to 6 inches away from the wall. Add approximately 2 inches to the width of the garment, 1 inch to either side of the rod or waterfall.

Hang-rods are usually 3 to 4 feet long; longer rods (unsupported) may dip or optically sag. Heavier garments, such as leather and fur coats and jackets, are best hung on shorter, supported rods.

SINGLE-ROD HANGING

If using **single-rod hanging**, rods should be from 5 to 6 feet, 6 inches from the floor, depending upon the length of the garments being hung.

DOUBLE-ROD HANGING (ONE ROD OVER THE OTHER)

The top rod should be from 6 feet, 6 inches to 6 feet, 9 inches from the floor when **double-rod hanging**. The lower rod should be 42 inches from the floor. (See Figure 15.10.)

Visual Merchandising and Dressing Fixtures: Trade Talk

aisle tables

back wall

bargain square

brand names

coordination

dominance factor

double-rod hanging

dressed leader

dump tables

economy square

endcap displays

end use

face-out hanging

feature tables

front-to-back display

gondolas

hang-rod

price

shoulder-out hanging

single-rod hanging

size

stock holders

T-stand

taste

vertical presentation

visual presentation

Visual Merchandising and Dressing Fixtures: A Recap

+ Visual merchandising is the presentation of stock on the selling floor. It takes place where the shopper and the product come together in a real, hands-on situation.

+ To produce good visual merchandising, the visual merchandiser must know both the product and the shopper and be able to arrange the merchandise in a customer-friendly way that makes sense to the shopper.

+ Visual merchandising seeks to make it easier for the shopper to locate, self-select, and accessorize merchandise; to provide information on sizes, colors, prices, and such; to take the stress out of shopping; to save the shopper time; and to make the shopping experience more comfortable, convenient, and customer friendly.

+ When preparing a visual merchandising layout, it is desirable to give emphasis to some special aspect of the product—this is the dominance factor. Dominance may involve color, coordination, brand name, size, price, or end use.

+ In a display that emphasizes dominance by color, all of the same color items of a particular style should be presented together, grouped by size from smallest to largest. Then the next style should be presented.

+ In a display that emphasizes dominance by coordination, various items that can be mixed and matched to create an outfit are grouped together by color or pattern.

+ The best visual merchandising pattern is one that shows stock from the front to the back, from the main aisle to the rear wall.

+ Visual presentation is more than just an orderly, systematic, logical placement of stock on the floor—it is display: the imaginative use of atmospheric lighting, color, and arrangement that breathes life and excitement into the product.

+ Visual merchandising benefits retailers by increasing sales, especially add-ons; promoting efficiency; motivating the sales force and making it easier to satisfy customers' needs; saving time (for salesperson and shopper); making salespeople more effective; providing a "silent salesperson" to give information about and suggest uses for the product; and simplifying the inventory process.

+ The T-stand is an aisle-facer that should be trimmed lightly to emphasize a look, a collection, or a specific style. The garment that faces outward toward the approaching shopper should be completely trimmed. If garments of different colors are to be shown on a waterfall, the spectrum technique should be used.

+ The primary types of stock holders are the quad rack and the round rack.

+ When using stock holders, merchandise is hung from left to right, from the lightest color to the deepest, from the warmest color to the coolest, from the smallest to the largest.

+ A quad rack is a four-way face-out fixture usually found just past the T-stand, in the front of the selling area. It allows four frontal views of the merchandise and is especially useful in displaying coordinated ensembles because each of the four arms can hold a component of the coordinated outfit.

+ When color-coordinated groupings are arranged on the round rack, they go within a single color, from the viewer's left to right: tops, jackets, vest, and bottoms. This is followed by another color grouping in the same order. Between the two groupings, print tops that may be used with either of the coordinates may be shown.

+ The back wall is best used for coordinates, with top over bottom, or to create an impact for the classification of the merchandise contained within the area. A vertical presentation is used.

+ A gondola should be merchandised using the color-size procedure and a spectrum technique. Because merchandise on a gondola is usually folded or bagged, display is desirable, either on top or using an end display.

+ Display tables are promotional and are set in an aisle for impact selling. They can bring attention to a particular item or can be used to indicate a sale or bargain merchandise.

+ Clothing on hang-rods can be displayed shoulder out or face out on either single-rod hangers or double-rod hangers.

Questions for Review and Discussion

1. List the seven objectives of visual merchandising.

2. How could a display of different-colored skirts and coordinating print tops be stocked to demonstrate dominance by coordination?

3. Identify seven benefits of visual merchandising for the retailer.

4. How, and with what types of merchandise, should a T-stand be dressed? Why should merchandise on T-stands be changed frequently?

5. Explain the procedure for merchandising stock holders. Why is this technique commonly used?

6. For what kind of apparel display is the quad rack best suited? Why?

7. What is vertical presentation? When is it most effectively used?

8. Where should advertised sale merchandise be displayed? Where is clearance sale merchandise best positioned?

9. Describe how you would merchandise the back wall with a coordinated group of misses' red, white, and blue summer sportswear. The group includes shorts, pants, T-shirts, tank tops, and jackets. What types of fixtures would you use on the wall? How would the merchandise be arranged with regard to color and size?

10. What type of table would you select to convey a prestigious image? Why? What type of table would you select to convey a bargain basement image? Why?

Chapter Sixteen
Modular Fixtures and Systems in Store Planning

Joe Fresh, Fifth Avenue, New York. *Design by Burdifilek Toronto, Ontario, Canada.*

**AFTER YOU HAVE READ THIS CHAPTER,
YOU WILL BE ABLE TO DISCUSS**

- ✦ the major types of modular fixtures and systems in store planning
- ✦ the advantages of modular fixtures in creating a store design for a chain-store retailer
- ✦ the benefits of display systems
- ✦ what items to consider when purchasing a display system

Use of Modular Fixtures

As you travel across the country and visit malls and shopping centers in the different cities, you discover that many store brands are designed with consistency. A Zara is always a Zara, an H&M is always an H&M, and Starbucks in a different city somehow looks just like the one back home. When a chain-store operation calls upon a store designer to create a retail setting that will be recognized anywhere—in any mall or on any fashion avenue—the first step is the creation of a prototype store. The prototype is the first constructed unit; once it has been customer tested, and any problems worked out, the design is ready for **rollout**. This means using the same design for all the retailer's stores, but adapting it to the new locations.

For the same look—the same fixtures, materials, graphics, and lighting—to be consistent despite retail spaces that may vary in height, in length, in width, and maybe even in shape, the store's design and everything in it are planned to be made in **modules**. The modular concept means the pieces will be adaptable, movable, and rearrangable—and also cheaper to produce. Because they have the same basic measurements, shapes, and details, it is simpler and less expensive to run off a number of units at the same time.

Think of a module as a building block. Let us imagine a module that is 2 feet wide by 2 feet tall by 2 feet deep. Using these 2-foot-square modules, we could place five cubes in a row to make a unit that is 10 feet wide by 2 feet tall by 2 feet deep. It is also possible to add blocks vertically. By stacking the cubes three high, the result is a "wall" that is now 10 feet wide by 6 feet tall by 2 feet deep.

Most designers and store planners prefer to use 7 feet as the usual height for wall cabinets or fixtures, though these elements can go higher. If the merchandise is placed more than 7 feet from the floor, it is almost impossible for most shoppers to reach up to get it comfortably. A very tall salesperson—or a salesperson and a ladder—is required to reach merchandise stacked from 7 feet to 12 feet off the ground. As for the width of the modules, the most popular sizes are 3 feet and 4 feet, though the fixture designer/store

designer may also add 18-inch and 24-inch modules to go with the 3-foot and 4-foot units. Two 18-inch modules will make up one 3-foot module, whereas two 24-inch units equal one 4-foot piece. So, within one module we have smaller modules that can be combined to make up the module.

If storage space is required, the designers may design a cabinet unit that is 3 feet wide by 30 inches tall by 24 inches deep. Placed on top of this storage unit can be another shelf/hang-rod unit that is also 3 feet wide but only 4½ feet tall and 15 inches or 18 inches deep. Together, they become a 3-foot by 7-foot module that can be mixed with other 3-foot by 7-foot modules. The 18-inch module can be used when there isn't enough room for a full 3-foot module. (See Figure 16.1.)

Modules are most frequently constructed of wood and are designed to be adaptable and convertible. The same frame will adapt to holding shelves or hang-rods, so depending on the merchandise mix, the time of the year, and the amount of stock at any time, the **modular fixtures** can be changed to show off what is available. In adapting the prototype design to a particular rollout location, the store designer or the company architect will fit in the 3-foot and 18-inch modules along the perimeter walls, using the smaller pieces to break up long runs of 3-foot modules.

Often, the floor units are also designed as modules. This is especially true for sales and display counters and cash wrap desks. There may be a single 6-foot module (twice the 3-foot module) plus 3-foot add-ons. There may also be 18-inch corner or end pieces. Depending on the available floor space, the store layout person may create a 6-foot or 9-foot counter with an 18-inch end piece at either end.

With graphics so very popular as a decorative and lifestyle form of display (see Chapter 18), many designs will include a 3-foot by 7-foot framed panel that holds a large image or a light box of the same size for color transparencies. In one rollout, the designer may use two photo frames, whereas in another, depending on the store's merchandising needs, the designer may use one graphic frame and one shelf module. It is also not unusual for changing rooms or dressing rooms to be designed to fit within the same

same look and image for the vendor shop—no matter how large or small—is to use modular fixtures and fittings. (See Figure 16.2.)

Use of Systems

A system can resemble a set of building blocks, a sophisticated Tinkertoy, a jungle gym, or a "Lincoln Log" construction, grown to life size or larger. It can be a collection of rods, rails, tubes, panels, or vertical and horizontal elements that are assembled by means of assorted joints, joiners, and connectors. It can be clips or slotted joiners that secure plastic panels or sheets of glass, wood, or composition board. Systems are manufactured in steel, aluminum, wood, and various plastics. They can be fragile, weblike constructions that are all but invisible, or they can also be heavy-duty scaffolding able to rise two or three stories and sustain a heavy load.

What most good and practical systems have in common is the ability to be easily assembled, disassembled, reassembled, and rearranged in new and different ways, in new and different places. A good system is stable, versatile, adaptable, and modular and is designed with many accessories that enhance the unit in the store, aesthetically and functionally.

A system can be used to make a displayer, a fixture, and a stockable and selling merchandiser. It can be assembled to create a complete wall of hang-rods, bins, shelves, and even dressing rooms. It may be designed to contain its own lighting and signing elements. With a system, the store planner/ visual merchandiser can start with the perimeter wall and erect a whole selling environment without once needing to nail or screw into the wall, bolt down into the floor, or suspend or reinforce from the ceiling. A system may supply the wall hanging or the on-floor stocking. It may serve as a feature unit or be devised as counters, tables, and cash wrap desks.

The most remarkable thing about using systems is the relative ease with which one can put them together and take them apart. It usually requires few tools; the ones

FIGURE 16.1 A modular system is one designed in sections or pieces that can be added to or subtracted from as needed. This Vitrashop wall system combines 4-foot wall panels with 2-foot panels, and they are connected by vertical slotted standards that hold the assorted hardware available for the system: hang-rods, shelf brackets, books, bins, and so on. In addition, the panels are finished with drilled holes so that hangers or forms can be pegged into them for merchandise display. *Courtesy of Vitrashop.*

module for efficiency and simplicity when implementing the rollout plans.

Vendor shops or shop-in-shops have become more and more important as boutiques within department and specialty stores. The designers of vendor shops work almost exclusively with modules, as the spaces allotted to the shops in these stores will vary. The space may or may not have a perimeter wall; it may be an island between two aisles. In addition, the merchandise mix may vary from one store to another. With so many variables, the only effective and economical approach to getting the

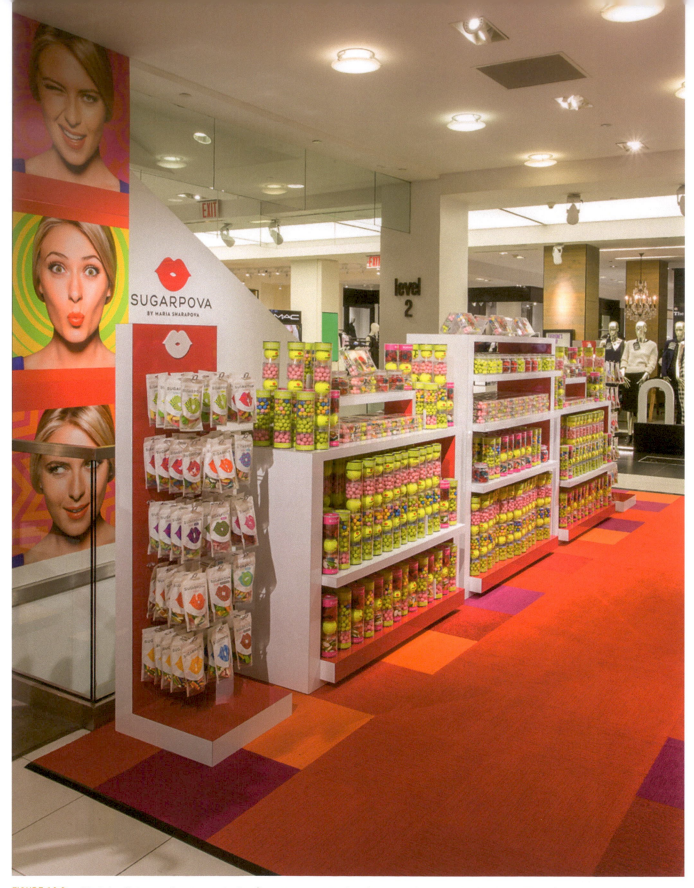

FIGURE 16.2   Modular fixtures align to create the Sugarpova sweet shop between the escalator banks at Bloomingdale's for Maria Sharapova's candy line. The white rectangular fixtures are stackable and have additional components to showcase the merchandise. The red interior adds a pop of color and coordinates with the carpet that defines the shop's perimeter. *Designed by RPG, New York, New York.*

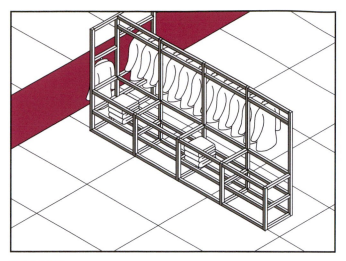

FIGURE 16.3   A modular system consists of same-size, interchangeable units or elements that can be combined to make up a specified modular size, for example, a 2-foot module made up of a single 2-foot unit or two 1-foot elements. Most important in a modular system are the strict adherence to the dimensions, the detailing of the connections and connectors, the availability of accessories, and the ability to rearrange parts visually and easily. *Illustration by Ron Carboni.*

most frequently used are a soft mallet (for pounding the finger joints into the tubes) and a regular or Phillips screwdriver. A few systems require an Allen or hex wrench. The visual merchandiser has to study the system, get to know what parts are available, and determine what the unit can do. We will outline in the text that follows some of the major categories of structural systems available today. (See Figure 16.3.)

Types of Systems

HOLLOW TUBES WITH FINGER FITTINGS

It is possible to obtain metal or plastic systems consisting of precut or standard lengths of hollow rods or tubes, round or square, and joiners or connectors that look like fingers. These **hollow tubes with finger fittings** fit into the open end of the tube and thus effectively "plug up" that end. At the same time, another finger in the same connector joint will fit into another tube. A two-pronged or -fingered joint can be used to form a right angle, or an L. Four equal lengths of tube joined by four **L-joints** will form a rectangle.

A T-shaped connector will join three pieces of tube in one plane. This will form what is essentially one long line with one line bisecting it. Another type of **T-joint** has two extensions at right angles to each other, and the third finger extends up or down. In effect, a corner can be turned with this joint and a continuation made with an open tube above or below. A cube could be constructed by combining twelve tubes with eight of these right-angle T-joints.

An **X-joint** brings together four lengths of pipe into a cross or X shape. Another four-pronged joiner forms a right angle and connects with rods above and below the angle. A five-fingered joint forms the X and has one finger open to connect above or below. A six-pronged joint forms the X and receives tubes or rods above and below it.

There are many variations on this type of system. Some use round tubes from ½ inch up to 2 or 3 inches in diameter. The sizes of the square tube systems are just as varied. (See Figures 16.4–16.6.)

CLAMPS

A vast collection of systems are available based on variations of a clamping device that holds or joins round rods

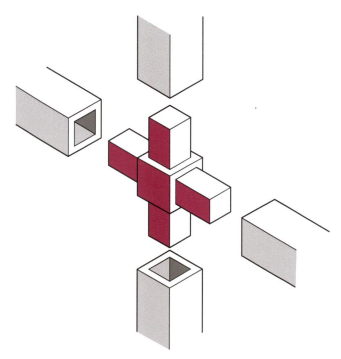

FIGURE 16.4   When the four hollow tubes slide over to join the four-fingered fitting, a cross, or X, is formed. *Illustration by Ron Carboni.*

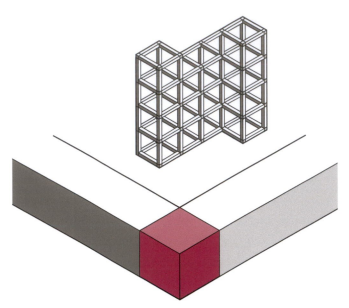

FIGURE 16.5　The system shown here uses square tubing of various lengths, with finger-projecting connectors of many configurations. It allows two to six tubes to connect at a single junction (see detail). *Illustration by Ron Carboni.*

or tubes. Often these **clamps** are hollowed-out spheres that come apart. They have shaped contours that will accommodate the proper size rod or tube. The rods are set into the proper "pocket" in the clamp and secured in place by means of setting a screw that closes the two or three parts of the come-apart clamp.

Other systems have clamps that are external units. Still other systems have vise-like clamps that work with sheets of plastic, glass, wood, or composition board. These joiners function like hinges and connect the panels at various angles so they can stand as walls, screens, or dividers. Some systems are available with colored tubes, but their painted surfaces are easily scuffed or scratched.

Some clamp systems are Opto System and Klem Panel Connector. (See Figures 16.7 and 16.8.)

EXTRUDED UPRIGHTS

Extruded uprights are a group of modular systems is based on vertical multifaceted and multi-slotted metal or plastic lengths into which horizontal elements, brackets, panels, or other structural elements are slipped and then secured. Some of these extruded metal (often aluminum) tubes are designed with four sides for assembling. Others have six sides, and still others have as many as

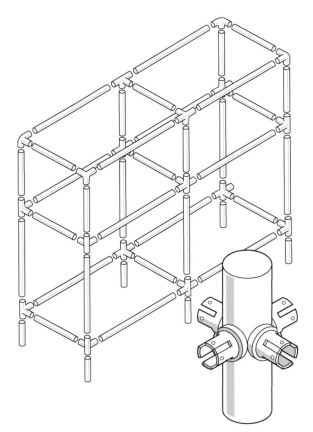

FIGURE 16.6　This system combines round metal tubes by means of fingered fittings (detailed in lower right). *Illustration by Ron Carboni.*

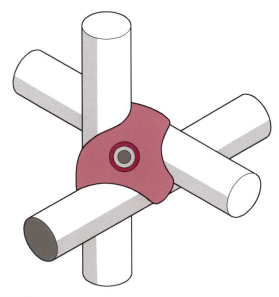

FIGURE 16.7　The Opto tube and clamp system. *Illustration by Ron Carboni.*

FIGURE 16.8 Opto's system can be used against a perimeter wall, or it can help create a freestanding partition or construct counters and floor fixtures. The assortments of parts and accessories makes it possible to create an entire shop of compatible elements all constructed out of the Opto system parts. *Courtesy of OPTO International.*

eight; with these, it is possible to form hexagonal or even octagonal structures. The store planner/visual merchandiser is not limited to right angle turns only. Again, the more accessories to be displayed, the greater the possibilities for variations in systems. ALU International, a leader is fixturing, has many varieties of extruded rail systems. This type of modular fixturing can be used for a variety of categories of merchandise such as grocery, beauty, apparel or home goods. The system is also used in museums and galleries to display photography and art. (See Figure 16.9.)

SLOTTED JOINERS

These are like Tinkertoys, only bigger, and are produced in an infinite variety of shapes, sizes, and materials. Basically, they are either cubes or spheres that are precision slotted or drilled with holes. Some **slotted joiners** are designed to accommodate sheets of glass, plastic, or composition board to form shelves, bins, or rectangular structures. Others work with rods and tubes to make skeletal frames.

There are many varieties available today because they are simple to use and even simpler to disassemble and store. Some of the most commonly used are from J. C. Moag and Sutton Design.

SLOTTED UPRIGHTS

Slotted uprights are not quite a system in the same way as those mentioned above, but they are certainly simple, adaptable building devices for fixturing and store planning. **Slotted uprights** are usually steel or aluminum squared tubes that are precision slotted on one, two, or four faces. The convenience and myriad uses of slotted upright standards that are secured onto walls and partitions have already been discussed in Chapter 15. These slotted uprights can be used with the finger joints to make self-standing units or can be secured at the floor and at the ceiling or spaced away from a wall or column by means of **outriggers** (horizontal members attached to a wall or column that serve to support and keep a horizontal or vertical element away from the bearing surface). The great variety of brackets and attachments that work with the slotted wall uprights will, in most cases, work on these square vertical poles.

Slotted upright standards are made by Garcy Stud, Kason Industries, and Crown Metal.

Selecting a System

There are other specialized systems on the market that cannot be put into one broad category or another. The visual merchandiser would be wise to review the manufacturer's catalog, which not only states what the system will do, but also will usually provide illustrations of the many

FIGURE 16.9 ALU's modular "Slider" system consists of a wall-mounted rail system and a variety of box configurations that attach and slide on the rails. The system accepts panels, shelves, and accessories that can convert the "wall" to suit any number of types of products or garments. The versatility of the system is evident used with Starbucks Coffee and Tazo Tea products. *Courtesy of ALU.*

components, attachments, and refinements. Some systems are produced in different diameters and assorted colors, and with accessories that might be available in some sizes, but not in others.

To use a system effectively, the visual merchandiser or store planner must know what it will and will not do. Because each system is somewhat different and has its advantages and disadvantages, more or fewer accessories, and different degrees of adaptability, the visual merchandiser should consider the following aspects before selecting a system for a specific use.

LOOKS

How will it look in the designated space? Will it look right with the type of merchandise that will be shown?

How does it go with the store's image? Will the system be too industrial or too juvenile, too metallic, or too heavy? Will the system appear overwhelming in the space it will fill? Will it blend with other fixtures or architectural elements already in the area? Will it scale properly with the architecture and the merchandise?

END USE

How long will this system be used in the specific area? Will it have to withstand heavy use or frequent reconfigurations? If the shop is temporary, a less complicated system may suit the constant reconfiguring; however, if the shop will remain in place and require only occasional, minor adjustments, the store planner or visual merchandiser may want to consider a system that locks or that can be secured rather permanently.

CONSTRUCTION

How much weight will this assemblage have to sustain? Will it be carrying children's clothing, lingerie, or separates, or will it be used for heavy outerwear and leather coats? Will the hang-rods and shelves be sturdy enough for the load intended, or will they sag or bow? Does the designer have to plan to use more uprights or shorter hang-rods to sustain the weight?

UPKEEP

Will the materials used in the manufacturing of this system hold up in daily use over a prolonged period of time? If it is made of metal, will the finish stay bright and shiny, or will it require polishing or replating? If it has been painted or lacquered, will the painted surfaces be subjected to rubs, scars, strains, and stains? Can the surfaces be retouched? If the system is made of wood, is it hard and scuff resistant? Can scratches, scars, and blemishes be easily removed in the store? If the shelves or bins are made of plastic or glass, will they break easily, discolor, sag, or bow? Will the edges be resistant to chipping? Will the exposed corners present a problem?

ADAPTABILITY

Is the system simple to assemble and reassemble? Is it too simple? Will unauthorized individuals have access to undo what a visual merchandiser has done? Are new washers or fillers needed every time a unit has to be put together? Does it require special bolts, screws, or nuts that can cause untold problems when a screw is missing? Are the replacement parts easy to get? Will the basic size and scale of this system work in most areas in a store, or is the system too specific? How safe is the unit? Will it stand without being reinforced into the floor, wall, or ceiling?

PRICE

Because price is such a variable, the selection must be based on the projected use and adaptability of the particular system.

It is only in the last few years that systems have been more commonly used by store planners and display persons in the United States. Over the years, environmental selling spaces, seasonal shops and pop-ups have become the responsibility of the merchandise presentation department. They are expected to come up with clever, trendsetting, ambiance-filled boutiques or shops in no time at all, often at a minimum cost. Visual merchandisers recognize the great advantage of these collapsible systems that can be quickly converted from a variety of rods, tubes, and connectors into a three-dimensional entity that houses and shows merchandise—and even carries its own decorative finish, signing, and lights.

Systems are practical because they are so versatile. Study the systems that are available. Consider all the advantages and disadvantages. Select the most convenient, practical, and adaptable one—for the price—and remember, save the parts. A system will serve only as long as the bits, parts, and pieces are cared for properly. Keep track of all elements, store them carefully, mark the cartons and boxes, and your system will be a worthwhile investment.

The design team at Plajer & Franz, an architectural firm in Berlin, used a simple tubular module system throughout its new Sogo Department Store in the St. Moritz Mall, in Jakarta, Indonesia. With this system it were able to effect a unified look for the store and still create definite and particular looks for different areas of merchandise. The heroic columns that are a major statement throughout the main floor were encased in grids made up

FIGURE CS16.1 As seen from the mall, the massive columns that support the floors above have been turned into merchandising fixtures by means of modular constructions that grid the columns. *Design by Plajer & Franz, Berlin, Germany.*

FIGURE CS16.2 In the cosmetics area, the floor units as well as column enclosures can be seen more clearly. Constructed of square tubing, the structures are readily assembled, and graphic end panels are easily added to the floor fixtures. *Design by Plajer & Franz, Berlin, Germany.*

of square tubes and then, with the addition of shelves and panels, turned into selling outposts for cosmetics, handbags, menswear, etc. Off the columns, the same system was used to form display tables, counters, and special fixtures. The use of the same tubular pieces made each area or department homogenous and yet unique. See Figures CS16.1 through CS16.4.

FIGURE CS16.3 The tubing can be finished in decorative colors or metallic, as shown in the handbag area. The use of the gold or brass finish combined with the white panels and shelves creates a lighter and more delicate look for this shop within the store. *Design by Plajer & Franz, Berlin, Germany.*

FIGURE CS16.4 Black tubing and deep gray with touches of coral turns the men's department into a truly masculine space. The column enclosures/fixtures combine face-out and shoulder-out hung garments along with folded and stacked merchandise of shelves. Brand names are indicated on black headers atop each unit. *Design by Plajer & Franz, Berlin, Germany.*

Modular Fixtures and Systems in Store Planning: Trade Talk

clamps	modular fixtures	slotted joiners
extruded uprights	modules	slotted uprights
hollow tubes with finger fittings	outriggers	T-joint
L-joints	rollout	X-joints

Modular Fixtures and Systems in Store Planning: A Recap

+ Modular fixtures—constructed of module building blocks in standard sizes—provide designers and store planners with flexible, adaptable units that can fit differently sized retail spaces.

+ These units enable store designers to create an identifiable look when rolling out; that is, introducing a new design for a chain-store retailer.

+ Modules are usually made of wood.

+ A system can be used to make a displayer, a fixture, or a stock-and-sell merchandiser. It can be assembled to create a complete wall of hang-rods, bins, shelves, and even dressing rooms. It may also contain its own lighting and signing elements.

+ With a system, a store planner or visual merchandiser can start with the perimeter wall and erect a whole selling environment without once needing to nail or screw into the wall, bolt down into the floor, or suspend or reinforce the ceiling.

+ A system requires relatively few tools and is fairly easy to put together and take apart.

+ Major types of systems include hollow tubes with finger fittings, clamps, extruded uprights, slotted joiners, and slotted uprights.

+ A visual merchandiser should consider the following aspects before purchasing a display system: looks, end use, construction, upkeep, adaptability, and price.

Questions for Review and Discussion

1. How would the use of modular fixtures help a store designer create a standard design for two differently sized retail spaces?

2. What are display systems? What materials are used to manufacture display systems?

3. What are the advantages of using display systems in store planning as opposed to using traditional display fixtures?

4. Why has there been an increase in the use of display systems over the past several years?

5. If you were in charge of the selection and purchase of a display system for the young men's sportswear department of an upscale department store, what factors would you consider? Describe the type of system you would select.

Chapter Seventeen
Furniture as Merchandisers and Props

Raining Chairs, Galeries Lafayette, Jakarta, Indonesia.
Plajer & Franz Studio, United Kingdom.

**AFTER YOU HAVE READ THIS CHAPTER,
YOU WILL BE ABLE TO DISCUSS**

- ✦ how furniture can be used to set the mood in a display
- ✦ uses for various types of chairs in visual presentations
- ✦ types of merchandise suitable for tabletop display
- ✦ how the interior of an armoire or a chifforobe can be "fitted" to accommodate a variety of merchandise

We explore the concept of using furniture as props further in Chapter 10. In this chapter, we will develop that idea and show how furniture can be much more. This chapter, among other things, will show you how a furniture piece can set the style or theme for an individual display or function as a fixture to show merchandise.

When furniture is used as a prop, its primary function is to define a particular style that is relative to the style of the merchandise or the overall setting. (See Figure 17.1.) The furniture piece can embody the brand's image and the aspirations of the shopper. Furniture can break up the monotony of fixturing on the selling floor by adding color, style, and innovative merchandising opportunities. Anthropologie stores are a prime example of how furniture can be used to tell a compelling visual merchandising story.

Chairs

A chair can be the essence of a whole room, an entire period or style or time, or a culture. A simple, single, easily

FIGURE 17.1   Furniture creates the setting and a story in this holiday window at Franzen, a luxury home and tabletop store. The design team re-created a hotel room filled with stylish furniture including shelves stocked with champagne. The furniture arrangement supports the theme, and the black-and-white décor enhances the beautiful glassware. *Franzen, Dusseldorf, Germany. Copyright WindowsWear PRO http://pro.windowswear.com; contact@windowswear.com 1.646.827.2288.*

FIGURE 17.2   It is such a cliché—but clichés make it easier to get a message across quickly. From association with the movies and things seen on TV, the tall, cross-legged canvas-seat-and-back director's chair says "Hollywood," and "Hollywood" is synonymous with "cinema." Here, the chairs set the scene for the Toronto Cinema Festival. *Le Château, Toronto, Canada.*

obtainable **director's chair** of colored canvas and wood can imply the glamour and excitement of Hollywood, of stars and famous names, and all of that in the confines of the display area. It doesn't take a whole sleek steamship to suggest "The Cruise"—a slatted **deck chair**, a bit of railing with a lifesaver attached (or in vinyl on the front glass), and a single "floating" porthole somewhere in the background will more than imply that this is the top deck of a luxury liner. Instead of attempting to re-create an entire designer's salon, a single elegant Louis XV or Louis XVI **fauteuil**[1] or **bergère**[2] (two French-styled chairs) can become what the shopper imagines that salon would look like. Ralph Lauren Polo and the image created in the Polo shops are easily identified by the classic Americana and late eighteenth-century furniture used in retail spaces, just as Early American pine chairs and furniture can be the visual essence of fine country classic woolens and tweeds. Thus, a chair can be more than a chair! (See Figure 17.2.)

There are numerous types and styles of chairs in a variety of furniture periods and finishes available—often for the borrowing from local furniture stores, antique shops, or local historical societies. Some dealers will loan in exchange for a simple credit sign in the window that identifies the donor or the source for the chair in the display. This is a great method for creating an assemblage that pays homage to one particular time period. (See Figure 17.3.) If there is space, a chair can be "accessorized," and the display area further enhanced, by adding a table, floral arrangement, bonsai tree, bundle of wheat, or bowl of natural dried spices.

A **yacht chair**, another type of director's chair, can provide the desired ambiance for active sportswear. This is a wood-framed chair with a changeable canvas seat and back and with legs that scissor front and rear. It is usually available in a wide range of colored canvas accessories. If the chair is set on a green grass mat or strip of green indoor-outdoor carpeting, it becomes part of an outdoor

---

[1] fauteuil—French for "armchair." An upholstered armchair with open sides, usually with upholstered arm or elbow pads.
[2] bergère—An all-upholstered low armchair, usually with exposed wood frame and enclosed sides. The upholstered arms are shorter than the length of the seat, and a soft, loose pillow rests on a fabric-covered seat.

or lawn setting. On a "wood" floor, it becomes part of a ship's deck. It is natural and logical to drape coordinates and accessories over the chair back or on the arms, or use the seat as an elevation to bring the accessories closer to the viewer's eye level. To expand or open up the setting, add more chairs and some sporting equipment, such as golf clubs, tennis racquets, a croquet set, or even a bow and some arrows and a big bull's-eye target. Most of these props are also available from sporting goods shops in exchange for a credit sign in the display.

To promote swimsuits, cover-ups, and beachwear, use a canvas-and-wood **beach chair**. It could be color keyed to match or complement the garment being shown. The mannequin doesn't have to stretch out on the chair; the chair could serve as an elevation for related merchandise or fashion accessories like jewelry, cosmetics, or beach bags.

To enhance the setting, drape a colorful but coordinated towel over the chair, add some inflatable beach balls, and maybe, on the floor, an island of sand with or without some colorful vintage metal pails and shovels. The pails can also hold the small accessories. If the display area is large, one can make a bigger splash with the addition of a large canvas beach umbrella. Beach chairs and beach umbrellas can be used in a window setting, on an interior ledge, or on a platform in front of a swimsuit shop. (See Figure 17.4.)

Slat-back **Adirondack chairs** are strong and sturdy and are representative of the great outdoors. They are designed to withstand the seasons, to go from autumn to spring,

FIGURE 17.5 Not only does this jumble/montage of spindle-backed opera chairs, now painted in myriad colors, attract the eye, but it does a great job of presenting the Gucci collection of fashion accessories in the open-back window in Milan. The set-up arouses the viewers' curiosity—draws them to the display and then treats them to a game of "hide and seek" and discovery. *Gucci, Milan, Italy. Stefania D'Alessandro/Getty Images.*

from spring through summer. They can show off sportswear, casual wear, sweaters, skirts, slacks, and menswear. Usually, the Adirondack chair is left in its natural woody state, but it can be whitewashed for summery events or pastel tinted for special occasions.

What is more nostalgic than **ice cream parlor chairs**? What could be more summery than ice cream sundaes and sodas? These quaint wire chairs, twisted and fragile looking, are excellent for a "parfait perfect" theme. White ice cream parlor chairs set the mood and place for pretty pastel-colored outfits. To complete the scene, add a white marble-topped table to match the chairs and some soda glasses and sundae dishes to "fill" with colorful accents and accessories, like scarves, belts, and costume jewelry. For Valentine's Day, wouldn't it be romantic if the cushions on the seats were red and if a red-and-white cloth covered the table?

Fall and back to college bring thoughts of traditional and tailored outfits to mind. One associates the career woman with her career-oriented clothes and **swivel chairs** or ergonomically designed **posture chairs**. There are executive chairs for the boardroom and big desks and round tables for the top-echelon woman executive. The display "set" designer can add water coolers and file cabinets. When showing women's suits and going-to-work outfits, the scene could be filled with folding chairs, **tavern chairs**, or **captain's chairs** to suggest that "doing lunch" is part of the workday schedule.

Let's switch to "going out"—to a night on the town—from dressy on up to formal wear. The right chair or cluster of chairs can set the scene and create the desired ambiance. French **Louis XV** (Rococo), **Louis XVI** (Neoclassical), and **Empire chair** designs are all elegant and lovely and so right with formal wear and bridal wear. The small, light-scaled chairs—often accented with gilt or rubbed with antique white—can be used to hold items, or they can play host to an artfully draped fur coat or a display of evening bags, gloves, slippers, scarves, perfumes, and jewelry. The mid- to late-eighteenth-century chair designs of England are also elegant and refined, but not as fine in scale as the French pieces. **Chippendale chairs**, which range from ribbon-back to Chinese-influenced to Gothic, are often better well matched to suits, tailored outfits, simpler designs and, of course, menswear. These chairs are usually finished in mahogany or walnut, and the upholstery is often deep and rich in color, whereas their French counterparts are mostly topped with pastel-colored, satiny upholstery. Add graceful palm plants or a wide-spreading lacy fern in a brass planter to fill the window. (See Figure 17.5.)

Another lovely, light touch could be a chandelier in brass or bronze, curly and swirly, dripping with prisms or swagged with crystal chains. It isn't necessary that the visual merchandiser match the chandelier to the chair; what is important is that the scale and proportion of one goes with the other and that they look right and comfortable together.

Let's not overlook the **country, or provincial, chair** styles: country French, country English, and Early American. These chairs are less detailed, simpler country cousins of the more ornate court styles mentioned earlier. These styles are usually interpreted in light-colored, natural woods, sometimes rubbed with white or gray and upholstered in textured fabrics in solids; plaids; and small, allover prints. These sophisticated rustics are complements for fine woolens, tweeds, and cashmeres, for designer separates for autumn and winter. They can add the Ralph Lauren look to a display with the aura of the countryside—and the essence of the landed gentry. No light and lacy palms or crystal chandeliers here! These chairs call for sturdier, leafy plants, like geraniums, begonias, asters, mums, and marigolds. Fireplaces, mantles, and trophies can further enhance the settings.

Today, anything that is Mid-Century Modern is considered in style because the silhouettes of the forties, fifties, and sixties complement men's and women's designer merchandise, and the **mid-century chair** (original or reproduction) can effectively sell the idea that something unique and of the moment is happening in the display space. Knoll and Design Within Reach (DWR) provide a gallery of options to inspire visual merchandising displays; however, this style of furniture is found readily in flea markets, in antique shops, and at estate sales. An **Eames** molded plywood chair, a sleek **Saarinen womb chair**, or a **Herman Miller** bench have the ability to transform a display into today's new classic retail environment. Clean lines, bold color, laminate or wood, the mid-century furniture collection has an allure that attracts a wide spectrum of shoppers from millennials to baby boomers.

Tables

Tables are not only props; they are fixtures too. These everyday pieces of furniture can create a sense of time and place; they can show off or hold merchandise in a more interesting, more personal, and intimate manner than a cold, steely fixture does. A table is an elevated platform. In a traditional window it will raise merchandise 30 inches off the floor of the window, which can be another 18 inches off the street level. When the window floor is level with the floor of the shop, tables definitely bring whatever is set out on them closer to the shopper's eye level. And to restate an old retail adage, "eye level is buy level." Small items or fashion accessories are more easily seen and appreciated if shown on top of a table. An arrangement of shoes, gloves, bags, scarves, jewelry, and cosmetics, plus a vase filled with live (or silk) flowers will create a decorative still life, and it will also let the shopper know what goes with what. If the 30-inch-high table is too tall, use a 16-inch "cocktail" table. The lower table is especially effective for the presentation of shoes and handbags. (See Figure 17.6.)

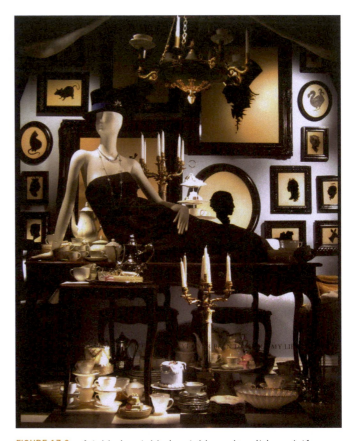

FIGURE 17.6 A table is a table is a table, unless it is a platform, an elevation, or a riser. Here, the table serves to elevate the reclining figure and bring some of the tea service pieces up closer to eye level. Note how the product display is shown on different levels so that the viewer may appreciate each collection before moving up and on to the next group. *Miss Jackson, Tulsa, Oklahoma. Design by Stacy Suvino.*

As previously discussed with respect to chairs, the period, style, and finish of the piece of furniture can help identify the class of merchandise as well as suggest where the items can be worn. A period piece may work wonderfully for luxury shoes, but casual or sporty shoes could be set out on mid-century modern or even rustic, rough-barked cobbler benches. Low woven rattan tables can present casual or sporty shoes for cruise and summer. A steamer trunk, lying on its side or back, could suggest shoes that travel places.

A repurposed table can be used successfully by painting a patina finish on it. A gardener's table will give way to a spring theme and, much like a wooden slatted picnic table, says summer. Tables can be merchandised with forms, accessory forms, or beautiful merchandise arranged in a lifestyle setting.

Armoires and Cabinets

Armoires, **chifforobes**, and **freestanding closets** all afford the shopper a glimpse at a coordinated lifestyle. It is like looking into the wardrobe of an organized, color-aware, color-conscious friend. In it one can see sweaters, blouses, skirts, slacks, and jackets just asking to be mixed and matched. If the closet is well designed, the top shelf will hold hats and handbags, whereas shoes will be lined up on the lowest shelf or on the floor of the closet. An armoire, chifforobe, or wardrobe steamer trunk is an excellent staple window prop or selling floor prop to feature merchandise. An armoire usually combines shelf space with hang space, whereas the chifforobe provides the hang space with drawers that can be partially opened and filled. A steamer wardrobe trunk has the same qualities with a bit more nostalgia in style. In an open-back window the armoire becomes the break or partition between the display space up front and the store's selling space beyond. Inside the store, on the selling floor, the armoire can be a mini-boutique, a specialized shop within a shop, or the focal display area at the end of an aisle. It can even be the entrance into a particular selling area. In a really small shop that sells mostly ready-to-wear, the open armoire can be the accessory "wall," with belts on an open, exposed inner door; scarves on the other; and on the shelves, an assortment of the accessories carried in stock.

To be really effective, this "fixture" should not be overstocked with merchandise. This is a display unit, and the garments need more breathing space—more space to show off. They need to be viewed. Coordinate a single color or color scheme, add a scarf or a belt, and then turn the hanger on the rod so that the shopper gets an almost full frontal view of the outfit. Search out second-hand stores and used furniture depots for salvageable pieces that can be painted a soft neutral color that will almost "disappear" into the surroundings. What really counts is what is on the inside, so do clever and interesting things with the interior and throw open the doors to reveal the contents. The inner sides of the doors and the interior space can be painted a contrasting color or wallpapered. Panels can be cut of board that can be wallpapered or covered with fabrics and serve as liners for the doors and closet interior. Interchangeable panels make it possible to change the color, the texture, or pattern of the armoire with the changing merchandise. Moiré fabric or papers that look like watered taffeta will make an elegant interior against which one can show gowns, furs, and fine intimate apparel. A soft, subdued allover paisley might be very handsome with woolens and cashmeres. Try ticking or stripes with casual sportswear and floral prints with pastel-colored garments. Although the basic piece is always the same, the interior, where the display goes, can be a changing stage set.

The original rods and shelves can be removed and replaced with slotted standards. (See Chapter 15.) These slotted standards can be almost hidden by the replaceable liner panels just mentioned. It is then possible to create different hanging and shelving arrangements. The wide range of brackets and accessories that fit into the standards will make it possible to have varying heights and lengths of hang-rods and shelves.

The style or period of the armoire, chifforobe, cupboard, or wardrobe trunk can say something about the merchandise within. Vintage styles are better suited for sportswear and separates, country-style woolens and tweeds, and classic casual garments. The more elegant period pieces are especially well adapted to lingerie, better dresses, and gowns.

Drawer Units

Drawer units—chests, bureaus, anything with pull-out surfaces—can be put to work in presentation and display, from tall units to low units, from highboys to lowboys, to nightstands. A closed drawer is a secretive thing and piques the viewer's interest and curiosity. An open drawer shows all, tells all, and can sell almost all. What do you put in drawers? Drawers are filled with small, all-important separates and fashion accessories such as shirts and ties, T-shirts, sweaters, scarves, socks, stockings, and all kinds of underwear.

When you pull open a drawer, you make a statement. Whether it is a color, a color scheme, or a full spectrum, it must combine show with stock. If showing blouses or sweaters, stack the neatly folded garments in the color range in the drawer while one open garment "casually" drapes from the drawer, onto the floor, or reaches up to a dramatic lay-down on the top of the chest. In using drawers for display, the eye level is important. The top drawers of a tall unit will not show off what is in the drawers, so that is the place to drape the single show item. The drawers at and below eye level are where the selling really takes place.

The top of a not-very-tall chest is also a valuable display elevation for a lay-down of garments that are not usually folded away in drawers: slacks, skirts, shoes, handbags, and toiletries. Thus, a traditional 36-inch-tall chest, ideally displayed, would feature garments laid out on top, maybe sharing the space with an array of thematic props or accessories to set the stage. A cluster of clay pots with a variety of succulents or a stack of books about bird watching or collecting may spark the interest of the viewer. The open drawers below could show off the range of go-with material available. As an example, for Mother's Day the chest could overflow with nostalgic black-and-white family images and an arrangement of objects that inspires the lifestyle of today's "Mom." (See Figures 17.7 and 17.8.)

Drawers are opened for a setting with an avalanche of sweaters, scarves, hats, and socks, and piled up on top are books and fashion accessories in precariously built-up stacks. Add several pieces of open luggage for cruise and resort wear. Luggage can be partially filled with the same merchandise that is filling the drawers. On top add a collection of sunglasses, and hats as well as images of faraway ports of call. It is really quite simple and logical. Imagine moving in or moving out, packing and unpacking, and then add some atmosphere for time and place, tell a merchandise story, and it's a display.

In addition to luggage, imagine what can be done with a vintage wardrobe or **steamer trunk** that is bigger. These beautiful antique trunks can be found in several different materials such as leather, wood or even a heavy

FIGURE 17.7 The small chest in this partial open-back window features a selection of the designer's shirts, ties, and fashion accessories. Using the top of the chest and a pulled out drawer, the designer has created different levels for viewing close to eye level. *Hermès, Boston, Massachusetts. Design: Lucy Anne Bouwman.*

FIGURE 17.8 Create a full room ambience with a few pieces of furniture and lots of imagination and fun. At Anthropologie, in New York City, a simple, collapsible table becomes a desk, a chair becomes a vehicle to carry an outer garment, and a shelf display unit supports the books, plants, and knickknacks a college-bound student might take with her to her "home away from home." The partial wall serves to divide the display area from the rest of the store. *Anthropologie, New York City. Copyright WindowsWear PRO http://pro.windowswear .com; contact@windowswear.com 1.646.827.2288.*

duty canvas with leather trim. In an open-back window an upright trunk with the drawers pulled out and filled with accessories, and one or two outfits hung on the wardrobe side, not only shows off a wealth of related merchandise but also creates a partial screen of the store's interior. The style of the trunk also suggests a time and a place; it gives the visual merchandiser a theme to work with. It would be a worthwhile investment to buy a secondhand or used trunk and fix it up with travel labels. Ignore the scuffs and

dents. What trunk is perfect after the first voyage? Paint it or paper it; make it decorative. With some clever draping, it is possible to hide the ravages of age and misuse. Because "theater" is always a great attention getter, the old steamer trunk could be turned into a theatrical trunk by stenciling on the names of theaters or opera houses, or even top musicals, on the shiny black or wooden finish. A big star could suggest celebrity status or that it it is "opening night."

Go Green 17.1: Upcycling Found Objects

If there is any place the visual merchandiser can "go green," it has to be with the props and decoratives that are used to create lifestyle settings or to attract shoppers to the windows or off the aisle, to the merchandise presentation. By carefully curating a few "found objects" into a display, a visual merchandiser can narrate a captivating story for the viewer. The texture and color of weather-beaten wood or warm rusted metals can add a sense of reality to the display, reminding the shopper of the brand's heritage or earthy nature. Calling up time periods from the past using an arrangement of objects naturally engages the eyes and senses of the shopper for a longer period of time.

Use every opportunity to attend flea markets and garage and tag sales. Every city and country around the world has a marketplace to sell a "treasure": something old and worn out but that still has life in it and that can be recycled, reused, or repurposed. An excellent example on the northeast coast of the United States is the renowned Brimfield Antique Show that encompasses 80 acres (or 20 football fields) of antiques, collectibles, and fabulous junk from all over the world (Figure 17.9).

Brimfield Market is a regular resource used by Anthropologie, Ralph Lauren, Pottery Barn, ABC Carpet, Whole Foods, and many other brands. Rome's Mercato Di Porta Portes is another popular style market with similar offerings abound.

Antiques go beyond residential objects and include architectural details from buildings, an old hotel balustrade, or an old store's faded and hardly readable sign; these may be the right nostalgic touch for a display. Old wooden movie house seats, a collection of verdigris glass medicine bottles, and weathered crates with a scatter of packing material will recall the past, accent a display, and entertain the shopper.

Props are all around you, and most do not cost anything. They require time, effort, and a dash of imagination. Visual merchandisers have the insight to see the beauty and value of deconstructing furniture and repurposing; a detailed spindle of chair or a handsome chiseled table leg can easily become a hang rod for merchandise. Low-VOC paints and adhesives can keep the project sustainable, and there are friendly paint finishes that can simply rub on to surfaces. As retail stores evolve, they require techniques that entertain and capture the viewer; by using found objects, furniture, and antiques the store takes on an adventure much like a visit to one's favorite museum.

FIGURE 17.9 Brimfield, Massachusetts, Flea Market offers a bounty of antique chairs and collectibles in a relaxed and friendly environment. Every object has a story and the vendors are more than willing to share the history of these fabulous finds. *Brimfield Flea Market, Courtesy of Anne Kong.*

FIGURE 17.10 Old, beat-up, and otherwise past-use chairs find a new use as they climb the heights in this tall window. The rickety collection of unstable chairs builds interest on the left, and one chair also serves as a precarious extra elevation atop the scarred and marred table. *Harvey Nichols Knightsbridge, London, United Kingdom.*

FIGURE 17.11 Take your old furniture, stepladders, dress forms—just about anything lying around—and do your own version of "wrap art." Readily available and recyclable bubble wrap—no matter the condition—plus some twine or tape can turn an everyday object into an artwork shrouded in mystery. A great way to suggest a new season, a new collection: a recent arrival being unwrapped for the viewer's pleasure. *Miss Jackson, Tulsa, Oklahoma, Design: Stacy Suvino.*

FIGURE 17.12 Home appliances and office equipment can also be readily recognized and create a setting. For this "green" window promotion, the washing machine and the water cooler, plus the neatly stacked towels, blue plastic bottles, and stacks of paper cups, help make a point about saving water. *Hudson's Bay, Toronto, Canada.*

Furniture as Props: Trade Talk

Adirondack chairs
armoire
beach chairs
bergère
captain's chairs
chifforobes
Chippendale chairs
country, or provincial, chairs
deck chairs
director's chairs

drawer units
Eames
Empire chair
fauteuil
freestanding closets
Herman Miller
ice cream parlor chairs
Louis XV chair
Louis XVI chair
mid-century chair

posture chairs
Saarinen womb chair
steamer trunk
swivel chairs
tables
tavern chairs
wardrobe trunks
yacht chairs

Furniture as Props: A Recap

+ Furniture can be used as props or fixtures or both.

+ A chair can suggest the essence of a scene.

+ Some chairs that can be used as props include director's chair, deck chairs, office chair, Louis XV or Louis XVI chair, French country chair, English country chair, Early American pine chair, and Mid-Century-Modern chairs.

+ Tables can also be used as fixtures as well as props.

+ Tables can be used for window displays to raise the merchandise to eye level.

+ Tabletop displays work well with small items and fashion accessories.

+ Using an armoire, steamer trunk, or closet for display can show the shopper a coordinated lifestyle and suggest mix-and-match choices.

+ An armoire, chifforobe, or closet display should never be overcrowded with merchandise. Items need breathing space and room to show off.

Questions for Review and Discussion

1. Give an example of how a chair can create an image in a window or interior display.

2. Describe the type of merchandise you would display with a wooden deck chair, an upholstered chaise lounge, and a porch swing.

3. Explain how the period, style, and furniture finish all come together to suggest the merchandise class and store image. Provide an example to illustrate your understanding.

4. How might an armoire be used as a selling fixture in a lingerie shop? A men's furnishings department? An accessory outpost?

5. Use decorating magazines to find five examples of furniture that could be used in display. Indicate the name and style of each piece, the type of merchandise you would use in the display, how the furniture piece would be incorporated into the display, and the reasons why you feel this piece of furniture would be appropriate for the setting.

Chapter Eighteen

Materials and Graphics Used in Visual Merchandising and Store Design

Giant Ribbons, Louis Vuitton, New York. *Copyright WindowsWear PRO*
http://pro.windowswear.com; contact@windowswear.com 1.646.827.2288.

AFTER YOU HAVE READ THIS CHAPTER,
YOU WILL BE ABLE TO DISCUSS

+ Types of materials used to produce displays
+ Types of materials used in store design
+ How cost and production time can affect material choices
+ Situations in which a material would be beneficial to use in a display

Materials and production processes are essential in communicating the essence of brands and the brand story. We realize that the store environment is more than a space to sell goods; it is a place for the shopper to connect with the brand socially; make memorable experiences; and develop a loyalty based on the look, style, and feel of the brand. Materials play a convincing role in brand recognition as they visually communicate through rich woods, bold color, invigorating texture, or soothing fabrics. Materials are essentially the ambassadors of the brand. (See Figure 18.1.)

In display settings that are temporary, materials can be money savers, problem solvers, and often a trigger for the design. The visual merchandiser embarking on a display project needs to be agile because materials can be used differently in displays than in store design. In a window or vignette, visual merchandisers have more opportunity to play, repurpose, and "distort" when using materials. They may also use materials in daring methods to "fool the eye" of the viewer. (See Figure 18.2.)

Knowing how and where to source materials, props, and florals for displays can present a challenge for the visual merchandiser. Each window display installation has a different need and budget, so finding the best value and the right quantity of elements becomes a big part of the job. Where does the visual merchandiser find hundreds of

FIGURE 18.1   Wood is one of the materials that help convey the concept for the Starbucks Roastery in Capitol Hill, Seattle, Washington. Reclaimed wood timbers are used on the ceiling to form a "cloud" above the bar. The contrast of a milled textural CNC pattern on the bar face is illuminated from below. The top edges of the wood bar add comfort for customers, and the handrails are wrapped in hand-stitched leather for warmth and finish. *Starbucks Coffee Company, Global Design and Innovation, New York.*

FIGURE 18.2   Hats off to the bright and shiny crowned head of Miss Liberty, which is certainly a recognizable American icon. Cleverly conceived and constructed of textured scraps of metal sheeting and roof flashing materials, the result is missing the green patina we usually associate with the Statue of Liberty but gains the crisp and clean look of the denim garments featured in the display. *Macy's, Herald Square, New York, New York. Copyright WindowsWear PRO http://pro.windowswear.com; contact@windowswear.com 1.646.827.2288.*

wheat bundles, faux stone tile, burls of wood, corrugated metal sheets, moss, pebbles, or scatter snow? Each year the professional organizations in the visual merchandising industry host trade shows and publish a "buyer's guide" to help designers find suppliers and manufacturers that suit their particular needs. (See Chapter 26.) There are suppliers that sell raw materials, imported props, furniture, florals, mannequins and fixtures, and much more. Other suppliers provide services such as printing, manufacturing, contracting, and more. Visual merchandisers can peruse supplier websites to learn more about the latest product offerings; this practice can spark inspiration and ideas to begin the design process. The resourcing process begins once the design for the project has been approved to move forward; a detailed drawing of the display with measurements and required quantities can guide the visual merchandiser through the ordering process. Besides finding the resources, the visual merchandiser needs to know the standard sizes of materials and how different materials are sold. For example, standard sheet size for most materials like wood, rigid PVC board, and Foamcore, is 4 feet × 8 feet. The thickness of the board might be ¼ inch or up to 1 inch. Sand and pebbles are sold in weights of 5- or 10-pound bags. When working with metal, we consider

the thickness or **gauge**. Foam products come in varied sizes, depending on where it is purchased—a lumberyard or a floral supplier, for example. Foam products have different textures and **densities**. It is important to inquire about the **standard size** of any material before calculating the square footage, yardage, length, width, or thickness. This ensures accuracy in the calculations of materials before purchasing. Suppliers' websites are not always updated as often as they should, so a call and conversation to check if the material is physically in stock is a good idea for a pending project.

Wood

The more a designer knows about the characteristics of wood and its source, the better he or she can understand the degree of warmth and beauty it can bring to the fixturing or store design. Every grain pattern is a unique masterpiece of design, texture, and wonder. These grain patterns also known as "figures or growth rings," describe the texture found in wood such as Birdseye, curly, or fiddleback. Wood can be warm and welcoming or cool and contemporary, depending on the grain, color, and finish. Birch, maple, and pine are the most common woods and can be found in most home improvement centers and lumberyards. Today, the popularity and availability of more exotic woods are inspiring store designers to use woods in unique ways than ever before—wood is used to create stylish accent walls, striking product displays, ceiling details, or whimsical lighting fixtures. Designers are mixing wood with other raw materials to achieve urban appeal or Zen style, or to send a message about sustainability to their clients. Hundreds of wood varieties have flooded the marketplace, including wood that is recycled or rescued. Wood rescued from beneath waterways, or taken from existing building structures, is currently one of the most popular materials for store environments and fixtures. Fortunately, reclaimed wood helps to reduce the need to harvest existing forests to meet the current demand. There are hundreds of varieties of woods, and even though many types are not always suited for making fixtures or cabinetry, the store designer can find a new and inspiring way to use it.

TYPES OF WOOD

Ash: Ash is a hard, heavy, ring porous hardwood. It has a prominent grain that resembles oak, and a white to light brown color. Ash burls have a twisted, interwoven figure.

Beech: Beech is a hard, strong, heavy wood with tiny pores and winding rays, similar in appearance to maple. This relatively inexpensive wood has reddish brown heartwood and light sapwood.

Birch: Birch is a hard, heavy, close-grained hardwood with a light brown or reddish color. Birch is often rotary or flat sliced, yielding straight, curly, or wavy grain patterns.

Cedar: Cedar is a knotty softwood that has a red-brown color with light streaks. Its aromatic and moth repellent qualities have made it a popular wood for lining drawers, chests, and boxes.

Cherry: Cherry, also known as fruitwood, is moderately hard, strong, closed grain, light- to red-brown wood, and resists warping.

Fir: Fir works easy and finishes well. Uniform in texture, it has a low resistance to decay. Used in furniture, doors, frames, windows, plywood, veneer, general millwork, and interior trim.

Hemlock: Light in weight, uniformly textured, hemlock is used for construction lumber, planks, doors, boards, paneling, sub-flooring, and crates.

Maple: Maple has a curly grain with burls, leaf figure, and bird's-eye figures; it is used extensively for veneers.

Mahogany: It has a reddish-brown color and may display a grain that resembles stripe, ribbon, broken stripe, rope, ripple, mottle, fiddleback, or blister figures.

Oak: Oak is a widely used hardwood that comes in two basic varieties; white and red. The red variety is also known as black oak, which is a reference to its bark.

Pine: Pine is a soft, white or pale yellow wood, which is lightweight and straight grained. It resists shrinking and swelling. Knotty pine is often used for decorative effect.

Rosewood: Rosewood is very hard and has a dark reddish-brown color. It is fragrant and close grained.

Teak: Teak is a yellow to dark brown hardwood that is extremely heavy, strong, and durable. Teak may show a straight grain, mottled, or **fiddleback** figure. It carves well, but because of its high value, it is often used as a veneer.

Walnut: It is strong, hard, and durable, without being excessively heavy. It has excellent woodworking qualities, and takes finishes well. The wood is light to dark chocolate brown in color.

Plywood is made of layers, or sheets or "plies" of wood glued together. The thickness and type of wood used on the outer surface will determine the actual cost per sheet. Plywood is commonly available in a variety of surfaces such as alder, aspen, birch, cedar, cherry, Douglas fir, hickory, mahogany, maple, oak, pine, poplar, red oak, walnut, or white oak. Plywood comes in many "grades" from rough to fine, and standardized thicknesses ranging from ¼, ⅜, ½, and ¾ inch.

Due to the high cost of solid wood, many designers choose to work with less expensive materials that have the same look as wood. Wooden **veneers** are thin sheets or slices of wood that are adhered to a less expensive material called a "**substrate**." A substrate is a board that is made from composite materials or particles of wood glued together. Authentic wood veneer can be glued on either one or two sides of the substrate surface, depending on the end use of the material. This affords the designer the strength and stability of wood, and the look of fine wood for a lot less cost. Most of the stylish furniture produced and sold today is made of composite materials with a wood veneer glued onto the surface. Substrates are **composite board**, **particleboard**, or **chipboard**. Composite boards have a smooth paintable surface; particleboard and chipboard have a rough surface made of compressed wood chips. Although substrate materials are considered raw and unfinished, they are a popular choice for fixtures and store environments of many lifestyle brands. (See Figure 18.3.)

Aspiring to attract young millennial shoppers, Urban Outfitters uses raw materials as a hallmark for its store interior and fixtures. These industrial-looking fixture solutions feature raw plumber's pipe in several configurations with sealed plywood, and pegboard to support the merchandise. (See Figure 18.4.)

FIGURE 18.3 The designers made effective use of assorted urban-type materials to create the rugged, masculine ambiance for the menswear area in the Springfield, Balboa, Spain store. The plaster that was removed from the walls revealed the rough brick structure that set the look along with the poured concrete floor. Enhancing the "hard city construction" look are the concrete blocks that support the plywood panel as a display table and the white tiles on the lower level displayer. Reclaimed wood completes the material/texture palette. *Caulder Moore, Kew, London, United Kingdom.*

FIGURE 18.4 The "Urban" in Urban Outfitters refers to the city and the raw, rough, and ready materials and textures one thinks of as being part of city life. Plumber's pipes fit the category, and when combined with raw, unfinished plywood, the table becomes not only a functional displayer but part of the decorative theme of the store and its brand identity. *Produced by Fleetwood for Urban Outfitters, Fleetwood Fixtures, Leesport, Pennsylvania.*

Fleetwood (http://www.fleetwoodfixtures.com) is a design leader in fixturing and store design; it offers exceptional custom, value-driven, high-quality fixtures for retail, hospitality, and unique workplaces. Fleetwood can craft from wood, metal, and glass, as well as advanced and sustainable materials.

New types of wood veneers have expanded the decorative surfaces that are now available in the marketplace. They include wood in woven, interlocked, or fused patterns to produce a variety of unusual textural surfaces. These products are available from Architectural Systems Incorporated (ASI) (http://www.archsystems.com), a global distributor and world renowned source for wood panels, flooring, decorative surfaces, and display furnishings. The New York City showroom and online gallery inspires designers, present and future. ASI curates a collection of the exceptional materials that includes materials recycled from chicken coops, barn wood, wine barrels, and more. (See Figure 18.5.)

Medium density fiberboard, better known as **MDF**, is a material with a smooth, paintable surface favored by retail design manufacturers and furniture makers due to the lower cost. MDF is an engineered material made of wood fibers blended with resin and bonded into sheets through a heat process. It is stronger than particleboard and can be routed on a CNC machine or "skinned" with a laminate. A **laminate** is a thin plastic skin or veneer that has a solid color, texture, or pattern such as a faux wood grain surface. MDF is durable, easy to cut and is available in ⅛-inch, ¼-inch, ⅜-inch, ½-inch, ⅝-inch, ¾-inch, 1-inch, and 1⅛-inch thickness. Not all of these are considered standard size. For projects that require a lighter weight material, **MDF Ultralight** is another alternative. MDF Ultralight is a medium density fiberboard that weighs about 30 percent less than standard MDF. Both standard and Ultralight MDF are available in 12–30mm, 4-foot × 8-foot through 5-foot × 10-foot sizes, depending on the supplier.

FIGURE 18.5 Fusión Wood Panels blend old-world craftsmanship and contemporary design with passion and imagination, delivering an organic architectural statement. This award-winning, sustainable collection is a mix of natural and reclaimed materials, including wine barrels, steel, and siding, for a textural and dimensional effect in a range of patterns. *Architectural Systems Incorporated, New York City, New York.*

When a curved surface is required for a design, there are several solutions to consider. Flexible MDF, or **tambour**, has precision-machined slots that run across the length or width of the panel, providing a smooth, curved surface. **Flexboard** is another brand name for a bendable MDF board for all types of projects that require a radius. Tambour can bend to produce a 10-inch radius and can be easily painted or laminated. Tambour is also a term used to describe other woods with bending capability, such as maple or cherry wood, so local research is recommended.

Another option is **bendable plywood** also known as Curve-Ply, FlexPly, and **wiggle board**. Bending plywood is normally made from hardwood with the layers all running in one direction; this allows bend-ability to the panel and can be applied on a curved radius. (See Figure 18.6.)

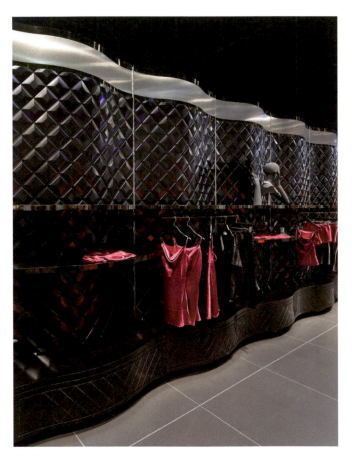

FIGURE 18.6 A beautifully curved plywood fixture is molded into a sensual wave shape and then routed with a soft quilted design to create a dynamic fixturing system for lingerie. The metallic painted surface gives the illusion of metal, matching the plated finish hardware. *JPMA Global Incorporated, Montreal, Canada and New York, New York.*

Luan is a thin, bendable wooden sheet with a grain that is used as a substrate under flooring or tile. It is also commonly used to achieve a curved design. Luan is usually manufactured in ¼ inch thickness, although you can find it as thin as ⅛ inch at times. It is relatively inexpensive and has many uses when curved surfaces are in demand.

Metals

Metals and metal finishes are an important part of the visual merchandiser's design vocabulary as well. The slick modern look of stainless steel shelving or the feminine glow of a rose-gold dress form base can elevate the look of a brand. More than ever, consumers are aware of these subtle environmental touches on the selling floor. Customization is the new standard in fixture design, and an exclusive metallic finish can speak volumes about a brand.

Metal as a material is available in flat sheets that are smooth, textured, or corrugated in various gauges or thicknesses. Metal sheets can be used as surfaces or cut into shapes using a table saw or laser- or die-cutting machinery. The die-cutting process is similar to a cookie cutter that punches out shapes using extreme force. Metal can also be "extruded" into shapes by heating and forcing the material through a shape. Many fixture systems utilize lengths of extruded metal bars, pipes, or rails. These fixture systems are extremely versatile because they are durable and can adjust quickly to accommodate merchandising changes. Interconnecting bars and rails construct into frames, boxes, and dozens of shapes to showcase merchandise. See Chapter 16. Signage and other materials can be integrated to customize the system even further. The international manufacturer ALU is a leader in the design of retail store fixturing solutions (http://www.alu.com/). It produces over a dozen unique systems that snap together quickly and efficiently to display merchandise hanging, on shelves, in hundreds of configurations. It is completely "tool-less" and works freestanding or attached to walls. One system, named Acrobat, anchors into the ceiling, allowing the merchandise to float in the retail space. ALU systems are used to display fine apparel, accessories, food, and much more. (See Figure 18.7.)

FIGURE 18.7 A sleek linear collection of cubes is actually a cleverly designed Slider fixture manufactured by ALU. The cubes and cubicles that are combined to create the desired effect are made of extruded aluminum rails. The fixture makes a unique wall unit where merchandise is seen at assorted levels, and some even get "star" treatment with solo appearances in their own cases. *Courtesy of ALU, Italy.*

Newly enhanced laser-cutting technology enables manufacturers to customize sheet metal and tubular metal shapes with a 360-degree laser-cut process. Using the latest computer aided design (CAD) software, manufacturers can produce 3-D models and color renderings throughout the design stages of products. CAD allows store designers to work closer with manufacturers through every phase of the design and production process—giving them the ability to make up-to-the-minute design changes that can impact cost, delivery time, and the outcome of the design. Working digitally also allows brands to create custom signature fixtures with their logos and design assets. (See Figure 18.8.)

The design industry is developing new finishes regularly. Standard metal finishes are classified using the terms **matte**, **high-gloss**, **leaf**, **antique**, or **patina**. Matte surfaces are dull with little reflective quality; gloss finishes are available in degrees of shininess. Leaf is a term derived from ancient gold leafing process. Gold leaf refers to hammered sheets of metal utilized in the traditional process of gilding; today's gilding is a metal alloy and is available in a wide selection of metallic colors such as silver, gold, copper, platinum, bronze, and brass. Leaf finishes are typically bright and polished; antique refers to aging the surface to appear distressed, and a patina suggests an oxidation process similar to the Statue of Liberty. Metal finishes are applied to surfaces using electroplating, plating, polishing, anodizing, and coloring. Just

FIGURE 18.8 Geometric shapes are intricately cut into the brass metal tube columns that border either side of this modern étagère fixture. The floor fixture accommodates both hanging and folded merchandise with room for accessories. This versatile fixture is available in an array of colors, finishes, and designs. *JPMA Global Incorporated, Montreal, Canada and New York, New York.*

as fashions go in and out of vogue, trends in store design run alike. When a consumer chooses to purchase an iPhone in gold instead of silver, that is a statement about his or her individuality, or style. A brand does the same by choosing a color or metallic finish for its fixtures and store interior. Some seasons we see the popularity of a particular metallic finish such as rose-gold for women, Spanish copper for men, or anodized aluminum for athletic wear. Customized finishes help brands differentiate themselves from their competition and support the brand identity.

Plastics and Foams

Another handy material for visual merchandisers is "plastic," commonly known as **acrylic**, **PVC**, **ABS**, **styrene**, or **Sintra**. All of these materials possess slightly different properties. Sintra is a brand of PVC that is extremely durable, rigid, and available in lightweight plastic sheets that can be custom dyed a color. Sheets range from 1 millimeter to 19 millimeters. Sintra is easily bent with a heat gun or molded through a thermo-heating process, making it a perfect solution for the waving flags in Disney Theme Parks. Its hard, smooth surface makes it easy to paint, print on, silk-screen, and laminate. It is easy to clean and has an attractive surface, and it is fire retardant. It can also endure a wide range of weather conditions, making it perfect for outdoor use including signage on the exterior of buildings.

Styrene is used for prototypes, signs, displays, enclosures, and more. It can be drilled, threaded, sawed, sheared, punched, and machined. It can also be painted and has excellent vacuum-forming properties. It is thermoformed into decorative panels or 3-D props and used in display or store interiors. Provost Display is the chief manufacturer of vacuum-formed plastic display panels used for theatrical, film, photography backdrops, window, and trade show displays. It has provided stock and custom vacuum-formed panels to the display and entertainment industry for over fifty-five years. (See Figure 18.9.)

ABS plastic has good impact strength, formability, stiffness, excellent aesthetic qualities, and toughness. It is a low-cost material and is used for making fixtures or parts of fixturing, such as bases, signage, fixture prototypes, and much more. ABS sheets can be easily heat formed using

FIGURE 18.9   The oversized vacuum-formed clamshell backdrops the Venus mannequin wearing an encrusted pearl necklace in an exhibition at Fashion Institute of Technology. The giant shell is one of many props available in flexible styrene plastic available through Provost Displays. *Provost Displays, Norristown, Pennsylvania.*

any conventional thermoplastic sheet–forming equipment. Acrylic refers to a plastic sheet that is completely transparent and flexible and that exhibits great resistance to breakage. Acrylic is an excellent material to use in place of glass for signage, fixturing, and displays because it is safer. It is lightweight—half the weight of glass—and is virtually unaffected by heat or cold. Fabrication is easy, as it can be sawed with fine-tooth blades, drilled with plastic drills, sanded and polished, and even laser-cut. It can be cemented with acrylic cement or formed using a thermo process. When acrylic is combined with the correct light source, it has the ability to conduct light on the edges.

Resins are commonly used for casting forms using a poured or rotational molding process. A strong material, resin is a liquid plastic that cures into a polymer and is used by consumers and professionals to make reproductions, props, and sets. Mannequin and dress-form companies use resins and fiberglass as a base material for molding and casting their forms. **Smooth-On**, a recognized supplier in the industry, sells its products on the internet and provides comprehensive tutorials on the casting process (https://www.smooth-on.com). Fabricators of themed environments all over the world use Smooth-On plastics, rubbers, and foams to bring fantasy and excitement to new heights for their thrill-seeking patrons. Their products are used in Las Vegas Hotels & Casinos, Place du Casino in Monaco, The Venetian Macao Casino, and theme parks like Universal Studios, Six Flags Amusement Parks, Great Adventure Amusement Parks, and Disney Orlando, Anaheim, Paris, and Tokyo,

Texture Plus is a supplier of faux surfaces. The company uses high-density **molded polymer** to create the look of real brick, stone, wood, bamboo, and metal without the cost and complicated installation of traditional building materials (https://www.textureplus.com). These easy-to-install panels can be used to replace expensive stonework and brick. Its products are used in retail settings, restaurants, and theme parks and have a resistance to hot and cold climates. (See Figure 18.10.)

FOAMS

EPS, or extruded expanded polystyrene, uses polystyrene pellets mixed with various chemicals to liquefy them. A blowing agent is then injected into the mixture, forming gas bubbles. The foaming, thick liquid is then forced through a metal mold. This is similar to the way styrene packaging is produced. Foam can also be sprayed from canisters with a spray gun. This type of foam is similar to the aerosol spray foam "Great Stuff" available to consumers in home improvement stores as a filler for patching cracks and gaps

FIGURE 18.10 Texture Plus manufactures long-lasting, lightweight, and affordable faux wall panels that are extraordinarily realistic in brick, stone, wood, bamboo, and metal designs. Made from a polymer-based building material, these panels are perfect for creating unique and attractive environments in store and window displays. *Texture Plus, Bohemia, New York.*

in homes and garages. Crafty display designers use it to create the icing on a giant cupcake or icicles in a window display. Display manufacturers use EPS on a larger scale to create many of the fantasy holiday displays. Once the foam has cured and dried, it can be painted. (See Figure 18.11.)

Extruded **polystyrene** is a high-density foam used primarily for insulation in homes and is sold in sheets. It is used to create many of the hand-carved figurines and sets found in the Christmas displays. Polystyrene foam comes in several densities, evident by the color of the foam itself. Pink foam is standard, and blue foam is higher in

FIGURE 18.11 Macy's brings the spirit of the season to life with its "Believe" holiday windows. The weird and wonderfully dimensional "family tree" was crafted from sprayed polyurethane insulating foam then artfully sprayed in luminous, fluorescent paints. The limbs of the tree frame rise up the hemisphere to the viewer's eye line. *Macy's Herald Square, New York, New York.*

density. The foam sheets are actually consumer products sold in home improvement centers; however, the material is widely used to create a custom design prop or prototype. The raw foam sheets are available in standard 2-inch × 4-foot × 8-foot and 2-inch × 2-foot × 8-foot sizes, and sheets can be glued together to achieve a greater thickness using foam board adhesive. This foam is easily carved using basic sculpture tools or kitchen utensils or can be cut on a CNC. The material can be painted, flocked, or covered with a fabric such as fake fur. (See Figures 18.12 and 18.13.)

Floral foam, also known as **Styrofoam**, comes in green or white sheets, blocks, and other shapes. It should not be confused with Oasis foam used in fresh floral arrangements. Floral foam is used in display and the DIY craft industry. It is easily cut, glued, and sculpted into shapes with a knife or cutting tool as a foundation material for dry floral arrangements or as a substrate to glue objects onto. Due to the rough texture of the surface, it is rarely used in view. Visual merchandisers find it helpful as a base material when building props such as a "field of wheat" on the floor or wall of a window display. (See Figure 18.14.)

PAPER AND BOARDS

Homasote is a brand name for a cellulose-based fiber wallboard, which is similar in composition to papier-mâché. It is made from recycled paper that is compressed under high temperature and pressure and is held together with an adhesive. Standard size is ½-inch thick in 4-foot × 8-foot sheets. Covered with an attractive fabric, it is commonly used in stores as a "pin-up" board for merchandise. It can also be used for floor or wall panels for window displays framed with 1-inch × 2-inch for support. **Upson Board** is a compressed paperboard used primarily to make jewelry

FIGURE 18.12 A holiday window in the early production stage shows the blue insulation foam that's been sculpted into fantasy creatures. Two beavers partially covered with faux fur material will later be motorized for this animated spectacular. *Courtesy of MMP/RVC, Dusseldorf, Germany. Photography: Gekko International Photo.*

FIGURE 18.13 A mother owl perched on her treetop nest, protecting her newborn babies, mechanically flexes her wings in a holiday window at Lord & Taylor. The owl and babies are another example of how extruded polystyrene rigid insulation foam sheets are transformed into fantasy characters for window displays and theme parks. *Lord & Taylor, New York, New York. Copyright WindowsWear PRO http://pro.windowswear.com; contact@windowswear.com 1.646.827.2288.*

FIGURE 18.14 An abundance of wheat pours from a fall portrait into the window display at Anthropologie. The wheat magically stands in place by using floral Styrofoam as a base material. The open cell Styrofoam shape underneath allows the wheat to insert easily and stay in place for the duration of the window display. *Anthropologie, New York, New York. Copyright WindowsWear PRO http://pro.windowswear.com; contact@windowswear.com 1.646.827.2288.*

FIGURE 18.15 Lengths of cardboard Sonotubes line up vertically to create a textural surface in the background of a window display featuring menswear. *H&M, Shibuya, Tokyo, Japan. Copyright WindowsWear PRO http://pro.windowswear.com; contact@ windowswear.com 1.646.827.2288.*

pads and panels. It resembles a thick cardboard before velvet or suede fabric is glued neatly onto the surface.

Often visual merchandisers have a need for a curved form, a base, or a pillar, so they opt to use a construction material that comes in the shape of a tube known as a **Sonotube** or concrete tube. Sonotubes are rigid fiber cylindrical forms meant for pouring concrete foundations for deck and porch supports.

In visual merchandising and display, these tubes are a solution for mannequin platforms, pedestals, props and more. They are sold in smaller sizes (8-inch to 15-inch) at home improvement centers, although select lumberyards can order these cardboard tubes in any length (greater than 20 feet) in a variety of diameters—24-inch, 36-inch, and 42-inch. They can be cut into slices to create rounded cubbies or lengthwise to create a half-round concave length. Store designers and set designers use them in hundreds of ways, depending on the need. They are sturdy, paintable, and easily cut on a table saw or with an electric jigsaw. (See Figure 18.15.)

FOAMBOARDS

Materials such as **Palight**, **Gatorboard**, **Ultraboard**, **MightyCore**, and **Foamcore** fall in to the category of display boards used by visual merchandisers and manufacturers to build displays, signage components, models, and prototypes of their designs. All of these materials differ in use and properties. The standard size for these boards are 4-foot × 8-foot; however, some are available 5-foot × 10-foot special order. Foam boards are three layers—an inner core with a face material on either side. It's important to read the websites and inquire if the material is suitable for the intended project or display; some boards are paintable and easily cut by hand, while others require a saw or have a warping factor. The difference in cost should be anticipated, and it is wise to see if a less expensive material will do the job. All of these boards contain a foam inner core; however, foam varies in density, and that determines if hand cutting or machine cutting the materials is necessary. The face of the board may be paper, fiber, or styrene, and most companies offer these products in black or white or color. Some offer an adhesive peel-and-stick face for mounting printed images, and others are available with a laminate on one side. Manufacturers and distributors for these products can be found on the internet; many can be purchased through home improvement centers, art suppliers, and craft stores.

Palight is Palram's brand for its broad line of flat foamed PVC products. It has several products used in the visual merchandising industry by independent designers, store design teams, and manufacturers. Palight ProjectPVC, cut to sizes, is typically used for DIY, maker, and craft projects. Palight EPS (Economical Print Substrate) is a high-quality, but value-oriented, substrate for digital and screen print applications for displays. Palight Premium is a line of boards optimized for use in the digital printing, fabrication, and display markets; both the EPS and premium version may be run through flatbed solvent printers and used for signage or environmental graphics. Palram also produces a version of Palight for outdoor use that is a thicker gauge with increased UV protection; it is used for outdoor and three-dimensional signage applications.

Gatorboard is another type of display board with an inner core of dense foam and a rigid exterior made of wood-fiber veneer. This exterior is water resistant and will not easily break or warp. Gatorboard is not easily hand cut and requires an elect hand or table saw for a clean straight cut. It is more expensive than regular foam board, but it has a paintable surface unlike Foamcore.

Ultraboard is a lightweight structural panel consisting of a rigid polystyrene foam inner core faced on both sides by a smooth, moisture-resistant sheet of solid polystyrene. The surface is excellent for painting, silk-screening, photo mounting, and vinyl application. These properties and a multitude of shaping methods make it an excellent choice for signage, photo mounting, exhibits' point-of-purchase displays, and routed letters. It is available in ³⁄₁₆-inch to 3-inch thickness. It is best cut by a saw, not by hand, and it can be routed and is available in colors by special order.

MightyCore is one of the strongest, most versatile rigid foam board products on the market today. Easy to work with and incredibly durable, MightyCore is the perfect choice for a variety of projects needed to be cut by hand. It is available in white in ¼-inch and ½-inch thicknesses. The ultra-smooth paper finish provides excellent ink coverage and adherence for flatbed printers. It accepts most glues, inks, and paints.

Foamcore is a strong, lightweight, easily cut material useful for backing, mounting photographic prints, model making, and creating three-dimensional displays. It consists of three layers—an inner layer of polystyrene clad with outer facing of a white-coated paper on both sides. It is easily hand cut with metal straight edge or T-square and an X-Acto knife or box cutter. It does not accept water-based paints and is prone to warping. It has more strength when constructed using hot glue or interlocking dovetail methods. It is an excellent material for creating prototypes of fixtures, props, and other components for window displays. (See Figure 18.16.)

FOAMCORE CUTTING TOOLS

Cutting and modeling Foamcore by hand requires using a metal straight edge and an X-Acto knife with a surplus of blades to achieve precision cuts. A unique set of cutting tools is available from Logan Graphic Products along with a line of YouTube tutorials to demonstrate the cutting process (https://www.youtube.com/watch?v=yYKa2RZTifU). **FoamWerks** is a revolutionary set of tools designed to use common foam board up to ½-inch (12.7 millimeters) thick as a three-dimensional medium for art projects, craft projects, architectural designs, 3-D modeling, topography projects, and anything else where foam board needs to be cut with precision and accuracy. There are FoamWerks tools available to cut circles, straight edges, beveled edges, v-grooves, rabbet edges, drilling holes, and more. The tools use easy-to-change razor blades, and many tools feature spare blade storage on the tool itself. FoamWerks line of creativity tools can in some cases be used freehand or in conjunction with the FoamWerks W3001 Channel Rail to guide the tools for perfectly straight cuts. Remember, a

FIGURE 18.16 A Foamcore prototype is used to test a fixture design and confirm the positioning of signage, price points, and the capacity of products. The strength and versatility of the Foamcore allows the design team to mock up the fixture accurately. Details such as draw-pulls add a realistic touch. The design team and client can review the fixture design before production and cite any necessary changes. *RPG, New York, New York.*

great visual designer is fearless, curious, experimental, and not intimidated by materials even when borrowed from the construction and building industry. Visual merchandisers are a breed of designers who will try their hand at anything!

Graphics

Along with the countless materials used for the fabrication of displays and fixtures, there is a world of graphic materials and graphic applications available to today's designer. Window graphics, environmental graphics, and signage for fixtures and branding have transformed the way we approach design. For many stores, it is the branding that drives the look we see in store design today, aimed to connect with the consumer on a higher level visually, architecturally, and culturally. (See Figure 18.17.)

The visual merchandiser or store designer may have spectacular design ideas for the store interior or window, but without the knowledge of graphic materials and capabilities they will not go very far with their designs. They need to be conversant in the latest technologies and materials to challenge the design process, and they need trusted industry partners (manufacturers) to make it happen. Any flourishing designer will divulge that his or her "secret advantage" is his or her industry resources. It is wise to connect with a local graphic manufacturer and visit its facility after exploring the company's website. Regularly attending trade shows and conferences as discussed in Chapter 26 is critical, because new materials and technologies are introduced to the industry frequently.

Visual Citi in the New York metropolitan area is a good example of a full-service graphic design house for retail displays, fixture rollouts, signage, and much more (http://www.visualciti.com). Another is Applied Image (http://bigres.com). It offers signage, printing, and fabrication for hospitality and retail environments: interior and exterior signage, wayfinding, fixturing and displays—a range of services an ordinary printer may not provide. Most of these businesses have a team of professional design engineers, graphic designers, project managers, and highly skilled fabricators.

A good graphic design company provides services that include prototyping and **value engineering**. Value engineering ensures the job is produced for the best value, with the appropriate materials using the most affordable process. For example, a job can be produced more inexpensively if the design utilizes the length and width of chosen material. Manufacturers can use may different methods, and the finished product will not appear any different to the consumer's eye, all while maintaining the design's integrity. In this line of work the visual merchandiser is often faced with the decision of going a few different ways to produce a job, mainly because of budget constraints, material size, or availability. Much of the work that is contracted is customized (not in stock), so it is important to discuss the turnaround time for jobs and inquire if most of the services are supported in the printer's facility.

As we view many of the images in this book we learn that the key to great retail design is customization, differentiating the look of your store from all of the others, creating an environment that elevates the shopping experience and impresses the consumer. Graphics are easiest way for retailers to achieve "personalization," even when their fixtures and merchandise may be similar to their competition. A retail graphic design manufacturer can assist the visual merchandiser and store designer in crafting the look and feel they desire for the store within the desired budget. The experienced designer who knows materials can negotiate the design by cutting just the right number of corners to

FIGURE 18.17   According to the design agency 2 × 4, the Prada Epicenter stores in New York and Los Angeles were created to transcend shopping and to engage public space and cultural programming. Both stores feature prominent wall areas where new graphic design content could be injected into the store on a regular schedule. Refreshed every six months and installed on a wall the length of a full city block, the wallpapers create an environment where culture, architecture, and fashion converge. *Prada Soho New York, New York. David LEFRANC/Gamma-Rapho via Getty Images.*

obtain the look for a lot less. For example, ABS can often substitute for acrylic on some projects for a fraction of the cost, and MDF can substitute for plywood.

Forging a good relationship with a manufacturer that has in-house production capabilities is essential to the success of the visual merchandiser/store designer; it is part of the design and planning process, and it pays off when that person can help bring your design concepts to life on the selling floor on time and within budget.

A retail graphic operation usually provides service that include:

- Window displays
- In-store displays
- Props/decor
- C-print and graphic rollouts
- Large-format graphics
- Foam
- Corrugated and paper displays
- Retail environments
- Dimensional logos and letters
- Custom fabrication
- Displays and fixtures in acrylic and wood
- Architectural signage

A good manufacturer works in a range of materials that include:

- Metal
- Laminates
- Aluminum
- Steel
- Display foam
- PETG
- Plastics
- Magnetic
- Graphics
- Paper and cardstock
- Polycarbonates
- Corrugated cardboard
- Electrical/LED
- Motors
- Eco-friendly and recyclable materials
- Acrylic
- Wood
- Sign foam
- Canvas, static
- Cling
- Vinyl
- Coroplast

ADHESIVE CUT VINYL

Adhesive **vinyl** is a high-performance material with varied strengths of tack or stick made to adhere to surfaces. It is available in hundreds of colors, and custom colors are available with large orders. Name-brand manufactures include Avery and 3M. Adhesive vinyl is used to brand a FedEx truck, an airplane, public spaces, museums, restaurants, stores, and—of course—window displays. It can withstand the outdoor elements for a long period of time. The vinyl product used for all of these applications differs slightly in performance and is rated by its durability and the length of time it needs to last on the surface on which it will be applied. This is extremely important to consider when ordering vinyl, because the vinyl used on airplanes and trucks is designed to last for many years, whereas the vinyl for a window display glass is temporary and much easier to remove. Vinyl for displays removes easily with a flat razor-edge tool and some window cleaner, while a heat gun with a chemical adhesive remover is needed for the grade that lasts longer. Vinyl is available in different opacities, from opaque to translucent; it may be high gloss or matte. Other finishes include reflective, metallic, glitter, etched, frosted, dusted, fluorescent, and solvent vinyl, which is printable. Small tabletop sized vinyl cut machines are available to crafters today, but most visual merchandising departments require a 36-inch to 48-inch machine for commercial use. Roland and Summa are trustworthy brand names, and your budget usually determines the one you

will purchase. These cutting machines typically run on a PC, although some software programs are Mac compatible. A proprietary software program or driver may be included with the package upon purchasing, and surprisingly some machines interface directly with Adobe Creative Cloud-programs such as Illustrator.

Once the media is loaded into the back of the machine and the desired design is sent via the software program, the machine cuts the media using a rotating tangential knife and ejects the finished job from the front. The vinyl will require **weeding** by peeling and removing the unwanted part of the design, around letters and inside the middle of the O, R, P, and B for example. Once the design is fully peeled, a layer of transfer release tape is applied over the design and burnished with a plastic paddle tool using uniform handstrokes. The design is then set into position on a surface wall or window and accurately measured to be sure the design or letterforms

FIGURE 18.18 The vinyl cut message on the window at H&M informs the viewer it's time to shop "Back to School." The repetition of letterforms creates a visual pattern and elevates the composition of the display. *Copyright WindowsWear PRO http://pro.windowswear.com; contact@windowswear.com 1.646.827.2288.*

are straight; a level is a handy tool to use in the process. Once in position, the design is taped to the surface and ready for installation; the transfer tape stays in tack (similar to applying a Band-Aid), and the paper backing is removed slowly, allowing the design to adhere to the glass. More burnishing follows with the plastic burnishing tool to ensure full adhesion and fewer bubbles, and the transfer tape is peeled away from the vinyl design. For larger jobs a professional installer may be needed. Signage and graphic companies provide both vinyl production and installation services for about $20 USD a square foot. (See Figure 18.18.)

Printing on adhesive vinyl is a solvent-based process, however it is quickly changing to eco-solvent inks that are more environmentally friendly. Solvent refers to ink that is not water-based, which is why vinyl cut prints can be used outdoors in all weather conditions. In order to produce printed vinyl cuts, a solvent printer/cutter machine is required. The printer/cutter prints the design first and then rolls the media back to cut around the design, typically on a roll of white, transparent, or cling media. The printed vinyl cut resembles a large "sticker," or label. Transfer tape is not needed to install the printed vinyl cut. Large or small,

the sticker is peeled partially, then applied to the surface and burnished slowly as the back material is released and the adhesive side is adhered to the surface. The result is a beautiful colorful graphic calling out to the shopper.

LARGE-FORMAT GRAPHICS

For the past decade **environmental graphics** have become a staple to the display window, the visual merchandising rollout, and the store interior. Trade shows and showrooms splash huge graphics to grab our attention, banners printed on soft fabrics gently blow and catch our eye, and backlit graphic lightboxes illuminate our walk past the shop window at night. (See Figures 18.19 and 18.20.)

We begin to recognize how powerful and widespread the use of graphic elements is in visual merchandising, largely due to the reduction in cost, accessibility, and the wide range of options in materials and technology. Environmental graphics uses imagery, graphic design, and color combined with the store's architecture to effectively communicate the essence of the brand, leaving a memorable impression on the shopper. Large-scale graphics provide the selling area with a look and an "attitude."

FIGURE 18.19 A giant graphic bouquet backdrops the mannequins and highlights the pattern of the tabletop products in the window display at Rustan's department store in the Philippines. The floral graphic is layered on a hanging panel to emphasize the design and add dimension. *Courtesy of Rustan's Department Store, Philippines.*

FIGURE 18.20 A wall-sized bamboo scene creates a Zen moment, inspiring the shopper to stop and reflect on the table setting at Rustan's department store in the Philippines. The image is printed on opaque fabric and applied onto an illuminated light box. *Courtesy of Rustan's Department Store, Philippines.*

The beauty of graphics is that they are temporary and can be changed to reflect the seasons or a promotion, allowing the store to have a fresh new look instantly. Graphics not only leave an impression; they have the ability to direct and move the traffic flow through the store. Floor graphics, column wraps, ceiling details, or a wall mural on a long span of wall help create the cohesive branded environment that motivates and excites the shopper to move actively throughout the store. (See Figure 18.21.)

FIGURE 18.21 The playful environment at Aéropostale entertains the consumer with merchandise and fixtures in a full spectrum of color. Architectural wall graphics of columns and archways add to the lively décor, topped off with an oversized vinyl cut message on the ceiling declaring, "Live, Love, Dream!" *Courtesy of Aeropostale, Roosevelt Field, New York. GHA Design of Montreal, Quebec, Canada.*

Many visual departments use a 42-inch to 60-inch inkjet printer to output day-to-day jobs and hire a print agency for larger quantity promotional work. An in-house wide-format printer can save the visual department turnaround time and money. Inkjet plotters print on a variety of medias. The media plays an important role in translating the design, and in some cases it can inspire the design itself. The following is a standard media selection:

◆ Bond and coated papers—lightweight to heavy presentation paper, technical paper, velum, brown paper

◆ Photographic paper—high-gloss, satin, or matte

◆ Backlit material—two-view adhesive and film

◆ Adhesive back polypropylene—light to heavy

◆ Banner and sign material—Tyvek® and polypropylene

◆ Fine art material—fabric—chiffon, canvas, cotton duck

A wide-format printer has a variety of uses in the visual merchandising department. Besides printing large-scale graphics for displays, it can generate quick templates for hand cutting designs out of Foamcore or wood. For example, if the visual merchandiser wanted to use a giant leaf shape in the display as a prop, he or she could design it on the computer, print it, and use it as an overlay to cut the shape by hand or with an electric saw. It is also an excellent tool for "prototyping or **comping**" to assist in the visualization process. For example, a large sign can be printed on inexpensive media and be tacked up in place to give a team of management a "snapshot" of an idea prior to installation. This process ensures everyone has a clear picture of the proposed design, and it provides a forum for discussion among stakeholders. The printer can also be used as a creative tool for creating dynamic props and decoratives in an in-house display department. (See Figure 18.22.)

In addition, it is a useful tool for printing presentation or inspiration boards to share with the design or management team. Some stores print their own store signage, props, banners, and wallpaper. The quality is extremely high, and designs printed on **adhesive back** media can easily be mounted on Foamcore, eliminating the use of toxic spray adhesive. The designs can then be used in a window display, on fixtures or for wayfinding. (See Figure 18.23.)

GRAPHICS IN THE STORE

Window graphics can function in several ways—to brand, to prop, or to inform the shopper about a sale, the designer's

FIGURE 18.22 These Power Puff Girls come to life with oversized printed heads mounted on Foamcore. The color boxes constructed of gator foam are painted to match the brightly colored Moschino fashion. *Moschino, Milan, Italy. Copyright WindowsWear PRO http://pro.windowswear.com; contact@windowswear.com 1.646.827.2288.*

The glass window storefront has become an increasingly valuable piece of real estate for the visual merchandiser thanks to the innovation of materials like vinyl and printable vinyl that adhere to the glass. Window graphics can reinforce an advertising campaign, provide directions, or transform the window into an environment.

Window graphics are effective in calling out to the consumer even before the window display has been fully recognized. Here is where the visual merchandiser must exercise knowledge of the brand positioning, color, typography, imagery, and materials. Some brands send prepared vinyl graphics and a planogram for installation to the visual team; however, in many cases the visual team has a graphics person who works on the production of vinyl in-house using the vinyl cutter and software on the computer.

Graphics and fixtures have become one and work hand-in-hand in today's store environment. In the past, a fixture may have had a large metal sign holder attached, where the graphic was inserted into a frame; today graphics and fixtures are fully integrated as one unit, where the graphic plays a more important role in the design of the fixture. Fixtures have evolved from racks to structural design elements that create the architecture of the store. (See Figures 18.25 and 18.26.)

name, a credit for an object used in the window, a price point, or exactly where the merchandise is located in the store. Vinyl applications can also be used to create a proscenium either to shrink the window's show space or afford it a decorative border. (See Figure 18.24.)

FIGURE 18.23 In a promotional window display at H&M, a Foamcore shopping bag with illuminated branding explodes with a giant image of Katy Perry. Stars, shapes, candy canes, and dimensional elements set the scene to celebrate her holiday campaign. *Copyright WindowsWear PRO http://pro.windowswear.com; contact@ windowswear.com 1.646.827.2288.*

FIGURE 18.24 The vinyl window graphics do a great job at Liberty of London to reduce the size of the window for the reclining mannequin. Directional signage informs the shopper where the treasures of merchandise can be found in the store. *Copyright WindowsWear PRO http://pro.windowswear.com; contact@ windowswear.com 1.646.827.2288.*

FIGURE 18.25 The Adidas brand logo is transformed into an oversized fixture to feature a promotional line of footwear in the Adidas Pop-Up for an NBA All-Star weekend event. The overall goal of the branded space was to amplify the partnership between Adidas and the NBA and showcase key product lines and launches. *Adidas Pop-Up Shop, Roundhouse, Portland, Oregon. Photography by Matt Dutile.*

Product signage and wayfinding is in a constant state of evolution, but there are few standards to abide by. In the age of customization, stores have developed very intimate ways to communicate their messages to the consumer. A sign is no longer a sign; it is apt to be an architectural element or a part of a fixture or wall. Still, there is a need to show price points and tell the consumer about the product features—transforming signage into a storytelling device that unveils the inner spirit of the product. A good sign should be clear, concise, and comprehensive. There are several types of signs used in retail settings:

- Wayfinding
- Promotional Signs
- Category Signs
- Sale Signs
- Price Points
- Institutional

If a sign is "selling" an item, it should say what the item is, what it does, why it should be purchased here and now, and how much it costs. In the fewest possible words and in the most understandable language, it should cover the questions a customer might ask. (See Figure 18.27.)

If the back of the sign will be visible, back it with either another sign or a graphic design. Try to keep all signs that

FIGURE 18.26 The red triangular Aéropostale sign on the side of the multilevel fixture has a cool vintage style resembling an antique or found object. The sign is integrated into the design of the fixture and enhances the assorted merchandise through the process of branding. *Courtesy of Aéropostale, Roosevelt Field, New York. GHA Design of Montreal, Quebec, Canada.*

appear in the same area or department consistent in color, size, and layout, so that the customer is not confused by too great a variety of conflicting signage. A category sign specifies the major classification of the collected merchandise rather than a specific design, pattern, or price. It could read, for example, "Women's Wool Sweaters," and under that one sign there could be a bin full of an assortment of varying prices, colors, kinds of wools, and manufacturers. As with the selling sign, neatness, accuracy, and simplicity count.

An institutional sign lists the services provided by the store: its hours, refund and exchange policies, delivery charges, alteration setup, and so on.

A store should not have too many signs, but items and categories should be identified to provide ease of recognition and relevant information. The more fully a store is "self-service," the more important good signage becomes. The signs help supply the answers the salesperson would ordinarily provide.

Wayfinding is a term that refers to directional signage or "finding one's way" in store design jargon. Wayfinding directs the consumer through a space by using floor graphics, ceiling graphics or a customized system. Department or category names are considered a part of wayfinding; typically this type of signage is located above the fixtures within the **sight line** of the store. The sight line is a term that refers to the line of sight or the unobstructed area of the store above the fixtures in a shop or department. In order to navigate intuitively, the eye must be able to travel distance and see

FIGURE 18.27 A simple sign with bulleted text provides consumers with all they need to know about the merchandise in a font size that is legible and easy to read. *Ulrich Baumgarrten via Getty Images.*

the directional signage that will lead shoppers to the desired area of the store. IKEA stores serve as an excellent example for good wayfinding. Pathways contain maps and exits to food and restrooms, and neighboring categories are clearly identified. Wayfinding should first provide the shopper with an orientation at the entranceway and work to identify each major location or department throughout the store. Landmarks such as escalators, stairs, or category gateways should be signed to create a natural flow or path for the shopper to follow. (See Figure 18.28.)

FIGURE 18.28 The entranceway to Aéropostale introduces the shopper to the brand through several graphic methods. The decorative brick wall on the left resounds the brand using a collage of imagery and chalkboard signage. The floor graphics speak boldly about the brand's heritage, and the illuminated brand signage merges seamlessly with the store architecture. *Courtesy of Aéropostale, Roosevelt Field, New York. GHA Design of Montreal, Quebec, Canada.*

DESIGN OBJECTIVE

When the Brinkworth design consultancy was commissioned to design the new AllSaints clothing store in Glasgow, Scotland, the location that it was fortunate to get was a former post office building. (See Figures CS18.1–CS18.2.)

Pam Flanagan, associate director at Brinkworth, explains, "The term 'Faded Grandeur' was conceived to describe the concept for AllSaints' retail environments. The aspiration was to create environments that were aligned with the aesthetic of the clothing range, resulting in a holistic conceptual approach exclusive to the brand. In many of the locations for the AllSaints stores, we were lucky to uncover existing architectural features during the strip out of the interiors. These features were integrated into the overall distressed aesthetic alongside the bespoke fixtures and fittings. The emergence of the 'found' within some of the initial sites was embraced as the approach for further development of the brand aesthetic and forming the unique

FIGURE CS18.1 The former post office building was converted to the AllSaints store, and much of the old was left visible in the new retail space.

identity of the stores. AllSaints wanted to keep clear of the cookie-cut, rollout design; therefore by uncovering and revealing the historical layers within the interior, each site developed its own unique story."

DESIGN SOLUTION

According to Ms. Flanagan, "The concept developed within an organic design process in which the client worked very close with Brinkworth on each store. Each store was viewed as a collaboration. There were no guidelines to adhere to, and AllSaints grasped the opportunity to be identified by the unification of the interiors and the clothing. So, for them the juxtaposition of the old and the new presented a unique aesthetic."

In starting the strip-out procedure in the old, neglected, early-twentieth century post office building, Ms. Flanagan says, "What was revealed were the original glazed brick tiles and traces of a staircase on one section of the wall that presented the opportunity to incorporate the palimpsest of the site into the new interior. Further uncovering of lathe and plaster sections of wall were retained within the overall scheme." (See Figure CS18.3.)

Amid the remnants of the decrepit building, the broken walls, and the raw construction elements, the smart, contemporary AllSaints clothes are presented on a variety of fixtures and displayers—some custom designed by Brinkworth and others, semi-antique and salvaged, "giving the store a strong eclectic feel, reflecting the strong ethos of the brand." (See Figure CS18.4.)

With the 23-foot ceiling, the Brinkworth design team took advantage of the height to create a unique lighting installation that consisted of seven 12-foot long horizontal crosses equipped with fairground light bulbs programmed to twinkle in various sequences and at variable speeds. The fitting system was made from drawn steel chains and was inspired by the industrial warehouse fixtures of the turn of the last century. The chains were fixed to the tall ceiling and became a decorative feature as well as creating a transparent division

FIGURE CS18.2   The double height arched windows parallel the AllSaints industrial style.

FIGURE CS18.3   Traces of the now long-gone staircase remain on the tiled wall of the store.

FIGURE CS18.4   The old doors and lead glass pane windows add further layers of integrity to the design concept and pair with the interior of the building.

FIGURE CS18.5 The drawn steel chain fixture system made from industrial warehouse fixtures of the turn of the last century are fixed to the ceiling. They double as a decorative feature to create a transparent division between the mezzanine and ground level.

between the mezzanine where the men's department is located and the ground level. Ms. Flanagan elaborates, "By sourcing industrial equipment from factory closures in the UK and further afield, we were able to build up a collection of fixtures and fittings that would otherwise be sent to landfills. For example, old weaving looms were taken from their original form, and by welding one or two steel rails to the frames of the looms, they were able to function as hanging rails for clothing." (See Figures CS18.5 and CS18.6.)

When Pam Flanagan was asked about the effect the reuse and repurposing of these materials had on

FIGURE CS18.6 The broken walls with the raw construction elements juxtapose the smart contemporary AllSaints clothes on a variety of fixtures and displayers.

the design process and the brand identity of AllSaints, she replied, "The old elements add further layers of integrity to the design concept through the exposure and honesty of the fabric of the interior of the building. In particular, the use of reclaimed Singer sewing machines with the shop front window design proved to evoke an emotional connection not with only the All-Saints customers, but also with passersby in the street who have an affection [for] and memories of the traditional sewing machines. The installation of the sewing machines in great numbers also became a motif for the brand, so much so that the shop fronts essentially did not require the application of any brand signage and were instantly recognized as AllSaints."

CONCLUSION

The client's reaction was, as usual, favorable, and thus Brinkworth continues to design these unique,

one-of-a-kind AllSaints shops. Ms. Flanagan sums it up like this: "The faded grandeur interiors and reappropriation of industrial elements have become entwined with the brand. The clothing and the environment have merged seamless to form a unique, memorable aesthetic for AllSaints as a brand. The use of the old became an essential component of each site. I don't think it was about making the design acceptable to the market; AllSaints wanted to stand out and be distinctive within the retail landscape, and they had faith that breaking away from that was the right move for the brand." (See Figures CS18.7 and CS18.8.)

CREDITS: *Design: Brinkworth. London, United Kingdom. Design Team: Adam Brinkworth, with Simon Ash, Kieran Morgan, Pamela Flanagan, and Kevin Brennan; Associate Director: Pam Flanagan. Photography: Louise Melchior, Brinkworth, London, United Kingdom.*

FIGURE CS18.7 The Brinkworth design team utilized the 23-foot ceilings with a unique lighting installation that consisted of seven 12-foot-long horizontal crosses equipped with fairground light bulbs.

FIGURE CS18.8 Design elements of the early twentieth century architecture add to the unique quality of the "faded grandeur" of the AllSaints store.

Materials Used in Visual Merchandising and Store Design: Trade Talk

ABS
acrylic
adhesive back
antique
bendable plywood
chipboard
comping
composite board
EPS
environmental graphics
fiddleback
Flexboard
floral foam
Foamcore
gauge
Gatorboard
high-gloss finish

Homasote
laminate
leaf
luan
matte
medium density fiberboard (MDF)
MDF Ultralight
molded polymer
PVC
Palight
particleboard
patina
plywood
polystyrene
resins
sight line
Sintra

Smooth-On
Sonotube
styrene
Styrofoam
substrate
tambour
Texture Plus
Ultraboard
Upson Board
value engineering
veneers
vinyl
wayfinding
weeding
wiggle board

Materials Used in Visual Merchandising and Store Design: A Recap

✦ Materials and production processes are essential in communicating the essence of brands and the brand story.

✦ Display and store designers must be knowledgeable about materials and processes to work with manufacturers.

✦ The basic materials are wood, wood composites, metal, plastics, foams, Homasote and various foamboards.

✦ Wood comes in hundreds of varieties; the choice has to do with style, cost, and end use.

✦ Plywood comes in many "grades" from rough to fine, and standardized thicknesses including ¼, ⅜, ½, and ¾ inch.

✦ MDF is a less expensive material than wood with a smooth, paintable surface and a standard choice for building fixtures.

✦ MDF Ultralight weighs less than traditional MDF.

✦ 48 inches × 96 inches is the standard size for materials sold as boards.

✦ Resins are commonly used for casting forms.

✦ Styrene and Sintra are thermoplastic materials.

✦ Sonotubes are circular forms.

✦ Wiggle board, tambour, or luan will achieve a curved surface.

✦ Veneers are skins or laminates that are applied to wood or composite board.

✦ Homasote is an excellent material for pin-up boards.

✦ Matte, high-gloss, leaf, antique, or patinas all refer to the finish of a surface.

✦ Foamboards are the standard material for mounting temporary graphics.

✦ Vinyl cut lettering is a standard for window display and signage.

✦ Printable vinyl cut resembles a large sticker.

+ Manufacturers can assist visual merchandisers and store designers with fabrication and material knowledge.

+ Fixtures and graphics are unified to better represent brands.

+ Signage is a storytelling device.

+ Wayfinding directs and familiarizes the shopper with the store.

Questions for Review and Discussion

1. Name three types of wood and what brands they would be best suited for.

2. What is the preferred substrate when using a veneer surface?

3. Describe the origin of rescued wood.

4. Name three uses for Sintra.

5. What is a good material for building a fixture prototype?

6. Describe a holiday display that could be manufactured with EPS foam.

7. What type of merchandise is best suited for a metal rail system?

8. How can fixtures assist in the branding the store?

9. What type of sign provides the store hours?

10. Define wayfinding.

11. How do environmental graphics affect the shopper?

12. What is a wide-format printer used for?

PART FOUR

Related Areas of Visual Merchandising

Fashion accessories are best shown in use. Chapter 19 focuses on how to show accessories in coordinated groupings and how to handle displaying accessories without outfits. Chapter 20 relates the unique techniques used for displaying home fashions, hard goods, and foods.

With the growth of self-service retailing and the increased competition for consumer dollars, point-of-purchase (or POP) displays have proliferated. Chapter 21 addresses the booming POP industry, focusing on the presentation of merchandise to the customer at the crucial point of purchase.

The ins and outs of trade show and exhibit design are explored in Chapter 22. This is a wide-open field for those with a background in display, commercial or graphic arts, or interior design.

Chapter Nineteen
Fashion Accessory Display

Eye Candy, Louis Vuitton, Barcelona, Spain. *Copyright WindowsWear PRO http://pro.windowswear.com; contact@windowswear.com 1.646.827.2288.*

**AFTER YOU HAVE READ THIS CHAPTER,
YOU WILL BE ABLE TO DISCUSS**

- ◆ the importance of accessorizing in fashion displays
- ◆ effective props for displaying accessories
- ◆ display techniques used in jewelry presentations
- ◆ the importance of lighting in accessory display

Fashion accessories are the little things that mean a lot in revenues for stores. In a fickle retail economy, accessories provide the affordable, accessible, and spontaneous sale. They complete an outfit. They add color where there is none. They infuse style that can turn a simple "nothing" dress or suit into a stylish outfit. The right accessories can update a dress or revitalize a suit and add sparkle to last year's outfit with the shimmer and glitz that appears in this month's *Style* blog or magazine. The fashion accessories—the shoes, bag, gloves, belt, hat, and costume or fine jewelry—are the exclamation point of a fashion statement!

Providing the Setting

One way to show fashion accessories is to make them part of the total look. This provides the shopper with a **setting**, or background, for those accessories, creating a sense of time, place, and occasion—and a distinctive and memorable style. The difference between a dress or suit carefully fitted on a form and the display of that same garment accessorized with a scarf, jewelry, and a bag slung over the shoulder, along with the right style and color of shoes, is the difference between "just a dress or suit" and a total outfit.

What was merely a garment on a three-dimensional form is magically transformed into an editorial fashion statement, an idealized presentation of what the garment can be and look like when properly accessorized.

For the specialty store or department store that sells ready-to-wear, but also has an array of fashion accessories, the visual merchandiser can add a secondary arrangement of fashion accessories into the display area next to the mannequin or form. It can be an additional bag, gloves, and costume jewelry. The visual merchandiser may even choose to add other lifestyle suggestions such as a bottle of cologne or perfume or hair accessory in a small still-life arrangement set out on a casually (but artistically) draped scarf at the foot of the mannequin (or form) that is already accessorized. The grouping on the floor can—for greater effectiveness—be raised onto a low table or pedestal; a transparent cube or cylinder; a classic capital or a piece of a column; a log or tree stump, if the merchandise and the season and the texture are all right; a mound of moss; a pile of flowerpots in either the natural terra-cotta or painted to blend in or complement the assemblage; a "rock"; a construction of bricks or glass blocks; or a low piece of furniture. The possibilities are endless. The use of elevation can step the merchandise up off the floor and bring it closer to the viewer's eye level. It can also add

FIGURE 19.1 Kleinfeld's in NYC has all the fashion accessories any bride might need and shows a sampling in the window along with the semi-dressed mannequin. The background of drawers—some pulled open—provides a neutral setting for the light-colored garments. *Kleinfelds, New York City.* Copyright WindowsWear PRO http://pro.windowswear.com; contact@windowswear.com 1.646.827.2288.

FIGURE 19.2 This black-and-white window is filled with dozens of shoe boxes, and several of the featured shoes have escaped from their containers and taken up prominent spots in the window. The display combines fashion with fashion accessories in a bold and dramatic manner. *Robert Ellis, Culver City, California. Design: Keith Dillion.*

a seasonal touch to the whole display setup, promote the image of the material, or even complement the color and texture of what is being offered. (See Figures 19.1 and 19.2.)

In menswear displays—and in some cases with women's wearespecially pant outfits—a complete suit or outfit can be

rigged on a suit or dress form, and the visual merchandiser can create the illusion of a total figure—headless—with just a form, a rod, and a base. An **auxiliary display** of fashion accessories, including shoes, can then be neatly arranged in a lay-down or on buildups next to the base of the form on the floor to suggest the right accompaniments for the outfit. Lighting is especially helpful in bring the viewers' attention to multiple locations in one display. It is important to light the auxiliary accessory group in a display, whether it is on the floor, on a chair, on a table, or arranged within open picture frames as a still-life composition. The visual merchandiser will usually light the chest area of a dressed figure, and the aura of light will take in any neck or lapel jewelry or earrings, shirts/blouses, and scarves/ties. When drapers are used, the trousers may hang off or over the slacks bar and reach down almost to the floor of the display area, where the shoes and other accessories can be clustered. The viewer's eye will travel from the jacket, shirt, and tie, down the length of the draped trousers, to the accessory grouping on the floor. (See Figure 19.3.)

Many of today's mannequins have a sculpted foot to suggest a shoe instead of a human foot that will accommodate wearing shoes. Occasionally the mannequin may need to use a foot spike to be held in a standing position, limiting

FIGURE 19.3 Scale plays an important part when promoting small items in full-size windows. To feature the assorted pieces of fine imported leather goods, the designers at Barneys New York created a giant head out of actual shoe boxes and finished off with gigantic glasses and used it as the "come-closer" attraction. The shoes are suspended throughout the window while other pieces rest on the boxes that line the floor. *Michael Loccisano/Getty Images for Barneys New York.*

the visual merchandiser to use shoes. It is not unusual, therefore, in Europe to see a beautifully accessorized, realistic mannequin—wearing hat, bag, gloves, scarf, jewelry, and so on—standing shoeless in the window, because visual merchandisers aren't able to drill holes through the shoes in order to put on the mannequin. The right and fashionable shoes are often shown standing on the floor next to the dressed figure. This tends to be a more acceptable way to display; however, it is considered poor "etiquette" to leave a mannequin barefoot in a display.

For the store or shop that specializes in fashion accessories without the ready-to-wear, one of the major challenges is that the products are usually small, and often there are many styles, variations, and colors to show. Most products look best at eye level—at 3 to 5 feet above the ground level. Elevations are effective in raising the products and putting them together into lifestyle clusters or compositions. (See Figures 19.4–19.6.)

FIGURE 19.5   Where possible, the display area should be scaled to the product being presented. At Saks Fifth Avenue, the framed elongated shadow box makes the ideal space for the designer shoes shown stepping lightly on gilded fronds. Each shoe gets special attention and its own space and a complimentary viewing angle. *Saks Fifth Avenue, New York City. Donato Sardella/Getty Images for Saks 5th Avenue.*

FIGURE 19.4   Instead of showing the actual product, which is small and really needs to be seen up close, the designers at Etalage B Display in Montreal went BIG—REALLY BIG! A gigantic string of faux pearls backs up the bride and makes a big statement about what to give the bride as a gift she'll remember and treasure. Now—step inside and see our beautiful pearls. *LSM Bijouterie, Montreal, Canada. Design by Etalage B Display.*

A raked, or ramped, floor panel in a window or display case (see Chapter 7) is an excellent device for raising the product off the ground. The inclined level of the **raked floor** puts the rear of the display space at a higher level than the space up front, near the glass. The viewer on the street can see more comfortably the pieces displayed in the back. Finally, window masking (see Chapter 18) may be another excellent way of focusing on small pieces. A traditional show window may begin about 2 feet off the ground, and the glass opening can be about 10 feet tall by 10 to 12 feet wide. That is just too much window—too wide, too tall, and too deep to show off items such as shoes, bags, gloves, jewelry, and so forth. The large

FIGURE 19.6 Urban styling and memories of West Side Story set the stage at Coach New York for the display of the assorted color offering of handbags. Featured in the center of the window and up close to the front glass, the bags are beautifully lit to enhance their color and importance. *Coach, New York City. Eugene Gologursky/Getty Images.*

window can be divided into two or three smaller windows with an adhesive vinyl proscenium, or frame, and with the floor of the new windows raised up and the ceiling dropped. This way, the new windows are more than shadow-box windows but much less than a traditional show window more suited to ready-to-wear. By dividing the space into smaller windows, it is possible to cluster and group individual color stories or trending fashion looks that in one larger window would conflict with each other. Additionally, a large graphic can be used on glass with a cutout or reveal that allows the viewer to see the smaller curated display. (See Figure 19.7.)

When working with small items, to get the desired viewer or shopper's attention, it is often effective to resort to contrast and scale and proportion (see Chapter 3). Because fashion accessories are the smaller parts of an outfit, making them the "stars" in the display often takes showing them in relation to larger elements or props. The larger items will draw the viewer's eye to the display and then, hopefully, lead the viewer's attention to the smaller but more important part of the display—the merchandise. The same technique can be effective by reversing the scale of the prop. The prop will need to command attention by the contrast of its relationship with the product; for example using something ordinary to contrast the extraordinary accessory. It is possible to contrast small jewelry with miniature objects such as dollhouse furniture or decorative elements that are unexpected. In addition, using contrast along with scale makes the presentation even more effective. An array of white shoes shown against a black, dark gray, or deep green setting will "pop" and be easily seen. Diamonds are brilliant and more intense in sparkling color when viewed against a

FIGURE 19.7 A standard size window is divided into a pattern of smaller "boxes" or shadow boxes where the Chanel-designed shoes and bags each get equal star billing. The dressed and accessorized leg forms add a stabilizing balance to the display and show how the pieces go together. *Chanel, Paris, France. Copyright WindowsWear PRO http://pro.windowswear.com; contact@windowswear.com 1.646.827.2288.*

deep, dark matte surface, like velvet, faille, or even a wool crepe. (See Figure 19.8.)

Importance of Props to Fashion Accessory Display

Props are the decorative elements in a display that add image and enhance the illusion of time and place and the appropriateness of merchandise to setting. They can and do get the shopper to stop and look at the display and at the merchandise being offered. In a display of fashion accessories, the prop can, by its size and scale, unify the assorted smaller pieces into a total, comprehensive composition. The prop, therefore, not only serves to attract the shopper; it also is the presence and force that "holds" the various elements together in an easy-to-see, easy-to-comprehend manner. (See Figure 19.9.)

In Chapter 17 we discussed just how a chair, a table, a chest of drawers, an armoire, a piece of luggage, or a trunk can hold the assemblage of accessories and coordinates

while elevating them off the floor to a better height for viewing from out on the street or in the mall. But there are also many other everyday items that can serve the same purpose. A good example is a folding stepladder, with each step presenting another group or cluster—a scarf can trail

FIGURE 19.9   No matter where you move on this chessboard you are sure to be a winner. Using a standard chessboard and chess pieces as the earring presenters, the scale is perfectly in sync. *Miss Jackson, Tulsa, Oklahoma.*

and drape down several steps, with gloves and a bag on one step; shoes a step below, with maybe a hat or jewelry; and a flower or bottle of cologne a step above. A 5-foot folding wooden ladder left natural for fall or painted white for summer or resort, pastel tones for spring, and maybe glittery gold for Christmas can fill up the main space of a window and hold a variety of small merchandise. It also helps elevate the fashion accessories. For a larger display, a pair of folding ladders can be used—maybe of different heights, for interest—and planks of wood or glass shelves can be stretched between them, supported by the steps, to show off a greater array of accessories in appropriate groupings. (See Figures 19.10–19.12.)

GLOVES AND BAGS

Just as handbags are usually comfortably padded with tissues to fill out the hollow interior and show off the bag at its best, so, too, can gloves be enhanced by stuffing with "poly-fill" polyester fiber used for pillow stuffing.

A softly draped pair of gloves casually displayed over a bag is effective too or in a lay-down arrangement, but sometimes a little animation is called for, a little

FIGURE 19.10 Bamboo dumpling steamers—inexpensive, readily available, and reusable—add an Asian and exotic touch to these red, poppy-strewn windows. Assorted small gifts and fashion accessories are shown in, on top of, and dripping out of the steamers, which are piled up to effect a variety of viewing levels for the small products. Some of the steamers have their tops off, and these are used to create other points of interest. *Christofle, Madison Avenue, New York. Design: Polar Buranasatit.*

FIGURE 19.11 What a clever, eye-catching, and eco-friendly way to show a great variety of toiletries or fashion accessories: using reused, recycled boxes of assorted styles and sizes. Here, the boxes create a bouffant skirt for the semiabstract mannequin, but they could also be used to form a Christmas tree if they climbed to a point and some ornaments were added for sparkle. Maybe throw in some gift-wrapped boxes with ribbon trim. New boxes need not apply. *Miss Jackson, Tulsa, Oklahoma. Designer: Stacy Suvino.*

FIGURE 19.12 Wooden cheese boards topped with fine wire mesh domes serve up assorted small pieces of jewelry and watches as a tasty treat on the green grass mat. The tilted domes manage to keep out the bees but still allow shoppers to feast their eyes on the delicacies being presented. *Cada, Munich, Germany. Design: Peter Rank, of Deko Rank.*

humanizing. The glove can be holding a piece of jewelry or the end of a draped scarf. It can be gripping a shoulder strap or clutching some foliage. All it takes is time and imagination.

Strips of tissue can be rolled into pencil-thin shapes and inserted into the individual fingers of the glove. For a little more control, the tissue can be wrapped around a piece of bendable wire. There are hand forms available on the market with articulated and bendable fingers, or mannequin hands designed to pull the gloves over. If leathers are soft, a rigid hand form may also stretch or distort a fragile glove and affect its possible sale when it is removed from the form and returned to the selling floor.

JEWELRY

In store interiors, fine jewelry is commonly displayed in locked glass cases on covered jewelry pads, risers, or saddles. These types of displays require less propping with elements and more attention to the covering on the pads, risers, and saddles. Here the brand can say "luxury" through the use of suede, chagrin, or skate skin. Soft materials work best: velvet is one of the default materials for jewelry displays however linen and suede are popular too. It is here that subtle colors, textures or even fine stitching can define a brand or the style of the jewelry designer.

The display of pearls can be enhanced against warm-colored fabrics. Avoid using fabrics in yellows or cream because these colors may make the pearls look yellowish and dingy rather than lustrous. If you want to show jewelry on a head or form, use an abstract head or one that has been painted a single deep, matte color. Don't make the jewelry compete against skin tones and makeup colors. There are forms available covered in jersey or flocked in a velvet like finish that work very well. It is possible to pull an opaque stocking over a head to temporarily change its color. If you are using tights, you'd be extra clever in converting the other leg of the hosiery into a chignon or braid or hair roll as an accent. These techniques, including the creation of paper hairstyles, were heralded by museums. One of the best resources for ideas is the social media website Pinterest.

Some visual merchandisers use pieces on body forms—showing where they can be worn. Using human anatomy as display props takes skill and careful positioning; otherwise they can feel "dismembered" in a display. Robert Lee Morris in Soho New York presents costume and fine jewelry on fragmented human anatomy with a great aesthetic. Abstract or sculptural forms are sometimes the better choice—something not quite so realistic. There are also custom jewelry pads and bibs that are marketed that can be used to show off pieces of jewelry.

The visual merchandising industry has many vendors that specialize in the display of jewelry. There are dedicated manufacturers that design custom **jewelry pads** with beveled edges and stitched details in a range of luxurious fabrics and leathers. Their capabilities include developing a fully branded line of fixtures, pads, forms and packaging. Chippenhook (http://www.chippenhook.com) in Lewisville, Texas, is a leader in the custom jewelry display industry for over 35 years. Its team offers design capabilities, logistics, manufacturing, and warehousing. Unique and impactful displays are paramount in the accessory industry; visual merchandisers understand smaller products require more attention.

Draped fabrics can be used to simulate a jacket or dress for a pin or brooch to be attached to or even to lay a necklace on. Bracelets can be shown over gloves that are flat or stuffed, and rings can be displayed over a glove with tissue-stuffed fingers. Velvet or fine kid gloves are especially good for the presentation of diamonds and other sparkling stones. There are so many innovative approaches to jewelry display today, including trays filled with white and brown rice. The organic nature and texture of the rice is visually appealing or may suggest a wedding theme. Small white beans or black beans are another thriving trend. This tactile texture allows the consumer to engage with the merchandise in the display. Sand in a tray is another approach; a tray of tiny beads, pebbles, or even wood shavings offers a natural approach if it fits with the jewelry's style and dimensions.

Fine pieces of jewelry or very expensive pieces of costume jewelry can be given a "Tiffany" treatment. The pieces can be dropped into a shadow-box setting, along with an attention-getting prop, like a piece of sculpture, a vase, a piece of quartz, a small painting, a collection of rare leather-bound books—or any prop that says "unique." Limiting the display space, accentuating the featured piece of jewelry in a beam of light, and using subtle illumination of the prop and the background makes the jewelry stand out. The piece can be draped over the books, sit atop a ridge of quartz, be displayed casually in front of the sculpture, or even be immersed inside a clear crystal vase (supported by invisible wires). However you do it, the viewer will see it and appreciate the class statement. A one-of-a-kind display usually means "expensive."

Silver jewelry can be treated more casually. It can be displayed against coarser-textured fabrics, like tweeds, burlap, wools, and linens. It can be laid out on floors covered with sand, pebbles, bricks, pavement tiles, or beautiful polished black stones. With the Southwest look so popular, and with Native American jewelry always in demand, why not show silver and silver-and-turquoise jewelry on sand "dunes" accented with succulent plants (real or artificial)? Real succulents require little watering or watching, you can use the real thing. Native American artifacts, like bowls, baskets, and woven blankets, can also add to the ambiance while underscoring the authenticity of the jewelry. The props can also be used as elevations and as a means of separating clusters of material into easier-to-see-and-understand groupings.

Lighting is of the utmost importance in the presentation of jewelry. Cold fluorescent lamps may be fine for blue-white diamonds, but they can be awful for gold settings and other colored stones. It certainly does not flatter skin tones when the diamond is tried on. Today, the small LED lights—the sharp, brilliant MR16 lamps—have an excellent color rendition and are ideal for jewelry displays. The narrow beams of light can be focused on the piece or pieces being featured and add fire to the brilliance of the stones and the setting. MR16 lamps can be used in shadow-box displays, in regular windows (maybe extended down on pipes), or in museum cases on the floor. They are small, available in various housings, and can be easily adapted to the showing of jewelry.

Fashion Accessory Display: Trade Talk

auxiliary display	props	setting
jewelry pads	raked floor	

Fashion Accessory Display: A Recap

Fashion accessories are best shown in use—as part of a costume. Fashion accessories should be shown together in coordinated groupings, either in a lay-down next to the costumed form or figure or raised up on a platform, elevation, piece of furniture, and such. When fashion accessories are presented without outfits, try the following techniques:

+ Reduce the window glass by masking into a smaller opening or into a series of shadow boxes.

+ Raise the floor level or use a ramp or raked floor.

+ Bring the merchandise up closer to the viewer's eye level.

+ Use props to unify small objects or to bring attention to the small piece shown in a large space. Props can hold, elevate, show off, contrast, complement, or even suggest the value and prestige of the pieces being offered.

+ Use the right lighting, and put the strongest light on the merchandise, while downplaying the ambient light. Colored lights can be used to "paint" the background and enhance the merchandise.

Questions for Review and Discussion

1. What are the key functions of fashion accessories?

2. If the store does not stock accessory items, what is the best way to obtain such items for displays?

3. Describe fashion accessory displays you could create around the following key props:
   a. An empty wooden picture frame
   b. A beach chair and umbrella
   c. Artificial ice cubes

4. How can large window displays be made smaller so as not to diminish small accessory items on display?

5. Explain the importance of contrast in the display of accessories.

6. What pointers would you give to an individual creating his or her first accessory display?

Chapter Twenty
Home Fashions, Hard Goods, and Food Displays

Rustan's Department Store, Makati, Manila, Philippines.
Courtesy of Rustan's Department Store.

**AFTER YOU HAVE READ THIS CHAPTER,
YOU WILL BE ABLE TO DISCUSS**

- ◆ effective methods for home fashions display
- ◆ the importance of creating lifestyle situations in hard goods presentation
- ◆ techniques used in food display

Visual merchandisers working with home fashions, hard goods, and foods can use many of the same techniques that are used in the display of fashion apparel. It is important to approach this type of display keeping in mind that the buyer of home fashion items and of home goods is the same person. An effective method for home product displays is the creation of vignette settings that unify assorted elements into a theme. Linens and accessories can be mixed and matched, and can be the focal point of a display or accoutrements for other home fashions. When working with hard goods, whether they are large or small items, it is important to create lifestyle situations for the products. This can be done through the use of props that will grab the attention of the shopper and eventual user.

Food displays need skillful lighting. Produce should be presented to convey a message of "natural" and "country fresh" and look as if bathed in sunlight. The clientele must always be considered, however. A more sophisticated rather than rustic look may be desired with upscale customers. Depending on the target market, the visual merchandiser can set the look and tone by selectively using certain accessories. A food display will always benefit from presenting the goods in a way that allows shoppers to envision their use. (See Figure 20.1.)

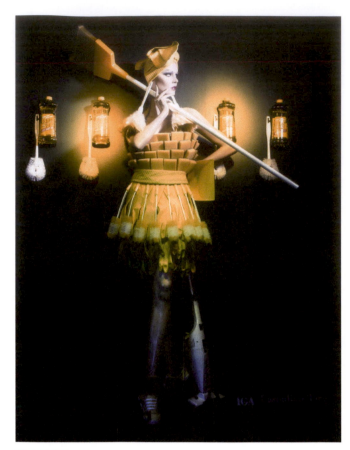

FIGURE 20.1   Fantasy and fun. The emphasis is on spring cleaning, and the mannequin is dressed in some of the brushes and cleaning aids available in the store. She wields a broom like a scepter, while a new vacuum cleaner stands beside her. The pinpoints of light and the product repetition on the back wall add to the display's effectiveness. *IGA, Montreal, Canada. Design: Étalage B Display.*

Home Fashions

Every year, the International Housewares Association (IHA) sponsors a giant expo at the McCormick Place exhibit space in Chicago, and literally thousands of manufacturers and vendors from around the world present their newest designs and wares to the thousands of merchants and global retailers that are involved in the home fashions business.

As a category, home fashions is more than just sheets, pillowcases, and towels. It is more than tablecloths, napkins, and placemats. This vast field includes china and pottery, silver, flatware and cutlery, crystal and glass, pots, pans and baking paraphernalia, and so on. Think of a well-furnished home—all the accessories and accents that go in after the furniture is in place. Home fashions is about the many choices and options afforded the shopper who is making purchases for his or her home. The presentation of these

myriad options is so important that IHA has established an annual international award for the display and visual presentation of these items. So, when we speak of home fashions, we are really talking about a vast array of products that need to be displayed. (See Figures 20.2–20.10.)

The numerous items that can be used to give a distinct personality to the home definitely require **lifestyle presentation**. They call for displays that bring assorted materials together into a single theme, and that theme usually fits a particular lifestyle.

Color and pattern are most important here. No matter if the products can be used in the living room, den, bedroom, bath, or kitchen, they can all be pulled together in a color, or color and pattern, story. The strength of the display of these assorted products depends upon the overall color story

FIGURE 20.2 Karaca Home is a Turkish department store for home furnishings, specializing in fabrics. The store's wide expanse of open-back windows requires partial walls and separations between each window's special color, pattern, or theme display. A large graphic element sets the mood on the back panel for the linen presentation, and wallpapered screens serve as neutral dividers. *Karaca Home, Istanbul, Turkey. Ayse Demirtepe, director of visual display.*

FIGURE 20.4 The Bay has a new and beautifully arranged floor in the department store for home furnishing. Pictured here is the china area with selections shown in vertical display fixtures and tables set with the featured plates, glassware, napkins, and more in the wide presentation aisle. *The Bay, Toronto, Canada.*

FIGURE 20.3 A closer look at a typical merchandised area in Karaca Home. Note the cross-over showing of related products and "go with" accessories on the back wall shelves. *Karaca Home, Istanbul Turkey. Ayse Demirtepe, director of visual display.*

FIGURE 20.5 Paper fans, a bamboo screen, and silk cherry blossoms set the scene for the small home fashions accessories. The pieces are presented in small clusters and at different viewing heights. *Christofle, Madison Avenue, New York. Design: Polar Buranasatit.*

FIGURE 20.6   An island platform display in the home furnishings department brings together a variety of furniture and accessories that are Asian—and exotic. A simple bamboo pole construction supports the sweep of fabric that forms a canopy over the setup, and the bursts of green foliage add a "live" and colorful relief to the lifestyle display. *The Bay, Toronto, Canada.*

FIGURE 20.7   Tabletop displays are important especially when a gift-giving holiday is approaching. At Lords in London, Mother's Day means an array of silk flowers, home toiletries elegant tea cups, and all sorts of feminine, flower-splattered products. *Lords, Westbourne Grove, London, United Kingdom. Rita Dewan, brand director.*

FIGURE 20.8   Scale makes a difference. These oversized papier-mâché vegetables draw the viewers to the display, where, at varying heights, the cookware is shown in color groupings, along with some actual-size vegetables. The green panel behind suggests "freshness" and complements the red and red-toned vegetables that are tumbling through the display. *Design: Étalage B Display, Montreal, Canada.*

that reaches out beyond the glass. With many designers and national brand name labels, like Ralph Lauren Polo, Calvin Klein, and Eddie Bauer, extending beyond their clothing lines into home furnishings, linens are definitely fashionable and can be presented in clever, amusing, and unexpected ways. We are long past the time when linens were white and were stacked in neat piles, tied with ribbons, and thus displayed. There is so much more color today, many more patterns, and lots and lots of **mixing and matching** of bed and bath linens and the go-with accessories. Here, again, simple **vignette settings** can set the scene with back panels, draperies, or even shower curtains serving as backgrounds and accentuating the color/pattern arrangement up front.

Propping can add to the lifestyle setting as well as serve as risers or elevations for some of the smaller objects being offered. As mentioned in Chapter 17, the use of tables, chairs, chests, armoires, outdoor furniture, bedsteads, and so on can all help effect a vignette setting for a particular lifestyle and the clientele or target market for that look.

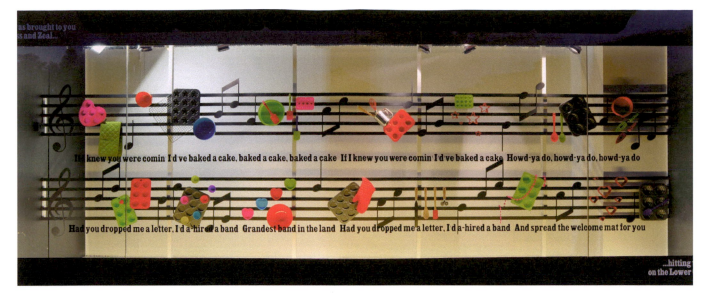

FIGURE 20.9 If you don't know the words you can hum it! Music makes the world go round and helps promote the home furnishings at Bentalls in the United Kingdom. As conceived by Tommy Aichison, regional visual merchandising director, each window featured another set of products superimposed over the "sheet music" that was appropriate, including "If I Knew You Were Coming" (bakeware, shown here), "Candle in the Wind" (candles and aromatics), "Slow Boat to China" (china and dinnerware), etc. *Bentalls, United Kingdom. Photography: Charlie Macdonald.*

FIGURE 20.10 A unique display to show off different sets of china in the same window. Cut-out figures "sit" on actual chairs at small, cloth-draped tables upon which sets of dinnerware are shown—raised up to the viewer's eye level. The mix of two-dimensional figures with three-dimensional props makes for a fun juxtaposing. The star-splattered background adds a romantic touch. *Design: Karina Barhumi, Lima, Peru.*

They also provide a variety of levels in the display to show-case the assorted clusters of products. However, the visual merchandiser must, usually because of budget restraints, learn to be resourceful in amassing the props needed. In situations that allow, working with neighboring retailers that are noncompetitive—that do not sell what you sell—is one solution. Develop a system whereby they lend you some of their stock for use in your window display, and in exchange you place in the window a card that credits the lender of these props. It serves them—the neighbors—by giving their merchandise window exposure in a different location. Their goods will be shown differently and used in a way they never could have.

Because many of the products are often soft, drapable, and textile in nature, the visual merchandiser should approach the display with the same attitude and make use of the same concepts suggested in Chapter 10. The nontextile items are "fashion accessories" of the home rather than an outfit, and should be layered into the composition in the same way one would add fashion accessories, only here they are part of a room or a place. The figures in this chapter, as well as others throughout the text, illustrate how fashion accessories can be adapted to home fashions and the particular market.

Hard Goods

Some people feel that the presentation of fashion is all glamour and fun because that is where the visual merchandiser can really take off and be different and do strange and wonderful things. Often, these people look at the prospect of displaying hard goods—nonfashion products—as dull and boring. Refrigerators, vacuum cleaners, auto parts, TVs, cell phones, and all sorts of small, handheld electronic devices aren't fun. Yet, as you may have noticed looking through this text, many of these "boring" and "dull" everyday objects have been used by talented visual merchandisers to add life and excitement to their fashion presentations. Again, it is important to note that although there is a difference between a casual sports outfit and an upright vacuum cleaner, it is the same shopper who buys both. The approach to the display of hard goods is therefore to treat them the same way you would a fashion product: humanize and dramatize—add color and texture—and use whatever display techniques you would with clothes to attract the shopper and interest him or her in the product.

Create Lifestyle Situations

Big, bulky appliances and small, handheld electronic and digital devices need the same thing in a display; they need to be humanized. They need to be shown in relation to the eventual user by creating **lifestyle situations**. Scale is important! Whereas large units can often stand on their own, smaller units need to have something dominant in the display composition—some focal element—that will catch the viewer's eye and bring him or her closer to where the smaller items can be more readily seen. In the case of handheld and small products, they also need to be brought up as close to eye level as possible, which means the use of risers, pedestals, or props that will elevate them off the floor. The dominant element can be a mannequin shown "using" the product or an enlarged lifestyle photograph showing the small unit in a gigantic, overblown size or in use. If possible, an overscaled model of the product, either dimensional or rendered in black and white as a line drawing on Foamcore, cut out and suspended in space, will work. The important thing to remember is the targeted shopper and his or her interest. Who is the shopper? What is the shopper looking for? How can this product be presented so that it appears to enrich or enhance the shopper's life—and lifestyle? So, we are back to lifestyle.

Small Items

Create everyday situations in the display space. Humor usually works best, even when the product is expensive. If the products are small or handheld, like electric shavers, tablets, cell phones, and so on, try using storytelling techniques to highlight the product's attributes. An example might be turning them into "people" by adding "arms" and "legs," à la Keith Haring drawings, in which the "head" or the "body" is the actual unit. Have these make-believe people doing activities such as the eventual shopper may be involved in: working at the office, cooking at home, jogging in the park. To make these "scenes" work, try masking the display window into a shadow box and raise the floor of the shadow box up closer to eye level. The little bendable, wooden models that artists use to get the look of a body in motion are readily available in art supply shops and are not only inexpensive but can always be used in interior cases as well. Have these miniature mannequins performing everyday activities as they carry these handheld products. The settings for these little people can be furnished and propped with mounted graphic materials that bring the environment to life. This will add another light touch as well.

Large Items

For the larger and often bulkier units, try to put them into lifestyle settings as well. Vignettes will do. You don't need to create the whole kitchen or the entire outdoors when a suggestion is sufficient. A piece of picket fence, a grass mat for the floor pad, and maybe some flower heads and a watering hose is certainly enough to create a backyard setting for barbeque equipment or outdoor furniture. Of course, it could be more attention getting with some humanizing details, like adding a life-size figure to the composition. If it isn't possible to borrow a casually dressed mannequin from a neighboring retailer, a cutout Foamcore figure can probably work as well—or even better—depending upon the target market. If the window is too large, try masking the glass with foliage drawn as a frame around the window or set cutout foliage drawings against the front glass. Maybe hang a line of "wash" across the back, if the window is open back, and write the message on the wash. Add some atmosphere, like children's toys, lounge chairs, and a doghouse—use mounted graphics to simulate an environment.

Treat the object itself as part of the lifestyle. Make it seem human, or turn it into an object of "awe and wonderment." Imagine an artist with a paint palette and canvas-covered easel painting the portrait of a refrigerator set up on a platform with drapery behind it. Add a "kid's" drawing of the Mona Lisa to the door for extra interest. Open the refrigerator door and fill it with unexpected objects, like baubles, bangles, beads, and lots of "bling" (shiny, sparkling stuff)—"rocks" overflowing the ice cube trays on the shelves.

Using Foamcore panels, cut them so that they fit around the appliance or large unit, and thus create an all-in-one setting with the product. Use colors to bring out the color or lack of color of the product. Draw a suggested room or place setting on the panels, but don't be too realistic or rational; be flighty, have fun, be a little over the top if it will work with the store's image and the customer's lifestyle.

Play with tag lines to get eye-catching displays: "Play It Cool," "Baby, It's Colder Inside," "Easy Living," "The Easy Life," "This Is Living!"

Food Displays

People have always been interested in food and how food looks, but lately, food presentation—raw or cooked, fresh or frozen, right out of the garden or off the chef's stove—has become a profession. Food magazine spreads, TV commercials, cooking programs, in-store displays, and demonstrations all require the visual merchandiser's know-how, talent, and imagination. Whether the food is on a supermarket shelf or in a gourmet food shop, on a roadside stand or in a specialty shop, or being set up for photo shoot or viewing by a TV audience, it is not enough just to show the food; it must be visually merchandised—and presented! (See Figure 20.11.)

FRESH PRODUCE

The imagery usually associated with the display of fruits and vegetables is of "country fresh," "just picked," or "from the

FIGURE 20.11   Old, recycled (and "green") crates and barrels, plus wicker baskets, bales of hay, and dried cornstalks, add texture and a vintage flavor to the in-store display of fresh fruits and vegetables. Add the striped canvas awnings and the live plants and trees, and it becomes a wholesome, old-fashioned outdoor marketplace where everything is fresh and right from the farm. *WWD/© Condé Nast.*

FIGURE 20.12   So pretty, it is almost a crime to bite into any of these beautifully prepared and presented items of takeout food. Each item is treated as a painting, and the colors and textures are balanced and enhanced. Lace paper doilies are placed under some of the less ornate items to soften the effect, while the sunflowers, green leaves, and halved tomatoes add colorful accents throughout. The all-white platters bring out the color of the foods and reflect the light from above. *Traiteur Gillet, Chalon, France.*

FIGURE 20.13   The meat shown here is uncooked but ready to go. Its rich red color is enhanced by the warm light in the counter and from overhead. The touches of green also complement the red, to make it seem redder. A rustic red-and-white checked cloth, in the background, also adds a sense of "country fresh" to the meat presentation. *Butcher shop, Milan, Italy.*

farm." It is **natural** and of the country; it is farmer's markets, roadside stands, orchards, and gardens. It is about color and texture, and it is mainly about light. Ideally, it is sunlight. Fruits and vegetables glow under warm yellow light, so avoid, if at all possible, cool fluorescent lamps. Incandescents are fine, as are some of the super-warm fluorescents, but the MR16 tungsten or LED lamps are better still in the rendition of crisp greens to rich reds and purples. (See Figure 20.12.)

Similar to merchandising clothing, it does make a difference which colors are presented next to each other. Sometimes, an analogous theme will work, with lemons next to limes that are next to oranges and red apples. However, to make fresh produce—and other foods—appear richer and fresher, it helps to complement the products with colors and textures. The rougher-skinned ones make the smooth-skinned ones seem more velvety by comparison. Green leaves or green foliage used to frame or highlight red apples, purple grapes, and any of the warm-colored produce will help them look richer and redder. (See Figures 20.13 and 20.14.)

To reinforce the "country fresh" concept, try to accessorize the produce with coarse linen or heavy checked cotton napkins, burlap bags, baskets of natural wicker or rattan, raw wood baskets, and bushels and barrels. Twigs, branches, raffia, and straw all work to promote the outdoor, just-picked look. Arrange fruits and vegetables in the assorted baskets and bushels lined with provincial printed napkins of complementary colors, and set them out on tiered, weathered timber shelves or food stands, or use bushel baskets—upright and upended—for a variety of heights. Put them out in baskets laid out on country-style tables or rustic hutches accented with colored fabric cloths. Add some natural elements—like sprays of leaves or flowers for color accents.

PREPARED FOODS

When setting out prepared foods and edible delicacies, depending upon the type of store and the clientele, the displayer

FIGURE 20.14 The meat is prepared and ready to take home and serve. The simple white platters are decorated with greens and sprays of rosemary and are accented with cherry tomatoes. The greens again serve to enhance the red in the meat. *Traiteur Gillet, Chalon, France.*

can set the **tone** and look with the choice of accessories—the types of linens, plates and platters, serving pieces, glassware, flowers, napkins, and so on. They are all part of the selling story. If the shop caters to a sophisticated, upscale market that thinks "country" is "kitsch," avoid the rustic and provincial look, and go for smart and stylish, with lots of white, stainless steel, glass, cool colors, and smooth surfaces. Bring out the silver wine coolers, candlesticks, and floral centerpieces. Use the designer china and tableware, all the linens and other accoutrements that you can possibly borrow or rent. Be ready to serve up the very best when only the very best will do.

You can also go casual—and still be smart and stylish—with hand-decorated pottery dishes and serving platters, colorful napery and linens—not too rough, but not too smooth either—and add some **terra-cotta** touches throughout for a nice, earthy quality. Maybe use terra-cotta floor tiles under the serving pieces, or add some terra-cotta garden statuary to the setups. When setting out the prepared foods, it should look as though company is coming—real friends whom you are trying to impress. Table settings with an imaginative mix of colors, textures, and materials work best. Flowers, leaves, fruits, and vegetables—all natural—make wonderful decorative accents for prepared foods.

For inspiration, check out food blogs, Instagram, and websites and publications like the Food Network, *Bon Appetit*, *Martha Stewart Living*, and *Cooking Light*, as well as catalogues from West Elm, Williams-Sonoma, Crate & Barrel, and other upscale household and houseware stores. They are filled with ideas and products that will enhance your displays.

Home Fashions, Hard Goods, and Food Displays: Trade Talk

lifestyle presentation	natural	vignette settings
lifestyle situations	terra-cotta	
mixing and matching	tone	

Home Fashions, Hard Goods, and Food Displays: A Recap

✦ Lifestyle presentations bring assorted materials together into a unified theme.

✦ Colors and patterns can be used to tell a color, or color and pattern, story. Linens and accessories can be mixed and matched against vignette settings to accentuate the arrangement up front.

✦ Lifestyle situations, which show hard goods, like vacuum cleaners, in use by mannequins or other creative human forms, can dramatize the products for shoppers. The important thing is to remember the targeted shopper and to make a presentation that demonstrates the viewer's relation to the products.

✦ Food displays benefit from images that say "natural" and "country fresh." Lighting that resembles sunlight is particularly effective for fruits and vegetables.

✦ Colors and textures are important for the composition of food displays. Rougher-skinned fruits can make smooth fruits appear even more so by comparison.

✦ Accessories like burlap bags, wood baskets, and colored fabric cloths will enhance the country-fresh image.

✦ A more sophisticated or stylish approach may sometimes be desired. Designer china and tablecloths with some terra-cotta touches can give the display an earthy quality while allowing shoppers to envision home and dinner scenes, with company over.

Questions for Review and Discussion

1. How is a color, or color and pattern, story created for a home fashions display?

2. What display methods can be used to humanize small, handheld items? Large and bulk units?

3. What imagery is associated with produce? List some accessories that are effective in conveying such a message.

4. In the presentation of food, what methods should be used to prepare the proper look and tone for different clientele?

Chapter Twenty-One
Point-of-Purchase Display

The Glossary, Barnes and Noble. *Design: Eric Williams RPG, New York City. Copyright © 2016 Barnes & Noble College Booksellers.*

**AFTER YOU HAVE READ THIS CHAPTER,
YOU WILL BE ABLE TO DISCUSS**

✦ displays that are considered POP (point of purchase)

✦ reasons for the use of POP by retailers

✦ functions of a POP display unit

✦ the product categories utilizing POP fixtures and materials

✦ materials used in the design of a POP unit

Point of purchase (POP) has been around since long before the cigar store Indian sculpted out of wood, clutching a handful of tobacco leaves, and garishly painted in green, red, and gold. It stood outside cigar stores and tobacco shops announcing to one and all on the street that tobacco products were sold just inside. Point-of-purchase signage probably goes back even further than the Middle Ages, when red cylinders bandaged in white announced the presence of the barber and bloodletter in the community. A walk down the crooked, cobblestoned streets of Salzburg, Austria, is a walk through two or three centuries of POP signage: three-dimensional objects that proclaim a product or service and even suggest its quality. Thus, giant keys hang over the locksmith's shop; gilded pretzels call to those seeking a bakery, just as the giant violin would entice a musician in search of a violin maker. For those who never learned to read—or those who could not make out the words from a distance—these giant replicas provided the information.

Point of purchase has become in recent times a complete and convoluted industry. It is display, fixturing, store design, and advertising all in one. It is the total image fabrication of a product; the attraction to the product as well as the provider of the product on the selling floor. It is the "shill" that stands out front and invites the shopper to come inside, where the product is on view. It is the silent or not-so-silent salesperson who points out where the product is once the shopper is inside, and it also explains what the product is all about. Point of purchase also stacks, stocks, holds, and coordinates the product or products in a manner that enhances the unit(s) and is convenient to the shopper. This full range of service to the shopper and the promotion of the product has made the POP industry the biggest and fastest growing extension of the display/fixture and advertising industries. In 1996 the total expenditure for POP advertising, signage materials, and in-store media provided to retailers by the vendors was in excess of $12.7 billion.

What Is POP?

Point of purchase used to be synonymous with "impulse shopping." It was associated with merchandise sold at the checkout counter or the cash wrap desk—the prepackaged, boxed, and shrink-wrapped items the shoppers didn't really need but were intrigued enough to pick up and buy. Today's POP is much more than the neon-outlined clock, the guzzling beer running from bottle to glass and back forever captured in a bas-relief of plastic, or the cardboard box that opens into a "dump truck" carrying a load of candy bars.

POP units can be displays, displayers, fixtures, and auxiliary items provided by the vendors or manufacturers to the retailers who stock and sell their products. The displays, fixtures, and assorted signage can appear outside the store—in the windows—and inside the retail setting on ledges, counters, shelves, or the selling floor or suspended

FIGURE 21.1   To promote the new Blossom line of toiletries in the Victoria's Secret Beauty stores, the company went all out with printed banners on translucent fabric, cardboard counter cards, and special tie-in shopping bags. These all carried the cherry blossom graphic art that appeared on the packages of the new line. The pink table covers and sprays of artificial blossoms helped carry through the pink-to-red color scheme. *Victoria's Secret, Water Tower, Chicago, Illinois.*

from the ceiling. The POP displays and fixtures can be made of cardboard, paper, wood, plastic, and metal, or any combinations of these materials.

More often than not, a POP unit is not designed to exist by itself but is part of an overall promotion or scheme that can involve dozens of coordinated elements—each located and doing its work in another area of the retail setting. The coordinated units are designed to promote the product or brand name, the customer's self-image, the image of the product, the advantages of the product over others similar to it, and the eventual stocking of the product. The campaign

FIGURE 21.3   POP materials can be sent to numerous retail spaces of the same company—or wherever the products are sold—to announce a promotion or carry a special message. As shown in this installation at a Verizon Wireless store, the strong red paper elements create a dynamic overall look in the store and tell a story. The red streamers indicate where the interactive POP displays are located. *Verizon, South Bend, Indiana. Design: JGA, Southfield, Michigan.*

or promotion can run the gamut from posters, cards, and banners to counter or ledge displays to mass merchandising fixtures on the floor. (See Figures 21.1 through 21.3.)

Why POP?

Following are some of the reasons for POP promotions and the use of POP materials:

1. The appearance of the sign or display in the retail setting where the product is available can and does often encourage the consumer to make an on-the-spot decision to purchase.
2. The sign or display flags the shopper—gains attention—and brings the consumer to the product.
3. POP not only enhances the product's image or its timeliness when part of a special promotion, like Halloween/Easter/Fourth of July, but can serve to explain the product and thus inform the shopper.
4. Coordinated promotions can stimulate the consumer to buy not only the product but also other products

FIGURE 21.2   With a wide variety of grooming tools for cats and dogs of every kind and size, this FURminator display was designed with effortless navigation in mind. Built for existing fixtures at PetSmart, this easy-to-install end cap uses printed styrene dividers to organize the product into clear categories and includes SKU info on the back panel to ensure simple restock. *PetSmart, RPG, New York City.*

that are being promoted along with it, such as combining a soft drink or beer promotion with snacks like nuts, pretzels, or potato chips.

5. The POP display or sign can reinforce a price message or stimulate an immediate action response from the consumer because "now" is the time to take advantage of a special promotion, a giveaway, a contest, and so on.

Therefore, POP displays and designs:

◆ Attract attention to the product

◆ Promote or reinforce brand name recognition

◆ Show and explain the product; educate the consumer

◆ Answer relevant questions: price, size, applications, and so forth

◆ Hold or arrange stock for the shopper's convenience

◆ Increase sales by coordinating items—or by "impulse sales"

Who Uses POP, and Where?

There are several major markets and manufacturers in those markets that are the most frequent purchasers of POP. They, in turn, give the material to the vendors to promote and sell their products. These groups are recognized by the **Point-of-Purchase Advertising Institute (POPAI**—pronounced "popeye"), an important industry organization of manufacturers and producers of POP material and purchasers of POP products. Following is a brief list of products within each market:

Food and paper goods—frozen and fresh foods, foods packed in cans, cases, cartons, tins, bottles, and bags. Anything from deli to salad dressings, from cake mixes to dog treats and snacks. Paper towels, napkins, picnic plates, soaps, cleaners, and detergents also come under this category.

Transportation industry—automobile showroom displays, gas and petroleum products, workstations, car accessories, tires, batteries, hubcaps, cell phones, and so on.

Personal products—shoes and shoe care, sportswear, active sports clothing, sneakers, sports equipment, bodybuilding equipment, eye fashions, costume jewelry, watches, pens, and related items.

Beverages—beer, soda, soft drinks, liquors, wines, and other such beverages.

Health and beauty aids—shampoos, hair products, skin care, vitamins, over-the-counter drugs, cosmetics, toiletries, perfumes.

Hardware/building materials—lumber, roofing, insulation, paints, lighting fixtures and lamps, wood flooring, carpeting, doors, cabinets, and related items.

Services and unclassified—fast-food operations, lotteries, educational products, books, paperback books, vending

FIGURE 21.4   This durable, functional, and restockable Coppertone self-standing fixture incorporates a changeable message board on top. It fits into the vacuum-formed, castle-like construction. The unit is double sided so that it can hold many products in its narrow footprint. *Design: Design Display Group (DDG), Carlstadt, New Jersey.*

machines, games and toys, airlines, cruise lines, hotels, travel, lawn care, and so on.

Household goods—garden supplies, dishes, pots and pans, coffee brewers, baking equipment, tools, TV, radios, VCRs, home entertainment, lawn and patio furniture, kitchen fixtures, and similar products.

Tobacco—cigarettes, chewing tobacco, and related products.

Considering the previous breakdown, it is apparent that POP signs, displays, and fixtures appear most frequently in the following retail outlets:

◆ Markets/supermarkets and hypermarkets
◆ Convenience operations
◆ Mass merchandisers, such as Kmart and Walmart
◆ Home improvement centers
◆ Drugstore chains and pharmacies
◆ Department and specialty stores
◆ Wine and liquor stores/packaged goods stores
◆ Sporting goods operations
◆ Office supply outlets
◆ Bars, taverns, and cafés
◆ Automotive aftermarkets: service centers combined with auto showrooms. (See Figures 21.4–21.6.)

FIGURE 21.5   The rotating floor unit makes self-selection simple. In addition to containing "how-to" booklets, color charts and samples, and even brushes, the unit is filled with small bottles of premixed Benjamin Moore paints that shoppers can use to try the colors on their walls at home. The curved metal handles make rotating the fixture easy, and more than one person can use the displayer at the same time. *Design: Design Display Group (DDG), Carlstadt, New Jersey.*

FIGURE 21.6   The Sony POP fixture all but talks back to the customer. Shoppers are invited to try, test, sample, touch, activate, and experience the numerous Sony electronic products set out on this handsome wood, metal, and plastic unit that serves as the focal Sony vendor feature in an electronics department. *Design: Design Display Group (DDG), Carlstadt, New Jersey.*

POP Longevity

POP units can be **permanent**, **semipermanent**, or **promotional or temporary**. Depending on the product's quality, styling, and end use, a POP counter display or store fixture can be constructed out of wood, wire, or plastic and be expected to last for a year or more in a drugstore or mass-merchandiser operation. A permanent fixture displayer may be considered when the product is not likely to change in design or in packaging very rapidly or when it is a more costly item than an impulse item. A permanent display may show off products like watches, fountain pens, samples of wood flooring, tires, or vacuum cleaners. If a new product is added, or a design is changed, often the displayer/fixture design of a permanent unit is generic enough to accommodate the new product, or it is designed to be adaptable to possible changes of stock. The displayer/fixture will be more costly to produce, and there may be fewer units produced, but what is made to stand up to wear and tear for a year or so will be considered permanent for that expected period of time. Included in this category are also items like neon and acrylic etched signs, electric clocks, and illuminated menu boards.

The semipermanent fixture or counter unit is usually expected to be in use for about six months to a year, and though it is constructed to be rigid and tough, the materials may not be as fine as those used in a permanent fixture/displayer.

The temporary, or promotional, unit has the shortest life expectancy. It is designed to serve on the counter, on the floor, or on the shelf for a few weeks, or a month or two at the most. Usually, it is a timely or seasonal piece that ties in with other media—such as ads or TV commercials. Promotional displays could be created for Halloween, the Super Bowl, New Year's Eve celebrations, Easter, a new color palette of cosmetics for fall, or the introduction of a "new and improved" product in a new and unfamiliar package. There may be life-size cutouts, dump bins, banners, dangles, shelf talkers, buttons, brochure holders, take-one pads, or sampling in store—all tied in with the single promotional theme. After the action or event is over, so, too, is the life expectancy of the promotional POP unit, which is often produced from cardboard, corrugated materials, or lightweight vacuum forming.

Designing the POP Unit

Before the designer can start the process of creating the desired unit, he or she must have the following information.

PRODUCT

What is it? Who can and will use it? What is the target market or the customer base? Is this a new product or a "new and improved" product? Is there a new formula—a new shape or size—or a new package? How is the product packaged? If this is not a new product, how has it been displayed before?

UNIT

What is this unit to do? Is it a display, a displayer, a stocking unit, a dispensing unit, a demonstration piece, or a sign? If it is a display, will it be used on the counter, in a window, or on the floor? How many products will it show? Does the unit need to incorporate a take-one pad, a brochure or leaflet holder, or a mock-up of the product?

If it is meant to contain and show stock on the selling floor, how many pieces of product will be supported? Will the unit have only one product, or does it have to show off a line of products—for example, a line of hair conditioners and shampoos designed for different types of hair or a selection of vitamins?

Where will this unit be used, and in what kind of setting: a supermarket, a drugstore, a department store, a café, or a convenience store?

TIMING

A very important element, not only in the designing of the unit, but in determining how the unit will be constructed or executed, is how long the unit is expected to function. Is the unit to be part of a special promotion event, something that will come and go quickly—something with a limited period of usage—or is it expected to serve for several weeks or a selling season?

Should this be a permanent unit that will be constructed of sturdy, durable materials that will stand up to the handling and traffic on a busy floor for an extended period of time?

Is the unit to be part of an advertising campaign and therefore relate to messages that will appear in TV commercials, in magazine and newspaper ads—and include the same images that will be appearing in the other media? Is it a promotional piece for Halloween, a Rose Bowl game tie-in, a golf tournament, or a Fourth of July celebration?

The amount of time the unit will be used will, to a large degree, affect how the piece is constructed: cardboard versus plastic, paper versus fabric, and so forth.

TIE-INS

The possible **tie-in** with an overall promotion was mentioned in the previous section. If the unit is to be part of an overall, all-inclusive promotion, like the launching of a new perfume or a Christmas campaign for a sparkling wine, what is the basic concept of the promotion? What images will be used? What copy or taglines? What promotional elements should be included in this POP unit? Who else is working on the promotion? What other POP units are being designed for the promotion? Are there magazine and newspaper ads being produced—TV commercials, radio spots, a celebrity tie-in, a new package being introduced, a color scheme, or a graphic image? Just how much are you expected to conform to the other elements in the promotion? You very likely may be bidding on several related parts of the promotion, such as banners, streamers, counter or window displays, table covers, and so on.

END USAGE

What kind of store will the unit appear in? High fashion? Popular priced? A department store or specialty store or mass merchandiser? Again, referring to the target market, is this a specialty targeted market such as Asian, Hispanic, African-American, or Irish (for St. Patrick's Day)? Knowing the specific market, if there is one, can provide the designer with guidelines and parameters; certain colors may be more effective for one ethnic group than another and some designs or elements may be taboo (many Asians

associate the number 4 with death, and in some societies white is a color associated with funerals).

PRODUCTION RUN

Of course, it is very important to know how many pieces will be produced. How large will the run be? What techniques will be best and most economical for that production number? Should it be vacuum formed or injection molded, lithograph offset printed or silk-screened? The size and number will affect the cost of the dies, tools, plates, and screens. If it will be a large run, then the dies and molds must be constructed of materials that may be more costly but that will hold up for the projected run and the large number of "shots."

SHIPPING

How are the units to be shipped? Where are they to be shipped, and in what stage of assembly? Will all the pieces be packed in several giant crates and shipped directly to the manufacturer/vendor and then distributed to several strategic locations before being sent to the retailers? Will the pieces be shipped unassembled, partially assembled, or fully assembled in individual cartons and sent directly to the retailer, timed to get there for the specific promotion, or will it go to another POP producer, where the units may be prepacked or have additional coordinated POP units added to these before being shipped? What kind of cartons or crates will be required? How big? How strong?

LIGHT AND MOTION

Is this unit to be enhanced with light, motion, or computer chips so that the shopper will be able to interact with the product or the display and perhaps get special information? These elements add to the cost of the unit. How much can the unit be enhanced with decoratives, appliqués, and so on, before overcosting the unit?

COST

And now—down to the basics: How much? You may not get a direct answer, but as a designer it does help to have an idea of the target market's price range while working in the design process and in selecting construction and finishing techniques. If no answer is forthcoming, look at the pieces its specialists. These are the authorities—the people who spend all of their time sharpening their talents and learning ever more and more about their specialties. These are the suppliers. These are the people who run the silk-screen operations, do vacuum forming and injection molding, the die cutters and the die tool designers, the casters, the molders, the printers, the stampers, and the suppliers of papers and plastics. A good POP designer is not expected to be a specialist in every technique. However, the designer should understand what the particular technique or process will do and how it will do it—when it will be most effective and efficient; when it will be the best solution for the design—and the cost. But the details, the little variations and adaptations of the actual process, should be worked out in conjunction with one of these specialists or technicians who really knows how to make a mold or die, how to get the most out of the material, and how to make whatever process is used cost-efficient. These are the "tricks of the trade," and these specialists know it. In the end, the designer is only as good as the specialists he or she works with.

FIGURE 21.7   The interactive POP fixture can be more than a fixture—it can be a decorative prop as well. In Zonik, a futuristic, out-of-this-world electronics store, the fixtures and POP materials are used to enhance the look and theme of the store. *Zonik, Dubai, United Arab Emirates. Design: Winntech, Kansas City, Missouri.*

that have been used in the past by this vendor for this product, "guesstimate" what it might have cost, and use that as a starting point. The designer does not have to be the estimator. The estimator is the person who puts all the probable costs and probable expenses together to determine a price per unit. It does help if the designer is knowledgeable about how much materials cost and what is involved in the various processes. In POP, thousands of units and nickels and dimes per unit can make the difference in getting or losing the job. If any field calls for care and efficiency in estimating and production, this is it! (See Figure 21.7.)

Specialists in POP Design

The POP industry, like many other fields in which there are technical processes and a complexity of materials, has

Materials Used in the Construction of POP Displays

Depending on the products, the intended use, the time it is expected to be on view, and the budget, the displayer or fixture can be made of a wide variety of materials: paper, cardboard, Foamcore, various thicknesses of wood, pressed board, plastic, or metal.

PAPER AND CARDBOARD

Probably the most popular medium for POP units is paper. Paper can be used for signs and banners, especially when permanence is not of the utmost importance, but cost is. Paper is available in many surface finishes and textures, in many thicknesses, and in a brilliant spectrum of colors. Paper can be applied, cemented, or laminated onto cardboard. Cardboard is also a form of paper and is available from thin pliable sheets to fairly rigid sheets, with a tremendous range in between. The thickness or density of the board—the ply—will determine how it is used in the POP program. Is it for a sign? Is it for a display or a brochure holder? Will it be a container and support several pounds of products on top of it? And if so, how much weight? Is the POP unit expected to be in use for just a week or two for a special promotion, or is it expected to be in service for a month or a season? The time the unit is to be used may also affect the ply of the paper or board.

There are also corrugated materials that are available in rolls and in sheets, in different surface finishes and thicknesses. Although lightweight, they do provide strength and support for units constructed out of them or reinforced with them.

Foam boards, though not paper, but rather a sandwich of two pieces of paper, with a filler of Styrofoam or some other foam material, appear on the market under a variety of trade names. Foam boards are produced in thicknesses that range from about ¼ inch up to 1 inch or even more. They are extremely versatile and dependable players on the POP production team because they can be die cut, scored, laminated onto, printed on, or used to construct small fixtures and displayers.

Paper is often flat—as printed sheets—but paper can be dimensionalized: folded; scored; cut into contoured shapes; cut and creased and folded into boxes, containers, or pop-up or pop-out displays; or appliquéd or layered for a dimensional effect. Paper products can also be embossed or treated to create three-dimensional textured surfaces. Some of the processes usually associated with paper, cardboard, and corrugated board will be discussed in the text that follows.

Printing Techniques

Digital printing has become a standard for the industry, and large flatbed printing has replaced the use of silk-screening for most POP manufacturers. Digitally produced artwork can be printed on large sheets of rigid materials such as wood, cardboard, acrylic, plastic, glass, metal, and many types of foam boards. The adjustable bed accepts up to an inch or more in thickness, and UV (ultraviolet)-resistant ink keeps the imagery from fading in direct sunlight. Banner and fabric materials can be stretched on a frame and printed in large format for billboards and building wraps. The printer has the capability to cut out a design following the printing process on cardboard and foam board; wood and metal can be cut using a CNC router.

Silk-Screen Printing, or Screen Printing Process

Another very effective technique for reproducing copy or artwork for displays and displayers is the silk-screening technique. In the past, the design for screens were cut by hand; however, today the screens are prepared photographically. What makes the screen printing process very special in the POP industry is that it is so adaptable and can be used on almost any material available.

In the screen printing, the screen may be as large as 8 by 4 feet or even larger if necessary. Screens used to be made of fine silk, but today most commercial printing houses prefer to cover their wood stencil frames with manufactured fabrics. Another plus for this technique is that one can print with a vast variety of paints, inks, and dyes, depending on the materials to be printed upon. The paints, inks, or dyes can have shiny or matte finishes; produce fairly flat or raised surfaces; be enhanced with glitter or flock; and be opaque or transparent, metallic, or Day-Glo. It is possible to print an opaque white over a black base or a real metallic gold or silver over any color. Glossy and flat colors can be combined on the same design, just as transparent dyes and opaque paints can be mixed to create the desired effects.

Dimensionalizing Paper and Cardboard Displays

Die cutting is the most often used method for adding a dimensional quality to a display, displayer, card, or poster. Die cutting can create interesting outlines and silhouettes and cutout openings from paper or board. It can be used to score the board so that it can be bent or folded in a variety of ways. It can create locks and tabs so that pieces can be folded along the score or crease lines and then assembled by locking the die cut tabs through the cutout slots to make boxes, trays, or easeled stands for cards, posters, or displays. Die cutting adds the third dimension to the unit, which adds interest to the total design. A well-designed cutting die can score and cut a piece of cardboard so that it can be folded or locked into a back panel with a pair of side panels and even a raised platform or tray or brochure holder in the middle—all out of the single piece of cardboard and without gluing. The silhouette of the side wings and the back panel can be decorated with curves or jagged lines or even die cut to look like latticework.

Dies are expensive and should be designed in conjunction with a die maker—a specialist who knows how to get the most out of each blade used in the die. Some dies are basic and can be used over and over again on many different jobs, such as an easel die or a box die, whereas others may serve only for one special display unit. In smaller runs, and when the cuts or silhouettes are not too complicated, the display producer may use a cut awl machine or band saw with a template as a guide. It is possible to get a fairly accurate cut, but there will be slight differences from stack to stack because of the human element involved. The cut awl operator can only cut a few boards at a time or a stack of paper about 1-inch thick. The result can be fairly crisp and clean, but when precision matching between slots and tabs is essential, or when intricate interior cuts may be required, this method is decidedly limited in its effectiveness.

Die Cutting Process The die cutting process requires a die—a cutting tool designed to suit the material being cut. The technique is similar to cutting out cookies from rolled dough. The shape of the cookie will respond to the contour, or outline, of the cookie cutter. Pressure will need to be exerted to allow the cutting edge of the cookie cutter to go through the layer of dough. The die in the die cutting process is placed on the stationary back plate of the machine. The paper or board to be cut is placed on the movable bed of the press machine and carefully lined up to correspond with the die. The bed is then raised to meet the die on the rear panel. Many tons of pressure are exerted, causing the machine to open and to cut the paper or board.

The die is actually a steel rule set in wood. To make the die, a piece of thick plywood is used for the base, and the die designer draws the cutting and scoring lines on the board. Using a jigsaw machine, the lines that have been drawn are cut out of the wood, leaving a groove, or channel into which the steel cutting blades can then be inserted. The curved and arced lines will be made by the steel blade being forced, in the channel, to conform with the desired curves and arcs. There are "bridges" left in the channels during the routing process of making the mold. These bridges are small stops in the channels that prevent the wood block from falling apart. The cutting blades that go over these bridges are called notches. When a score line is desired instead of a cut-through line, the blade that is inserted in the wood base is slightly lower than the cutting blade, and the scoring blade's edge is rounded rather than knife sharp. This blade can then make a "cut score," which actually cuts through part of the board for a sharp right-angle crease or a "crease score," which is softer, and a rounded bend in the board.

Rubber pads are set around the cutting blades so that the sheet can more readily be ejected after the pressure has been applied. It also makes handling the cutting dies somewhat safer. In the "make ready" die, the blade is dulled, purposefully, in several spots to leave "nicks," usually in the corners. The size of the nick will depend on the thickness of the paper or board being used. Nicks are made where the cutting blade has not penetrated completely. They hold the die cut pieces in place in the full sheet from which they were cut. "Stripping" is the step that follows, in which the die cut pieces are separated from the excess, surrounding stock. If the unit or units (the die cut pieces) will not be stripped until they arrive at the place where they will be used, such as at the retail setting, the nicks hold the pieces in place during shipping. When the die cut sheets arrive at their destination, the excess paper or board can be removed by pushing or tearing around the notches or perforated outline. A single die cut sheet may hold several dozen individual tags or cards or just one single unit or display.

The die cutting machine used for smaller runs is often the platen, or clamshell, press that has been described previously. Basically, it opens and closes like a clamshell. For larger runs and high-speed die cutting, there are more sophisticated presses that require a more complicated "get ready" die. These units work like printing presses, in which one sheet is automatically fed into the press at a time, pressure is applied on the die from above, and the machine then pushes out the die cut sheet of paper or board at the other end. At present, the largest die possible is a 50- by 74-inch finished sheet, as the largest bed on a press can only accommodate a sheet of 52- by 76-inch stock. (See Figure 21.8.)

FIGURE 21.8 The ultimate in brand promotion! The Coca-Cola shop on Las Vegas Boulevard, in Las Vegas, features myriad Coca-Cola products emblazoned with the company's logo. Shown here is a display of some of those branded products offered for sale as well as an oversized Coca-Cola bottle that anchors the setup and serves to recall the traditional Coke bottle. Hanging from the square column are die-cut cardboard cutouts of the Coke bottle and some of the other bottled drinks prepared by the company. This store is the ultimate vendor's shop and does a terrific job in projecting the brand's image. *Coca-Cola, Las Vegas, Nevada.*

Lamination Lamination is a process whereby two or more materials are joined together into a single piece, using glue or cement. The process refers to the bonding of a printed sheet of paper or a decorative finishing paper onto a sturdy, undesigned cardboard. The supporting board provides weight, strength, substance, and body, whereas the printed—usually lithographed—paper on top contains the graphics or message.

In the process, glue is distributed evenly on the back of the sheet, which is then bonded to the supporting board. Pressure is exerted on the sandwich, as well as some heat, and then the piece is allowed to dry overnight. The

moisture evaporates, and the two pieces are now one and inseparable.

Decorative foils are often bonded onto coarse chip boards, and then they may be embossed in another dimensional process. Fine veneers of wood—fractions of an inch thick, almost paper thin—are also laminated onto heavy, serviceable, and nonglamorous plywood backing.

Other Dimensional Effects

Appliqué A flat POP display can be given greater depth and interest with the addition of some three-dimensional appliqué or attachment. Some examples of appliqué include paper lace glued on the edge of a fan, a paper flower placed behind the ear of a photographed Polynesian beauty, or a piece of fabric tucked into the pocket of a silk-screened pinstripe jacket. Because this is usually a manual process, it can add quite a bit to the cost of manufacturing the unit, but because it is so effective, it can be worth the added cost.

The appliqué serves to break up a flat design, making it more of a dimensional display and less of a poster. Sometimes, these softening elements are sent along with the unit, and the retailer is requested to add a boutonniere or to pin on a piece of bridal net. In this case, the producer does not need to handle each unit separately. The packing is simplified, and the appliqué looks fresher for the viewer. The retailer, however, must be agreeable to adding these final touches.

Layering Dimension also can be achieved by superimposing different shapes, one on top of the other, to add a sense of depth to the POP display. These layers can be set one directly on another, or they may be separated from each other by blocks and tabs. Using a tab or a fold-back flap to attach a layer will give the effect of greater depth, but the POP unit will still pack fairly flat.

Embossing A raised, embossed, or relief impression can be made on a piece of artwork when, during the printing process, specific lines are etched into a die, so as to appear on the printed surface. Or, sometimes, a die is placed underneath a piece of artwork, and pressure is applied from below, creating a raised pattern on the surface of the artwork. The embossing, in either case, creates a raised, textured surface.

Blind Embossing A method of adding dimension to a surface and creating a raised design without the use of inks or paints.

Paper Sculpture A technique for creating full-round, or bas-relief, decorative designs and objects by means of scoring, folding, cutting, curling, and applying papers of assorted colors, textures, and weights—for example, the Japanese art form of origami.

Papier-Mâché A technique for producing three-dimensional objects, such as mannequins, by means of molding pulped paper. The pulped paper is mixed with glue and, sometimes, with a whitening substance. This "mushy" material can then be shaped, filled into molds, or formed around shapes or forms. As the mâché dries, it becomes harder, stronger, and more durable. Strips of paper can also be moistened with paste and layered over and over in a mold or around a form to make a papier-mâché reproduction of the unit. There is some shrinkage as the unit dries. It is also called paper stucco when used to create architectural details such as moldings or frames. This is a hand process and is not recommended when there are long runs or many products to be reproduced.

Rubber Mâché A rubber, latex-like compound is poured into a specially made hollow mold and allowed to dry or set or is force dried by being heated in an oven. The excess material that did not set or harden is poured off, and the "rubber" unit is allowed to cure and become fully rigid. It usually requires a minimum of smoothing, rasping, or sanding to finish the surface that was formed by the inner surface of the mold. When finished, the piece should be fairly firm and resistant to breakage. The piece can then be painted, gilded, textured, and made to resemble natural materials, such as wood or stone. This, too, is basically a hand operation that is not suited to big, commercial runs.

PLASTICS

Plastics are very important in the manufacturing processes used in making POP displays, displayers, fixtures, and signage. They afford a great variety of materials used in POP production, including sheets that can be cut out and used to construct complete units shelves on wire or wooden units backgrounds for displays; platforms or risers; materials that can be bent, formed, and shaped; and materials that can be molded or extruded from molds or dies. Some plastics are available in sheets of different thicknesses and colors. They have certain unique properties, such as being resistant to water, breakage, or shattering; strong to support great weights; or soft and pliable. Some plastics are available in granule or powder form and need chemical catalysts or heat to expand and fill in hollow mold cavities. Some plastics respond to heat; others resist it.

There are two very important categories of plastics: thermoplastics and thermosetting plastics.

Thermoplastics

Thermoplastics are resins or plastics that can be repeatedly softened by the increase of temperature—that is, the application of heat. When the thermoplastic material is in a gel-like, or softened, state it can be formed, shaped, or even reshaped. To harden or set the material in its new form/shape, the material has to be cooled. When cooled and "cured," the thermoplastic retains the shape until it is once again subjected to great heat. This material is very important in the vacuum forming processes. Some thermoplastics are polythylene, polypropylene, PVC, polystyrene, acrylic, and ABS.

Thermosetting Plastics

In contrast, **thermosetting plastics**, when cured and set, become infusible and insoluble. In some stages of the production, the thermosetting material may be liquid in form. The curing process—whereby the softened material hardens in the desired shape or form—can be accomplished by the application of heat or the addition of chemicals. After that shape is assumed, the material cannot be reshaped or reformed, like thermoplastics. Some thermoplastics can be converted into thermosetting plastics by being cross-linked with other plastics or chemical additives. Some thermosets are polyesters, alkyds, melamines, epoxies, and phenol formaldehyde.

In selecting a plastic material for POP production, the designer must know what the desired end product will be. What is it expected to do, and for how long it is expected to be in use? Cost is also a major factor to be considered. Plastics are usually more expensive than paper products, but they can do things that paper cannot—and they can last longer. Plastics are used for outdoor signs, indoor signage of a semipermanent nature, fixtures with bases, and shelves that will be exposed to wear and tear on the selling floor. Fixtures that need to be theft proof, with a look-but-don't-touch-or-take attitude, may require plastic envelopes or enclosures.

Processes for Producing Plastic POP Units

Semidimensional units can be vacuum formed or made by an injection molding technique, sonic seal, or hot stamping.

Vacuum Forming Process Vacuum forming is an "extreme" form of embossing. In this technique a lightweight, thermoplastic material is used. The plastic sheet is capable of being shaped and formed when heated and when cooled will retain the new shape or form. The plastic sheet is heated and softened and then forced over a mold or die usually placed beneath it. Pressure is exerted from above that causes the now pliable plastic to take on the contour and shape of the mold below. Suction, also applied from below, ensures the skin-like fit of the plastic to the mold; it also helps to cool off the plastic so that it will keep the new shape. When the plastic is "set"—returned to room temperature—it maintains the shape of the mold. The process is then repeated with another sheet of plastic.

There are four types of plastics used in the vacuum forming process, and they are all thermoformable materials; that is, when heated, they leave the solid state and become malleable, pliable, or formable. Most popular and most inexpensive are the styrenes and polystyrenes. The sheets are available in a variety of thicknesses and in many colors, both shiny and matte. The main problem with this group of plastics is that they can shatter, and the clear sheet is not truly clear. The other classifications used in this process are the acetates, the vinyls, and the polychlorides, which are really clear and available in a range of colors and thicknesses. They are basically stronger and more durable than the styrenes. Where the vacuum formed unit is required to support weight, such as a cantilevered shelf or the base of a fixture, the latter three materials are probably better to use in the vacuum forming process.

The all-important element in the vacuum forming process is the mold. The mold can be constructed originally of wood, putty, clay, or any combination of materials and then hardened. Because the pressure exerted by the vacuum forming press is anywhere from 6 to 8 tons of pressure, the original mold or construction can only be used to make several sample units. One of them will be turned into a production mold by being reinforced with a wood frame and filled with cement or epoxy.

In preparing the production mold, the plastic shape—one of the sample pieces—is placed in a box lined with plaster of paris. The epoxy (or cement) is then poured into the hollow shell or form. Pins are inserted into the epoxy-filled mold to create the air holes that are necessary for the vacuum and suction to work during the shaping process. The new epoxy mold is then sanded, smoothed, and polished and made ready for use in production.

Each time a sheet of plastic is brought down under heat and pressure to conform with the mold, it is called a shot. Depending on the number of shots or pieces required to be made from the mold, the mold has to be corrected. For shorter runs—a few thousand—the epoxy mold is effective, efficient, and relatively inexpensive to make. For more shots, poured or liquid, aluminum molds may be preferable, but they are more expensive to generate. The most durable mold is one made of cast aluminum. It is also very important in designing a mold that there be no undercuts or indentations that will hinder or even make it impossible to lift the molded piece of plastic off of the mold.

After the sheet has taken on the form of the mold, it must be trimmed and the excess material removed. This is often done with a die (see "Die Cutting Process," earlier in this chapter). The die may be placed in with the mold so that the pressure exerted from above to soften and shape the plastic will also cut off the excess material of the sheet. If there are any internal cuts or openings needed in the mold such as a slot or a shape, another die may be used to effect those cuts.

Usually, the molded piece is half or partially rounded. It may be anything from a low relief to a half ball. When a full-round or totally three-dimensional piece is required, two halves or two separate molded pieces that will then be glued or notched or stapled together are used. For example, if a giant Christmas ornament is desired, then two half rounds will be formed and then joined together. This is a separate process. The die that is designed to trim off the excess material may be made with a lip or extension that can be used in the joining process.

Injection Molding Techniques All the processes used in the injection molding and vacuum forming of three-dimensional pieces for POP require heat plus pressure. The amount of heat and pressure will vary with the specific technique or machinery used. In most instances, the plastic material is heated in a barrel or chamber in the machine, and then it is pushed through, in measured quantities, to fill in the hollow cavity of the mold. Heat may be applied when the molds containing the material are inserted into the hopper—the opening that feeds the machine. For the plastic piece to be formed, the mold has to be cooler than the material injected into it.

Pressure may be exerted by pushing or ramming the heated or softened material into the mold, or while the plastic material is in the mold, to guarantee that the plastic material fills in all parts of the cavity of the mold. Some pressure may be exerted in the removal of the finished molded piece from the mold.

Injection Molding Tool The usual injection molding tool is made of aluminum because it is easier to tool, costs less, and takes less time to make. However, when very large runs are anticipated, the tool can be made of steel. The typical mold is made in two parts: the cavity side, which is the face of the desired product, and the ejector side, which is the back. The shot of melted plastic passes through a nozzle in the injection molding machine into the sprue, or opening, in the cavity part of the mold. The "gates" control how much material goes through the "runners." Pressure is maintained on the mold till the gates "freeze." The plastic material is, therefore, trapped in the hollow space between the cavity half and the ejector half of the mold, and it takes on the shape of that hollow form. The material is cooled in the mold, and when it has set sufficiently to hold the desired shape or form, the ejector pins in the ejector part of the mold push the finished piece out.

Sonic Seal Very often a product that is made by injection molding will require two or more separate molds to make up the finished piece—for example, a shaped box with removable top. The box, the cover, and the bottom of the box are each molded separately and then hand assembled. The cover will be set on top of the box, but the base may have to be welded on. Instead of cement or chemical bonding agents, this process is accomplished with a sonic sealer. This machine electronically fuses and melds the pieces together so that they are not only secure but, if necessary, waterproof as well.

Hot Stamping A process for applying the product's name or logo, decorative designs, or copy onto dimensional plastic pieces, such as shelves, platforms, or back panels, is called hot stamping. This is accomplished by placing the plastic surface to be decorated underneath a sheet of colored plastic film of the desired color. The artwork is raised on a rubber plate that is set in the heat-and-pressure machine above the coloring film. When pressure and heat are combined, the rubber plate is pressed down on the color film, which in turn leaves the desired colored imprint on the plastic piece that is held in place below. It is not unlike a rubber stamp leaving its imprint on paper, but instead of ink, colored film is the medium.

Sometimes the logo or design is raised and is part of the molded plastic piece. In that case, the rubber plate is flat and has no design. The heat and pressure force the colored film to yield the color to the raised design on the piece of plastic and, at the same time, bond the color.

When two or more colors are used, the process is repeated with another rubber plate and the other desired colors of film.

WOOD AND METAL

Along with some plastics, metal and wood are used for more permanent POP displayers and fixtures. They are stronger and more durable than paper and cardboard or extruded plastic shapes. However, they are more expensive to use.

Wood has a natural look and provides a sense of warmth to the product as well as a residential quality to the design of the fixture. Shoppers associate it with furniture and with the shop furnishings or fixturing of better shops and boutiques. Home fashions and home products look more intimate on wooden fixtures. Very often, wood or a wood-finished piece (covered with a wood veneer or laminate) is used in vendor shops—especially when the manufacturer wants to achieve an upscale look or wants to appeal to the rugged, masculine lifestyle. Because wood suggests a better or finer product, watches, pens and pencils, jewelry, and other expensive items may be housed in wood on the floor or on the counter. Outdoor products are given a more rustic look from a wood-finished displayer.

However, because some solid woods are too expensive to use in mass-merchandised POP items, it is likely that the fixtures and displayers will be made of some of the wood look-alike materials and possibly finished with a veneer or very fine sheet of fine wood. The inexpensive solid woods, such as pine, may be weakened by the knots, or the finished pieces may end up looking too provincial, or country-style. Also, soft woods will scratch or dent when kicked or mistreated by the shoppers. In working with wood, the designer also has to consider the back of the unit: Will it be visible? Does it have to be finished? Sometimes the back of a single-faced piece can be finished with a lesser wood or a more utilitarian substitute rather than the same wood used on the face of the unit. Not only is this economical, but it may also strengthen the finished piece.

It is not unusual to see wood combined with metal in permanent fixtures and displays. Welded metal pieces may be used for the framework and then combined with wood shelves or panels or signs. A wood fixture may be equipped with metal grills, grids, or expanded metal shelves that look lighter and are lighter than wood. Also, grids or grills will permit the ambient or targeted light to pass through the floor fixture or wall unit so that the products on the lower shelves are illuminated.

Wood dowels or metal rods can be used to carry or support vacuum-formed or injection-molded shelves, bins, or trays, thus making the units more permanent on the selling floor.

POP Design Checklist

The designer has now accumulated the necessary data and is ready to proceed. It is advisable to consider every POP unit as part of an overall promotion and as the ultimate message of the advertisement. The POP unit can support a shrinking sales force by answering customers' questions, supplying the necessary information, giving prices and construction details, and showing the available selection and range. It can offer a sample, supply a taste, or be tested. It can be, if well designed, an asset to the merchandise retailer with limited sales help or fixtures. The customer is where the sale is made!

When designing, the following checklist may be helpful because it asks all the questions that the unit will be expected to answer.

1. When is the unit to appear? What is the timing?
2. Toward whom is the product or service directed? What is the target market?
3. What is the purpose of this unit? Is it to introduce a new product? An improvement? A new style?
4. Is there an ad or TV campaign planned in conjunction with this unit? Will the POP design carry the same ad message?
5. Does the unit have anything to do but carry the message? Is it a sampler? A tester? A stocking or restockable unit?
6. What POP units have been done in the past for this product or manufacturer?
7. What are the competitors doing with their POP programs?
8. In what types of retail operations will these units be used? Where will they be located in these stores? Will other POP units be used in conjunction with this piece?
9. What quantities will be required?
10. What is the budget?
11. How long will this unit be used? Is it to be reusable?
12. Will the finished unit be bulk shipped or individually packed and shipped? Will it be sent by public conveyance or personally delivered by a company representative?
13. Should the unit include samples? Dummy boxes or bottles?
14. If the unit is to be stocked and prepacked, how many items should the POP piece carry?
15. Would the client like light or motion? Is there room in the budget for special effects: appliqué, vacuum forming, embossing, complicated die cutting, and so on?
16. What materials and techniques would the client prefer?
17. Who installs the unit—the customer? A sales representative?
18. Would the client like to see rough sketches? A comprehensive ("comp")? A model?
19. How is the client to be charged for the designs or comps?
20. Would the client like to see some auxiliary design concepts that would reinforce the message being presented in the POP unit; for example, table tents, shelf readers, overhead banners or streamers, decals, buttons, or T-shirts?

DESIGN OBJECTIVE

This was a "first." Clae was a new brand of men's shoes being introduced to the Polish market as simply and as inexpensively as possible, but—at the same time—it was to be a memorable introduction. As Jerzy Wozniak and Pawel Garus, the owners/architects of design firm mode:lina architekci, based in Poznań, Poland attest, "Our task was to launch a new brand in the Polish market by creating a memorable project. The design objective was to maximize the shopping experience using the lowest budget possible because the shop is temporary." The architects were to design a pop-up shop for Clae that would serve as their introduction to the new market

A pop-up shop is just that; a shop that appears suddenly—makes an impact—and then disappears, hopefully leaving behind a vivid memory. Since it is not expected to last for any real period of time, the design solution must be creative and imaginative and make do with easily procured and often easily disposable materials. For the Clae company, this 'now it is here—now it is gone' retail space was to be located in the relatively new Galeria Malta mall in Poznań, surrounded by well-designed and popular shops. The pop-up shop space had to stand out as visually appealing, while not appearing too makeshift. The appeal of the shop and the window display story had to attract the male shoppers in the mall through its rugged, masculine, rough, and raw textured appearance. The big problem was getting the right material—at the right price—that would accomplish this goal.

DESIGN SOLUTION

The designers at mode:lina selected a gray palette, rough wood, and used-and-reused pallets. The designers had used these sturdy elements only a few years before and had more than enough of them to cover the floor, line up against the walls, and create risers and display fixtures to highlight the shoes. Pawel Garus said, "Reused pallets redefined the whole store's interior in the shopping mall. They created individualized presentation spaces and imparted a raw and manly ambience to the space."

FIGURE CS21.1 The natural gradations of the gray color palette were contrasted with some that were white-washed to create a pleasant neutral ambiance. Pallets were laid as a floor, stacked to become risers, platforms, seating for trying on shoes, and even as a cash wrap desk. As a wall covering material, the openings between the slats served to support the display of featured shoes.

FIGURE CS21.2 Old wooden pallets became the solution. They were being reused, easily available, and inexpensive, and the rough texture was well-suited to the product and the shopper. Also, it was a "green" product.

FIGURE CS21.3 To introduce a new brand of men's shoes, the designers were challenged to create a pop-up shop that would attract the shopper and be memorable but inexpensive to produce.

"It was an unusual interior for a shopping mall and the concept was most bold. You occasionally see a pallet or two used decoratively as an elevation or as a displayer, but this time the whole space was covered with pallets," added Jerzy Wozniak.

Mr. Garus continued, "The architect or designer always faces a challenge of low budgets in designing a temporary store. That was true with this Clae store. Using the second-hand pallets helped to optimize the budget and create a recognizable and memorable interior. We used old material in an atypical way—lining walls and even as a counter. It also was an ecologically sound thing to do since reusing these already-several-times-used pallets we did not have to get anything new to cover the walls, serve as display fixtures, or platforms or contrast so effectively with the mall setting."

Mr. Wozniak agreed and added, "It was interesting to find that lining the walls with the pallets also reduced the noise level in the store and absorbed the echo, which was a big plus in a store of only 60 square meters—especially when several people are in the shop at the same time."

CONCLUSION

Not only did this pallet-filled shop draw lots of shoppers to the unique and rustic setting that was clearly

FIGURE CS21.4 When the shop was dismantled, the used pallets were further reused as display platforms and risers in window displays. Forever "Green."

visible through the display windows that fronted the space, but it got a tremendous response from the design media. It certainly fulfilled the client's wishes, and the strong impression created by the use of the worn, gray wooden pallets has become *the* recognizable icon for the Clae brand. Try Googling Clae, and the palleted store image will appear.

DESIGN CREDITS: Architects/Designers: mode:lina architekci, Poznań, Poland. Design Team: Pawel Garus, Jerzy Wozniak, Kinga Kin. Client: Clae Shoes. All photos courtesy of mode:lina architekci.

Point-of-Purchase Display: Trade Talk

appliqué	layering	rubber mâché
blind embossing	paper sculpture	semipermanent unit
die cutting process	papier-mâché	sonic seal
embossing	permanent unit	thermoplastics
hot stamping	point of purchase (POP)	thermosetting plastics
injection molding techniques	Point of Purchase Advertising Institute	tie-in
injection molding tool	(POPAI)	vacuum forming process
lamination	promotional, or temporary, unit	

Point-of-Purchase Display: A Recap

+ Point of purchase (POP) is the total image fabrication of a product.

+ POP units can be displays, displayers, fixtures, or auxiliary items provided by vendors or manufacturers to retailers.

+ Some reasons for using the POP display are as follows: It encourages the consumer to make an on-the-spot decision to purchase, it gains attention and brings the consumer to the product, it explains the product and informs the shopper, it can coordinate with other promotions and induce sales of related products, and it can reinforce a price message.

+ Product categories utilizing POP include food and paper goods, personal products, beverages, health and beauty aids, hardware and building materials, fast-food operation, lotteries, hotels, vending machines, household goods, and tobacco.

+ POP units can be permanent, semipermanent, or temporary or promotional.

+ When designing a POP unit, the display person must consider the type of product; the target audience; where the unit will be used; whether the unit will be permanent or expendable; the life expectancy of the unit; promotional tie-ins; the type of store in which the unit will appear; the number of units to be produced; the method of shipment; whether light, motion, or computer chips will be involved; and how much the unit will cost to produce.

+ The POP unit can be made of a wide variety of materials: paper, cardboard, Foamcore, various thicknesses of wood, pressed board, plastic, or metal.

Questions for Review and Discussion

1. What is the function of POP display in retailing today?

2. List five items that could be considered POP units.

3. Why has POP become such a growing and important business in the past decade?

4. What can POP do that "regular" display cannot?

5. Which industries are heavy users of POP? In what types of retail outlets do POP units commonly appear?

6. Explain the three categories of life expectancy for POP units.

7. In designing a POP unit, what factors are taken into consideration?

8. What is a POP specialist?

Chapter Twenty-Two
Exhibit and Trade Show Design

The National Museum of Toys and Miniatures. *West Office Exhibition Design, Oakland, California. Photo © Aaron Dougherty.*

AFTER YOU HAVE READ THIS CHAPTER,
YOU WILL BE ABLE TO DISCUSS

✦ the differences between exhibits and trade shows

✦ the unique characteristics of the various types of exhibits

✦ common traffic patterns created in exhibits

✦ the considerations involved in planning and selecting an exhibit system

✦ the use of graphics and lighting in attracting attention and enhancing an exhibit

Exhibits are designed to showcase objects or collections with the purpose of stimulating interest and educating viewers about a particular product, idea, or organization. And while the exhibit itself is organized and orchestrated for enjoyment, enlightenment, and experience, it may also be used to market and advertise a sponsor.

A trade show is a commercial display of new products, services, or concepts presented to a select group of prospective buyers or consumers at an organized show or event. The sale may be direct (with purchases being made at the site of the exhibit) or indirect (may lead to eventual purchases). Keep in mind that many of the principles of exhibit and trade show design, described as follows, apply equally to merchandise display and visual presentation.

FIGURE 22.1   In a permanent exhibition at The National Museum of Toys and Miniatures, unique displays compare toys from the past with similar, more contemporary toys, introducing visitors to the museum's vast collection. *West Office Exhibition Design, Oakland, California.*

Types of Exhibits

PERMANENT EXHIBITS

The **permanent exhibit** is usually reserved for content of a historic or artistic nature in a museum or corporate headquarters. (See Figure 22.1.) Many museums have permanent exhibits in which paintings, sculpture, and other artwork are framed, hung, and encased as a core exhibit for that institution. Consider the welcoming nature of the prehistoric dinosaurs that greet the viewer at the American Museum of Natural History. Permanent exhibits serve as a backbone for a museum—something to be shared over generations of viewers. Museums undertaking large renovations will occasionally revisit a permanent collection for the purpose of maintenance, updates in lighting or seating, or a total restoration.

A permanent exhibition may also be housed in a corporate headquarters or visitor center where the information displayed about the company or geographical location is not changing on a regular basis. An example is a famous winemaker in Napa Valley California; this company has an exhibition displayed at the entranceway that tells a story about the company's history in the form of a timeline. The display includes various shapes of wine bottles, wine openers, casks, and personal artifacts. The display familiarizes visitors with the heritage of the winemaker and instills a

sense of pride about its corporate culture for employees. (See Figure 22.2.)

A visitor center exhibit may convey the history or story of a particular locality and highlight the area landmarks that are available for visiting. The exhibit can offer information about sights, tours, wildlife, and lodging and point visitors to local businesses such as retail shops and restaurants. This type of exhibit is often

FIGURE 22.2   Flaunt the corporate brand! As part of an exhibition at the Robert Mondavi Winery's Visitor Center, in Napa Valley, California, a timeline was designed to communicate the company's history and heritage. The display includes imagery and vintage labels and bottles all artfully presented on a wrought iron armature of grape leaves and vines. *West Office Exhibition Design, Oakland, California.*

funded by local government or a BID (business improvement district). It will remain the same over the years and require only minimal updating to reflect changes in local businesses. In some cases, the building itself may be a notable and novel landmark, such as a lighthouse or log cabin.

TEMPORARY EXHIBITS

A **temporary exhibit** is usually the presentation of an item or items that are on loan for a limited time. The show schedule is announced and the duration of the showing is advertised and publicized. The arrival and showing of the treasures of China at a local museum for a one-month showing is an excellent example of a temporary exhibit. The limited stay creates the necessary impetus to have the public come to see the exhibit while the artwork is on loan.

A community room in a library, town hall, or department store might house temporary exhibits sponsored by local clubs, artists, or artisans of the community. A public service area in a large corporate building or a shopping center may also hold temporary exhibits that could be either educational or promotional (e.g., a Red Cross lifesaving exhibit or an automobile show). Temporary shows can often fall into the category of a traveling exhibit that makes several stops around the globe to educate the public about a brand or raise awareness about a particular cause (e.g., solar power, cancer prevention, or clean water). A temporary exhibition in New York called the Museum of Feelings invited consumers to engage in a round of sensory activities using an app and their olfactory senses to determine how color and scent could affect their feelings. This temporary museum, which was sponsored by SC Johnson, intended to introduce Glade products to a younger generation of nesters. (See Figure 22.3.)

Trade Shows

Trade shows are commercial ventures wherein a brand manufacturer or distributor will show a line of merchandise, introduce a new product or service, or exhibit purely for the company's image. Trade shows are marketed to specific audiences or industries and may be open to the public for the duration or on a select number of days.

FIGURE 22.3   While the exterior of the Museum of Feelings changed color to reflect the mood of people in the city, visitors inside explored their emotions through a series of interactive experience built to showcase the beautiful connection between scent and emotion. *Museum of Feelings by Glade, Brookfield Place, New York. Timothy Fadek/Corbis via Getty Images.*

Trade shows are produced in large exhibition halls that house several hundred exhibitors at the same time in an open floor plan of blocks and aisles. Each vendor has the option to rent a different size "booth" or space on the show floor. Spaces typically run 10 feet x 10 feet or 10 feet x 20 feet and upwards in size. Larger shows may allow two-tier show booths that accommodate a second-floor area for private meetings or demonstrations. Booth rental fees are determined by size and location; entrance and corner locations are considered more desirable. The management of the exhibit hall or the organization sponsoring the show may set restrictions concerning the design of a booth or exhibit, the height of walls, fireproofed materials, lighting and sound equipment, and overhead signs. The trade show designer must follow the guidelines provided by the management to comply with the union regulations that govern the setup, lighting, trimming, and eventual dismantling of the show since every venue differs in policy. Exhibiting at a public trade hall is costly and often affects the way designers approach the exhibit design. The designer must consider how long and often the booth will be used; the weight, method, and cost of shipment; and the time it takes to assemble the booth on site. Some vendors will try to utilize the framework of a booth design for several years and factor ways to update the booth. Once the booth is set up, the shipping cases and crating material needs to be stored for the duration of show before repacking.

Traveling Exhibits

A **traveling exhibit** is a broad, all-inclusive term for portable, or movable, displays. A traveling exhibit is conceived and designed to be moved from one location to another and to be assembled quickly, with few changes and a minimum of professional assistance. Some traveling shows are actually large buses or vans that have been converted into "galleries on wheels." The viewer enters at one end of the vehicle and exits from the other, after having seen the complete showing. Often, the government will produce a traveling show that will visit schools and libraries. The van or bus may be parked in the parking lot or out in front of the institution, and the students will be invited in to see the special collection.

Other traveling shows are not designed to conform to one location. These shows use collapsible or modular systems, panels, frames, or stands that can be reassembled and that will adapt to a pre-established plan or pattern in an area of a specific size. Sometimes the designer may have to supply several alternate arrangements for the systems in order to accommodate variations in floor layouts or space allocations of a venue.

This basic concept behind traveling shows is their capability of being assembled and resembled; this concept is often the very principle upon which many trade show systems are based. Because the manufacturer or exhibitor may have to show in several different markets (different trade shows in different cities) within the same short selling season, the exhibit may have to be assembled and used for a week or less, then be broken down, crated, and shipped off to the next exhibit hall, where the following week it has to be reassembled and ready for the new trade show. The exhibit designer may have to add or subtract panels or frames from the exhibit depending, again, on the allotted space and restrictions set by the new exhibit management. (See Figure 22.4.)

Outdoor Exhibits

An **outdoor exhibit** may take place in a public space such as a garden, a park, a parking lot, or in the middle of an open shopping mall. Depending on the content to be shown, this can be the most challenging type of exhibit. The garden or park setting is ideal for sculpture and other

FIGURE 22.4   Simple but interesting molded plastic modules in several colors that can be used singly, side by side, or back to back make for a great traveling exhibit. The modules can be arranged and rearranged to suit the physical and spatial specifications of each new venue. *Titan Display, India. Design: Collaborative Architecture, Mumbai, India.*

dimensional objects that are not affected by heat, cold, rain, snow, or animals. The natural light and setting can be a great asset to the outdoor exhibition and play an important role in the design.

When the exhibit can be contained under a roof—a pavilion or a tent—it is more manageable. With an overhead enclosure, the designer can make plans despite the sun, gusts of wind, or unexpected showers.

Planning the Exhibit

The primary job of the exhibit designer is to tell the story about the objects on display; as previously described, these objects can be a collection of artifacts, products, or services or a brand identity. The designer must distill all necessary information before beginning the design process. Once familiar with the content and information, he or she may begin building the storyline. The process does not begin with an exhibit system, pedestal, or panels; it begins with a sketchpad and the designer's insights. Crafting the exhibit's story begins by establishing a clear and understandable narrative that contains undulating highlights as it guides the viewers through the exhibit journey. Much like reading a good book, the exhibit must have an exciting beginning, a climax, and summation.

AUDIENCE

As in all displays, the target market is a prime consideration. What is the age and intelligence level of the viewing audience that will come to see this show? Are they children, teenagers, adults, or all of the above? Are they knowledgeable on the subject, or must they be directed and oriented to the material to be presented? Are they coming with a pre-established interest or curiosity about the subject, or must they be stimulated to rouse their interest in the show? What is their average interest span? How much material will they be able to absorb in one visit through the show?

Understanding the answers to these questions and other information supplied by the exhibitor, the designer can then build the exhibit story with the anticipated length of the visit to the show and consider the best method to communicate to the viewer audience. Depending on the material, and the show space, the designer can help set the pace for the viewer by determining the best communication device. Will digital media tell the story best? Large imagery? Interactive devices? Sound? The designer must consider the best form of communication to reach the audience, depending on its age and education level, even using more than one device to keep the viewer interested.

SUBJECT

The better organized the exhibit, the more readily it will be understood and accepted. If the exhibit is based on a single, unifying theme, and all the content is related (e.g., fashions of Coco Chanel), the background information can be explained or illustrated only once, at the beginning. Then the story can unfold by curating the collection chronologically, by color, by season and so on.

At a trade show it is simpler and more effective to show one product or a related line of items rather than present a complete spectrum of unrelated and sometimes conflicting merchandise. When many diverse items must be presented, the good designer will use some device or gimmick (color, line, dividers, graphics, and so on) to unify the dissimilar and individual pieces into a harmonious and controlled flow. At a recent trade show, the manufacturer of a diverse line of mannequins (from very realistic to very abstract, from child to adult) had all the mannequins dressed in black and gold. Although the fashions and styles were varied, in keeping with the type of mannequin used, the black-and-gold color scheme made a strong, unifying impact.

Whatever the subject matter of the exhibit, the exhibitor and the designer must supply an avenue of interest for the audience to follow, in which the theme, product, or premise is presented in an appealing, coherent, and compelling manner. There should be a point of view expressed, and that point should be presented up front, at the beginning, so that all that follows is an explanation and an elaboration on the basic theme. A good exhibit presents, stimulates, and leaves an impression, but never confuses. Even if it is a goodwill, prestige, or institutional type of exhibit, the exhibitor still has the opportunity to publicize, either directly or indirectly, his or her product and to stimulate a demand for his or her services.

SIZE

The size of an exhibit is commonly a great variable. When dealing with a particular gallery, museum, library, or exhibit area, where the space devoted to showings is relatively constant, the exhibit designer "knows the territory"—what can be done and how much can be shown effectively. On the other hand, the designer of a traveling exhibit supplies an exhibit system of panels, frames, and stands that will require a certain amount of square footage to set up the show correctly. The individuals who receive the exhibit (the staff decorators) must then make the design work within their actual configuration of space. (See Figure 22.5.)

A well-designed traveling exhibit will have a degree of flexibility drawn into the plan. The design will either expand or contract as space permits. It might require omitting some secondary material in order to make the best presentation of the major items. A display that will travel and be set up in any number of spaces should have auxiliary floor plans, alternative arrangements, and sketched recommendations accompanying the exhibit. The show that is "mobile" (i.e.,

FIGURE 22.5 Large trade show exhibits often consist of several units or modules that can be arranged to suit the needs of the brand and to accommodate the space. Here, a tall, circular, drum-shaped unit serves as the reception area, alongside individual one-on-one test stations and sampling booths. In addition, the tall, illuminated rectangles can be arranged into semi-enclosed spaces of various sizes. *P&G Beauty, Buenos Aires, Argentina. Design: Anthem Worldwide, New York.*

FIGURE 22.6 Here, the Amuneal company uses its namesake aluminum surfacing to face the exhibit that houses the Amuneal product line. The exhibit is designed like a house, with windows and doors through which visitors sneak peeks. The windows are see-through, and the wide, wood-framed door welcomes show-goers to see and sample the products on display within. *Amuneal GlobalShop, Las Vegas, Nevada. Photo: Alistair Tutton.*

set on a train, bus, or van) is already limited in size by the unit that houses and carries it. (See Figure 22.6.)

The design of the individual trade show exhibit will vary with the particular exhibit hall and its space allocation. The exhibit floor is divided into blocks or booths that may be 8 feet by 8 feet, 10 feet by 10 feet, or 12 feet by 12 feet, depending on the module of space that is most economical for the hall's management. The exhibitor reserves a booth or a combination of booths, such that the exhibit area (based on a 10-foot module as an example) may be anything from a 10-foot by 10-foot space (one booth); to a long, narrow rectangle measuring 10 feet by 40 feet (four adjacent booths); to a square block, 20 feet by 20 feet (two booths wide by two booths long). The size and shape of the total space will determine the layout and traffic pattern of the total booth area, the location of the entrance and exit from the display area, and the amount of material that can be shown.

Ideally, the space should relate to the subject matter. Statues and large architectural pieces need open spaces so that they can be viewed from all sides as well as from a distance. Coins, jewelry, manuscripts, and small collector's items are more effective in smaller, more intimate surroundings.

When the amount of material (like a retrospective showing of Picasso's works or the full line of General Mills

products) is staggering and requires lots of space and material, it is advisable to have a digital app show guide, or catalog available for the visitor. As the viewer threads his or her way through the maze of myriad objects, the app or catalog will supply the basic information and the necessary background material that would have only cluttered the exhibit if additional signs had to be included. It also provides a route for the viewer to follow. The guide provides the viewer with a means to locate what he or she actually wants to see and to spend time where he or she feels it will be most beneficial and instructive.

The size of the exhibit is especially important when the exhibit must be crated to be shipped to the next show place. The cost of crating and shipping is a very big part of the exhibit budget, and the designer must consider this in the original plan. It will affect the framework used for the show and the manner in which the show is set up and taken down.

DESIGN AND LAYOUT: THE TRAFFIC PLAN

After the storyline is developed, the size of the exhibit is specified, and the content to be shown is selected, the designer starts by plotting the traffic patterns within the space. This is most important and may determine which structural materials are used.

The traffic plan is the basic consideration in moving people through an area. The layout may be in long lines following the perimeter walls, creating a gallery effect with series of straight lines, panels, or "walls." The gallery effect may be accomplished with freestanding panels displaying exhibit content on both sides.

The path may follow a zigzag of screens folded into a series of V-shaped bays. These bays, or alcoves, may be used to separate or highlight certain content, contain a case or riser, or create a setting for a dimensional object. Or, the floor plan can be a pattern that combines straight panels with an occasional V for emphasis or as a change of pace.

The maze is another option in exhibit design. In this case, the traffic flow is directed by "pointing arrows," and the viewer is swept along by a series of angles and turns. He or she has no alternative but to follow along the prescribed route. The maze allows more content to be shown because the aisles are usually narrower, the content is shown on two sides of the frame or panel, and the convoluted floor pattern permits the use of more panels in the allotted space. Although the viewer is shepherded through the presentation, there can be bottlenecking, where people get "stuck" in funnel-like openings. A viewer who decides to go back to look at something previously passed can cause a problem in the traffic flow. Rarely does the maze layout allow the viewer the freedom of selecting a course through the show at his or her own tempo. Some viewers may resent the "herding" quality and the closeness of this type of exhibit layout.

Whatever type of traffic plan or floor plan is used, a change of pace should be built in. Long gallery runs, although exceptionally well suited to certain content, can be enhanced when balanced with a few side bays or aisles for added interest or emphasis. An occasional maze might supply just the right ambiance for other content or work to separate groups of products. However, if the visitor feels restricted, inhibited, or confused, the purpose of the exhibit may be lost.

STORY

A good exhibit has a great story, **theme**, or unifying element. For example, the American Museum of Natural History hosted a show named "Poison," targeted at a wide audience of viewers. Consider for a moment that poison can be found in plants, animals, the environment, household items, food, and folklore of the past. The theme gave way to a dynamic degree of storytelling that called up fictional characters (Snow White and the Mad Hatter) as well as important historical figures (Cleopatra and Napoleon) who had a brush with poison. The exhibit design team took theme of poison and expanded in a way to appeal to young and old, piquing the viewer's interest with antidotes, curiosities, and folklore. The story or theme must support and build depth into the exhibition; it has the ability to build in more content by using images and interactive features to engage the audience. (See Figure 22.7.)

The exhibit should start with the main idea and then elaborate and illustrate the premise behind the show. Something should get the visitor's attention or pique the curiosity, enough to make him or her want to go on and see more.

If graphics are used to narrate the exhibit, they should start out with an effective statement and carry throughout the exhibit. If the area lends itself to it, a dramatic and

FIGURE 22.7   This interactive "enchanted" book allows users to bring their stories to life through media projection and touch sensor technology, featuring animations and a soundscape. Visitors explore the origin myths of these poisons and annotations explaining how they were used in the past. Based loosely on Leonardo da Vinci's notebooks and Dioscorides' De Materia Medica, this interactive book also highlights each plant, where it is found, and the effects of its poison. *Poison Exhibition, AMNH, New York. EMMANUEL DUNAND/AFP/Getty Images.*

enticing entrance is always effective. MOMA's (Museum of Modern Art) Tim Burton exhibition invited viewers to walk through the mouth of a frightening character with large fangs. (See Figure 22.8.)

The exhibit entrance is like the overture to a musical: stimulating and exciting, with just a bar or two of what is to come and enough to set the feet tapping and the senses moving in the right direction. The entrance can be heightened by using lighting effects, a dynamic color, or animation. If there is copy, a headline, or a quote that sets the theme, it should be easy to read and provocative.

COLOR AND TEXTURE

Color is always vital to a presentation, whether it be by its presence or its absence. If an exhibit is mainly black and white (such as printed materials or photographs), then the

FIGURE 22.8 A giant "Burtonesque" character greets visitors at the Museum of Modern Art for the Tim Burton retrospective. The dynamic entranceway exudes all of his cinematic style as the giant monster teeth threaten overhead, setting the tone for excitement that follows. *Bennett Raglin/WireImage/Getty Images.*

designer may have to use colored backgrounds to add pace and pizzazz to the show. A change of color may serve as a "punctuation mark" to indicate the end of one idea or phase and the introduction to the next one.

Colored or neutral backgrounds may be necessary to overcome the existing background color of the exhibition area. If the exhibit hall is white and airy, and the presentation requires deep, dark colors and dramatic shadows, the designer may accomplish this by means of colored panels, dropped ceilings, or special lighting effects. Optically, color can stretch walls, bring them closer together, or open or close areas and, thus, seemingly affect the architecture of the show area. (See Chapter 2.)

Texture is also a tool that can be used by the designer. Color and texture can be used on the walls, panels, ceilings, and floor to set the traffic pattern of the show. The designer can lay a path of carpet or tiles that contrasts with the existing floor of the display space. Imagine a red velvet runner leading around a painting or sculpture exhibition or a green "grass" matting used to set a crafts show inside an enclosed brick or stone space.

Branding and Graphics

BRANDING

The brand identity for an exhibitor will carry through its theme by means of an identifying and well-sized **logo** or **trademark**. The logo may brand the total exhibit structure, a sizable back wall, floor graphics, or digital media on giant screens. It may be part of the catalogue cover design or on the brochures or giveaways. Souvenirs, like T-shirts, reusable shopping bags, or phone cases will often be identified by the same logo. A dramatic, dimensional representation of the logo can be the entrance to the exhibit. (See Figure 22.9.)

Any additional branding information used, whether for headlines, captions, or general information, should be in a style that is consistent with all other brand collateral. The brand exhibitor will supply a "style guide" for the use of typography or other digital assets and even a recommend a vendor for signage and printing needs.

FIGURE 22.9 Graphics and signage are vital for identification on the crowded show floor and for visualizing the brand image. A sign depicting the Dr. Martens logo floats high in front of the double-tiered exhibit, while graphic images of the product and Dr. Martens "customers" add to the appeal of the brand. *Courtesy of Dr. Martens.*

ENVIRONMENTAL GRAPHICS

A long, straight, unbroken gallery wall can become an exciting and moving background by using large-scale environmental graphics. The designer may plan a dynamic wall pattern to suggest movement in the background. Visually, bold, large-scale graphics can be used to direct visitors subconsciously in a space and lead them through the floor plan. The dynamic movement suggests the "path" for the presentation, and the viewer is "led" along by it. The large graphics also work on banners, freestanding frames, and modular constructions.

Oversized photographs and enlargements of detailed drawings and printed material can be used effectively in promoting the theme of an exhibit. A greatly enlarged graphic, greater than life-size, adds impact to an idea and turns a minute phrase into a mighty statement.

In a showing where crowds are anticipated, the photographic enlargement makes it possible for the viewers in back to see what is going on up front. The surprise of seeing a 6- or 8-foot close-up of a face or pattern, as one turns from one aisle into another, can be just the thing to add impetus and rhythm to the next group of objects

to be viewed. A grainy or grayed photomural may be the right tone and texture for appliquéd cutout letters with a message.

In a crowded exhibit hall, where many exhibitors are competing for attention, large imagery or **photomurals** can be very effective. Murals, or long, continuous pictorial illustrations, can serve as a bridge between groups of ideas, explain the passage of time or a change of locale, or supply a historical setting. The mural can supply the atmosphere or background that will make what follows more readily understood. A giant map can set the scene for what comes next.

HEIGHTS AND ELEVATIONS

Eye level is a very important consideration in planning an exhibit. It is not enough simply to place material to be viewed at 5 to 5 1/2 feet off the ground. When there are crowds or several layers of viewers lined up to view the exhibit contents, the designer should hang the work above regular eye level. This is an accommodation to the people in the back who may have to look over the heads and shoulders of those in front. It also adds a change of pace to what otherwise might be a routinely hung show.

There are no restrictions or rules for the height or level of presentation at a showing. Basically, it should be determined by the individual object being presented. Some things look better when viewed from above—that is, when the viewer looks down on them (e.g., coins, jewelry, manuscripts, or miniatures); other objects are best displayed when the viewer can look up at them; while still others need a straight-on view. Thus, the presentation will depend on the content, the type of exhibit, the construction of the exhibit, and the main object, or thrust, of the show. If a dramatic story is being presented, or the development of a product or theme, then a straight-on show may be best. If it is an exhibition of artwork of various materials and techniques, the exhibit can be made more interesting when a variety of heights are used in displaying or setting up.

In any long presentation, whether it be a gallery run or an unbroken lineup of panels, a change of pace is necessary. The viewer's eye needs a rest, a pause. It is quite monotonous to see object after object on the same background color, lit with the same intensity. In such a case, after a while, all the objects on view tend to blend together. Varying sizes can break this routine pattern. One large unit might be balanced by several smaller ones that fill the same amount of space. (See Chapter 3 for a discussion of balance and symmetry.) A break in the imaginary top or bottom line will cause the piece that extends above or below the others to receive more attention. Interspersing an occasional panel of a contrasting color will also relieve the overall sameness of the presentation and focus in on the uniqueness of the one that has been treated with special emphasis. Lighting variations will also help reduce the potential for monotony.

The use of museum cases and pedestals can add momentum to the pace and rhythm of a show. If photos and manuscripts have been carefully mounted on a vertical surface (a wall, panel, and so forth), then placing a book, manuscript, or photo on a pedestal, at a different eye level, will emphasize the importance of that particular object. The viewer is "forced" to look at this part of the show in a different way, switching eye level, the angle of the head—in fact, his or her entire focus. Subsequently, the viewer registers that this is something special, different, and more important.

Clusters of platforms of assorted heights are effective for exhibiting three-dimensional objects. A riser can bring an otherwise unimpressive object to new "heights" of importance in the viewer's eye. For example, a clay vase on a pedestal is special and unique. A clay vase along with several others, at the same level in a display case, is just another vase. Separate and apart, it becomes extraordinary.

A dimensional cube or riser can also become an island in an aisle and serve as a separation in a traffic pattern. The riser can also be used to direct traffic around a run of panels or frames. The platform serves to break away from a flat gallery presentation, or to fill in the bay, or V, formed by a folded screen. For a traveling exhibit, cubes can be designed with open bottoms and made to nest so that they will stack and ship more easily. (See Figures 22.10 and 22.11.)

Exhibit Systems

Exhibit systems used for store planning and display were discussed in Chapter 16. Although they were introduced as a fixturing concept, many were brought on the market specifically to serve the exhibit industry. As previously mentioned, systems are available in steel, aluminum, wood, and heavy-duty plastic. Most systems are designed with an infinite collection of joiners, end caps, and accessories. Some even come with built-in lighting. The systems may be super sleek, ultrachic, or high-tech, or look like a warehouse construction. Some are designed to "disappear," be all but invisible, whereas others are meant to make a decorative statement. Systems go from simple ladder constructions to very complex webs and grids.

Some systems are preset regarding their use, and there is little the designer can do to alter the physical setup. Other systems offer a varied collection of modular, multisized, notched panels that can be creatively built into an intricate "house of cards" that stands, or into folding screens, cubes, and such. In selecting a system, especially one

FIGURE 22.10 Another example of a supersized exhibit constructed of semitranslucent fabric and aluminum rods. The huge design salutes Mexican history, and the semitransparent fabric panels are printed with script and painted in the style of noted Mexican artists. The seemingly solid structure becomes illusory and ephemeral when the viewer shifts position. *Guanajuato Exhibit, Acapulco, Mexico. Design: Arrca Exposiciones, Leon, Mexico.*

FIGURE 22.11 Getting attention to what is inside the exhibit space is very important, especially when the booth is semi-enclosed. Converse sports shoes made quite an impact on visitors in the aisle with this bold American flag made of red, white, and blue Converse sports shoes—a "shoe show stopper." *Converse at the Bread & Butter Trade Show. Designed by Checkland Kindleysides.*

that will be used for temporary setups and for traveling or trade shows, the following criteria should be considered:

◆ Is it compact?
◆ Is it light?
◆ Is it easy to assemble and dismantle?
◆ Is it easy to maintain?
◆ Is it flexible and adaptable?
◆ Is it modular?
◆ Are replacement parts and accessories readily available?

Exhibit designers would do well to check with organizations such as the SHOP! Association, *Exhibit Builder Magazine*, and larger trade show venues, for lists of current manufacturers of portable trade show booths.

Theft and Vandalism Control

Unfortunately, theft and vandalism are challenges that the exhibit designer must help control. The designer has to plan for the safety and protection of any irreplaceable materials on view. Sometimes it requires enclosed museum-type cases with locks.

Security guards may become part of the exhibit landscape, not only as symbols of authority but also to admonish viewers who touch. In some cases, the appearance of security in the form of television cameras, sensor equipment, and locks on cases may be enough to protect the exhibit. Ropes and stanchions can also be used to keep the exhibited material out of arm's reach. The rope-and-stanchion combination can also be used to control and direct traffic.

Light, Sound, and Motion

Lighting is such a crucial element that it often makes or breaks an exhibit. The kind of lighting used in exhibits is often determined by the type of content to be displayed and the type of exhibit or trade show. **Ambient lighting** is the mood-producing light used in an area or exhibit. Colored filters can be used, adding warmth and depth where needed, or strong, sharp accents of color to excite or stimulate the viewer. Ambient lighting is part of secondary lighting and makes use of floodlights, filters, and wall washers. It can include indirect lighting devices: lights hidden behind a riser or a baffle or valance dropped from overhead. The combination of natural and artificial light can complement an exhibit space if the natural light is controlled or indirect.

Task lighting is the all-important spotlighting and highlighting of an exhibit. It strategically places the light where it really counts and makes the items stand out and show up at their very best. Some exhibit areas or rooms are equipped with ceiling track lighting, which can facilitate the spotlighting and floodlighting of a show. In this setup the designer may be in control of both the general lighting and the special lighting. In museums and galleries, archival content will require the use of measured light (foot-candles) by a professional lighting designer.

Small objects in cases can be lit with miniature LED or fluorescent tubular lamps. Some objects are especially attractive when lit from behind or below. Frosted glass panels and shelves are good to use in these instances. Wherever and whenever possible, the designer should try to hide the source of light.

Backlighting objects or photographic transparencies can be especially effective when the area in which they are to be used has low-level lighting. Illuminated cases appear more brilliant when the surroundings are darkened. Rear projection and rolling video need controlled, general lighting to work. The use of "dissolves," whereby one object seems to fade away, and another object takes its place, requires a timer device.

Thus, lighting can help tell the story, set the scene, and emphasize or enhance an object. It can isolate one item or unify a group of unrelated pieces. It can create the mood or ambiance, add drama and excitement. Lighting can create a sense of direction or a path for traffic to follow, and set a pace and tempo. On a trade show floor, with dozens or hundreds of exhibits vying for attention, good lighting can be the beacon that brings in the crowds. The exhibit designer, just like the retail merchandise presenter, must balance the primary, or general, lighting with the secondary lighting.

Acoustics can present challenges in large exhibit spaces due to marble or concrete floors, high ceiling heights, and lack of insulation. The exhibit designer can control the use of sound and music in multiple ways, beginning with the use of materials for the design of the exhibition. Fabric walls, panels, and materials (such as Homasote), all possess sound reduction properties. Music or sound bites can be introduced through headphones or in small viewing rooms. Sound can also be introduced through directional speakers or "sound domes" that the viewer stands beneath; this eliminates the need for public headphones. It is wise to seek the services of a sound engineer when acoustics play a central role in the exhibit design. (See Chapter 4.) (See Figures 22.12 and 22.13.)

Motion can be more eye-catching and startling than a stationary display. The **movement** can be smooth and

FIGURE 22.12 Lighting makes a big difference in an exhibit, especially when it is used to draw—to attract and lead visitors to or through the stand. At the Level Green exhibit the lighting adds to the drama and dynamics of the design, as the fluorescent tubes, embedded in green plastic super-construction, drive the directional design. Note the interactive stations entombed in the green floor units set on the patterned floor. *Level Green, Wolfsburg, Germany. Design: J. Mayer H.*

FIGURE 22.13 Although Teknion had a large space, the giant fabric-and-metal cube that encompasses the display area below looms even larger—and more dramatically. The glowing panels that make up the hanging cube are evident from anywhere on the convention hall floor and yet come apart for ease of shipping. The Teknion office furniture appears in vignette settings on the floor, and the display areas are adaptable and easy to change. *Teknion, IIDEX/NeoCon Canada, Toronto. Design: Burdifilek, Toronto, Canada.*

subtle, such as a turntable slowly rotating and showing an array of items, or a complete front-to-back of a single mannequin. The turntable may be a heavy-duty floor unit made to sustain a great deal of weight, a tabletop unit for smaller and lighter pieces, or one that is suspended from above to put a mobile into a spin. Ceiling motors can be used for a variety of motion effects.

Miniatures attract and fascinate audiences. Scale models are informative as well as intriguing and might do a better job of instructing than a full-size replica. For the exhibit designer faced with space restrictions and traveling and shipping schedules, the model setup and the use of miniatures can be extremely useful.

Digital Media and Interactivity

Digital media and **interactivity** are essential components in exhibitions today. Although the cost of equipment and creating content can challenge the exhibition budget, media and interactivity create the highpoints—the buzz! Today's

viewers expect technology. Virtual reality can transport visitors into the future through space or allow them to become a superhuman for a brief few minutes. Visitors can experience flying, diving, or bungee jumping from the highest cliff, or test their aptitude against the entire population without leaving the museum. At the Cleveland Art Museum, museumgoers can insert themselves into famous works of art and travel through time to communicate with historic figures of the past. An exhibition at the Brooklyn Museum honoring the designer Jean Paul Gautier used simple projection on a blank mannequin face to animate the designer giving a monologue for museumgoers. Other mannequins wearing the designer's fashion winked and grinned at viewers. This special effect mesmerized viewers, prompting a blitz on social media and brought crowds to the Brooklyn Museum to view the living mannequins.

More and more exhibit designers are finding that an exhibit or display that involves the viewer physically is very effective and leaves a long-lasting impression on the participant. When a person makes a personal connection with the content on view; turns a crank; pushes a button; makes a recording with his or her phone; changes the location of an object; tastes, smells, touches, or in any way makes actual contact with the content, he or she becomes personally involved with the display, and the displayed items become part of his or her experience.

Museums are presenting more hands-on exhibits than ever before. The hands-on experience allows the observer to pace the show according to his or her own level of interest. The participant will spend more time at some displays and less at others. Today's designer has to be aware of the many approaches to technology in order to produce exhibits that not only attract but also impress.

Live performance in an exhibit can provoke interactivity; however, it must be carefully curated. A live demonstration can quickly draw an audience if orchestrated well. People will stand around, intrigued and delighted, watching a mime, a magician, a mad scientist, or performing animals.

Greater anticipation and excitement is generated when the live performer is not always "on," but makes scheduled appearances. In this way, the exhibitor can gain an audience in the exhibit area and "sell" the product or idea to those who are waiting to be entertained or to those who have just been amused. It can also be used as a means of controlling traffic.

DESIGN OBJECTIVE

JGA, the design firm, was asked to create a trade show unit for the Timberland brand that would be featured at the Outdoor Retailers Winter Market in Salt Lake City. According to Ken Nisch, chairperson and project principal at JGA, the booth had "to reflect the attitudes of a 'new generation' of outdoor consumers—the millennials. The target consumers' idea of the outdoors is not a passive world, but one of challenging technology and adventure." In addition to showcasing the assorted Timberland brands of clothing and accessories in the 3,000-square-foot space, the space had to reflect the company's commitment to "environmental accountability, leveraging its 'nutrition label' concept." That meant a "green" or sustainable design that included the use of reclaimed, recycled, and "found" materials or objects while "minimizing negative environmental impact," added Mr. Nisch. (See Figure CS22.1.)

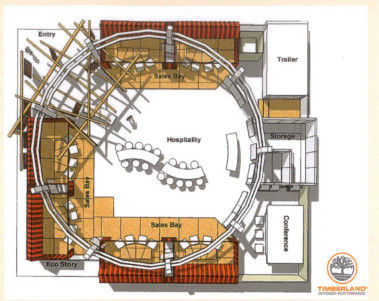

FIGURE CS22.1   A floor plan depicting the layout of space and fixtures for the two-tier Timberland tradeshow booth.

DESIGN SOLUTION

The designers created a two-level unit constructed mainly of reclaimed industrial materials like the shipping containers. They now serve as "rooms" or select merchandise areas in the scheme as well as units in which loose props and furniture can be stored and shipped to other show locations. Mr. Nisch goes on to explain, "The outside of the booth featured a three-dimensional 'nutrition label'—a signature element that is part of the outdoor performance packaging and is translated into a large panel element—highlighting the various materials and an environmental 'scorecard' for full transparency and accountability." The now brightly painted orange shipping containers form the surround, or outer rim, of the stand and visitors are welcomed in at the corner entrance. A highly visible Timberland sign floats over the entry. The visitor is greeted by panels covered with graphics of featured products and the reception desk. Once inside the enclosed area, the visitor finds her- or himself in "a community gathering space with stand-up counters. It is an easy 'meet and greet' place. A hospitality element transforms into a stand-up table for beverage or for buffet lunch service." Hemp fabric and translucent acrylic panels are used to separate an enclosed conference area, and the acrylic panels also "provide the feeling of natural lighting and are set as joints between the booth's modules (the orange shipping containers) and also work as vertical skylight elements." The assorted containers served as mini showrooms for the various Timberland products and, in addition to shelving and/or hang-rods for product display, they were furnished with custom tables made of natural materials that were used as work surfaces for customers and comfortable chairs. Though essentially open to the common area, they did provide some privacy as work areas.

A merchandising trailer was "docked" into the stand. It had its signature crow's nest, and the interior was fully fitted out as a selling space. Nisch adds, "A 6-inch elevation of the selling deck created a physical and visual separation from the social, common area of the booth. A galvanized handrail and the previously mentioned marketing panels further delineated the border." (See Figures CS22.2–CS22.6.)

FIGURE CS22.2 Bold brand signage and a mobile panel system with colorful brand imagery greet show attendees at the entranceway. The orange-colored "rooms," or extensions, are shipping containers that have been refreshed and refurbished for a new use.

FIGURE CS22.3 Timberland's commitment to going green extends the choice of materials. Natural wood, stainless steel, and the brand's bold orange color reveal the DNA of the Timberland brand at the entrance.

FIGURE CS22.4 The mini showrooms are furnished with custom tables that elevate to display the merchandise from a distance.

FIGURE CS22.5 The show space is outfitted with tables made of natural materials that are used as work surfaces for customers to explore merchandise and write orders.

FIGURE CS22.6 The entire space functions as an open marketplace, inviting visitors to come in and explore the array of Timberland's merchandise.

Conclusion

The booth was selected as "best in show" for its design and outstanding look and its ability to serve the Timberland brand and what it represented. Among the numerous "green" or sustainable products the JGA design team used were hemp, cork, recyclable sound absorbing material, panels made of wood scraps without the use of formaldehyde, biodegradable flooring materials and recyclable and resourced aluminum—and, of course, the shipping containers.

DESIGN CREDITS: *Design: JGA, Southfield, Michigan. Chairperson & Project Principal: Ken Nisch. Exhibit Contractor: Exhibit Works, Livonia, Michigan. For Timberland: Senior Director: Bevan Bloemendaal. Project Leader & Senior Manager: David Curtis. Fixturing Manager: Jean Wood. Senior Manager of Corporate Meetings & Events: Stephen King. Senior Manager of Visual Merchandising: Amy Tauchert. Photography: Mark Steele Photography, Columbus, Ohio.*

Exhibit and Trade Show Design: Trade Talk

ambient lighting	movement	temporary exhibit
exhibits	outdoor exhibit	theme
exhibit systems	permanent exhibit	trademark
interactivity	photomurals	trade shows
logo	task lighting	traveling exhibit

Exhibit and Trade Show Design: A Recap

+ An exhibit is the display and showing of special materials that have been collected and edited for presentation. The major purpose of an exhibit is to stimulate and create interest for a particular product, idea, or organization aimed at a special audience.

+ A trade show is a commercial display of new products or concepts presented to a select group of prospective buyers or consumers.

+ Types of exhibits include permanent, temporary, trade show, traveling, and outdoor.

+ The size of an exhibit can vary greatly, and the designer must determine what can be done within a space and how much can be shown effectively.

+ A traveling exhibit must have flexibility so that it can expand or contract as space permits.

+ Trade show exhibits will vary with each exhibit hall and its space allocation. The exhibition may require a number of modules put together to accommodate the material or may be contained within one module.

+ Common traffic patterns at exhibits include long lines following perimeter walls; a zigzag of screens folded into a series of V-shaped bays; and a maze layout where the viewer is swept along by a series of angles and turns.

+ When planning an exhibit, the following must be considered: size of the exhibit, design and layout of traffic patterns, theme or story of the exhibit, and color and texture of the presentation.

+ Graphics can identify an exhibit, call attention to it, promote the theme, supply atmosphere and background, and add a change of pace to a routinely mounted show.

+ In selecting a system, the following criteria should be considered: compactness, lightness, ease in assembling and dismantling, maintenance, flexibility and adaptability, whether the system is modular, and whether replacement parts and accessories are readily available.

+ Theft and vandalism may be controlled in a number of ways: setting of objects in museum-type cases, hiring of security guards, security cameras and sensor equipment, ropes and stanchions, and good lighting.

+ Types of lights used in exhibit design include daylight, or natural light; fluorescent light; incandescent light; ambient light; spotlights; and track lights.

+ Movement and animation, audiovisual effects, and live action are special effects that can enliven and enhance an exhibit.

+ Special amenities can bring attention to an exhibit as well as satisfy the aesthetics or personal comfort of the viewer.

Questions for Review and Discussion

1. Identify exhibits that you may have visited or that have been hosted in your community.

2. Give an example of a trade show that you may have attended or that has been held in your community.

3. Distinguish among permanent exhibits, temporary exhibits, and traveling exhibits.

4. What problems must be overcome in the design of outdoor exhibits?

5. Explain the relationship between the size of the exhibit and the potential traffic pattern that will be created.

6. Why are height and elevation such important factors in exhibit design?

7. What is an exhibit system? What criteria should be used in the selection of an exhibit system?

8. What is the difference between ambient lighting and task lighting? Give examples of each.

9. What special effects might be used to add excitement to an exhibit?

PART FIVE

Visual Merchandising and Planning

Chapter 23 discusses the presentation of stock on the selling floor and how visual merchandising takes place where the shopper and the product come together in a real, hands-on situation.

Floor space is a primary concern of fixturing. Because a store's success is often computed in terms of sales per square foot of selling space, the floor plan, including the positioning of departments and fixtures within the store, is vital to the ultimate success or failure of the store. Guidelines for store planning and interior layout are explored in Chapter 24.

A budding new type of store—community retailing—is discussed in Chapter 25 along with the experiential store.

Chapter Twenty-Three
Visual Merchandise Planning

Aéropostale, Roosevelt Field, Long Island, New York.
GH & A Design, Montreal, Canada.

**AFTER YOU HAVE READ THIS CHAPTER,
YOU WILL BE ABLE TO DISCUSS**

+ how metrics play a role in visual merchandising
+ the importance of a retail calendar
+ the importance of merchandising directives and planograms
+ how aesthetic sensibility plays a role in visual merchandising
+ the steps in visual merchandise planning

Visual merchandise planning can mean different things to different people working in retail. For buyers, merchants, and store management, visual merchandising is about metrics or the average revenue a retailer generates for every square foot of sales space. ROI, or **return on investment**, is an indicator retailers use to calculate the performance of retail space. Retail **metrics** are gathered using numerous methods—traditionally stores relied on the total sales per day or year using their cash register figures to measure performance. Today, the collection of retail data is a multimillion-dollar industry that allows retailers to track everything from current stock levels by the shelf to the total number of visitors in real time, their traffic patterns, demographics, and even the number of "looks" a mannequin receives. Retail metrics is becoming a more valuable tool as stores acquire the technology to record and understand consumer trends and how they affect sales. This data affects many of the important decisions retailers make about merchandising and product placement. The other central planning element is the store's retail calendar. The retail calendar divides the year into segments, or selling seasons that include holiday sale periods, promotions, local events, and other annual activities that affect "when and what" is displayed in windows and the store interior. The calendar also enables the store management and merchants to work more efficiently with store planners and visual merchandisers. A well-thought-out schedule keeps displays and merchandise moving freely, in and out of the windows and on and off ledges and platforms. These predetermined time slots keep the store looking new, fresh, and exciting as new merchandise continues to arrive. (See Figure 23.1.)

Successful visual merchandising begins with establishing a well-thought-out **floor plan**. (See Figure 23.2.) Depending on the type of store, the floor plan may be the job of a visual merchandiser or the store planner or both. Smaller stores and specialty stores often depend on a visual merchandiser, while larger stores will have an in-house store planning department. The floor plan indicates the placement of merchandise, fixtures, display platforms, and the flow of traffic through the store. Most importantly, it determines the product **adjacencies** or the arrangement of product categories in a logical and natural formation for consumers to navigate the store. For example, the jewelry

area may be located next to watches, eventually leading to other accessories before entering the apparel area. Categories refer to the group of products or brands that meet a particular consumer need. Towels, shower curtains, bath mats, and soap dispensers all fall into the category of a bath area. Good merchandising requires aligning categories adjacent from one another using logic and consumer behavior as a guide to ensure the shopping experience is simple and intuitive yet fun and inviting. Searching too long for a product can leave a shopper dissatisfied and angry. When a category is merchandised on a fixture or wall, leading brands supersede lower-level brands.

The visual merchandiser and store planner work year round expanding and contracting the floor plan to accommodate merchandise and displays that fluctuate in size due to seasons, holidays, trends, or stock levels. They will develop **merchandising directives**, **planograms**, and **visual standards** to circulate this information to all stores to continuity of the stores image. (See Figure 23.3.)

Directives and planograms contain detailed diagrams and drawings of the displays and merchandising from all views (floor plan and elevation), so that the visual team in each store can interpret how to implement the setup. It will include **merchandising standards**, which convey the "formula or hierarchy" for the location and display of merchandise. Standards developed by the corporate visual team often correspond with agreements made with brands or vendors. Merchandising directives help determine the optimum installation time and merchandising methods to feature products in windows or on the selling floor. Display and merchandising configurations that are preplanned are often referred to as a **rollout**. (See Figure 23.4.)

Some areas on selling floor are considered more desirable than others, such as the areas near the main aisles, entrances, or escalator banks. These highly coveted locations divide the floor plan into zones. **Zones** differentiate areas of **priority** or those parts of the selling floor that are premium. An area within a display that is elevated or most evident to the consumer's viewing point is also considered a priority zone.

Directives and planograms map the arrangement of fixtures and merchandise based on priority or a particular brand strategy, taking the number of styles, sizes, flavors,

FIGURE 23.1 Retailers plan for the year ahead by knowing key dates and events that will impact their retail business. The retail calendar allows the time to strategically plan for more sales, more profit, and a more successful year. *The 2017 BrightPearl Retail Calendar, Courtesy of Bright Pearl.*

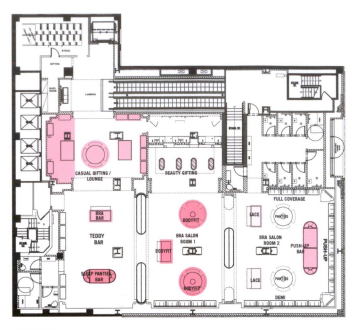

FIGURE 23.2   The floor plan is a flat representation of the length and width (or depth) of an area as seen from overhead. It indicates the location of entrances, dressing rooms, fixtures, and other merchandising elements. It should also identify the placement of merchandise categories or adjacencies. *MMP/RVC.*

and colors into account. Visual merchandisers can use a variety of methods to create a merchandise planogram, including digital software programs; for example, JDA is one of the most popular choices, and MockShop is another. There are many programs featured at the NRF Show (see Chapter 26). Once the template of the store's fixtures is in the software program, the visual merchandiser can enter the number of SKUs or units of merchandise. The planogram program can calculate and place units into the appropriate bay of a fixture in multiple configurations. Stores that use this technology hope to organize the merchandise to optimize sales to the highest potential. However, the merchandise must be arranged sensibly, so the consumer understands how to navigate the fixtures and the selling floor. The visual merchandiser can use the program to reveal more innovative opportunities to attract consumers by facing merchandise out, cascading the merchandise

FIGURE 23.3   A merchandising directive sets a standard on the placement of merchandise and displays. It clearly maps the number of products featured on shelf and the placement of marketing. *MMP/RVC.*

FIGURE 23.4   This rollout illustrates how the display table is a central focus on an aisle bordered by cabinets and dress forms. It is part of a multipage directive that informs the visual merchandiser about the placement of merchandise, mannequins, and props. *MMP/RVC*.

in color order, or layering. Planograms and standards are sometimes produced using other programs such as PowerPoint® or Adobe Creative Cloud®.

Techniques such as **cross-selling** promote more sales by suggesting "related or complimentary merchandise" together. Cross-selling strategically positions products that are often purchased together on the same fixture to create a stronger merchandise story. It suggests what consumers normally "mix and match," making shopping more fun and convenient. Imagine the customer's frustration at finding the perfect pant and jacket, but no coordinating blouse in a career apparel area.

A good example is finding all the makings for "s'mores" together on one fixture. Chocolate, marshmallows, and graham crackers are typically located in different aisles of the grocery store. By cross-selling, they come together on an endcap fixture or tower display to deliver the message—"Hey, It's Summer, Have a S'more!"

Placement is another key strategy. The height at which a product is positioned on shelf will positively influence sales. Retailers can use sales data to identify high- and low-performing merchandise and then reposition that merchandise either at eye level to the consumer or where the best sales have historically taken place. **Fixture capacity** is another consideration for the visual merchandiser. How can the fixture be utilized effectively to maximize the number of units? This discussion typically begins earlier in the fixture design and manufacturing stage. The **capacity** of a store fixture is defined by the number units it holds and the number of the sides the fixture uses to sell merchandise. Fixtures can be approached from various sides, better known as a quad, three-way, two-way, or head on. Occasionally retailers will "add on" to a fixture. **Wings** or **fins** can attach to fixtures to increase capacity to sell more products, cross-sell, or call out to the consumer with signage.

Signage is the single most important component in visual merchandising. Without signage the consumer is lost in a maze of fixtures and merchandise. Signage, or **wayfinding**, directs and informs the consumer about the merchandise story; it communicates the product's key attributes that often differentiate the brand from its competitor. Signage can softly lure the consumer with a tempting sales pitch of "buy one, get one free" or "limited edition" while conveying brand identity with color, graphics, imagery, and price point.

Lighting is another essential consideration. The design of a specific lighting technique can distinguish a visual merchandising rollout or store brand. By underlighting interior platforms or featuring mannequins in pools of strong downward spotlights, the display can be more striking and memorable for the shopper. (See Chapter 4 on Lighting.)

Setting the display up for a "trial" to work out the kinks is another popular visual merchandising practice. Many retailers set up a "**mock shop**" in their corporate offices or headquarters to experiment and photograph the displays before sending the merchandising directives to the other chain stores. A mock shop is a large space that houses multiple styles of fixtures used in all stores. Visual merchandisers can arrange the fixtures and merchandise in the mock shop to design the rollout that will later be implemented in each store. The mock shop process allows merchants, buyers, and store management to weigh in on the design so all parties are in agreement. Once the merchandising configuration is approved, it is documented and dispersed to all stores as a directive for a particular length of time or season.

Even though metrics, computer programs, and calendars play a major role in the planning process, visual merchandising planning is a still creative process that requires an **aesthetic sensibility**. Simply stacking and hanging merchandise on a fixture will not promote sales; the merchandise must tell the consumer a story by using display strategies, tactics, or attention-getting devices. There is no replacement for the power of stunning imagery, bunches of dried leafy sunflowers, rustic clay urns, or a Navajo blanket wistfully cascading from the shelf, in other words—"display." Merchandising without display is just that—merchandising! Merchandising with display is visual merchandising! A software program can never replace the human touch of creating a visually arresting and inspiring display. The execution of a good display comes from knowing in advance what trends, colors, and type of merchandise are scheduled for future display so that some thought and preparation can be made for the eventual visual presentation of that new merchandise. It also requires a close working relationship with the retailer or buyer, the promotion department, advertising people, and display manufacturers and suppliers.

Good displays come from the visual merchandisers' knowledge of what is available and where by maintaining good resources. It requires an awareness of what is going on in the community, in the city, in the country, and in the world and then being able to draw on that awareness to create attention-getting, image-building, and merchandise-selling displays.

Visual Merchandise Planning

The following are some of the points to consider in planning:

◆ Is there a theme or an idea that will complement the merchandising directive and stimulate sales, but also inspire the consumer to connect with the brand to establish a long-term relationship? Can the visual merchandiser blend an advertising story, national news story, or social media campaign in to tie in with the theme for greater impact and exposure?

◆ Consider the approach to the promotion or individual display presentation. Will it be limited to a single garment; a single classification of garments or merchandise; or a single pattern, color, or featured designer? Is the promotion to be storewide, or will only one department or type of merchandise be featured? Will the window display be coordinated with the interior of the store—on major ledges, columns, platforms, and counters and along the traffic aisles? How will the visual merchandiser unify all these areas into a cohesive, dramatic, and dynamically flowing presentation? Remember, the simpler and more direct the approach, the easier it will be for the shopper to comprehend the message.

◆ Ideally, the whole idea or theme of the display should be summed up in some form of signage that appears in the display area. Consider different methods to energize the signage. It can be placed in a sign holder, on glass using vinyl, or printed on a flowing transparent banner hanging near the display. Durable floor graphics can lead the shopper into an area. Lightboxes, backlit signage, and wall murals can direct and inform the shopper about trends, promotions, products, and price points.

◆ If there is to be a series of windows, will the merchandise all have the same look? Will there be variations on a theme? Will all the windows show only swimwear and cover-ups, or will it be a promotion about color and include men's, women's, and children's fashions and accessories—in color—as well as home furnishings, linens, kitchen gadgets, gift items, and so on in that featured green? The visual merchandiser may want to use the same decorative theme in all the windows—no matter what the merchandise classification—or vary the decorative elements from display to display but retain a flow and easy movement from window to window. The store management will decide how many windows to give to a promotion and how those windows will be apportioned among the various departments in the store. This is part of scheduling. The schedule indicates which merchandise will be given emphasis and "star" exposure, up front, and which will be subordinated to the secondary windows (on a side or less trafficked street) or to the shadow boxes.

◆ How can this display setup be different from the previous one? Can a different set of mannequins or an alternative to the regular mannequins be used? Can the background and floor colors be changed for this display? Can something new be done with the format of a window? Could the window be masked or cut down in size? Could a valance or vinyl proscenium be added to create a "come-and-look-at-this" frame around the glass? How about adding plants to the front of the window or placing trees or bushes between the windows?

◆ Can the type of lighting be varied? How can customers be made aware that something new and different is going on before they are close enough to really see it? (See Chapter 10 for techniques used in visual merchandising.)

◆ How do we reinforce the store's image with this display? Is it possible to enhance the store's reputation while promoting the merchandise? Some noted stores today show only image-promoting window displays, assuming that shoppers will be fascinated enough to want to enter the store in order to be transformed into what was promised outside—in the window.

Visual Merchandise Installation

Let us assume that the schedule was blocked out in advance and that the theme, signage, and marketing for the installation were already roughed out. Three months before the scheduled installation, the visual merchandiser will order whatever props or backgrounds are necessary from an outside supplier. He or she will then begin **scheduling** those parts of the display presentation to be done in the display studio of the store (e.g., covering floor and wall panels, signs, banners, and mounted graphics).

A week or two before, the visual merchandiser and buyer should check that the merchandise is in or on its way and that everything is set to go as planned. The visual merchandiser should check those areas in the store to be tied in with this installation—the counters, ledges, platforms, and so on—to be trimmed. The necessary signage, the pads to be changed in cases and under counters, the backgrounds to T-walls, the walls over ledges, and the column treatments also have to be considered.

The following is a suggested checklist for installing a display.

1. *Merchandise.* Is it in the store? Is it ready for the display: selected, correctly sized, and steamed? Is it the merchandise that was expected? If not, will any changes from the original plan be necessary? Have all the accessories been pulled together?

2. *Mannequins.* If mannequins or alternatives are used, have the correct mannequins been selected on which the merchandise is to be displayed? Do they have the appropriate look? Will the body positions work with the garments? Are they clean? Do they have any noticeable chips that need to be repaired? Will the shoes fit properly? Does the mannequin base need any special covering or repair? Are all the parts in one place and ready to be assembled?

3. *Lights.* Are all the necessary lights working? Does anything need to be replaced? Have the right filters been found and set aside? (It would be wise to have a few additional spots available should the setup need more lighting than anticipated.)

4. *Props, fixtures, and backgrounds.* Are all the pieces necessary for the presentation in the store? Does anything still have to be picked up? The visual merchandiser should refer to his or her floor plan and display checklist, checking off the items. Are the props, platforms, and risers that are to be used in top condition? Are any scratches, or ragged edges visible? Can a quick paint job or touch-up remedy any damage? What is the condition of the fixtures to be used? Do they require a clean-up? Are the floor pads covered? Are the wall coverings ready? Will the display area be cleaned, inside and outside, on the day of the trim? If the walls of the window show, in what condition are they?

5. *Signs.* If any signage will be needed, are they ready?

On the day of the **installation**, the previous trim is pulled (removed), and the merchandise is returned to the proper departments. Much of this preparatory work becomes second nature after the visual merchandiser has had some experience planning, setting up, and trimming displays. The best professionals remember to check out and take care of all the little details; most of the big ones are obvious and will be easily seen and checked. Remember: Someone out there is looking—judging the merchandise and the store. It is the responsibility of the visual merchandiser to ensure that everything being shown is presented in the best of all possible ways.

Case Study 23.1: WithMe Mobile, Chicago, Illinois

Design Objective

The founder and CEO of ShopWithMe of Chicago, Jonathan Jenkins, really threw down the design gauntlet when he commissioned Giorgio Borruso of Marina del Rey to design a store that could service almost any genre of merchandise in a turnkey-ready, interactive space. The noted and much lauded architect was expected to provide a "white box" filled with new technology and style that could accommodate a retailer's entry into the active business scene by just bringing in his own graphics, merchandise, and displays. As Mr. Borruso explains, "The WithMe mobile is to provide a durable framework for adaptable experimentation, which gives us an evolutionary model where key systems are strong enough to carry ambitious and continually evolving components directly to customers." (See Figure CS23.1.)

The WithMe Mobile prototype was first introduced in Chicago as a 3,000-square-foot retail space flanked by the Wrigley Building, the Tribune Tower, and Mies van der Rohe's One Illinois Center—"at one of America's primary epicenters of commerce and modern architecture." Mr. Borruso continues, "The WithMe Mobile will challenge traditional models of retail architecture by allowing innovative brands to

FIGURE CS23.1   Located "at one of America's primary epicenters of commerce and modern architecture," the WithMe Mobile shop of the future, as designed by Mr. Borruso, "challenges traditional models of retail architecture." It gives "a glimpse of a future where hierarchies of industry have been disrupted by new technologies, ideas, and ways of life."

inhabit a technologically advanced space for a brief period of time and provide scalability, rapid deployment, and testing new ideas in any market, with ever-evolving cutting-edge technologies, and the highest level of design and architectural aesthetics, giving us a glimpse of a future where hierarchies of industry have been disrupted by new technologies, ideas, and ways of life." In some ways, Giorgio Borruso was being challenged to create a pop-up shop for the Store of the Future. (See Figure CS23.2.)

Design Solution

In an all-white space with light-colored wood floors and giant windows that put almost all of the store on view from the street, Mr. Borruso adds, "The interior is comprised of various interactive elements that lend online and physical experiences. Shapeshifter is a kinetic wall that exhibits a new way of thinking about spatial boundaries, adaptable reactive merchandise displays, and personalized digital communication." This floor-to-ceiling pixel wall consists of 900 screens that act independently and can be used as merchandising shelves or hang rods. The different screens also respond to instructions from the ShopWithMe mobile app. A virtual reality dome is an in-the-round theatrical device that allows brands to extend the capabilities of their space into the digital realm. Mr. Borruso adds, "Advance fixtures like the ReacTable provide interactive product information by placing

FIGURE CS23.2 The interior—all white with light wood floors and many full-height windows—"is comprised of various interactive elements that blend the online and physical experiences" according to Giorgio Borruso. The ReacTable is an example of an advance fixture that provides interactive product information by placing merchandise along the display surface.

merchandise along the display surface, while telescopic fitting room enclosures blend ancient natural materials with the technological. Mirror displays and mirror-clad fitting room cabinets allow visitors to request and purchase products to try on in-store as well as browse online inventories for same day delivery. An express check out kiosk allows customers with the ShopWithMe app to swipe and pay on their way out."

And with the world ecology a vital element for the younger generation, Mr. Borruso reassures them with, "WithMe Mobile addresses sustainability by creating a completely reusable space which is highly customized via 'Change the file—not the fixtures.' Tenants bring their own databases, update graphics, and can rearrange fixtures and lighting in a matter of minutes." (See Figure CS23.3.)

Conclusion

This kinetic space has already housed objects from the scale of jewelry to motorcycles, and several WithMe Mobiles are currently traveling around the country playing host to various retail brands at prominent locations. Says Mr. Borruso, "They provide a durable framework for adaptable experimentation, which gives us an evolutionary model where key systems were strong enough to carry ambitious and continually evolving component directly to customers. Advanced mobile and tensile architectural systems blend the orthogonal and the fluid to permit construction and disassembly anywhere in the planet in a matter of days." (See Figure CS23.4.)

CREDITS: *Design: Giorgio Borruso, Marina Del Rey, California. Client: ShopWithMe, Las Vegas, Nevada, Jonathan Jenkins, Founder & CEO. Photography: © Fotoworks/Benny Chan.*

FIGURE CS23.3   The Shapeshifter is a striking example of what Mr. Borruso describes as a "kinetic wall that exhibits a new way of thinking about special boundaries, adaptable reactive merchandise displays and personalized digital communication." The pixel wall unit consists of 900 screens that act independently and can be used as merchandising shelves or hang-rods.

FIGURE CS23.4   "A virtual reality dome is an in-the-round theatrical device that allows brands to extend the capabilities of their space into the digital realm," Mr. Borruso says. Mirror-clad fitting room enclosures allow shoppers to request and purchase products to try on in store or browse online inventories. Customers with the ShopWithMe app can quickly swipe and pay for their purchases as they leave.

Visual Merchandise Planning: Trade Talk

adjacencies	fixture capacity	mock shop	scheduling
aesthetic sensibility	floor plan	placement	signage
capacity	installation	planogram	visual standards
categories	lighting	priority	wayfinding
cross-selling	merchandising	retail calendar	wings
directives	merchandising standards	return on investment	zones
fins	metrics	rollout	

Visual Merchandise Planning: A Recap

◆ A good display depends on planning, coordination, and cooperation.

◆ The display calendar is a well-thought-out time schedule that keeps displays and merchandise moving freely in and out of windows and on and off ledges.

◆ A change of windows can be set for every ten days to two weeks, but should never be longer than one month.

◆ The display schedule should be blocked out a year in advance.

◆ The visual merchandiser should plan advance preparation time for big promotional and sale events. These should be developed in cooperation with retailers and the promotion and advertising staffs for possible themes, slogans, concepts, and directions.

◆ The display person should order whatever props or backgrounds are necessary about three months before the display is scheduled. The display person will then schedule the parts of the display presentation to be done in the store's display studio.

◆ A week or two before the promotion day, the display person and buyer should check that the promotional merchandise is in or on its way and that everything is set to go.

◆ The display person should check the following for planning a new display installation: merchandise, mannequins, lights, props, fixtures, backgrounds, and signs.

◆ On the day of the installation, the final countdown should include checking the merchandise for loose buttons, uneven hems, and so forth and ensuring that the tool kit is fitted properly and completely, the lights are clean and working, and the floors and windows have been cleaned.

Questions for Review and Discussion

1. Why is it important for a visual merchandiser to have local, national, and international awareness?

2. How can cross-selling work to increase sales?

3. Why are product adjacencies important on the selling floor?

4. How far in advance should the display schedule be roughed out? What items should be included on the display calendar?

5. Create a yearlong display calendar for a small specialty store. Be sure to include all major sale events and seasonal merchandise deliveries.

6. Beginning three months before a promotional event and ending with the installation of a major display, outline the process the display person should follow.

7. In display planning, what questions should the visual merchandiser answer regarding the following items:
   a. Merchandise
   b. Floor plans
   c. Mannequins
   d. Lights
   e. Props, fixtures, and background
   f. Signs

Chapter Twenty-Four
Store Planning and Design

Primark Gran Via Madrid; Madrid, Spain. *Courtesy of Primark.*

**AFTER YOU HAVE READ THIS CHAPTER,
YOU WILL BE ABLE TO DISCUSS**

◆ the duties and areas of expertise essential to successful store planners

◆ the concept of engagement and placemaking

◆ the process of store rehabilitation

◆ scale, in relation to floor planning

◆ the basic architectural and store planning symbols used in floor plans

◆ the differences between an elevation and a floor plan

As retail continues to evolve so will the roles of visual merchandisers and **store planners**. Yesterday's store planner is today's "experience-maker." The store planner is more than a space planner, decorator, and divider of the selling floor space; he or she is responsible for understanding inventory, allocation, expense control, interactive technology, strategies to increase basket size, and consumer demographics, all while communicating the corporate identity and brand values. A store planner is also a lighting expert, a color connoisseur, and a visual merchandiser with knowledge of mannequins, fixtures, furniture, and forms and the know-how to sell the merchandise. He or she must also understand the psychology of consumer behavior and the concept of placemaking. Most of these individuals we now call store planners have a background in architecture or interior design, but more and more visual merchandisers are bringing their special talents into the store planning field, as the approach to store planning continues to evolve.

Today, shoppers want more than just to shop; they are on a never-ending journey for new experiences that excite the senses. What are these customers searching for? Only the store planner of the future truly knows. Store planners know that shoppers want entertainment, comfortable furnishings, charging stations, internet connections, social interaction, diverse cuisine, and immersive technology, and they enjoy experimenting with products. Retail nirvana includes coffee, cocktails, temporary exhibits or pop-up shops, and online offerings in a brick-and-mortar setting. Generation Y and Z want to learn more; they seek situations and environments that present new challenges, engagement, and education. The "take away" or product is not necessarily tangible for this generation; it is based more on feelings and an attitude. All of these concepts promote long-lasting memories that resonate with shoppers and reverberate on social media— but do they result in sales? Store management is beginning to understand that retail's "new encounter" ignites a relationship, one that can be shared with friends, family, or community—and no one can put a price tag or "knogo" on that! The new store environment is about placemaking. The term **placemaking** refers to the design of public spaces that bring people together. It applies to the development of retail spaces that reflect a sense of community, discovery, and the aspirations of today's consumer. (See Figure 24.1.)

FIGURE 24.1 Urban Outfitters' three-level lifestyle store in Herald Square offers millennial and Gen Z shoppers more than merchandise. The 56,000-square-foot store has a beauty salon offering everything from makeup and skincare to men's grooming products. The store hosts events, product launches, and partnerships with cool brands, and shoppers can order online and pick up merchandise in-store. The eatery serves up a healthy mix of options, and collaborations with top chefs have been publicized for the future. *Eugene Gologursky/Getty Images.*

FIGURE 24.2 PERCH Interactive unites physical products with digital content to engage shoppers and analyze their behavior. PERCH acts as a dynamic product spotlight, grabbing customers' attention with animation, sound, and rich media while educating and entertaining them with curated content. *Courtesy of PERCH Interactive.*

Digital integration is the heart of the store experience; store planners must be agile with their knowledge of how technology can articulate their vision. The retail landscape is now a play park, a museum, or an event; it is no longer a store. (See Figure 24.2.)

Functions of the Store Planner

The job of the store planner encompasses space planning and much more. Here are some of the current store design considerations:

- To design an efficient and attractive selling environment that provides a fulfilling customer experience, maximizes sales per square foot of selling space, and saves in labor and energy costs.
- To combine the selling space with the "back of house" service area, where stock is maintained and the non-selling activities of the store are carried on. Happy employees result in happier consumers. The space dedicated to employees should provide a fair amount of space to function.
- To set up traffic patterns that will promote customer movement from areas that get the greatest exposure (near entrances, elevators, and escalators) to remote corners and back areas, where the more expensive items are usually located. (See Figure 24.3.) Entrances give way to landing areas, or "thresholds," for consumers to pause before beginning their journey into the store. Pathways and signage should provide simple navigation. Grids and circular pathways allow the consumer to backtrack or locate departments with ease. Hot spots, outposts better known as "speed bumps," promote impulse buying, allow the consumer to pause and focus on feature merchandise.
- To promote and sell using appropriate strategies for the brand. For example, sensory techniques promote a stronger brand experience. Branding the environment with a scent gives the store an "attitude"—exotic, clean, or sexy. Socially connected displays promote "a buzz" and appeal to shoppers who are dedicated

FIGURE 24.3 The stairway is more than a link between two or more levels; it is an important part of the shopping experience. It becomes a stage for mannequins to appear in or near or part of an adventure with discoveries anticipated ahead. *Wormland, Berlin, Germany. Design by Blocher Blocher Partners, Stuttgart, Germany.*

to sharing their experiences with others. Kiosks and other interactive selling devices offer the consumers engagement. Invite consumers to "sit down and stay awhile," and relax with their devices. All of these increase time and "basket size" or sales. Temporary selling spaces enhance the store environment. Much like the trunk shows of the past, today's pop-up shop is a reason to revisit and re-engage. Promotions, socially conscious partnerships and events, designer collaborations, or introducing products sold exclusively online for a limited time are all ways to attract or bring the shopper back again and again.

- To stock and show. The store planner selects the selling vehicle or fixturing for the specific merchandise being offered. Fixturing signifies the style and character of the store environment; it is another opportunity to emphasize the brand. (Consider how reclaimed materials can make a statement about a particular brand.) Fixtures not only organize the merchandise; they make it "desirable." They are a stage for products, and display is the choreography.

● To enhance the store's image and, thereby, add stature to the merchandise being offered. The store planner is the "interior designer" for the store; by orchestrating all of the design elements and activities they create the store's impression for the consumer.

The store planner works closely with the store management, the merchants, and the buyers. Based on previous sales figures, or on projected sales figures, the store planner, together with the executives, will prepare a **block plan**. This is the first allocation of space on the ground plan and the designation of selling areas on that selling floor. This apportionment of space is based on the merchandising needs, proposed traffic patterns, proximity to related merchandise, and anticipated sales. By roughly blocking in the areas, management gets a visual picture of how much space is actually needed and how much is left for growth. The back of house areas (service elevators, storage, employees'

changing rooms, toilets, offices, and so on) and the social amenities (restrooms, vistas, galleries, restaurants, meeting or community rooms, and so on) are fitted into the remaining space. The floor plans are then redrawn, always in scale, with more and more details and specifications added on.

The final floor plan will have all the counters, cases, tables, and freestanding floor fixtures (round racks, quad racks, T-stands) drawn in place and will show the aisles, passageways, dressing rooms, exits and entrances, escalators, elevators, and more. Islands for display arrangements, platforms for mannequins, and T-walls to separate areas will be indicated. The store planner will locate the "impulse items" (merchandise purchased on impulse rather than by plan, such as cosmetics, candy, or inexpensive but faddish novelties) in the high-traffic areas, leaving the customer to find his or her way to the "demand merchandise" (the necessities: household goods, appliances, and so on).

The effective store planner directs the shopping action that starts right at the entrance. He or she plots the lighting, creates the changes in color and texture as the shopper moves from area to area, and is responsible for the raising or lowering of ceilings over aisles or boutiques. It is also his or her responsibility to place mirrors for reflection or

FIGURE 24.4   The designers at Checkland Kindleysides firm of London created a focal wall and area that is a showstopper. The blacked-out ceiling suddenly rises to new heights by the addition of a mirrored canopy that extends out over the space, making this area visible throughout the shop. Mannequins and merchandise presentations fill in the cubicles of the wall while other mannequins sit on the floor fixtures loaded with product in front. *New Look, United Kingdom.*

glitter, to suggest changes in flooring materials between aisles and shops, and to arrange for dividers, plants, and artwork. One of the duties of the store planner is to establish adjacencies or the order in which classifications are featured on the selling floor. Related merchandise is placed close together so, for example, shoes can be matched to a handbag, or skirts to sweaters.

Whether the store planner is designing a small specialty store or dividing up floors or areas in a large department store, the basic responsibilities, as enumerated above, are still the same. However, the small store presents particular challenges, as space is especially precious, and each cubic foot is expected to earn a certain number of dollars in gross sales. In the larger operations this is still a factor to consider, but sometimes the gracious sweep of a wide aisle or a vista is worth the expenditure of space in favor of store image and the ambiance that is achieved. (See Figures 24.4 and 24.5.)

desirable or, for the sake of a different look, more advantageous to start with an existing structure and restyle it to their own requirements. Many department and specialty stores discover that after some years their operations have become dated, and they no longer function as efficiently as they did five or more years earlier. Since shopping has become more about experiences, the challenge of offering new information and technology requires regular updating to remain current.

When an existing structure is modernized, redecorated, and rearranged, but not necessarily gutted and rebuilt, the store planner/architect is involved in rehabilitation, or "rehab." **Rehabilitation** is the remodeling, redecorating, and refixturing of an existing structure, often by the store planner. The "rehab" will still have the interest, the spirit, and the architectural details and flavor of what it once was, but it comes out fresh and ready to function for today's consumer experience.

Rehabilitations

Not all stores are built from the ground up, new and ready to accommodate the needs of a particular retail operation. Some merchants seem to find it more economical and

Floor Plans

Store planning begins with plans—sketches, drawings, bubble diagrams and block plans, and renderings. Bubble diagrams and block plans help the designer synthesize

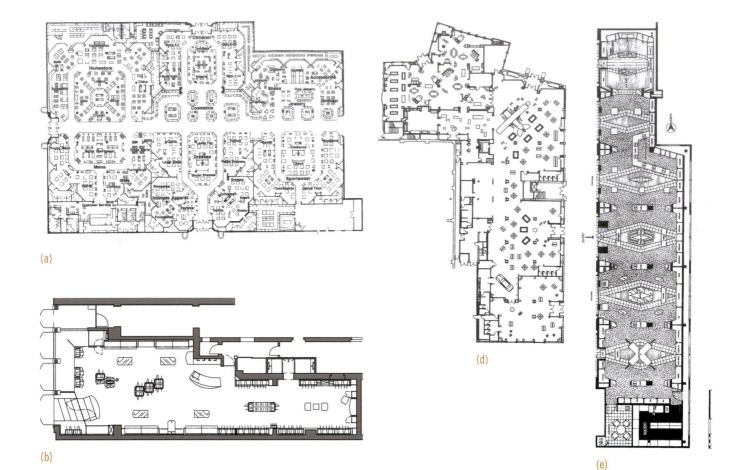

(a)

(b)

(d)

(e)

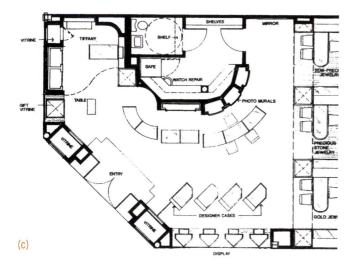

(c)

FIGURE 24.6 Some typical floor plans showing the layout of departments, fixtures, and the traffic patterns that direct shoppers through the spaces.
(a) Proffitt's, Johnson City, Tennessee. *Design: Schafter Associates.*
(b) Kluchen, Germany. *Design: Umdasch Store Fitters, Germany.*
(c) Yamron Jewelers. *Design: Brand + Allen Architects, Houston, Texas.*
(d) Eddie Bauer, Illinois. *Design: Mithun Partners, Seattle, Washington.*
(e) Duty-free/tax-paid store, Sea-Tac International Airport. *Design: Sunderland.*

the relationship between shops, departments, or fixtures; they are commonly used in all types of space planning as a method for experimentation. They consider all of the details, the special requirements, and the limitations. (See Figures 24.6a–e.)

Most of the challenges are usually solved before the start of construction or installation. The store planner must communicate with store management, consult with buyers and fashion coordinators, and get construction done through the carpenters and painters before ever stepping into the window or onto the ledge. It takes planning, plotting, and programming. It takes *preparation*.

Just as architects and engineers work with mechanical drawings to correct errors before they become full-grown and costly mistakes, the store planner should also work with scale drawings of the areas for which he or she is responsible. Visual merchandisers and store planners should not only know how to read and interpret a floor plan or building plan, but also be capable of drawing a plan—to scale—in one of the many CAD programs used by architects, engineers, and designers. Today, the store planner is often given a set of drawings for a new store, or a revamped department, or the designated space for a shop within a shop, and told to lay out the fixtures, counters, counter fixtures, furniture, and so forth to be used, or is asked to plan the aisles, the traffic flow, and the display areas to see what will and will not work in the allotted space. It is also possible, using these preliminary drawings, to estimate the amount of background or flooring material required and the sizes of the platforms or risers, the partitions, or dividers that will be used. The store planner can preplan the lighting requirements as well. He or she must render these ideas in scale, in a plan, and with an elevation and sometimes a perspective so that contractors or carpenters can finish the area.

CAD programs have proven remarkably helpful in this type of work because it is possible to "draw" the space and "move" fixtures, furniture, and other items around in the established parameters to get the desired traffic patterns and merchandise layouts. The designer can also create a "walk through" of the space to visualize the flow of movement within it. In some cases, a physical model of the space may be required. Although it is an ambitious undertaking, a model is made in proportion to the actual finished design. This is done to get a visual image of how things will look, how things will fit, and how they will work.

Let us, first, be sure we understand what a **floor plan** is. It is a flat representation of only two measurements—the length and width (or depth) of an area or object, as seen from overhead. It is as though one were viewing the area from far up in the air, and all that could be seen is a graphic representation of height, with everything flattened out.

By using a scaled floor plan, it is possible for the store planner to experiment with platforms, fixtures, display cases, and so forth, of assorted sizes and shapes, without ever actually having to lift or push them.

DESIGNING IN SCALE

When we speak of scale, we are referring to the relative proportion of one object to another. When we say something is "overscaled," we mean it is too big, too overwhelming, too dominant, in relation to the objects around it. *Relation* is the key word here. **Scale**, in mechanical drawing, or in the preparation of floor plans or models, is the proportion that is used by the designer or draftsperson to designate the future actual size.

For example, let's imagine an architect is going to build on a 100-foot by 300-foot space. Rendering in scale allows the designer to work with a large space in an organized method in CAD. He or she begins by selecting a scale to work in—a proportion—and the designer works on the assumption that each foot of actual space will be represented on the drawing by ⅛ inch or ¼ inch, for example. The contractor or engineer looks at the corner of the designer's finished drawing—in a box usually found on the lower right side of the drawing—to find the proportion or scale used in the drawing. Thus, at a scale of ⅛ inch = 1 foot, the plan drawing of a space measuring 100 feet by 300 feet will be drawn at 12½ by 37½ inches.

Reading a Floor Plan

Figure 24.7 is a composite of a store floor plan, and it gives us the opportunity to point out some of the usual as well as more unusual **architectural symbols** and markings found in floor plans.

BASIC ARCHITECTURAL SYMBOLS

A. A heavy, solid fine line (or two lines that are not filled in—see AA) indicates a structural, exterior wall. It is a part of the basic construction of the building. (This can also be a common wall that is shared with an adjacent building.)

B. A solid line, thinner than A (sometimes two lines that are not filled in but that are closer together than A) indicates a floor-to-ceiling interior wall, partition, or solid divider. The

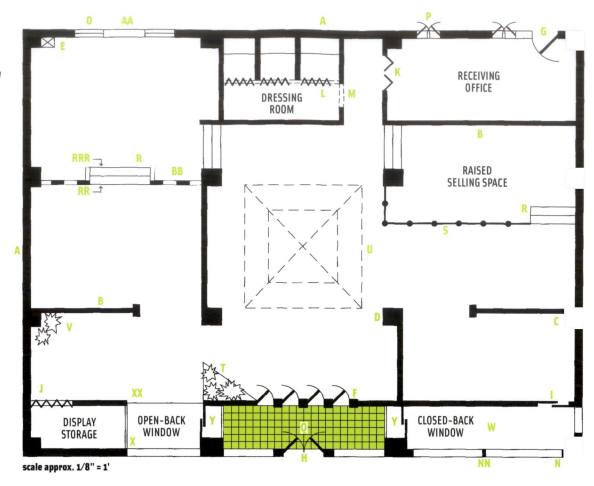

FIGURE 24.7 A composite floor plan of a small retail operation. *Illustration by Ron Carboni.*

scale approx. 1/8" = 1'

wall or partition may or may not be structural, but usually the columns or piers on the floor plan (see C) will indicate where the weight-bearing, structure-bearing elements can be found. This thin line indicates a division, or separation, between departments or areas as well as where the on-the-floor selling operations end and the behind-the-scenes activities begin. In this way, it is possible to recognize how much space has been devoted to fixturing and on-the-floor stock, compared with the area reserved for backup stock, dressing and fitting rooms, receiving, packing, offices, and so forth.

When the partition or wall does not go up to the ceiling, it is represented by narrow lines, partially filled in (BB). This is sometimes called a **partial, or dwarf, wall**.

C. A heavy, solid (or shaded) rectangle extending out from either the thin or heavy solid line indicates a pier, a **beam**, or a **buttress**—reinforcing elements used to add strength to the wall's construction or to help support the weight of the

floors above. When the rectangle is attached to an internal or external wall, but is not shaded or filled in, it can represent a vertical conduit or duct for water pipes, electric or gas lines, and so on. This is part of the building's functioning structure and cannot be removed or disregarded by the draftsperson laying out a store or a department.

D. A solid rectangle, out in the middle of the floor, usually in a set grid pattern with other such rectangles, represents a **column**. (A column stands free, out in the open and unattached, whereas a pier is actually a thickening or an extension out from a constructed wall.) In many cases, interior walls will be constructed to tie in with the independent columns and thus make them appear as piers. A supporting I beam will appear on the floor plan looking like a capital letter I.

E. A rectangle with an X through it will usually indicate an unusable area that is part of or essential to the construction or maintenance of the building. It is unusable floor space for the purpose of the draftsperson. It is a situation similar to the vertical conduits mentioned previously (see C).

F. A thickening at the end of a wall indicates a doorjamb or a molding, or a frame around a window. In either case, the thickening will be to either side of a break in a wall, thus indicating some sort of opening.

G. A thin line plus an arc indicates a traditional door. The line represents the door in plain view; it is hinged to one side or the other of the doorjamb or frame. The arc shows the direction and extent of the door swing. This is important to the space planner because it will limit what can be or should be placed on the wall onto which the door will swing back. Traditional doors will vary from 24 inches to 27 inches for closets and toilets, and from 30 to 36 inches for main entrances.

H. A double door—two doors that swing open, one to each side—is indicated by a double arc representing two swings. If it is a foyer or vestibule, and there are a series of doors—and they all open into the store—all the doors will be hinged, usually swinging in the same direction.

I. For a sliding door, because one panel slides behind the other, there are two lines shown, one for each panel. There is no loss of wall space with this type of door. It is usually used to cover closets or storage space.

J. An accordion fold door—a corrugated vinyl or slatted wood screen that folds back over and over again on itself and often does not extend out beyond the door frame—is represented by an inverted V. The same symbol could represent a movable, folding wall or partition between areas.

K. A pair of folding doors, hinged to fold back on themselves, is represented in the same way as an accordion door. These can be solid panels or louvered doors; they may be used as a single pair or two pairs to the single opening. Each pair folds back to the side of the door frame to which it is hinged. Because they fold back on themselves, they take up less back wall space than a traditional door.

L. A curtain closing over a doorway, such as might be used in a dressing room area, is represented by a double dotted line that indicates a hang-rod; a snaking line is the curtain. (At this point, it should be mentioned that a broken

or dotted line usually indicates something that is above ground or floor level, i.e., does not rest directly on the floor but is still an integral part of the floor plan.)

M. An archway or wall opening that has no door or any other covering or closing device is represented by a broken line. It could also be a pass-through from one area into another, similar to a pass-through between most kitchens and dining rooms. The broken line indicates that there is some wall space above the opening and below the ceiling. If sliding panels or a corrugated screen were installed inside the wall opening, it would be indicated on the floor plan, as in I and J. (As previously mentioned in F, the thickening at the end of a wall could indicate a window frame as well as a doorjamb. It is much more likely that windows will appear in perimeter or outside walls rather than in internal walls or partitions.)

N. A plate glass window, similar to a picture window or a display window that cannot be opened, is represented by two fine lines that abut and fit inside the heavy line representing the exterior wall. Sometimes, three fine lines, close together, will represent the glazed unit inside the thickness of the wall. In architectural drawings in which the wall is not shaded in, the non-opening windows (N) are represented by three lines within the two lines indicating the exterior wall. (See AA.)

NN. A **mullion**, a metal divider between a run of several plate glass windows that facilitates the replacement of glass when necessary, is represented in the floor plan by a solid area between the two fine lines of the plate glass window.

O. Windows that can be opened usually are represented by three fine lines set inside the wall construction. The three lines actually make up the two window frames that can be raised or lowered. (In a casement window it takes an upper and a lower frame to cover the window area.) The framed windows are usually 30 to 36 inches wide.

P. A casement window with two vertical frames hinged onto the window frame, with windows that swing in and out rather than ride up and down, has a symbol that is similar to the one for swinging doors (H), as the action is basically the same.

Q. A tiled floor that could represent vinyl, asphalt, ceramic, or even marble squares set in a geometric pattern is indicated by drawing a similar pattern.

R. In this plan, steps with only two treads (RR) are indicated by three fine lines. Because a riser is usually 8 inches high, the three risers (RRR), the elevated area or platform, are 24 inches high.

S. A balustrade or railing with stanchions or uprights set 3 feet apart is represented by a solid line broken at regular intervals with a dot.

T. A planter containing plants is indicated with a fine line.

U. A skylight or glazed ceiling is represented by the dotted (or broken) line, which indicates something above ground level.

V. Plants are drawn as a circle of jagged lines.

W. A closed-back display window area with a full wall is indicated as a solid line and a sliding door (I) with two lines, one for each panel.

X. An open-back window with a full view of the store beyond is represented by two fine lines. The thin line in the back (XX) indicates the end of the raised platform. If there were no line, it would mean that the display window was at ground level, not elevated at all.

Y. A shadow-box display case with a glass front (solid fine line) and sliding panels in back (two lines, one for each panel).

STORE PLANNING SYMBOLS

Figure 24.8 is part of an actual fixturing floor plan of a department in a large retail store. It is drawn and reproduced to a scale of ⅛ inch = 1 foot. The architectural symbols are the same as those used in any architectural floor plan. As discussed and illustrated in the previous section, the following are the basic construction elements:

A. The heavy line represents a constructed wall that serves as the perimeter, or enclosing, wall of a particular area or department.

FIGURE 24.8 A section of an actual department store floor plan with the floor and wall fixtures. *Illustration by Ron Carboni.*

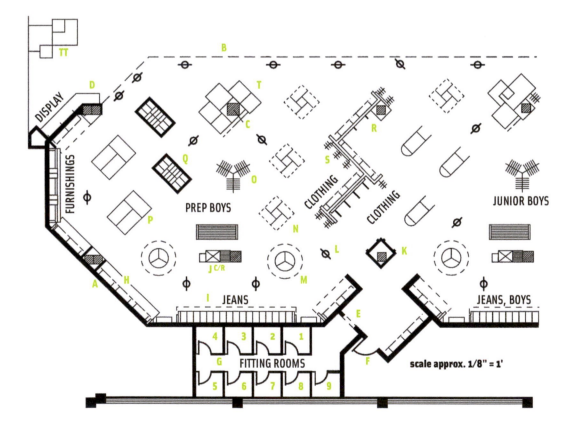

B. The thin, straight, broken line is the boundary of the department and the delineation between the selling area and the walkway or aisle. In the store layout, that line could also indicate a change in flooring materials: hard floors (wood, ceramic, asphalt, or vinyl tiles) for the aisle and soft floors (carpeting) in the department.

C. The shaded-in rectangles represent the columns necessary to the building's construction. As one looks at this plan, it is easy to see the pattern and spacing of the columns.

D. A platform, facing the aisle, designed to hold a display setup is represented by fine lines drawn in the shape of the setup. Directly behind are two columns enclosed within a semi-triangular partition.

E. The two dotted lines indicate an archway or opening in an otherwise straight wall. This is the entrance into the fitting room area.

F. The traditional symbol for a door is a thin line plus an arc.

G. The individual fitting rooms are drawn with solid lines for the walls and a thin line plus arcs for the doors. The arc shows the direction and extent of the door swing.

The fixtures on the floor plan are represented as follows:

H. Wall-hung merchandise: The two thin lines, perpendicular to the constructed wall, are brackets that are connected into a slotted system set in or on that wall. Many perimeter walls have slotted uprights. The broken line between the two brackets indicates the hang-rod. It is depicted by a broken or dotted line because it is above the floor level. The dotted line that is spaced about 1 foot out from the hang-rail is an overhang or valance extending out from the wall. It covers the hang-rods and is probably equipped with secondary lighting for merchandise and the back wall.

I. Binning on the perimeter wall: The dotted line in front of it is an overhead fascia or canopy with lighting.

J. A cash register and wrapping station, known as C/r, or cash/wrap desk: It is often combined with a column, as shown here represented by a shaded rectangle. The column provides an electrical outlet, necessary for most new registers, as well as visibility. A shopper can see a column from across the floor, and thus more easily find the cash/wrap station. The register and wrapping station are represented by fine lines. "X" marks the space for the register. A large shaded-in rectangle is immediately behind the cash register and wrapping station configuration.

K. A column enclosure: It is a shield or mask built around an actual column and used either decoratively or functionally. It is represented by a shaded-in rectangle for the column and fine lines in the shape of the enclosure. Other times, the sides are mirrored to provide ambiance as well as to enable shoppers to examine the merchandise. Sometimes, they are used as a backup for a mannequin platform (see N) or to hold merchandise from attached hang-rails or waterfalls.

L. A T-stand: The small, special item or featured attraction displayer often used to line the aisle as a "come-on" is indicated by a small circle, with an angled fine line drawn through it. They are also used throughout the department as "reminders."

M. A round rack, in this instance, on a Y frame: Depicted here is a standard unit, 3 feet in diameter. The broken circle that extends out another foot from the inner ring indicates how the outer edges of the hanging garments will fall beyond the fixture itself. Thus, a 3-foot round rack will actually take up a space on the selling floor measuring 5 feet in diameter.

N. A quad rack, or four-armed fixture that shows four face-out groups of merchandise: Again, the broken square encompassing this fixture indicates the outer edges of the hanging garments extending beyond the floor unit itself.

O. A Y rack: It takes up a large area on the floor and does not hold nearly as much merchandise as might be fitted into that same space on a different fixture. It does, however, present a different look, a different directional setup in merchandise presentation. The short bars extending from the three major arms of the unit are the hangers, and again suggest the amount of space they will require.

P. A group of three tables in a cluster: Sometimes, these tables will have drawers or cabinet space below the tabletop for extra stock.

Q. A multiple binning raised up on a base or a table: This is indicated by a rectangle. Fine lines are drawn within the rectangle in the configuration of the bins.

R. A low partition, not a floor-to-ceiling, constructed wall: The short lines that are perpendicular to the "wall" suggest that they are brackets that fit into slotted uprights.

S. Waterfalls or a face-out arrangement for merchandise: The three arms that extend out are crossed with "hangers" to show that the merchandise will face forward.

T. An arrangement around a column of platforms, pedestals, or cubes for a mannequin presentation: This is represented by a pattern of squares surrounding a column.

TT. Another cube, or pedestal buildup: This buildup is shown as large and small squares in the shape of the buildup.

OTHER TYPES OF DIMENSIONAL DRAWINGS

It is also recommended that the store planner make an elevation of an object or area. Whereas the plan view gives the length and width (or depth) of an area, the elevation, or flat, front-on view, is another two-dimensional view that shows the width and the height. The elevation is used in conjunction with the plan. It supplies the missing measurements and answers questions like these: Does the table have drawers or cabinets below? Does the unit have legs, or does it sit directly on the floor? How many bins or shelves will fit on the wall?

The store planner can also make a simple **isometric perspective**, or projection, which is a type of scale drawing that gives all the measurements (height, width, and depth), thereby providing a more natural, three-dimensional representation of an object or area. It is actually a form of shop drawing, and a carpenter or builder could take the measurements directly from the drawing and see what the unit will look like. This type of dimensional representation starts with a correct and well-drawn floor plan.

Store Planning as a Career

Store planning is a growing field that visual merchandisers can enter. There is no way that one chapter or even an entire book will create a store planner, but many of the techniques that store planners use have been discussed in this text.

A knowledge of CAD drawing and drafting is essential. The store planner must be able to communicate in the language of plans and elevations—and all in scale. An awareness of the importance of color and texture (see Chapter 2) and the impact of light and lighting (see Chapter 4) on color and on the merchandise is essential to the store planner. He or she must understand also how color, light, and texture will suggest certain clichés of ambiance (see Chapter 2). A strong knowledge of materials and the manufacturing processes is vital; a good designer needs to know how to design it, spec the materials, and understand the production and building as well. (See Chapters 18 and 21.)

Fixtures are the "furniture" of the store (see Chapters 14 and 17), and the store planner must know the various types that are available and what they will do for the merchandise and the store's image. It is a function of the store planner to use the floor space (and the air space) to its fullest. He or she must devise economical and creative methods for housing stock and highlighting displays. Sometimes the store planner will use real furniture and antiques (see Chapter 17) as fixtures or props in order to get a desired effect for a unique shop or department.

Mannequins and forms (see Chapter 12) are the "silent salespeople" of display, and they serve the store planner well. They can be used instead of signs to designate what is being sold in an area or to add a high point in an otherwise flat merchandise presentation. Mannequins add drama as aisle liners or as centers of interest in island presentation; they are invaluable to the store planner, especially when a store has no display windows.

Any visual merchandiser who wishes to become a store planner should consider studying, in depth, interior design, materials and methods of construction, perspective rendering, the history of furniture and decoration, furniture construction, and lighting techniques. There are some schools that do grant degrees in store planning. This is a relatively established field and one that has much to offer the visual merchandiser who wants to advance in retailing. Individuals interested in store planning might contact the local chapter of the Retail Design Institute (RDI) or the American Society of Interior Designers (ASID) for more information on schools with store planning curricula.

Go Green Box 24.1: Green Design Techniques

Almost daily there are announcements, brochures, and public relations material about new products and techniques that are "green" and that will make going green not only simple for the designer but energy and money saving for the retailer as well. Lighting companies are coming up with new, longer-lasting, energy-efficient and color-effective lamps, dimmers, and sensors that are readily adaptable to new retail designs or rehabbed ones. There are firms producing unique finishes of plastic resins and decorative panels that are mainly composed of recycled materials, are biodegradable, and that add to the look of a space while being kind to the planet. In the United States and in other countries there are organizations, like the Forest Stewardship Council (FSC), that certify which woods can be used because they are readily regrown and replenishable—such as bamboo and aspen. In addition, designers have available to them numerous boards made from recycled wood scraps and materials that would otherwise have to be discarded. Wood and timber that once was used for flooring, beams, and siding of demolished buildings are reclaimed and now available to add interesting textures to environments. Paints, adhesives, and finishes that are low VOC and that do not emit noxious fumes or odors are available in a multitude of colors and finishes. So, going green is becoming more feasible, economically and otherwise, for designers and their clients. (See Figures 24.9 and 24.10.)

Readers may want to peruse Martin M. Pegler's *Green Retail Design*, published by ST Media Group, for numerous examples of green designed retail spaces from around the world.

FIGURE 24.9   Recycled lumber and reused timber find new expressions and uses in this store interior. From flooring, to wall covering, to hanging beams for holding the lighting equipment, to stacks of planks turned into mid-floor elevations—the use of the used is all part of the company's commitment to sustainability and world ecology. *Timberland, Westlake S/C, London, United Kingdom.*

FIGURE 24.10   Discarded movie house seats and wooden shoe forms are useful again. The chairs not only add a touch of nostalgia but also serve as try-on seating for the store's young-at-heart shoppers. The shoe forms—overhead—become a decorative "sign," indicating where the shoes can be found in the store. Note the clever use of the wood hand forms as scarf displayers. *Timberland, Westlake S/C, London, United Kingdom.*

Case Study 24.1: Carlo Pazolini, Brompton Road, London, United Kingdom

Design Objective

Along with the recent Carlo Pazolini shops in Venice and the New York City flagship store in Soho, Giorgio Borruso designed this store on Brompton Road in London. No two Carlo Pazolini shops are ever the same; there is no cookie-cutter scheme involved, though there are many similarities. In each store's design, Giorgio Borruso is aware of and sensitive to the existing architectural shell within which he will create the new environment using the signature forms and lines and adapting the same color palette as he has used in previous Pazolini stores.

Design Solution

Designer Giorgio Borruso shares, "Carlo Pazolini, Brompton Road is a 120-square-mile space in Knightsbridge housing men's and women's shoes and accessories. The design marks an evolution of the Carlo Pazolini worldwide store concept integrating specificities of site. While investigating the history of the area and the building (from the early 1900s), it was discovered in planning archives that the neighboring historical Brompton Arcade was converted into a retail space in the last decade, installing a new roof structure and remodeled mezzanine. Our design sought to recognize the memory of this arcade by re-creating a contemporary barrel (or tunnel) vault ceiling as well as the illusion via a mirror wall that the space opens to the exterior at the back. An historical detail in the facade was used (in conjunction with the seating and wall shelving) as a generative 'seed' for the interior geometric language and led us to a pointed rather than semicircular barrel vault design. The memorialization of this neighboring arcade space led to a tunnel-like twisting of the interior in such a way that the floor, walls, and ceiling become wrapped into one another, creating a vortex of movement from front to back in which design elements flock like schools of fish moving through a turbulent fluid environment."

FIGURE CS24.1   The designer/architect, Giorgio Borruso, used this store to further "the evolution of the Carlo Pazolini worldwide store concept that integrates specificities of site." He created this very contemporary shop next to the historic Brompton Arcade in London, United Kingdom.

FIGURE CS24.2   By installing a new ceiling, the designer recreated a modern version of the barrel-vaulted or tunnel ceiling of the original neighboring arcade. The addition of the mirrored wall adds to that illusion as it opens to the exterior at the back.

FIGURE CS24.3 The memory of the original arcade "led to a tunnel-like twisting of the interior, creating a vortex of movement from front to back." The floor, walls, and ceiling come together and become wrapped into one another.

FIGURE CS24.4 The shelving and seats were formed by a molding process with bonded natural wool and resin to create a new structural composite that combines "old and new, natural and technological."

"The design of the interior programmatic elements for this shoe store (seating, display, storage, and point of sale) recognize that there is an ambiguous distinction between our bodies and the things we wear. Like the buildings we inhabit, we shape our clothing and it shapes us. Attempts at accurately sculpting the shape of the human foot in Egyptian, Classical, and contemporary art imply that footwear literally shapes our feet over time. As newborns, our toes quickly take on the shape of the shoes we wear, but for a brief time are remarkably dexterous, like plaster ready to be cast by muscle memory. This is the nature of the space we sought to create, and with that in mind, used the shape of an infant's foot as a Platonic or iconic 'cell' in an emergent network of display shelving and seating."

"To further refine this concept, we looked to the principle of Swarm Intelligence, which digitally abstracts phenomena in the natural world like insect swarms, schools of fish, flocks of birds, etc. These natural examples of swarm intelligence form loose cellular networks that negotiate an ephemeral distinction between object and space."

Conclusion

"The synthesis of old and new, of the biological with culture and technology, was reinforced by material innovations that brought together new structural resins with one of the most ancient materials: natural wool felt. The shelving and seating cells in this project used an innovative molding process which without glue bonded the natural wool and the resin at a molecular level and formed a new structural composite that synthesized old and new, natural, and technological."

CREDITS: Design: Giorgio Borruso Design, Marina Del Rey, California.

Store Planning and Design: Trade Talk

architectural symbols	column	partial, or dwarf, wall	scale
beam	floor plan	placemaking	store planners
block plan	isometric perspective	rehabilitation	
buttress	mullion		

Store Planning and Design: A Recap

- ✦ Duties of a store planner include the following:
  - To design an efficient and attractive selling environment that will promote maximum sales and savings in labor and energy.
  - To combine the selling space with the behind-the-scenes service area, where stock is maintained and the non-selling activities of the store are carried on.
  - To set up traffic patterns that will promote customer movement from areas that get the greatest exposure to remote corners and back areas.
  - To promote and sell, stock and show. The store planner selects the selling vehicle for the specific merchandise being offered.
  - To enhance the store's image and, thereby, add stature to the merchandise being offered.

- ✦ Rehabilitation is the remodeling, redecorating, and refixturing of an existing structure but does not necessarily involve gutting or rebuilding.

- ✦ Scale is the relative proportion of one object to another.

- ✦ A floor plan is a flat representation that gives the length and width (or depth) of an area, as seen from overhead, whereas an elevation is a flat, front-on view that shows the width and height.

- ✦ A knowledge of CAD is essential to a store planner. He or she must also be aware of color and texture; the impact of light and lighting on merchandise; and the types and availability of fixtures, mannequins, and forms.

- ✦ A prospective store planner should study, in depth, interior design, materials and methods of construction, rendering, the history of furniture and decoration, furniture construction, and lighting techniques.

Questions for Review and Discussion

1. What are the main roles and responsibilities of a store planner?

2. How has placemaking influenced the store designer's approach?

3. With which individuals will a store planner need to work closely to achieve the best possible results in store design and layout?

4. List the "back of house" areas and social amenities that must be included in the floor plan.

5. Describe the preparation and communication that must take place before drawing the floor plan for a store.

6. If a store planner is going to design a plan for a 100-foot by 200-foot specialty store, how large will the plan be using ¼-inch scale?

7. What is a scaled floor plan and what are the benefits of its use?

8. How does scale work?

9. What is a template and how is it used in floor planning?

10. Describe the symbols used to illustrate the following features:
    a. steps
    b. a mullion
    c. a column
    d. a sliding curtain
    e. a door
    f. a cash/wrap station
    g. a round rack
    h. a quad rack

11. Explain the differences between a floor plan, an elevation, and an isometric perspective. What is the purpose of each?

12. In what areas must a visual merchandiser be knowledgeable to be a successful store planner?

Chapter Twenty-Five
Community and Experiential Stores

Shinola Pet Accessories Launch, New York City.
Theo Wargo/Getty Images for Vanity Fair.

**AFTER YOU HAVE READ THIS CHAPTER,
YOU WILL BE ABLE TO DISCUSS**

- ✦ spaces that promote a sense of community
- ✦ the concept of placemaking or multi-use spaces
- ✦ how food and other activities can enhance retail experiences
- ✦ stores as educational experiences
- ✦ key strategies for attracting consumers

As discussed in Chapter 24, the rules and formulas for store planning are changing. Consumers no longer need to go to a physical store to buy products, and as a result, the strategies for designing stores are no longer the same. Today's retail strategies revolve around **consumer engagement**, **experiences**, and **placemaking**. It is clear that yesterday's retail hallmarks of "comfort and convenience" are easily found by shopping online, so store designers have added emphasis on establishing new connections that appeal to the senses of today's shopper. Don't underestimate how the online shopping phenomena quickly changed consumer perceptions about shopping the physical store; the mix-up or variety of categories offered online erased many shopping barriers of the past. In some ways it caused shoppers' expectations to change faster than retailers could respond, generating uneasiness by retailers about "what's next."

Community, **conservation**, and **experiential retailing** are just a few of the current trends rising on the retail horizon. We see fashion, furniture, music, art, and books alongside food, friends, and digital media. A recent *New York Times* article written by Steven Kurutz titled "Shopping That Is About More Than Sales" referred to a retail operation that opened in the Venice area of Los Angeles. It was opened by Blake Mycoskie, the founder of TOMS shoes, who thought that the term "store" did not fit his brand or the products he was offering. He wanted a name for his retail areas that created "a lifestyle for the brand." The term he selected was "community outposts." In the article he was quoted as saying, "An outpost seems like more of a meeting center—an area for information—almost a political rallying point. This is a place where things are happening." He opened his first over three years ago and now has seven—with more on the way.

Instead of space filled with racks and shelves that are loaded down with products, or the hushed atmosphere of a lush designer's boutique that seems to turn off affluent young shoppers these days, these outposts are community centers. They are places where one can relax in a Wi-Fi-enriched environment on comfortable couches—maybe with a cup of freshly brewed coffee or a light repast of organic fare—with casually arranged clusters of merchandise artfully arranged for the visitor's perusal. There may

be a lecture or musical recital going on somewhere in the space, or a yoga class in session. Walls may be enhanced with changing exhibits of artwork produced by young, local talent interspersed with areas of hung garments. The focus for the visual merchandiser is still primarily to show and sell product, but the presentation techniques are more subtle and challenging. Here the product presentation has to be more organic and original. It has to blend in yet stand out; it has to grow within the space and yet not overwhelm it. It appears that today it is no longer enough just to be involved with local students or schools, support community charities and events, or serve as a space for neighborhood activities; creating an experience—an emotional one—is now a necessary part of doing business in the community and an essential part of the retailer's brand identity.

As Alex Eagle, the creative director of "The Store," a multifaceted, multipurpose retail space in Berlin, was quoted as saying, "With everything being so easily available a click away online, you have to offer an experience. People want something for their time."

Going along with the feeling of community, and offering comfort and convenience as well, is the blending of food service and shopping experiences. For some time now shoppers in upscale stores or boutiques were accustomed to being pampered with offers of coffee, tea, or maybe wine. Soon department stores found that light food service was a fine way to keep shoppers in the store for a longer period and thus spend more time shopping. Retailers are now finding that taking space way from product display may be more profitable if that space is used for food and beverage service. Additionally, store owners are recognizing that the opening and store closing times have to be changed to accommodate the shoppers and their schedules—late night and early morning hours fit the diverse lifestyle of today's consumers.

One emerging concept attracting a steady flow of visitors is the shopping environment that simulates an art gallery or museum by hosting a temporary show. The Dover Street Market Store model crafted by Rei Kawakubo of the Japanese fashion label Comme des Garçons is a multi-brand retail experience that features a new selection of designers each season. Each designer creates a unique art installation to accommodate his or her collection alongside Comme des Garçons' menswear lines. Other well-known designer collections populate the space too. The store environment has been described as "chaotic beauty"—an immersive environment resembling an art installation, coupled with the most innovative brands of merchandise in the world. The visual merchandising is a daring mix, extremely avant-garde, inspiring the visitor to return regularly for the next installation much like a museum or art gallery. The ground-floor Rose Bakery café is homey and healthy with community-style seating. Dover Street Market is a retail institution that captures the treasure hunting spirit of today's fleeting customer. (See Figures 25.1 and 25.2.)

Sustainability and conservation is another focus of many millennials, as well as older shoppers who are concerned about the environment. They are more interested in where a product was made, who made it, how it was made, what it is made of and how much energy was used in getting it from where it was produced to the shop than they are the cost. When they make a purchase they want it to mean something—make a difference—maybe affect the life of a worker somewhere in the world or save a tree in a rainforest in the jungle. These social-minded consumers have many questions that must be answered by the visual merchandisers in their means of product presentation.

Shinola is another great example of a brand with a sense of community. Shinola is more than a brand; it has positioned itself as a beacon of hope for the American economy or the return of the American dream. It started as a small accessory and watch business bent on reviving the future of the city of Detroit, Michigan, and has grown to 20-plus brick-and-mortar stores employing over 600 workers. Shinola has created a heritage brand in the era of disposability, gaining customer loyalty through its beliefs and practices. It has expanded its line of goods to include handmade leather goods, bicycles, apparel, and gadgets for the home and even

FIGURE 25.2 The repurposed wooden boxes encircle the shopping environment at Dover Street Market, creating a maze-like experience for the consumer. Each nook frames and features a single piece of merchandise, and the element of surprise keeps the eyes in motion. *Dover Street Market, London, United Kingdom. Ed Reeve/Getty Images.*

FIGURE 25.1 A giant mirror carefully angled on the wall reflects a surreal display at Dover Street Market in London. The illusion features a mannequin dramatically sprawled out on a classic loveseat surrounded by accessory merchandise. The theatrical nature of the display mimics an art installation. *Dover Street Market, London, United Kingdom. Ed Reeve/Getty Images.*

its own bottled cola; its retro style resounds with the millennial and Gen Y shoppers. Stores locations aimed to revitalize the community are off the beaten path, encouraging the design for each store to take inspiration directly from the building it is housed in. The result is a store that beautifies the neighborhood while remaining a part of it. All of the stores exude a relaxed "cool factor," unpretentious and appealing to those who appreciate a utilitarian style with a taste for fewer but higher quality items in their lifestyles. Shinola connects with the local community on a personal level by recognizing the area history where it builds it stores and the people who live there. It sponsors regular events that recognize local "makers" and workers in the community and seeks ways to find a working relationship.

Shinola's branding evokes true American spirit and innovation. Its tag lines "Where American is made" and "Built in Detroit" are not only heart-warming, but have stimulated the company's brick-and-mortar sales. The sales force is trained to make the consumer feel right at home without the pressure of making a sale, recognizing that the stores are a showplace for the company's goods. The brand is comfortable with the idea of the consumer leaving empty handed and ordering later online. "Let's Roll Up Our Sleeves" is a newer campaign featuring a series of ads with inspiring messages. It rallies people from across the land to unite and work together for the greater good of our country. In a keynote presentation at Globalshop, President and Founder Jacques Panis discussed the five senses of the guest experience and what it means for the Shinola retail space. "The narrative is vital in telling the brand story in-store and connecting with the consumer," he said. Sight, sound, touch, and taste are essential elements of the guest experience, in addition to smell, which is the most important since it is the only sense directly connected to the brain. (See Figure 25.3.)

FIGURE 25.3   Shinola hosts regular neighborhood gatherings to promote new products and connect with community. To celebrate the grand opening of the Brooklyn flagship, the brand released a limited-edition Jackie Robinson watch and hosted a block party that was DJ-ed by The Roots' Questlove, among others. *Cindy Ord/Getty Images for Shinola.*

Stores can foster the idea of community through education. For example, a Texas wine discounter offered his customers early-evening classes on how to purchase wine, the wine making process, and varieties of grapes and flavors. He empowered his customers with more information than they could find on the signage or wine bottle label. The ROI was extremely profitable. Customers got excited about putting the new information to use by purchasing more wines to taste and test. The classes sparked a new generation of "regulars" on their way coming home from work.

K'OOK! is a flourishing retailer with a freestanding kitchen, a large collection of cookbooks, a coffee bar, and plenty of space for everything to do with cooking, kitchen products, and fine dining. Positioned as "people-centered," K'OOK sells much more than kitchen products—it sells the cooking experience. (See Figures 25.4–25.7.)

Today's visual merchandisers have to educate while showing and entertaining. They not only have to create spectacular displays for the merchandise but also understand how to present food that excites the eye and stimulates the appetite. Display designers have always been "quick-change artists"—being able to switch from promotion to promotion—from holiday to holiday, from season to season. Now they must also be able to turn

FIGURE 25.5 The "heart" of the shop is the fully equipped kitchen where myriad activities are planned. Workshops on cooking and baking are limited to ten, and on Saturdays "there are product demonstrations and tastings so the store becomes a place for people to gather socially." *Courtesy of K'OOK!*

FIGURE 25.6 The annual Italian Food Weekend—which lasts for four days—is done in conjunction with the Pasta al Pesto Cooking Studio of Italy and a wine tasting. It is combined with a pop-up restaurant with room for even more people to enjoy the Italian cuisine. *Courtesy of K'OOK!*

FIGURE 25.4 The owners of K'OOK!, Anne van der Spoel and Karen Schoen, agree that the store's main focus is "on making our customers happy." "Happiness" can be enjoying a cup of freshly brewed coffee at the coffee bar at the end of the cash/wrap counter and easily seen from outside, or enjoying any of the many other things on offer at this housewares/homewares shop in The Netherlands. *Courtesy of K'OOK!*

FIGURE 25.7   The Food Festival, held in July, brings hordes of avid foodies to this little town. In its third year it attracted over 12,000 visitors and more than sixty food trucks offering a great variety of foods. This endeavor encompasses many other shopkeepers and the community as a whole. *Courtesy of K'OOK!*

the shops around for exhibits, social gatherings, evening events, and a mixed collection of products.

Placemaking is a **people-centered** approach to the planning and design of spaces. Comfortable, accessible environments that promote social interaction and allow for a variety of activities to take place are the key characteristics of placemaking. Placemaking is the buzz for younger generations. It spawned through local events like flea markets, festivals, community events, and trend of going "local." The idea can develop through an organization such as a BID or a design firm making its stake, or be facilitated by the community members themselves. A Business Improvement District (BID) is a public or private partnership in which property and business owners elect to make a collective contribution to the maintenance, development, and promotion of their commercial district. Many young aspiring designers concerned about underutilized "dead" space are advocating for more spaces and places within their community. Their vision aimed to benefit downtown retailers, business with services, and local street vendors will connect and create a stronger retail presence in the community. (See Figure 25.8.)

The Experiential Store

Imagine an interactive store on steroids! If you can imagine a store that excites and stimulates all of your senses and entertains you and actually helps you make your buying decisions, then you are in an experiential store.

More and more as buying on the internet becomes easier, some people prefer to do their shopping online while still in their bathrobe and slippers. The brick-and-mortar shops have to do even more to make getting dressed and coming into the store to shop worth their while. It has to be an experience; it has to be a sensual and emotional happening. Online shopping may appeal to your sense of sight and maybe hearing, but what about the other senses. What about taste, touch, and smell? What about actually holding, stroking, feeling the fabric? How does the garment really fit? Where is the fun in shopping?

Rebecca Minkoff's flagship stores in New York and Los Angeles uses digital technology to interact and play with shoppers. A large smart wall with a handwritten message invites the shopper to Tap! and begin their journey. The smart wall offers a free beverage choice and suggests merchandise to try-on.

A salesperson, ready with an iPad, will deliver the items to the dressing room, and you receive a text letting you know your fitting room is ready. Should you require a different color or size or want to get a sense of how that dress will look in the evening, you can tap the magic mirror in your dressing room to let it know. Lighting can change the look, and a list of the items you've tried on in the "session" will be saved and sent to your phone so you can order later online. According to Uri Minkoff, the brand's CEO and co-founder (and Rebecca's brother), the enhanced fitting rooms have both increased customers' time spent in stores and boosted clothing sales since the store opened.

In an experiential shop you not only see the real product under the best light and coordinated with the best accessories, but you can try it on if you prefer or through an oculus rift device "see" yourself in the garment

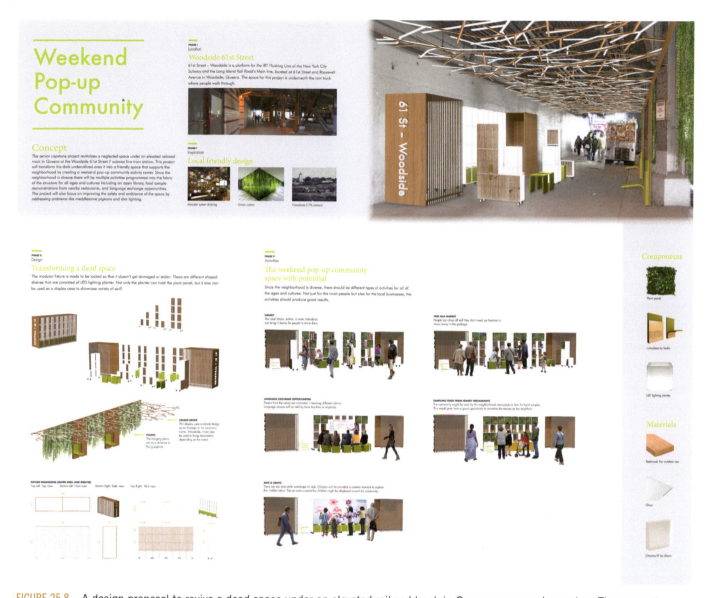

FIGURE 25.8   A design proposal to revive a dead space under an elevated railroad track in Queens near a subway stop. The concept aspires to transform a dark, underused space into a friendly space that supports the neighborhood by creating a weekend pop-up community activity center. Activities include library day, a language exchange, arts and crafts lessons, and local food sampling. *Courtesy of Chihiro Fujiwara, 2016 BFA graduate of Visual Presentation and Exhibition Design, Fashion Institute of Technology.*

of choice without actually removing your clothes to try it on. For fun, you can photograph yourself in the "new" outfit and send the image off to friends who might be just outside the dressing area or at their homes. To keep your texting fingers flexing and in working order, there may be interactive units in the store where you can use them to get information about products—like choice of colors, sizes, availability, price, or alternate recommendations. Soft drinks may be available or even light repasts or samplings of edible products. The trip to the store can be an adventure or a game where you win the jackpot even if you don't make a purchase.

Case Study 25.1: McCormick World of Flavors, Harborplace Light Street Pavilion, Baltimore, Maryland

Design Objective

It is not a surprise that McCormick's 3,818-square-foot space in Baltimore's Harborplace Light Street Pavilion is called the World of Flavors since McCormick is a global leader in flavor. The company, under various brand names, manufactures, markets, and distributes spices, seasoning mixes, and condiments throughout the world. The objective as presented to the architectural design firm JGA of Southfield, Michigan, was "to create an experiential showcase featuring McCormick global leadership in flavor through three platforms: cooking, baking, and grilling." This is the company's first branded retail destination and allows visitors to interact with some of the McCormick brands like Lawry's, Old Bay, Zatarain's, Thai Kitchen, and Grill Mates.

Design Solution

Signature McCormick identity elements begin on the store's facade. There is the McCormick brand block that extends into the center with a "flavor band" and illuminated signage that offers a view into the shop's interior. The loft-like interior is reminiscent of the McCormick plant and headquarters that existed nearby from 1920 to 1989. It was important that this space serve not only as a corporate brand showcase but further identify with McCormick's roots in Baltimore. The store is organized by a series of zones focusing on branding in key product categories and activity areas. In addition to cooking demonstrations and product sampling, there are assorted activities and digital experiences for visitors to enjoy. The

FIGURE CS25.1   The objective was to create a space where McCormick Spices could introduce its many products that enhance the cooking, baking, and grilling experiences and reinforce the brand name and signature color. Shoppers enter under a canopy of oversized McCormick red screw bottle caps.

FIGURE CS25.2   As visitors move through the space that is organized by zones featuring key product categories, their senses are delighted by sights, aromas, samples to taste, and messages gently promoted on touch screens and keyboards.

barbeque area resembles a dream backyard setup where the Grill Mates products are featured with the natural light adding to the outdoor feel. Experiential moments are showcased in vignettes, and the familiar red caps that cover the McCormick spice jars become giant brand signature elements clustered in the Red Cap alcove and as a canopy to highlight areas. There is also a history wall that proudly presents the company's heritage and tradition.

Ken Nisch, chairman and project principal of JGA explains, "McCormick was focused on the concept of flavor—a portfolio of flavors supported by a series of things such as demonstration kitchen, interactive—all which reinforce the flavor positioning, while recognizing the distinctive nature of each. Each of their brands is revered in their own genre as well as by those who appreciate the visual culinary heritage of each of these spices and their cultural roots." To be truly effective in creating the brand identity the design should appeal to all the senses, and Mr. Nisch agrees. "Branding is 360 degrees. Today branding starts before the customer comes to the store. There is the traditional advertising as it might have done in the past—catalogs, newspaper ads, and such; today there is also social networking like YouTube, Facebook, and blogs, and we get the opinions and influences of friends and family as well as thought leaders who comment about essentially every point of life. The sensory cues of aroma, music, tastings, displays, etc. can bring these opinions to life, but more importantly, they embed these opinions beyond the front of the mind into the deeper emotional fabric of memory."

Mr. Nisch continues, "A key component is the personal touch. Shoppers who purchase online miss the emotional and sensory cues. We call this the 'soft experience' and in this case it is easy as there is no more emotional or evocative category of retail than food, as it is totally embedded with tradition and culture and memory. In this shop everything from food demonstrations with the cultural heritage of each brandto the sampling that takes place and even the 'virtual sampling' through things like 'Flavor Print' which allows people to connect and match recipes and flavors and spices reinforces the sensory cues."

In addition to the striking accent of the signature red of the red cap, the palette includes culinary-inspired finishes such as stainless steel, aluminum, marble, and natural wood. To further the loft-like appeal, the polished concrete floors and open ceiling use the "bones" as a background element to contrast with the recycled, reclaimed wood that serve as tabletops. The red tile facade distinguishes the demo kitchen with its unique marble top.

Conclusion

In summing up this project Mr. Nisch says, "This concept was created as more of an experiential base. It essentially becomes kind of a common ground for testing, prompting, and validating ideas. Its focus is on how to talk to this cross-section of influencers in a real world, in real time. It does it so both explicitly in terms of soliciting consumers, but more importantly implicitly through data gathering across five interactive developments that allow McCormick to measure consumer

FIGURE CS25.3 The sensory cues, such as aroma, music, tastings, and displays can bring the brand to life and can embed the memory of the product and its qualities in the visitor's mind.

FIGURE CS25.4 Per Kevin Nisch, project principal: "The designers have created a sensory-laden playground for customers or would-be consumers where they are introduced to the whole McCormick family of products."

interests, areas of confusion, areas of opportunity—all through the 75 percent consumer usage of the store's interactive network.

"This project is really a portfolio of brands, and within this portfolio are brands that are appropriate to different uses, occasions, adventures, and traditions. They promote the idea of experimentation, openness, and adventure with food. So the whole idea of the store basically says that they all carry the McCormick promise of quality, and they do so in a way that is unexpected and really takes you beyond your everyday pepper, cinnamon, etc., into cultures, cuisines, history, and combinations. The experience center/store

is designed to basically get people comfortable with the idea that all things within the McCormick brand umbrella are available to make your life more interesting [and] your friends happier, while creating new traditions of entertainment."

CREDITS: *Design: JGA, Southfield, Michigan; Ken Nisch: Chairman and Project Principal; For McCormick: Lori Robinson: Vice President, Corporate Branding and Communication; Kathleen Haley: Director, Corporate Branding and Communication. Retail Consultants: Brand Theater: Frank Dinunzi and John Ariotta; Bentz-Papson Associates: Rick Bentz. Interactive Exhibits: 5th Screen Digital Services: John Curran and Keith Kelsen. Specialty/Theatrical Fixtures: Blue Genie. Art: Kevin Collins. Photography: Laszlo Regos Photography, Berkley, Michigan.*

Community and Experiential Stores: Trade Talk

community
conservation
consumer engagement

experiences
experiential retailing
people-centered

placemaking

Community and Experiential Stores: A Recap

✦ Consumers no longer need to go to a physical store to buy products, and as a result, the strategies for designing stores are no longer the same.

✦ Retail strategies revolve around consumer engagement, experiences, and placemaking.

✦ Community, conservation, and experiential retailing are just a few of the current trends rising on the retail horizon.

✦ Sustainability and conservation is an important aspect for today's consumer.

✦ Today's consumers want their purchase to mean something—to make a difference and benefit society in some way.

✦ Community shopping activities revolve around exhibits, social gatherings, evening events and a mixed collection of products.

✦ Sight, sound, touch, and taste are essential elements of the guest experience, in addition to smell, which is the most important since it is the only sense directly connected to the brain.

✦ Placemaking is gaining popularity through local events like flea markets, festivals, community events, and trend of going "local."

✦ Shoppers who purchase online miss the emotional and sensory cues; the store design should appeal to all the senses.

Questions for Review and Discussion

1. Why is community retailing gaining popularity today?

2. What caused the shift in retailing to integrate a greater sense of community?

3. Compare and contrast the community/experiential store and a traditional department store.

4. Why are consumers concerned about the meaning of their purchases?

5. What caused consumer expectation to change?

6. Give five examples of how a store can work with local students or schools or charities or serve as a space for neighborhood activities.

7. Describe what products suit community retailing best.

8. Why are experiences in retail valuable? How can they impact sales?

9. Explain how experiential retailing can impact the sale of food products.

10. How can brands use experiential stores to boost online sales?

PART SIX

Industry Resources

The final segment of this book is devoted to industry resources and areas of employment that are a part of, or closely related to, visual merchandising. Chapter 26 provides a list of the wide variety of magazines, websites, and trade show opportunities. Most visual merchandising professionals find that involvement with industry trade organizations provides them with the support, resources, and inspiration necessary in their occupations.

Chapter 27 identifies career opportunities in visual merchandising and related areas.

There is a wide-open field for those with a background in display, fashion merchandising, interior design, commercial or graphic arts, and architecture. The importance of a résumé, portfolio, and website is also discussed as a vehicle to seek jobs and network with potential employers.

Chapter Twenty-Six
Trade Organizations and Sources

NRF Show at the Javits Center, New York. *Courtesy of Shop Association.*

**AFTER YOU HAVE READ THIS CHAPTER,
YOU WILL BE ABLE TO DISCUSS**

+ how professional organizations can help support the efforts of visual merchandisers

+ the leading visual merchandising trade organizations

+ the services and benefits available to members of the various visual merchandising trade organizations

+ other sources of information and ideas for individuals in the field of visual merchandising

+ why visual merchandisers should maintain research files

Although visual merchandisers are often artists and craftspeople involved in aesthetics and the arts, they are also essentially businesspeople. They are in the business of presentation, and their purpose is to sell the store and the merchandise within it. As businesspeople and craftspeople with specific talents, there are professional organizations available to them. These trade organizations are different from trade unions. Whereas unions might have a widely diversified membership, the **trade organizations** to be discussed here were formed specifically for the creators and/or the end users of the mannequins, fixtures, props, decoratives, foliage, point-of-purchase displays and fixtures, store furniture, and so on.

Most of these organizations sponsor trade shows and events in various locations once or twice a year. The trade show is an exhibit of products and services as well as the new innovations conceived by designers who are employed by the manufacturers. These products and concepts, it is hoped, will enhance the presentation of merchandise, suggest new trends in store fixturing, or reinforce a promotion, or a combination of these. The shows are generally scheduled for times of the year that are convenient for the supplier and the buyer, while still allowing the end user sufficient time to order for an upcoming season, a store opening, or a new promotional year.

Very often, buying offices, resident buyers, and fashion forecasters will plan group meetings for these show times. Visual merchandisers and their staffs as well as store planners will be invited to attend these industry meetings in the same city, at the same time. These meetings add another dimension to the trade show and make attendance even more worthwhile.

Major Organizations

The following describe some of the major organizations that are essential to the craft and profession of visual merchandising and store design.

SHOP! Association
http://www.shopassociation.org

SHOP!Association is a global nonprofit trade association dedicated to enhancing retail environments and experiences. SHOP! represents more than 2,000 member companies worldwide and provides value to the global retail marketplace through its leadership in the following areas:

- Research (consumer behavior, trends, and futures)
- Design (customer experience design, store design, display design, and fixture design)
- Build (manufacturing, construction, materials, methods, logistics, installation)
- Marketing (in-store communications, in-store marketing, technology, visual merchandising)
- Evaluation (ROI, analytics, recognition/awards)

SHOP! is the new name for Association for Retail Environments (ARE) and the POPAI Association. Formerly known the National Association of Store Fixture Manufacturers, the organization has served the industry since 1956. SHOP! Association publishes and distributes a buyers' guide, a membership directory, and a SHOP! *Retail Environments* magazine.

Planning and Visual Education Partnership (PAVE)
http://www.paveglobal.org/

PAVE was founded in 1992, and from its inception, its objective was to encourage students to study retail design and planning and visual merchandising. Each year PAVE sponsors design competitions for college students studying retail design, with cash awards in the categories of store design, fixture design, and visual merchandising. PAVE also seeks to encourage retail management, store planners, visual designers, architects, and manufacturers to interact with and support design students, through seminars, workshops, and PAVE's annual fund-raising gala, the proceeds of which are dedicated to financial aid and internships for qualified students. (See Figure 26.1.)

Retail Design Institute (RDI)
http://www.retaildesigninstitute.org

The **Retail Design Institute (RDI)** is composed of many levels of creative professionals in the retail industry. It was founded in 1961 as a collaborative community where ideas, knowledge, and passion could be shared at a local level and enable members to fulfill the fast-paced

FIGURE 26.1 Now in its twentieth year, the PAVE Gala is a major fundraiser that awards over $150,000 to students and schools throughout the year in support of retail design studies. The event, held each December, seeks to forge links and build bridges between the students of today and the professionals they seek to emulate. *Courtesy of PAVE.*

FIGURE 26.2 Each year RDI sponsors the Iron Design Challenge—this design charrette allows executives from design firms and retailers to interact and work with the students to complete a contest that will benefit an NFP organization. The students have two hours and plenty of donated resources to build a concept. *RDI, Courtesy of Richard Cadan.*

planning and design needs of retail. Today their membership includes architects, graphic designers, lighting designers, interior designers, store planners, visual merchandisers, resource designers, brand strategists, educators, trade partners, editors, publishers, and students. RDI has an active education program, sponsoring scholarships and design challenges for students in store planning programs in schools across the country. There are also newsletters and other publications and many regional and joint meetings that are often combined with presentations by trade members. There are several local chapters, which plan special programs for their groups. (See Figures 26.2 and 26.3.)

Path to Purchase Institute
http://www.p2pi.org

Formerly known as the In Store Marketing Institute, this membership-based "think tank" organization is dedicated to satisfying the needs of the in-store marketing professionals and point-of-purchase field in general, and provides them with a constant update of what is happening in the retail field. Since 2003, this global association has been serving the needs of brand manufacturers, retailers, agencies, and all types of solution providers along the path to purchase. It fosters best practices and a deeper understanding of all marketing efforts that lead to a purchase in-store or online. The institute publishes the *Shopper Marketing* magazine and sponsors bi-yearly leadership

FIGURE 26.3 The organization also sponsors workshops for professionals at showrooms and retail stores. *RDI, Courtesy of Richard Cadan.*

events—League of Leaders and Forum of Merchandising Executives. The Shopper Marketing Summit is held annually in New York along with the Effie Awards.

EHI Retail Institute
http://www.ehi.org

A rather new entry into the international scene is the EHI Retail Institute, centered in Germany but reaching across the world. With a membership going on 600 international retail companies and their industry associations, manufacturers of consumer and capital goods, and service providers, the organization is gaining an outstanding reputation as a think tank for the retail industry.

EHI operates its own publishing house and promotes research on topics concerning the future of retailing. EHI is also closely associated with colleges and universities around the world and is a cosponsor of EuroShop, and international trade fair (discussed in the following section).

International Sign Association (ISA)
http://www.signs.org/

The International Sign Association (ISA) is a 2,300-member trade association, the members of which are manufacturers, users, and suppliers of on-premise signs and other graphics products from the United States and fifty-four countries around the world. ISA supports, promotes, and improves the graphics industry, which sustains the nation's retail, distribution, service and manufacturing industries.

Sources of Information and Ideas

TRADE SHOWS

EuroShop
http://www.euroshop-tradefair.com

Without a doubt, and with trade shows for retail interiors and visual merchandising materials literally happening around the globe, the biggest, best, and most widely awaited and attended is **EuroShop**, which occurs only once every three years (2017 is the most recent) in Düsseldorf, Germany. By the latest count more than 2,500 exhibitors from more than sixty-three countries show their wares to more than 110,000 visitors—shoppers—from more than ninety countries. It boggles the mind to imagine fifteen oversized soccer or football fields or more (actually, 200,000 square meters, or more than 2 million square feet) devoted to a presentation of products and services concerning retail environments. To help visitors find what they are looking for and what is of interest to them, the products are divided into four major categories: the major area of food and nonfood retail, consumer and capital goods industries,

wholesale skilled trades, and finally, chain gastronomy. There are also curated tours offered by Euro-a-go-go to help visitors navigate the show.

EuroShop prides itself on being the leading and the biggest show for retail environment and the trend barometer for innovations in the field. In addition, leading figures in the industry from around the world speak or are otherwise involved in seminars during the five days that the show runs.

National Retail Federation (NRF)
http://www.nrf.com

The National Retail Federation is the world's largest retail trade association. Its membership includes department stores; specialty, discount, catalog, internet, and independent retailers; chain restaurants; and grocery stores. Members also include businesses that provide goods and services to retailers, such as vendors and technology providers. NRF represents an industry that contains over 1.6 million U.S. retail establishments with more than 24 million employees. The 501(c)(3) nonprofit arm of the National Retail Federation builds awareness of the industry through statistics and stories; develops talent through education, experiences, and scholarships; and fosters career growth among people who work in retail. The NRF holds an annual conference/convention in New York each January. (See Figure 26.4.)

FIGURE 26.4   Retail's big show is the National Retail Federation's flagship industry event, its annual convention and expo held each January at Jacob K. Javits Center in New York City. The four-day event offers unparalleled education, collegial networking, and an enormous expo hall full of technologies and solutions. *Courtesy of Anne Kong.*

GlobalShop
http://www.globalshop.org/

Currently, the biggest and by far the most inclusive annual trade show in the United States for the store designer/visual merchandiser and retailer is **GlobalShop**. Sponsored by the editors of *Design:Retail* magazine, the show has grown until it now fills over 1 million square feet in conference center venues in Las Vegas or Chicago. The show usually occurs late in March, and 1,000 exhibitors from around the United States, Europe, and Asia show their latest and most innovative materials, fixtures, lighting, techniques, and technology. The show lasts only three days and is attended by chain operators, department and specialty store personnel, consumer product manufacturers, discount and mass merchandisers, and, of course, store designers, architects, visual merchandisers, and display persons.

GlobalShop, today, is actually five trade shows in one. It combines the Store Fixturing and Visual Merchandising shows with the Store Design and Operations, the Digital Store, and the At-Retail Marketplace. With one admission, visitors can tour all the exhibit spaces and find ideas, materials, or products in unexpected places.

The centerpiece of each show is an exciting retail speaker conference that highlights consumer behavior and other key topics. Leaders in the retail industry, famous architects and designers, outstanding visual merchandisers, or "people in the news" make presentations at the conference. For anybody interested or involved with retail presentation, this is a show not to be missed.

Retail Design Collective
http://www.shopassociation.org/retail-design-collective/

Sponsored by SHOP! Association, the Retail Design Collective is an annual show held in early December in New York City. In addition to the exhibits held in showrooms around the city, there is sometimes a central location designated for out-of-town exhibitors to show. The showroom exhibits are set up for the occasion to show off their spring lines and newest wares. There are numerous showrooms devoted to mannequins, fixtures, and decoratives; many of these are open to prospective buyers all year long. The showrooms host lively events and parties during the evening to kick off

FIGURE 26.5　The Retail Design Collective showrooms roll out the latest and greatest innovations in new products and exciting finishes each December. Visual merchandisers and store design teams come to New York in search of fresh ideas for their stores and leave inspired. *Courtesy of Glenn Sokoli, creative director, Global Visual Group.*

the show, allowing industry members to gather and network in a social environment. (See Figure 26.5.)

The International Contemporary Furniture Fair
http://www.icff.com

The ICFF is held over a four-day period at the Javits Center with more than 35,000 interior designers, architects, retailers, representatives, distributors, facility managers, developers, manufacturers, store designers, and visual merchandisers. On the last day of the show the ICFF opens its doors to the general public as well.

More than 750 exhibitors from all points of the globe display contemporary furniture, seating, carpet and flooring, lighting, outdoor furniture, materials, wall coverings, accessories, textiles, and kitchen and bath for residential and commercial interiors. This remarkable throng of exhibitors creates an unparalleled opportunity to view a broad yet highly focused selection of the world's finest, most innovative, and original avant-garde home and contract products side-by-side, under one roof.

The ICFF hosts representatives from Australia, Austria, Belgium, Brazil, Canada, China, Colombia, the Czech Republic, Denmark, Egypt, El Salvador, France, Germany, Guatemala, Italy, Japan, Lebanon, Lithuania, Mexico, the Netherlands, Norway, Philippines, Portugal, Scotland, South Africa, South Korea, Spain, Sweden, Switzerland, Taiwan, the United States, the United Kingdom, and Venezuela.

Making their yearly pilgrimage to the celebrated design hub are contingents from Austrian Federal Economic Chamber, Brazilian Furniture, British European Design Group (BEDG), Ceramics of Italy, Design Philippines, Furniture New York, The Furniture Society (U.S.), Inside Norway, Interiors from Spain and Portugal Brands.

ExhibitorLive
http://www.exhibitoronline.com/

Exhibitor Live is an annual conference for professionals in the exhibition, trade show, and corporate event industry held at Mandalay Bay, Las Vegas each March. The show features five days of emerging trends, tactics, and technology and the newest exhibit marketing and management techniques. Visitors can attend programs from world-class exhibitors where veteran experts share their best practices. They offer an exclusive university-affiliated professional certification and essential training for: trade show managers, exhibit and event managers, marketing managers, and all others responsible for their organization's trade show and/or event programs.

ISA Sign Expo
http://signexpo.org/

ISA Sign Expo is the largest trade show dedicated to the sign, graphics, and visual communications industry. The event is held annually and alternates between Las Vegas, Nevada, and Orlando, Florida.

TRADE MAGAZINES AND WEBSITES
Design: Retail
http://www.designretailonline.com/

Design:Retail (formerly *Display & Design Ideas*) is a monthly magazine published by Emerald Expositions that contains design strategies, in-store marketing, new products, and global trends. *Design:Retail* is also the major sponsor of the aforementioned GlobalShop trade show. The publication is free to subscribers, and it contains stories on new retail operations, current trends in retail store formatting, fixturing, and lighting concepts. The editors will often poll their readership on questions relevant to their work. These surveys may focus on budgets, personnel, education, what products readers use, what products they would like to have, and so on. In addition, the magazine is filled with colored ads for all types of products and materials related to store design, visual merchandising, and display.

An inquiry card is included in each issue for the convenience of the reader. By circling the number corresponding to the number on the ad, the reader will, for the price of a single stamp, receive brochures, booklets, and samples from numerous manufacturers and suppliers. Each year the Design:Retail Forum brings together the top leaders from the retail design industry, including store design, architecture, and visual merchandising retail executives. This event covers topics and discussions of the most pressing issues in the retail design community. The publication also sponsors CitySCENE, a series of local networking events across the country designed to bring like-minded peers from the retail design industry together for casual conversation and cocktails. The invitation is open to interns and junior designers on up, as *Design:Retail* wants to bring together all levels of industry experience.

VMSD
http://vmsd.com/

The visual merchandiser should subscribe to **VMSD (Visual Merchandising and Store Design)**, published by ST Media Group. In this monthly magazine, in addition to articles relevant to merchandise presentation and store planning, there are dozens of ads for the many elements necessary for the successful installation of windows and interiors. By filling in the numbers on the request card that is inserted at the back of the magazine, the visual merchandiser/store designer is ensured a steady flow of brochures, booklets, and illustrative material on new products and designs. VMSD sponsors the IRDC International Retail Design Conference each year. It is a premier educational and networking event for the store design and visual merchandising community. IRDC brings together over 400 attendees from all across the world to engage in design dialogue centered on best practices, evolving trends, and fresh strategies for engaging shoppers.

WindowsWear Pro
http://www.windowswear.com

WindowsWear PRO is a premier subscription website for the window display and visual merchandising industry, providing inspiration to the world's leading brands to innovate and create more engaging visual displays. The site features proprietary trend reports, analysis, information, and exclusive access to the world's fashion windows (25,000-plus analyzed windows and more than 500 exclusive brands from around the world).

OTHER PUBLICATIONS

Sign & Digital Graphics Magazine
http://www.SDGmag.com

The business of visual communication, signage, graphics, and point of purchase.

Creative Magazine
http://www.creativemagazine.com

Point of purchase, exhibit design, and sales promotions.

Chain Store Age
http://www.chainstoreage.com

Brandweek
http://www.brandweek.com

Point of purchase and sales promotions. Published along with *Adweek*.

Interiors+Sources
http://www.interiorsandsources.com

Materials, furnishings, flooring, and trends.

Exhibit Builder
http://www.exhibitoronline.com

Best practices in trade shows and events.

RESEARCH

Visual merchandisers and store designers should keep active research files and books as a method to personally foster their own creative style and resources. They can collect information on their computer and collections amassed at trade events or museum shows or during travel journeys. Books, catalogues, brochures, photographs, swatches, and any other bits and pieces can inspire the designer or help make a project simpler to execute. It is never too soon to start your own personal resource library; most design firms dedicate an area with similar resources.

Because this is an ongoing sort of collection, it should be reexamined often, updated, and kept viable. Often, an idea that was filed away can stimulate a design project in some way or another. Images; articles from magazines, websites, or blog posts; Pinterest boards; and Instagram can often suggest new inspiration for shop-in-shops, mannequins, color schemes, or even fashion accessorizing.

Keeping a reference library is an absolute must. It gives the visual merchandiser/store designer a place from which to start. Ideas evolve from other ideas.

Trade Organizations and Sources: Trade Talk

Design:Retail magazine and website
EuroShop
GlobalShop
PAVE (Planning and Visual Education
 Partnership)

Retail Design Institute (RDI)
SHOP! Association
trade organizations

*VMSD (Visual Merchandising and Store
 Design)* magazine and website

Trade Organizations and Sources: A Recap

✦ Professional organizations support the efforts of visual merchandising by sponsoring trade shows during the year. Such shows will feature concepts and products that will enhance merchandise, suggest new trends in store fixturing, and/or refine an ad campaign.

✦ Trade shows often give visual merchandisers and their staffs the opportunity to attend industry meetings being held in the same city.

✦ The leading visual merchandising trade organizations are:
  • NRF National Retail Federation
  • SHOP! Association
  • Retail Design Institute (RDI)

✦ Visual merchandising trade organizations offer various benefits, as follows:
  • Path to Purchase offers seminars and workshops dealing with challenges and new trends, makes awards, maintains an information center, publishes guidelines and bulletins, and maintains a public relations program.
  • SHOP! Association presents various awards at trade show events sponsored once a year in New York;

participates in research programs; works closely with schools that offer visual merchandising curricula; offers scholarships, grants, and cooperative work plans; maintains an accurate and complete mailing list, available to members only; and offers free employment information.

✦ Other sources that may be used by individuals in the field of visual merchandising are trade shows and trade magazines. The biggest and most inclusive trade show is GlobalShop, held each year in Las Vegas. It attracts exhibitors from around the United States, Europe, and Asia.

✦ The visual merchandiser should keep an active research file of booklets, brochures, photos, ads, swatches, and any material involving design and display. Subscriptions to magazines and trade journals can also provide useful information and help stimulate ideas.

✦ Research files can help the display person keep up with new ideas in the field and might stimulate a whole new promotional concept, suggest new arrangements for displays, or lead to the evolution of new ideas.

Questions for Review and Discussion

1. Why are visual merchandisers considered businesspeople as well as craftspeople?

2. State the meaning of the acronym and the main purpose for each of the following trade organizations. What activities are conducted in order to achieve each organization's goals?
   a. NRF b. SHOP! c. RDI

3. Name three trade publications directly related to the field of visual merchandising. In what ways might trade publications be used by visual merchandising professionals?

Chapter Twenty-Seven
Career Opportunities in Visual Merchandising

Architects and store designers reviewing floorplans.
Hero Images/Getty Images.

**AFTER YOU HAVE READ THIS CHAPTER,
YOU WILL BE ABLE TO DISCUSS**

+ other areas of opportunity for individuals with a background in visual merchandising
+ educational requirements
+ the basic areas that a résumé should cover
+ the purpose of the website and portfolio
+ employment networking techniques
+ the attributes of a good visual merchandiser

To a person considering visual merchandising as a career, the term too often implies merely doing displays in a department or specialty store. Visual merchandising or display is much more than that. The career possibilities and the fields in which one can practice the techniques of "showing" and presentation are myriad. Although trends in fashion have great influence on what the visual merchandiser is showing, be it books, luggage, or even Starbucks coffee, visual merchandising is more than the business of fashion.

Over the years many people have found their way into the world of display and visual merchandising through studies in fine arts, communications, interior design, or fashion. Today, more formal education is required. The good news is that many colleges with design programs are offering specialized courses and degrees in visual merchandising and retail store design. Today's designer needs a design foundation in basic graphic design skills and the Adobe Creative Suite in order to handle branding elements properly. Visual merchandising is still a "hands-on" business that requires knowledge of materials, tools, and the building process. Communicating concepts and design development is fostered through courses in sketching, model-making, and at least one or two computer aided design programs such as Sketch-up, AutoCAD, 3D Studio Max, Vectorworks, or Rhino. Visual merchandisers must also study art history and furniture design periods. All of these disciplines support working in the visual industries.

Visual merchandisers with the proper training can find careers in the following fields:

- Display design in a department or specialty stores
- Store planning and fixture design
- Point-of-purchase design
- Graphic design and branding
- Event design and brand activation
- Museum, exhibit, and trade show design
- Home fashions and food presentation
- Styling
- Party design
- Set and stage design for fashion shows, festivals, and events
- Display design for a manufacturer of display fixtures or props

- Freelance design for individual stores or manufacturer showrooms

Display and Visual Merchandising

Retail display is often a starting point for many visual merchandisers. Installing weekly window displays and maintaining the store interior is a rewarding career choice for the person who enjoys working "hands-on" in a creative environment with variation in day-to-day responsibilities. Visual merchandisers work cross-functionally with merchandising, marketing, store planning, and store management. Since consumer behavior is changing faster than the speed of light, stores need to provide more experiences for visitors. Creating and implementing these brand interactions is rewarding, especially when you personally witness the excitement on the selling floor. Working within the store also requires patience and understanding of the general public.

Malls

Mall management hires visual merchandisers to mount the spectaculars that are usually staged in the rotundas, in the central atriums, or on stages set up around the mall. Here, the designers are dealing with two, three, and sometimes four stories of vertical space; to be effective, these "production numbers" have to be *big*. Designers are dealing with oversized, overscaled, and overwhelming display concepts. Visual merchandisers will combine and coordinate merchandise from many retailers into one theatrical extravaganza—in a setting to match.

There are also opportunities with the producers of the overscaled displays and props that are designed especially for areas like malls and large public spaces—particularly at Christmas and Easter. All those Santa houses, Santa's thrones, gumdrop forests, 8-foot ornaments, and 20-or-more-foot trees have to be designed, constructed, decorated, and then installed—and that all takes people with taste, talent, flair, and a background in display.

Store Planning and Fixtures

The store planner will find himself or herself interacting with many of the same individuals as the visual merchandiser (visual merchandiser included). Store planners spend much more time working in CAD on the computer to establish floor plans that prioritize merchandise and traffic flow. They design fixtures, furnishings, and lighting plans. They work with all levels of management and individual brands to develop appropriate strategies to support each brand's image. The lead requirement is understanding space planning, allocation, capacity of fixtures, traffic flow, and the specific regulations for designing public spaces with regard to safety, egress, fire codes, and ADA conditions. (See Figure 27.1.)

Point-of-Purchase Design

Point-of-purchase designers come from different design backgrounds. Often industrial designers, packaging

designers, and graphic artist find their way into this highly specialized field of fixture design. POP designers can work directly with a brand or a POP design manufacturer. POP supports temporary, semi-permanent, and permanent types of fixturing solutions. Knowledge of materials, cost, fabrication, branding, and 3-D modeling is vital for the POP designer. It's an extremely detailed job that focuses heavily on the capacity of fixtures, brand recognition, callouts, price points, and differentiating products from the competition. POP designers interact with brand marketers, account executives, engineers, and controllers to "value engineer" the design. (See Figure 27.2.)

Graphic Design and Branding

Graphic designers with formal training and a proficiency in Adobe Creative Cloud work in visual, event, trade, or exhibition design creating branding, signage, price points, promotionals, banners, environmental graphics, and wayfinding.

FIGURE 27.1   A day in the life of the store planner includes rendering on the computer, reviewing plans, communicating with vendors, and reporting back to the team. Store visits and meeting with manufacturers are a regular part of the week's activities. *Thomas Barwick/Getty Images.*

FIGURE 27.2   Maria Sharapova's candy line, Sugarpova, featured at Bloomingdale's, makes a strong impression in this custom pop-up shop environment that includes colorful graphics. The giant lips and colorful packaging was the perfect way to attract both tennis and candy lovers. *Designed by RPG, New York, New York.*

Event Design and Brand Activation

Event and promotion design is a growing career choice for visual designers today. Brands are willing to allocate sizable budgets for events such as promotions, product launches, and pop-up stores. The online store may be all the talk, but there is no beating the physical store experience. "Clicks to bricks" is trending, and online retailers recognize the need for consumers to understand the scale, look, and feel of their products from time to time. The rise of online shopping is, in many cases, encouraging the development of new and innovative retail events and experiences. Brand activation, sponsorships, design collaborations, and charity affairs all require a special event or experience. Visual merchandisers are highly skilled in this area because they understand how to work on a tight deadline, with budgets, space, and many other constraints. (See Figure 27.3.)

Museum, Exhibits, and Trade Show

In addition to trade show designing, there is a need for exhibit designers for museums, historical societies, art galleries, airports, and other public spaces. The trade show or exhibit designer works with limited space to showcase visually a particular product (or products); a name or company image; or paintings, sculpture, photographs, or graphics. It's about telling a visual story. In some ways trade show and exhibit design is closely allied with showroom display and merchandising, which is another excellent field for display

FIGURE 27.3   Event designers design it, plan it, and install it! Imagine a Miami Beach scene complete with palm trees and lounge chairs popping up near Bryant Park at 6 a.m. in midtown Manhattan. This Lily Pulitzer Pop-Up Shop for Target had shoppers lining up at 3 a.m. for a chance to shop the collection before it was available in stores. *Rob Kim/Getty Images.*

FIGURE 27.4   The bright yellow doors are open and the house of "Wilton" welcomes buyers to peruse Wilton's latest baking line at the International Housewares Show in Chicago. Inside, buyers will entertain everything for baking and decorating including a giant "candy sprinkle" wall. *The International Housewares Show, Chicago, Illinois. Courtesy of Anne Kong.*

designers and visual merchandisers. Very often the showroom is tied in with trade shows, and as each season is introduced or as new products are revealed as part of a market week, the showroom is reorganized, rearranged, refixtured, and retrimmed to enhance the look of the products and suggest to the buyers in the showroom that something new is happening here and now. It is a combination of display, stage setting, and visual merchandising. (See Figure 27.4.)

Home Fashions and Food Presentation

With the increased interest in home fashions and changing attitudes toward how to present furniture and home furnishings, this vast field has become another area for career opportunities for the visual merchandiser. Furniture is now sold in lifestyle displays or vignettes, not as chairs and sofas, but like coordinated pieces of an outfit. Pieces are shown with all the accessories and decoratives in a setting that suggests a particular look—or lifestyle: the casual, pastel Southwest look; the relaxed New England cottage style; the contemporary, sophisticated urban scene; high-tech;

eclectic; and so forth. It takes a visual merchandiser to design these abstracted or vignetted stage sets that create an ambiance for the furniture and accessories. There are jobs available in wholesale furniture showrooms, in department stores, and in furniture and home fashion retail stores.

As mentioned in Chapter 20, the presentation of food—fresh or prepared—has expanded the opportunity horizon for display persons. Supermarkets as well as specialty food shops, gourmet takeouts, and *traiteurs* are all in the business of showing foodstuffs at their very best. It is more than the final touches added by the chefs and bakers; it is now what the visual merchandiser can add to the look with lights, color, textures, and imaginative decoratives. TV commercials, cooking and food magazines, and the ever-growing number of cookbooks need stylists, or presenters, who really know how to make the foods come alive.

Styling

Individuals with visual merchandising skills and training often get involved in styling as a career. There are different kinds of stylists, including those for films, commercials, magazines, or catalogues. There are also fashion show stylists, manufacturers' stylists, advertising stylists, and photographers' stylists. A stylist styles the shoot, the event, or the line according to the image that is to be projected. Designing is usually not part of the job of a stylist. Rather, a stylist will put together the fashion and apparel looks to be presented. Working with a theme specified by the director, the stylist will coordinate the separate pieces, accessories, models, and props to be presented. Most stylists work on a freelance basis and have a specific specialty (such as film, advertising, or food). These jobs require a high level of creativity and flexibility in scheduling.

Party Design

Party design is another relatively new and very big market with job openings for visual merchandisers. It includes conceiving a theme for a party; designing or selecting the invitations, the table linens and service, the centerpieces, the decorations in the room, and the favors; and sometimes even planning the menu and food service. Whether it is a birthday, bar or bat mitzvah, engagement, wedding, anniversary, charity affair, or testimonial dinner, this is big business. Everybody who hosts a party wants that party to be unique and memorable. The party designer can turn an ordinary event into an affair to remember. This type of design can extend into the commercial field with planning and executing receptions at trade shows, gallery openings, and anyplace where "taste" is important and a lasting image is to be produced. (See Figure 27.5.)

Set and Stage Design

Have you ever thought about how many parades, fashion shows, and music/art festivals there are each year? These events call for spectacular, overscaled presentations and sets that may include stages, sound, digital media, light shows, and custom-designed one-of-a-kind props. Glastonbury, Coachella, Fuji Rock, Benicàssim—these are just a few of the notable global music and art festivals. It takes visual and display talent to innovate and design these large extravaganzas. Theme parks are opening all over the country, and they need visual merchandising talent, just as many malls do.

Display Decorative Manufacturing

Most people on the street don't realize that the decorative props, the unusual elements in a display, the dancing mechanical figures at Christmas, or the handmade collage panels are often designed and produced by display manufacturers and

FIGURE 27.5 Events and parties typically evolve from a theme or special occasion. The job of the party planner may include booking the location to creating an English garden on a Manhattan rooftop to selecting the table wear, the centerpieces, linens, menu, and even the invitations and the souvenirs and the bags to carry them away in. *Courtesy of Josh Tierney.*

The job of the designer is challenging especially when the buyers are seasoned designers themselves, in search of inspiration and new products for their stores. The creative director who works for a manufacturer must entertain and create a buzz during market week with larger-than-life displays. *Glenn Sokoli, creative director, Global Visual Group.*

then purchased by visual merchandisers for use in windows and store interiors. This is a very big business, as anyone who has ever attended an industry trade show, such as GlobalShop or EuroShop, knows. This is a different challenge for the display designer: to be a prop designer, a prop maker, or even a salesperson on the road or a showroom "rep" for a display manufacturer. (See Figure 27.6.)

Tools for Getting the Job

RÉSUMÉ

A thoughtfully planned and well-written **résumé** may not get you a job, but it may certainly succeed in getting you the all-important interview. The résumé is "you on paper." It acquaints the reader with your goals, qualifications, education, and experiences. For positions in visual merchandising or related areas, the résumé might be written in a very standard manner or in an individualized, more imaginative style. However, don't underestimate the power of a neatly organized résumé.

Depending on experience and accomplishments, a résumé will vary in length. However, your résumé should cover these basic areas:

- Name, address, cell number, email, and website
- Occupational goal
- Education
- Work experience
- Special accomplishments, skills, and interests

LINKEDIN

LinkedIn is an online global resource for hiring, networking, and connecting people. The résumé is the first step; creating a profile on LinkedIn is second. Don't regard this social media platform casually—it is strictly business. Post an image of yourself styled in proper business attire, as you would dress for work. Keep all of the information you enter in a formal tense and link as many personal resources as possible. Besides linking your personal **website**, or **Behance** site, research and join the professional industry groups and alliances offered. Many of the professional trade organizations sponsor online group activity. Follow and stay active in these groups. The best way to get noticed is to engage in the daily online dialogues—post ideas and questions of your own on the LinkedIn homepage. This is the most valuable networking you can do to find employment. LinkedIn will automatically suggest introductions and connections; learn more and take advantage of all LinkedIn can do.

PORTFOLIO WEBSITE

Aside from the standard résumé for most jobs in the field of visual merchandising, the candidate is requested to present a **portfolio** to the prospective employer. A portfolio should represent a collection of an individual's best and most creative work, including previous displays, sample sketches, process images, floor plans, and fixture designs. The portfolio should be available on a personal website or Behance site. A designer can easily access Squarespace,

Wix, or any "build your own website" host and design his or her own digital portfolio. For interviews, bring a tablet or laptop accompanied by a sketchbook or bound booklet of published and printed work.

When on the job, smart individuals will continue to build their portfolio in preparation for new job opportunities or possible promotions within the company. For freelance visual merchandisers, a quality portfolio is essential. It becomes a "calling card" and a reference showing prospective customers what you are capable of doing for their store, showroom, or exhibit.

A balanced representation of abilities is recommended for inclusion in the portfolio. Of course, employers expect to see only the candidate's very best work.

An Effective Visual Merchandiser

One should select the direction or field that seems to offer the greatest potential for personal development and financial gain. This decision should take the following into consideration: the individual's temperament and talent, degree of creativity, willingness to interact with people, and ultimate goals and ambitions.

Some people want to lead or direct. They are organizers and administrators. The visual merchandising field needs people who can organize, arrange, plot, and plan in an orderly manner with one eye on the budget and the other on the calendar and the time schedule. These talents are necessary to the creative process of display.

Some display people, on the other hand, have "star" personalities. They need to razzle-dazzle, to sparkle, and to erupt in creative outpourings. They are filled with imagination, touched with flair, and tingling with excitement. For them, the planning, scheduling, bookkeeping, and nitty-gritty of following the "book" can be utter torment. It would be a waste to misuse or misdirect their unique talents.

Other display people may find the mechanical aspects of drafting and the specifics of space and layout more to their liking. They could be in tune with interior design and all it entails. For them, a career in store planning or the designing of commercial interiors might provide the greatest satisfaction.

Personal gratification is most important in the development of a career. Because so much of our time is spent on the job, it is imperative that we like what we do, that we are happy and enthusiastic doing it. With so many diversified and fascinating areas from which to choose, no display person should ever be bored or unhappy.

No matter in which direction he or she goes, first and foremost, a visual merchandiser is a merchandiser, a person whose business it is to sell or promote by means of presentation. Whether presenting a garment, an organization, or an idea, we expect a display person to be an artist or a designer, or both. Creativity and imagination are his or her major attributes. Most people not involved in the industry tend to take window and interior displays for granted. They do not realize the time, thought, planning, and preparation that go into creating a display. It takes talent to dress a mannequin or rig a form and to create the semblance of life or animate inanimate objects.

The display person is a fashion coordinator and should be au courant, knowing the trends, the looks, the newest styles. He or she needs to know from where, in the long history of fashion design, these "new" designs evolved. He or she must find the settings, props, and accessories that will enhance these new trends.

The visual merchandiser should be a connoisseur, a collector, an avid reader, and a student of the world, past and present. In trash heaps, in secondhand stores, and at house razings, he or she may find tomorrow's display setting or a prop or a fixture that was not originally designed to be a fixture. The visual merchandiser should be able to see beauty where others may not and then be able to make that beauty visible to all.

A good display person should be an interior designer, a space planner, a lighting expert, a landscape gardener. The display person may even be called upon to brighten up and lighten up an architectural colossus perpetrated by an architect with an "edifice complex."

Some builders have been known to construct monuments rather than marketplaces. They build in and leave little room for change, and change is the life force of fashion.

The store planning and visual departments are called upon to do seasonal shops and special selling environments.

They are expected to come up with clever, bright, and inexpensive ideas that change a "blah" department into a stimulating selling ambiance. The ebb and flow of the traffic within the store, and the direction of that traffic past the eye-stopping displays and into sales areas, are part of the store planner's art form.

The visual merchandiser must be involved in a store's advertising, copywriting, signage, and graphics. He or she must be able to communicate with coworkers, management, and potential customers. This communication is written as well as oral. The visual merchandiser should be able to write simple, direct, understandable sentences. Often, the visual merchandiser is called upon to write the copy line and card heading that add meaning, and sometimes humor, to the merchandise presentation.

And always, the good visual merchandiser is learning. He or she is always studying the world past the display window, outside the store, and beyond the parking lot. It requires constant preparation to do a good and thorough job.

Let us assume now that you already are a visual merchandiser. You have selected a particular field in which you feel comfortable, happy, and fulfilled. What are you going to do to maintain that feeling? Are you still growing, learning, and stretching your talents? Here is a checklist for you to consider every once in a while, especially when you feel your job is not quite what you think it should be.

♦ When is the last time you read a book that really stimulated you to think? When did you last feel that you learned something and expanded your horizons?

♦ How long has it been since you have been to a museum, a gallery, or an art show? Have you been keeping up with what is new in the world of art or with what was very old but is suddenly new and fashionable? Are you keeping up with the new media, new techniques, and new approaches to presentation?

♦ When did you last involve yourself with the new directions in the field of graphics; with posters, layouts, signage techniques, and devices; and with new typography and methods of graphic reproduction? Are you keeping up with the advances in photography, holography, and calligraphy?

♦ Do you remember the last experimental play or movie you saw? Even if you hated it or were totally confused by it, did you try to get something out of it?

♦ If you have traveled, what have you seen and absorbed that you cannot get from a picture, a postcard, or a guidebook? Did you wander through foreign streets picking up sounds, smells, and sights that someday may serve as inspirations for displays? Are you really looking, or are you just sightseeing without really absorbing the sights?

♦ Have you taken any courses lately, not simply for credit, but just because you wanted to know more about something—anything? Are you still growing intellectually? Are you learning more about your profession and the world?

♦ Where is your inspiration intake coming from? Google? Do you ever leave your computer to peruse books or magazines anymore? Do you allow yourself to get "lost" in these books? What do you do to increase your knowledge of language so that you may communicate better with those around you?

♦ What are you doing on social media? Are you inspiring others, and do the images you post say something about your personal design direction? Are you expanding your horizons beyond your immediate surroundings? Do you demonstrate global citizenship and awareness on social media?

♦ Look in the mirror—the full-length one! Take a real, long look. Do you look like a person who is involved with fashion and with the presentation and promotion of new looks and ideas? Do you look, feel, smell, act, and react like a person who is a trendsetter? Are you sending off "sparks"? Are you sending out messages? Are you communicating?

♦ And, in a quiet moment, think about this: Are you growing as a person? Are you honest, ethical, and sincere in what you do?

Are you satisfied with your answers? You may find some of the problems with your job are really problems within yourself. You are in the showing business. You are supposed to be an image maker, but your own personal image must also be created, fostered, and developed.

Career Opportunities in Visual Merchandising: Trade Talk

Behance   portfolio   website
LinkedIn   résumé

Career Opportunities in Visual Merchandising: A Recap

+ Visual merchandisers can pursue careers in the fields of commercial exhibiting, museum and graphic arts exhibits, staging of fashion shows, point-of-purchase design, store planning, and packaging.

+ Visual merchandisers may also work as trimmers, decorators, or designers in a department or specialty store; for a manufacturer of display fixtures or props; as freelancers in individual stores; for a manufacturer's showroom; or for trade shows.

+ Further career options for the person with visual merchandising training lie in the fields of home fashions and styling for films, commercials, magazines, catalogs, and photographers.

+ Party design is a fairly new field open to the trained visual merchandiser, as is the area of special events such as parades, beauty pageants, fashion shows, and theme parks.

+ Basic areas covered by a résumé should include name, address, telephone, occupational goal, education, work experience, and special skills and interests.

+ A quality portfolio is essential because it becomes a person's calling card and reference. It should represent a collection of an individual's best and most creative work, including photos of previous displays, sample sketches, copy design, floor plans, fixture designs, and such.

+ In selecting a career within the field of visual merchandising, one should choose the direction or field that seems to offer the greatest potential for personal development, job satisfaction, and financial gain.

+ The decision to enter a particular field should take into consideration the individual's temperament and personality as well as his or her degree of creativity, willingness to interact with people, and ultimate goals and ambitions.

+ Creativity and imagination are the major attributes of a visual merchandiser.

Questions for Review and Discussion

1. For each of the following career areas, explain how visual merchandising skills could prove to be beneficial.
   a. Trade show and exhibit design
   b. Home fashion field
   c. Styling
   d. Party design
   e. Special events
   f. Fixture design
   g. POP

2. What are the two basic tools needed to get a job in the visual merchandising field? Describe each thoroughly.

3. What items should be included in a visual merchandising portfolio?

Glossary

A

abstract mannequin—A sophisticated and versatile figure that represents the ultimate in style and decoration; the abstract mannequin is more concerned with creating an overall effect than with reproducing natural lines and proportions.

abstract setting—Presentation in which merchandise is the dominant feature, and the arrangement of lines, shapes, and forms supports and reinforces the message.

accent lighting—Used to highlight key objects or focal points; metal halide lamps are usually for this type of lighting. See also **secondary lighting**.

acrylic—A resin based material used for fixtures, signage and other display needs; also known as Plexiglass, it is available in many colors and sizes. Transparent acrylic imitates the look of glass, is safer to use, but has a shorter lifespan due to scratching and fogging.

adhesive back—Refers to a media used in large-format printing. Stronger than paper, polypropylene has a sticky backed surface covered by a peelable release paper that avoids using toxic spray adhesive to mount prints.

Adirondack chairs—Rustic wooden chairs with a slatted back and a seat that is lower in the back than the front.

adjacencies—Refers to the logical and natural arrangement of products that are related to one another; positioning related merchandise together on the same fixture or in close proximity.

aesthetic sensibility—Refers to the skill and experience that enables a designer to evaluate and make judgments about composition, color, and all forms of design.

aisle table—Feature table that is set in an aisle for impact selling.

ambient lighting—The mood-producing light used in an area or exhibit. Ambient lighting is part of secondary lighting and makes use of floodlights, filters, and wall washers.

analogous color scheme—A harmonious arrangement of color created by clusters of colors adjacent to one another on the color wheel; these colors are compatible and reinforce one another.

angled front—A type of storefront in which the store entrance is recessed from the street, and the display windows lead back from the street to the entrance, creating an aisle for the shopper.

ankle-rod fittings—Attachments on the back of the mannequin's leg into which a supporting rod is inserted.

antique finish—A look of aged beauty. It refers to aging a surface, object, or fixture to appear distressed or weathered by time and natural elements.

appliqué—A three-dimensional attachment; gives depth to a flat point-of-purchase (POP) display.

arcade front—A type of storefront set back from the street consisting of a series of windows with backs and three sides of glass, coming forward from the entrance wall; the shopper enters between protruding window displays.

architectural symbols—Written or printed marks used in the creation of plans and designs, such as for a store.

armoire—A tall cupboard or wardrobe usually combining shelf space with hang space; in display, an armoire can be used as a prop or a fixture. See also **freestanding closet**.

Art Deco chair—A small chair, rounded in form, sensuous and stylized and designed in the Art Deco style of the 1920s and 1930s. It can also be characterized by its linear, geometric lines and luxurious materials.

articulated artist's figure—A lifesize form or abstract mannequin based on the small wooden miniatures used by artists and designers to get correct anatomical proportions and poses for figure drawing. It lends itself to decorative and undressed applications as well as fully dressed and accessorized setups.

assets—Graphic elements such as a typeface, logo, colors, patterns, and designs.

assortment display—The showing and display of a merchandise collection of unrelated items that happen to be in the same store; see also **variety display**.

asymmetrical balance—Distribution of design elements in which the two sides appear to be of equal weight but are not replicas of one another; it is more informal and often more interesting than symmetrical balance.

audiovisuals—Custom video or audio computerized electronic devices used in display to provide shoppers with messages they can see or hear, or both; relatively expensive, these are used when the information being conveyed is specific or complicated.

auxiliary display—A variety or assortment of product that may or may not have a relationship by category. An auxiliary display can also refer to a group of merchandise displayed alongside a mannequin on risers or a fixture.

awnings—Rooflike covers of canvas or other material extending over a doorway or from the top of a window; they make viewing a window display more pleasant for the shopper by providing shelter and reducing glare; they may also add color and eye appeal to a storefront.

B

back to school—These displays are enhanced by alphabet blocks, owls, blackboards, pens and pencils, notebooks, dictionaries, books and bookcases, and dunce caps.

back wall—The perimeter wall or a freestanding partition wall; this is the highest merchandising area and is best used for coordinates, with top over bottom, or to create an impact for the classification of the merchandise contained within this area. Ideally, the back wall should be broken into coordinated groupings or color patterns to stimulate the customer, please the eye, and alleviate uniformity and boredom.

baffle—Any device used to direct, divert, or disseminate light.

balance—The distribution of elements across a design.

bank of windows—A run of two or more windows separated by a divider, such as a doorway, a pier, or a small shadow box.

banners—Colorful pieces of fabric, plastic, or treated paper—often triangular in shape, and usually with grommets or holes punched on top—used as attention-getting decorative devices outside and inside the retail setting; they may carry the imprint of a name or logo.

bargain square—A grouping of aisle tables used to display sale merchandise; see also **economy square**.

beach chairs—Folding chairs of canvas or slatted wood for use outdoors.

beam—A reinforcing element used to add strength to a wall's construction or to help support the weight of the floors above.

Behance—An online platform to showcase and discover creative work by designers. Behance acts as a hub specifically for designers, enabling clients and others to discover them.

bendable plywood—Also known as Curve-Ply, Flexply, and Wiggle board, bendable plywood is made out of wood veneers with the layers running in one direction; this allows the panel to bend on a curved radius.

bergère—An all-upholstered French period chair, usually designed in the style of Louis XV or Louis XVI.

big-box store—A giant, hangar-like retail space covering an area ranging from 20,000 to more than 100,000 square feet, in which is gathered a vast assortment of merchandise ranging from apparel to grocery, sports equipment, and cars; also known as superstore.

bins—Containers or boxes for holding products or merchandise; they can vary in size, shape, and proportion and can be constructed of cardboard, plastic, metal stampings, or wood.

blind embossing—A method of adding dimension to a surface and creating a raised design without the use of inks or paints; it gives depth to a point-of-purchase (POP) display.

block plan—Prepared by the store planner, together with the executives, this is the first allocation of space on the ground plan and the designation of selling areas on that selling floor. This apportionment is based on merchandising needs, proposed traffic patterns, proximity to related merchandise, and anticipated sales.

body trunk or trunk form—A male form that generally starts at the diaphragm (above the waistline) and continues to just below the knees; shorter forms are cut at midthigh. It is used to show shorts, underwear, swimwear, and so on.

bra form—A headless, armless form that ends just below a defined bustline, with or without shoulders. The forms are usually scaled to wear a size 34B. Junior bra forms are proportioned for a size 32A bust.

brand identity—Refers to the use of brand colors, a brand logo, and other identifiable graphic assets that appeal to the perception of consumers about a brand.

brand image—A consumers impression of a retailer, a brand or a product. It describes how a consumer perceives the brand.

brand names—A manufacturer, designer, or product name that is immediately recognizable and promotional, such as Adidas, Nike, and Dior.

branding with light—The use of a lighting technique to differentiate a store brand. Examples include wall washing the store with color (inside or out), the use of singular spotlights on merchandise, or using a specific style of light fixture.

brass—Second in popularity to chrome, brass finishes can be applied over steel or nickel or even on soft brass itself. This finish requires extra protection and care.

bridal—These displays are promoted by use of symbols such as antique chairs, strewn carnival lights, floral crowns, tulle drapes, and wildflower bouquets.

bronze—A brown and dark finish with a mere metallic glint; it requires special care, special handling, and special lighting on the selling floor.

buildup display—Merchandise presentation in which items sit atop an assortment of cubes or cylinders clustered together, causing the viewer's eye to travel upward.

bust, blouse, or sweater form—An armless, headless form that ends just below the waistline; it has a defined bust and is used to show ladies' blouses and sweaters.

butt-rod fittings—Attachments on the mannequin's buttocks into which the floor rod is inserted so that the mannequin can stand.

buttress—A reinforcing element used to add strength to a wall's construction or to help support the weight of the floors above.

buzzwords—In the creative process, buzzwords reveal information about the personality of the product or brand and how a consumer perceives it.

C

CAD, or computer aided design—Refers to drawings or renderings used to communicate a design that are generated on a computer using programs such as AutoCAD, Vectorworks, or SketchUp.

capacity—Refers to the total number of units (products) that a fixture can hold and the number of the sides the fixture uses to sell merchandise. A high-capacity fixture holds a large quantity of products.

captain's chairs—Chairs with a rounded back resting on vertical spindles that come forward to form the arms.

categories—Categories refer to the group of products or brands that meet a particular consumer need. Towels, shower curtains, bath mats, and soap dispensers all fall into the category of a bath area. Good merchandising requires aligning categories adjacent from one another using logic and consumer behavior as a guide.

category sign—A sign specifying the major classification of the collected merchandise, rather than a specific design, pattern, or price.

ceiling grid—A suspended lattice of metal pipes, wires, or wood used for hanging objects in a window display.

chifforobes—Combination wardrobes-chests of drawers; in display, a chifforobe can be used as a prop or a fixture.

child mannequins—These range from tiny tots to the preteens and teens in a variety of ethnic groups, facial expressions, poses, and makeup styles; depending on the child's size and the target market, the choices are many.

chipboard—Substrate material that comes in panels or sheets made from compressed

wood chips often used to fabricate fixtures when covered with a veneer. It is used raw by brands that prefer an urban unfinished style.

Chippendale chairs—An eighteenth-century style of chair usually finished in mahogany or walnut, with deep, rich-colored upholstery; styles can range from ribbon-back, to Chinese-influenced, to Gothic.

Christmas—Symbols of this holiday are almost endless and include Santa Claus, garlands, Christmas trees, snow ornaments, snowmen, candy canes, reindeer, sleighs, bells, music boxes, Christmas music, and stuffed stockings. For a religious emphasis, a crèche, stained-glass windows, organ pipes, angels, or choirs can be used.

chrome—Currently the most popular finish for fixtures, chrome is used for counters, floors, and walls. It is made by electroplating chromium onto another metal. Stronger and often superior fixtures have a base of steel with an electrolytic deposit of chromium on it.

clamps—A mechanical device or tool that is used to hold objects together.

clearance sale—This type of sale can be promoted by cleanup symbols, such as mops, brooms, pails, crates, plastic bags, and cartons; empty hangers or shelves, or a giant scissors "slashing" prices can also be used. Clearance sales demand dynamics and direction.

closed-back window—The typical display window, with a full back wall, sides, and a large plate glass window facing the pedestrian or street traffic.

closed facade—A type of storefront in which the windows are completely blocked off, painted out, wallpapered over, or wrapped in graphics, and only the entrance to the store is visible.

CNC—(Computer Numerical Control **router**) is a computer-controlled cutting machine for cutting various hard materials, such as wood, composites, aluminum, steel, plastics, and foams by using a digital design generated by a designer.

coat, or suit, form—Traditionally, a headless, legless, and often armless gray

jersey-covered torso made of papier-mâché; the unit is supported by a rod attached to a base.

color—The biggest motivation for shopping. Color is what we see first, what attracts us to an object; it can be used as a device used to draw shoppers to both window and interior displays.

color of an object—The color seen as the result of the object's selective absorption of light rays; for example, a blue object absorbs all the wavelengths of light except blue.

color psychology—The study of the effects of color on people and their moods; important to visual merchandising for helping influence shopping behaviors.

color rendering index (CRI)—A measure of how a light source renders colors of objects compared with how a reference light source renders the same colors.

colored lights—Light bulbs that are tinted on the outside to produce different colors when illuminated, or the use of colored gels in front of regular bulbs to produce the desired color of light. LED controllers allow LED bulbs to change and project color automatically.

columns—Supporting pillars that are an integral part of a store's construction; they can be used to hold merchandise or to show merchandise decoratively.

community retailing—Refers to mixed-use retail space that benefits local businesses and encourages consumers to interact with community. It can include merchandise, furniture, music, art, and books alongside food, friends, and digital media.

comping—Refers to the process of making a prototype, mock-up, or example for review before going into production.

complementary colors—Colors that are opposite one another on the color wheel.

composite board—A material available in panels or sheets that is a mixture of wood fiber, plastic, and a binding agent. These components are mixed and extruded to form a sheet material that is stronger than wood. Composite board may be covered with a veneer, and it is used to fabricate fixturing.

composition—The organization, or grouping, of different parts, or elements, used to achieve a unified whole.

conservation—A brand philosophy, sustainable practices are at the forefront of the consumer's perceptions about brands. Consumers are forming emotional bonds with businesses that align with their beliefs and rewarding them with loyalty.

consumer engagement—Methods, strategies, or activities meant to involve consumers in the physical store to extend their visit time or promote enjoyment by connecting in a unique way. The goal is to create a positive memory so that customers return or to inspire them to use social media to share the experience.

contrast—The perceived difference among adjacent forms, lines, or colors in a composition; placement of these elements so as to intensify their different properties.

cool colors—Receding colors: blue, green, violet, blue-green.

coordination—In display, the mixing and matching of merchandise by color, pattern, and print; or, for the display person, the effort to create a harmony of functioning, for the purpose of creating and implementing the display calendar; it requires knowledge of what is available and where, what is in stock or in the warehouse, and what can be borrowed from neighbors or institutions.

copper—A pink or rusty-gold finish that goes well with natural, light woods, to create an earthy, traditional, provincial, or masculine setting; it requires special care, special handling, and special lighting on the selling floor.

copy—The information carried by a sign using worded information or slogans.

corner window—Faces two corners that are perpendicular to one another; a window with double exposure and double traffic.

correlated color temperature (CCT)—A measure of a lamp's color appearance when lighted. All lamps are given a color temperature based on the color of the light emitted.

costumer—A freestanding fixturing unit used on a floor, ledge, or counter; it has a hanger set onto the top of an adjustable upright, which is set into a weighted base, and usually a skirt bar.

counters—Major areas for merchandise presentation; the place where the merchandise is presented and the sale is concluded.

country, or provincial, chair—A country French, country English, or Early American chair. These chairs are less detailed, simpler, with light-colored, natural woods and textured upholstery in solids, plaids, and small, allover prints.

courtesy sign—A placard crediting the borrowed pieces for a display or presentation; see also **credit sign**.

C-rack—One-half of a round rack, this display unit consists of an arc-shaped base with a similarly arc-shaped hang-rod above it; the two arcs are connected by two adjustable uprights. The C-rack can be used for dresses, coats, suits, and coordinates. See also **half-circle rack** and **semicircular rack**.

creative process—The process for creating design work that begins with a design brief, followed by inspiration, ideation, sketches, models, and prototypes. It culminates with a presentation of material resources and CAD drawings to the client. Implementation and installation of the project follow the creative process.

credit sign—A placard crediting the borrowed pieces for a display or presentation; see also **courtesy sign**.

cross-selling—Mixing product categories to increase sales. Cross-selling strategically positions products together on the same fixture or in a display to create a stronger merchandise story.

cruise and resort—These sales are enhanced by symbols of beautiful environs: blue skies, green grass, blue water, and bright yellow sunshine. Seascapes, beach and picnic scenery, fans and air conditioners, pool and barbecue equipment, and travel posters are good backgrounds

and props for displaying this type of merchandise.

curved line—A soft, voluptuous, snaking or arced line, as opposed to a mechanically drawn straight line. Often suggests femininity.

cut awl—A lightweight power tool that is designed to cut out intricate profiles from boards and fabrics of assorted weights. It comes with a variety of blades and attachments.

cutout figure—A silhouette of wood or heavy board. Clothes are pinned or draped over it for a frontal view of the merchandise. Because the figures are two-dimensional, they provide very little form to the merchandise.

cutout form—A wooden silhouette to which life-size photographs of frontal views of men and women are applied. The arms are sometimes removable. It is sophisticated and trendy; a boutique look rather than a department store approach.

D

deck—A digital document containing several pages that provides all phases of a proposed design initiative. It can originate internally within the company or externally with a contracted design firm working in coordination with the company. Decks are a tool to communicate all pertinent design information to corporate, marketing, merchandising, and visual departments.

deck chairs—Folding chairs, often with a leg rest, traditionally used on a ship's deck.

deep window—Window in which the back is far from the front glass; to reduce depth, the display person may erect a self-standing screen or hang drapery from a ceiling track.

design brief—A written statement describing the design concept and the deliverables for a project or client.

design concept—A creative idea for the design of a project.

design process—The steps in fulfilling a design concept, including ideation, sketching, modeling, rendering, preproduction, and implementation.

Design:Retail **magazine and website**—design:retail is an industry resource for tracking trends, products, and projects that are crafting tomorrow's most innovative retail environments. Store planners, visual merchandisers, retail designers, independent architects, and contract designers working with retail chains, as well as designers, planners, and architects, depend on design:retail for inspiration and information on what is driving retail design into the future. http://www.designretailonline.com/

diagonal line—A line that is angled like the hypotenuse of a right triangle; it suggests movement, action, and a sense of excitement.

die cutting process—The method most often used for adding a dimensional quality to a display; the technique requires a die, a cutting tool designed to suit the material being cut, and is similar to cutting out cookies from rolled dough.

digital billboard—an electronic display screen controlled by a computer designed to deliver motion graphics, images, and messages for the purpose of advertisement.

directives—Planograms or sets of instructions for implementing a display or design project.

director's chairs—Folding chairs of wood and canvas, traditionally used by Hollywood film directors.

display calendar—A schedule of a store's upcoming displays, generally blocked out a year in advance. The schedule should be worked out with merchants and buyers, determined by when they buy new merchandise, seasonal and holiday promotions, and yearly sale events.

display cases—A major area for merchandise presentation; today's most common, basic display case design has a glass or transparent plastic top and at least three sides of glass.

display cubes—Laminate or wood-finished blocks found on the selling floor; cubes can be used to elevate merchandise

presentations, as a display surface for a lay-down of accessories, or for demonstrations.

dominance factor—The emphasis of one unit or object over another in a composition; can be achieved by color, size, or position.

double-rod hanging—Two parallel hang-rods or rails—one over the other—spaced approximately 3 to 3½ inches apart. Often used to show tops on the upper rod and bottoms on the lower rod or rail.

draper—Consists of a gently curved hanger on top of a rod and serves to show a dress, sweater, jacket, and so on; see also **hanger top**.

drawer units—Pieces of furniture with pull-out surfaces, such as a chest or a bureau; in display, these units can be used both as a prop and a fixture, especially with small separates and fashion accessories.

dress form—An armless version of the three-quarter form typically mounted on a movable stand.

dressed leader—Can be either the first face-out hanger on a four-way fixture or the first garment shown on a waterfall off of a wall system. That first hanger can be the visual explanation of how the assorted parts come together and how the prints and solids can be combined to create a variety of looks.

dump tables—A type of aisle table used for displaying sale or special merchandise.

E

Eames—Refers to furnishings made of molded plywood and leather, designed by Charles and Ray Eames for the Herman Miller furniture company. The designs were produced from the early 1940s to the late 1950s and have resurged in popularity for use in residential, commercial, and store design over the past decade.

easel—An adjustable folding frame or tripod; small easels may be used in a display or a store window to hold a price card or message, larger ones, to hold a shirt and tie at an angle.

Easter—Easter is symbolized by cuddly bunnies and chicks, decorated eggs, Easter bonnets, white lilies, daffodils, and tulips. The spiritual side of an Easter display can involve church scenes, stained-glass windows, sunrise services, and pipe organs.

economy square—A grouping of aisle tables used to display sale merchandise; see also **bargain square**.

elevated window—A window in which the floor is higher and thus closer to the eye level of the average viewer; it creates a boutique-like atmosphere and allows the store to show more merchandise, especially separates and fashion accessories; it is good for lay-down presentations and sometimes buildups, for special interest.

elevations—Buildups used to provide interest and to help separate merchandise in mass displays; they can be tables, chairs, and/or other pieces of furniture that raise up a mannequin, a form, a stand, or an arrangement of merchandise or a platform that covers a large portion of a display floor.

elevator-type windows—Windows in which the floor is actually an elevator platform that can be lowered to the basement level, where the display is prepared and set and then raised to the desired level.

embossing—A raised or relief impression that creates a textured surface; it gives depth to a flat point-of-purchase (POP) display.

Empire chair—A chair from the Empire period, characterized by its heavy, masculine appearance; these chairs have a wooden back and an upholstered seat.

enclosed displays—A type of display used to show merchandise in a protected area, usually a fully glassed-in platform; they may be located at the entrance to a department, line an aisle, or be part of a perimeter wall.

enclosed window—A large, closed-back, plate glass window facing pedestrian traffic; has a full back wall and sides.

endcaps—Fixtures attached to either side of a gondola fixture facing out toward the aisle. The endcap emphasizes one particular product or line of products and highlights the brand. The aisle is considered a premium location due to the traffic flow and attention.

end use—The ultimate use for which something is intended; products that will end up being used together or that will appear near each other are often displayed in a way that shows how they fit together.

environmental graphics—Environmental graphics use imagery, graphic design, and color combined with the store's architecture to effectively communicate the essence of the brand, leaving a memorable impression on the shopper.

environmental setting—A merchandise presentation that shows an assortment of related items in a setting depicting how and where they may eventually be used.

EPS—Expanded polystyrene is dense ridged foam available in sheets, panels, or a spray; it is used to create props and custom design elements. It can be carved, painted, or used as an infrastructure material.

étagère—An open, multishelf display fixture; most often used to show china, glass, home furnishings accessories, and small gifts.

European display techniques—Small shop, or boutique-type, display techniques.

EuroShop—The leading and biggest trade show for retail environment and the trend barometer for innovations in the field. Held once every three years in Düsseldorf, Germany, the five-day show last hosted more than 2,500 exhibitors from more than sixty-three countries, who showed their wares to more than 110,000 visitors from more than ninety countries.

exhibit systems—Systems that go from simple ladder constructions to very complex webs and grids, in a variety of materials and styles. Although they were introduced as a fixturing concept, many exhibit systems were brought on the market specifically to serve the exhibit industry.

exhibits—The display and showing of special materials that have been collected and then edited for presentation. The major purpose of an exhibit is to stimulate and create interest for a particular product, idea, or organization. Exhibits are orchestrated for the enjoyment of a special audience or market and may be used to educate, advertise, or propagandize.

experiences—In retail, the integration of activities that go beyond shopping. Some examples are eateries, bars, entertainment, DIY areas, or sensory and digital experiences.

experiential retailing—Refers to creating a memorable customer experience that goes beyond the display of products. An immersive retail environment that invites the customer to experience a total lifestyle within a physical store, it may include digital integration.

extruded uprights—A group of modular systems based on vertical multifaceted and multislotted metal or plastic lengths into which horizontal elements, brackets, panels, or other structural elements are slipped and then secured.

F

face-out hanging—A type of display in which merchandise is hung with the front fully facing the viewer.

fall—Autumn symbols include fruits and vegetables; red and gold fall leaves; asters, mums, and marigolds; and pumpkins, and gourds, and jack-o-lanterns. Baskets, leaves, rakes, and any sort of earthy materials are also good for display in this season.

fantasy setting—A highly imaginative presentation; it can be as detailed or as suggestive as time, budget, and the display person permit.

fascia—A horizontal board or panel that can be used to conceal lights or as a background for merchandise displays.

Father's Day—Familiar symbols are sports equipment, chess pieces, playing cards, and trophies and awards for years of giving; old-fashioned props can bring memories of the "good old days."

fauteuil—A French period-styled armchair.

feature tables—Promotional tables.

fenestration—Window placement; how and where we display depends largely on this and on a building's architecture.

fiddleback—A grain found in wood finishes that has many curves and lines that are very close together. It may consist of swirls, curls, or resemble a flame shape and makes the wood more desirable. For example, birds-eye maple wood has a distinctive pattern that resembles an eye shape.

fins—Projecting panels or other separating elements on a fixture.

fixture capacity—Refers to the amount of products a fixture can hold or successfully merchandise. A capacity fixture is designed to hold bulk merchandise without seeming visually heavy.

fixtures—Merchandisers; units to hold and show product.

flexboard—Also known as tambour; a bendable substrate with a hardboard face that can be formed first and laminated or painted last.

floor fixtures—Units designed to hold and show merchandise out on the floor; the major types of fixtures include round racks, T-stands, and quad racks. Also known as a **freestanding fixture**.

floor plan—A flat representation of the length and width (or depth) of an area or object, as seen from overhead.

floral foam—A form of Styrofoam with open cells used as substrate for dry floral arrangements or custom display elements. Floral foam should be disguised by the arrangement and never be visible to the consumer. It can be cut or shaped with a cutting tool.

fluorescent light—A flat, even light that offers few shadows and provides little depth or textural interest; often a popular choice with installers and retailers because of their low cost and efficiency, fluorescent fixtures are not always the best choice for many categories of merchandise.

flying—A technique for showing merchandise whereby, through the use of wires, pins, and tissue-paper padding, garments seem to be soaring through a display window.

Foamcore—The simplest and most efficient mask or proscenium can be made from this material, which is available in 4-foot by 8-foot panels. It is lightweight and fairly rigid, especially in the thicker sheets. There are also newer, denser, and more rigid styrene-covered boards.

focal point—Any place in the retail setting where emphasis has been placed to attract the shopper.

font—An assortment of type all of one size and style.

foot rod—This 4-inch foot rod, sometimes referred to as a foot spigot, comes attached to the mannequin's baseplate. The mannequin's foot with the opening slides onto the 4-inch foot rod, keeping it standing upright.

form—A three-dimensional representation of a part of the human anatomy, such as the torso, the bust, or the area from shoulder to waist or from hips to ankles.

formals—These displays are about fantasy and dreams; symbols include railings, balustrades, columns, arches, stairways with red velvet runners, velvet-covered ropes, photomurals of famous opera houses or concert halls, gold opera chairs, and a view of a night skyline.

formulas—In visual merchandising, formulas are merchandising methods and techniques that have been proven successful. Examples are repetition, color blocking, or the use of nostalgia, surrealism, or fantasy.

four-way face out—See **quad rack**.

freestanding closets—Portable closets, usually combining shelf space with hang space; in display, a freestanding closet can be used both as a prop and as a fixture. See also **armoire**.

front-to-back display—A display technique in which items are shown from the main aisle to the rear wall of the space; should be used whenever creating a visual merchandising pattern in any area of the store.

full-figured mannequin—The size 14–16 woman, with bigger bust, waist, and hip measurements; this mannequin represents a woman who wears large or plus sizes.

G

Gatorboard—A type of display board with an inner core of dense foam and a rigid exterior made of wood-fiber veneer. This exterior is water resistant and will not easily break or warp. Gatorboard is not easily hand cut and requires an electric hand or table saw for a clean straight cut. It is more expensive than regular foam board but is paintable.

gauge—The thickness of a material.

general, or primary, ambient lighting—The allover level of illumination in an area.

glass facade—A type of storefront in which there are display windows to one or either side of the glass doors that are usually open during business hours; the glass panels of the windows extend from floor to ceiling, and there are usually no raised floors in the windows.

GlobalShop—Currently, the biggest and most inclusive annual trade show for the store designer/visual merchandiser and retailer. The centerpiece of each show is a presentation of new vendor shops especially created for some of the country's best-known brand marketers.

gondola—A long, flat-bottomed merchandiser with straight, upright sides; it is usually designed to hold adjustable shelves and may be combined with cabinets or storage areas below. Gondolas are commonly used in groups on the selling floor and oriented toward aisles or walkways.

graphics—In today's store design and display, generally refers to oversized photographs, blowups, or light-box art, although artwork, sketches, and enlarged prints are also used.

H

half-circle rack—See **C-rack**.

half sheet—A board measuring 14 inches by 22 inches that is used for window displays or to identify merchandise in an interior display.

Halloween—Witches, owls, black crows, ghosts and goblins, skeletons, and horror films are the perfect symbols for Halloween; it is associated with the colors orange and black.

hanger—A device for hanging garments; it can be an alternative to the mannequin. Ideally, a dimensionalized, or padded, hanger should be used to ensure that the garment drapes better.

hanger top—See **draper**.

hang-rods—Rods or rails from which garments are hung. Hangers rest upon and slide along this rod.

hard wigs—One of the two major types of wigs used for mannequins; a hard wig is highly lacquered or plasticized—never to be restyled; the hard wig usually features coarser hair, less subtle colors, and more elaborate and decorative styles and is generally better suited to the semirealistic or highly stylized mannequin.

headless mannequin—This mannequin has a full-size, realistic, or semi-abstract body with arms and legs but no head; it will work in windows in which height is a problem.

Herman Miller—A major American **manufacturer** of **office furniture** and home furnishings. It is one of the first companies to produce modern furniture under the direction of design director **George Nelson**, who is one of the most influential producers of **modernist** furniture. Herman Miller nurtured the work of Charles and Ray Eames and many other notable furniture designers.

HID—High-intensity discharge lamps; these lamps are used for general store lighting; they are smaller than fluorescents and, like incandescents, provide shadows and highlights.

high-gloss finish—A surface that contains a shininess or luster. It often refers to paint that dries to a shiny finish. Laminates and woods can have a clear coat applied to obtain a highly polished surface.

high-traffic area—Locations throughout the store that get very heavy foot traffic: in front of and around escalators or elevators, at entrances or exits, and near major featured spots; displays in these areas should be changed frequently.

highlight—An area with the most intense light; an important aspect of secondary lighting.

hollow tubes with finger fittings—Metal or plastic systems consisting of precut or standard lengths of hollow rods or tubes, round or square, and joiners or connectors that look like fingers.

Homasote—A brand name for a cellulose-based fiber wallboard, which is similar in composition to papier-mâché. It is made from recycled paper that is compressed under high temperature and pressure and is held together with an adhesive. It has many uses including pin-up boards and floors in store windows because it is easy to pin into using a T-pin.

horizontal lines—Long lines parallel with the ground or the floor of a window. They are relaxed lines, restful and peaceful.

hot stamping—A process for applying the product's name or logo, decorative designs, or copy onto dimensional plastic pieces, such as shelves, platforms, or back panels.

humor—In display, an attention-getting device. The use of the comical and the amusing can be attractive to shoppers.

I

ice cream parlor chairs—Chairs of heavy wire, with a round, wooden seat.

implementation—In the design process, implementation or installation is the completion phase of a project. It is the final stage where all design elements are installed and secured and any last-minute solutions are worked out.

incandescent light—These lights are used for warmth, emphasis, and highlighting; these lights are more expensive to install and use, and they give off more heat.

injection molding techniques—Processes for molding of three-dimensional pieces for point-of-purchase (POP), requiring heat plus pressure.

injection molding tool—An aluminum, or sometimes steel, tool used for molding of three-dimensional pieces for point-of-purchase (POP). The typical mold is made

in two parts: the cavity side, which is the face of the desired product, and the ejector side, which is the back.

inspiration storyboard—Also known as a mood board, the inspiration storyboard is either a digital or handmade board that conveys the design concept. It may consist of imagery, graphics, and material samples. It illustrates the designer's style and approach for the client.

installation—The act of setting up a display and arranging the props and dressing the mannequins or of placing the fixtures and arranging the merchandise in a store.

institutional display—Promotes an idea rather than an item or product; for example, a large Christmas display or a promotional window for a charity or cultural institution helps foster a positive image for a store.

institutional sign—A sign listing the services provided by the store: its hours, refund and exchange policies, delivery charges, alteration setup, and so on.

intensity—The purity and strength of a color.

interactive fixture—A merchandising unit that may include an electronic element, a keyboard and a computer screen that the shopper can operate to get product information.

interactivity—Refers to a digital device, digital media, or digital experience that promotes customer engagement in a retail setting. Interactivity can also be used to describe other social activities that influence the brand experience.

intermediate colors—The colors that result from mixing a primary color with a secondary color, in varying degrees.

island display—A featured display space viewable from all sides.

island, or lobby, window—A window that has glass on all four sides, allowing the merchandise presentation to be viewed from any angle and any direction.

isometric perspective—A type of mechanical, scale drawing that gives all the measurements, thereby providing a more natural, three-dimensional representation of an object or area.

iterations—Describes additional versions of a project, display, or store design. It can refer to tweaks or revisions of a design plan.

J

jewelry pads—A thick Upson board shaped panel covered in velvet or the customer's own material used to display jewelry.

jigsaw—A handheld power tool that is excellent for cutting curves, scrolls, and irregular patterns. It is possible to adapt this tool to make both inside and outside cuts.

junior mannequin—A size 5; the figure averages about 5 feet, 7 inches, to 5 feet, 9 inches in height and is a bit shorter in the waist than the missy mannequin; many juniors are positioned and made up as young and active figures.

K

kiosk—A self-standing booth or structure on the selling floor that may accommodate a salesperson as well as merchandise; it can be used as a mini-boutique, an outpost, or an enclosed information desk.

knock-down (KD)—A fixture or display designed to be shipped unassembled in parts. The KD design reduces the cost of shipping but requires assembly on site.

L

laminate—A decorative plastic skin or overlay for a surface that is glued.

lamination—A process whereby two or more materials are joined together into a single piece, using glue or cement. In display, it refers to the bonding of a printed sheet of paper or a decorative finishing paper onto a sturdy, undesigned cardboard; the supporting board provides weight, strength, substance, and body, whereas the printed paper on top contains the graphics or message.

landing area—An area at the entrance of the store specifically designed to slow down shoppers, occasionally targeting them with promotional merchandise. Big box stores will position food services and value-based offering to interrupt the pace, whereas department and specialty stores entertain consumers with large displays.

large-scale imagery—A photo enlargement often appearing as either a framed or an unframed background panel or in a light box illuminated from behind. In lifestyle displays, sometimes the mannequins or forms in the foreground are dressed in exactly the same outfit reproduced in the large-scale image; the photo may also show some alternative or coordinating items.

lay-down techniques—The folding, pleating, and placement of garment next to garment and accessories next to the featured garments. Lay-down requires all the basics of good composition.

layering—The superimposition of different shapes, one on top of the other; gives depth to a point-of-purchase (POP) display.

lead time—Advance planning time.

leaf—Leaf is a term used to describe a finish of a surface or object. It is derived from ancient gold leafing process. Gold leaf refers to hammered sheets of metal utilized in the traditional process of gilding; today's gilding is a metal alloy and is available in a wide selection of metallic colors such as silver, gold, copper, platinum, bronze, and brass. Leaf finishes are typically bright and polished; antique refers to aging the surface to appear distressed, and a patina suggests an oxidation process similar to the Statue of Liberty.

ledges—Larger and more imposing than a counter fixture; they require a space at least 5 feet high.

LED—Light-emitting diodes; solid-state devices that, unlike incandescents, do not require heating of a filament to create light.

lifestyle graphic—A graphic, such as a photographic background panel, used to convey a particular lifestyle; a selling tool.

lifestyle presentation—The bringing together of assorted materials into a single theme that usually fits a particular lifestyle; necessary for the presentation of home

fashions. It may be a realistic setting or even an abstract one, in which objects relating to the lifestyle are intermingled with shapes and forms.

lifestyle situation—A type of scenario that humanizes merchandise by showing it in relation to the eventual user; it is important for the presentation of hard goods.

light—In display, light leads shoppers into and through the store, directing them to featured presentations, with stops along the way for highlighted focal points and displays; it can separate one area from another, one boutique or vendor's shop from another.

lighting—A device used to draw shoppers to both window and interior displays.

line—Valuable attention-getting devices in window and interior displays. Vertical, horizontal, curved, and diagonal lines can be used in different ways to arrest the attention of the passerby to the display. When brought together effectively, with composition, lines lead the eye to the entire display as well as to each of its parts.

line-of-goods display—The showing and display of only one type of merchandise (e.g., all blouses or all pots and pans), although they may be in a variety of designs or colors.

LinkedIn—A professional networking website. It is an excellent tool for industry news, job searches, and recruitment. It enables the user to connect with colleagues and clients professionally using a profile image, resume, skill set, and endorsements.

live action—A demonstration by a live performer at an exhibit; it must be carefully planned, as this can quickly draw an audience but just as quickly lose one.

L-joints—Two-pronged joints used to form a right angle, or an L.

logo—A trademark, emblem, or insignia that represents the individual manufacturer, vendor, product, and so forth. It may be a decorative grouping of letters that are part of the name of the company or product or an ideograph or stylized symbol or character that represents the company or item—for example, the Pillsbury Doughboy.

Louis XV chair—A chair from the Rococo period, characterized by curving lines and ornate decoration.

Louis XVI chair—A chair from the Neoclassical period, characterized by an oval or rectangular seat back and straight, fluted legs.

luan—A thin, bendable wooden sheet with a grain that is used as a substrate under flooring or tile. In display it is used to achieve a curved structure. Luan is manufactured in ¼-inch and ⅛-inch thicknesses, making it a good solution for creating curved structures.

M

male mannequin—The male mannequin is about 6 feet tall and wears a size 39 or 40 jacket, size 32 trousers, and a size 9 to 10 shoe; today, active-sports figures are appearing on the market that have better muscular definition than previous models.

mannequin—A representation of the human form, used especially for displaying clothes.

marquees—Permanent awnings extending out over the entrance to a store; an integral part of the building facade.

masking—The partial concealment of a window presentation's view; can be used to create shadow boxes.

materials—Refers to fabrics, foamcore, dry florals, panels, metal, tile, and anything used as an ingredient in a design or display.

matte—Matte surfaces are dull and muted with little reflective quality. Matte refers to paint or laminate finish with a nonglossy flat appearance.

MDF Ultralight—Medium density fiberboard Ultralight is a paintable material available in sheets or panels; it is lighter in weight than regular MDF. Air is pumped into the material during production, making it 30% lighter. MDF is used to manufacture fixtures and surfaces in store interiors.

medium density fiberboard (MDF)—Medium density fiberboard is a paintable composite material available in sheets or panels. MDF is used to manufacture fixtures and surfaces in store interiors.

merchandising—The creative arrangement of merchandise in a retail setting.

merchandising standards—The principles and techniques used in the arrangement of merchandise set by a brand, store management, or visual merchandiser.

metrics—The measurement of retail performance in sales, stock levels, and activity.

mid-century chair—A chair characterized by the style of mid-century modern design period (early 1950s). Clean lines, angular composition, and bentwood are a few elements that define the era's modernity.

mind map—A mind map is a design method used to formulate ideas by using written words to create a diagram or map. It is a brainstorming process that is helpful for initiating ideas.

mirror—A reflecting surface, usually of glass and often set in a frame; mirrors can add depth, width, and height to a display. A weighted mirror with an adjustable or tilt-table frame is a must in cosmetic and jewelry areas.

misses, or missy size, mannequin—Wears a size 4 to 8, depending upon the cut and the mannequin's proportions; can stand anywhere from 5 feet, 8 inches tall, to almost 6 feet tall.

mixing and matching—Assembling coordinates in different ways.

mock shop—a physical space in a corporate headquarters designed to stage displays and merchandise presentations. The set up is documented to generate a planogram that can be implemented in a group of stores. Additionally, there is mock shop software that allows the visual merchandiser to do this virtually on a computer.

mocking up—Refers to the process of making a model or prototype of a design to assess its value. The mockup may be in true scale, half scale, or smaller and may be constructed of foamcore or another appropriate material. Mocking up allows the designer to see the design dimensionally and make the necessary changes in the early stages of design.

model—A replica of an original design made to evaluate the design's success. It can be produced by hand in an inexpensive material such as foamcore or 3D printed in plastic. Sometimes a prototype model is manufactured in the original materials to test on a selling floor.

modular fixtures—Fixtures composed of modular elements.

modules—Series of standardized units in specific shapes or sizes used together. In store planning, the modular concept means the pieces will be adaptable, movable, and rearrangable—and also cheaper to produce.

molded polymer—A resin-based material that is poured into a mold to produce a custom design element or prop. Molded polymer has a long life span, can be used outdoors, and is paintable.

mood board—A design tool used to communicate a design concept through a collage of images, text and sample materials. It may be digital or dimensional.

monochromatic color scheme—The development of the full range of a single color in a design.

Mother's Day—An annual celebration honoring mothers and motherhood each May. A soft feminine color palette and symbols such as lace, ribbons, florals, and fragrances are traditionally used to define the holiday celebration in stores.

motion, or movement—In display, an attention-getting device that employs the use of a motor, a fan, or another mechanical device.

MR16 and MR11—Miniature, low-voltage tungsten–halogen lamps that emit sharp, bright light and produce a color balance close to sunlight; two of the most popular accent/focal lamps.

mullion—A metal divider between a run of several plate-glass windows that facilitates the replacement of glass when necessary.

museum cases—Display cases that can, on occasion, serve as a counter or demonstration area; they consist of a column or pedestal (usually rectangular) with a five-sided glass case on top. They are often taller than a counter, and the merchandise, precious and special, is raised up closer to the viewer's eye level.

N

natural—From nature; a concept associated with food display, especially of fresh fruits and vegetables. Warm yellow light, with its association to sunlight, helps put across this idea.

natural materials—Natural materials, such as twigs and branches, or anything that comes from nature.

neutral colors—Colors that can be either warm or cool; warm neutrals: off-white through all shades of beige to the deepest brown; cool neutrals: black, white, all the shades of gray.

NFP, or not-for-profit—An organization that does not earn a profit by its owners; instead it funds a worthy cause or mission by enlisting volunteers, members, and donors to assist in fundraising activities.

nickel-plated—A surface similar in appearance to chrome plated, but not as durable or efficient. Nickel-plating is not frequently used for better fixtures; this finish may have a yellowish cast when compared with the cool, silvery-blue color of chrome.

nostalgia—A longing for the past or something contained therein; evoking this feeling in shoppers, through use of elements of the time gone by, can be a valuable selling tool.

National Retail Federation (NRF)—The National Retail Federation is the world's largest retail trade association. Its membership includes department stores, specialty, discount, catalog, Internet, and independent retailers, chain restaurants, and grocery stores. Members also include businesses that provide goods, and services to retailers such as vendors and technology providers. The NRF holds an annual conference/convention in New York each January.

O

OLED—(organic light-emitting diode) Bendable light panels made from organic materials popular for displays due the soft natural light quality, color, low heat and longevity.

omnichannel—describes the numerous methods a consumer can shop, by using a digital device, website, catalog or visiting a store.

one-item display—The showing and advancement of a single garment or any single item.

one-off—A singular display where the inspiration is derived from the merchandise without a design brief. With the one-off, the physical attributes of the merchandise such as color, texture, or style are the key focus of the design.

open-back window—A window that has no back wall, thereby offering a direct view into the selling area beyond.

open facade—Type of storefront in which, unless there is a change of flooring material, there is no separation between the shopper on the mall aisle and the store, except the threshold.

outdoor exhibit—A display taking place in a garden, a park, a parking lot, and so on. Depending on the material to be shown, this can be the most challenging type of exhibit, owing to the effects of the elements.

outdoor lighting—Display in which lights are draped, swagged, or wired on building canopies and facades; it is effective for holidays and store events but uses a lot of energy.

outpost—A freestanding, self-contained selling unit that contains a stock of a given type of merchandise, along with display and signing relevant to that merchandise. The outpost features merchandise not ordinarily sold in the department in which it is set up.

outriggers—Horizontal members, attached to a wall or column, that serve to support and keep a horizontal or vertical element away from the bearing surface.

P

painted finishes—These include baked enamel, lacquered, and epoxy paint finishes. They are also becoming increasingly popular in hardware, gourmet, and kitchen supply areas. For many years, painted fixtures were white, black, or metallic gold, but today there is no limit to the range of colors available.

Palight—Palight is a brand name for 4' × 8' flat PVC plastic panels or sheets that can run through a flatbed printer. Palight is an excellent material for signage, thermoformed props, and many other display applications.

pants, or slacks, form—A male or female form that goes from the waistline down to, and including, the feet. Men's forms will usually wear size 30 trousers with a 32-inch inseam. Female pants forms are designed to wear a size 8. If the legs are crossed, one leg will be removable to facilitate dressing the form. It is often provided with a foot spike that will hold the form in a standing position.

panty form—A waist-to-knees form for showing panties, girdles, or bikini bottoms. These forms are about 2 feet tall and are usually used for counter and ledge displays.

paper sculpture—A technique for creating full-round, or bas-relief, decorative designs and objects by means of scoring, folding, cutting, curling, and applying papers of assorted colors, textures, and weights, such as the Japanese art form of origami; it gives depth to point-of-purchase (POP) displays.

papier-mâché—A technique for producing three-dimensional objects, such as mannequins, by means of molding pulped paper; it gives depth to point-of-purchase (POP) displays.

Parabolic Aluminized Reflector (PAR) bulbs—High-voltage incandescent lights, usually used as secondary lighting; also known as **spotlights**.

partial, or dwarf, wall—A partition or wall that does not go up to the ceiling.

particleboard—A composite board made of wood particles and a bonding agent used to manufacture furniture and fixtures. It can also be used as a substrate. Stores like Urban Outfitters use it as a surface material in store design.

pastels—Soft, delicate shades of color.

patina—A finish that suggests age or the oxidation process on the surface of wood or metal caused by weather, wear, or time. The Statue of Liberty has an oxidized patina surface known as **verdigris.**

patriotic—Symbols for holidays that promote patriotism. In the United States these are flags (Presidents' Day, the Fourth of July, and Election Day); eagles; fireworks; the White House; the Statue of Liberty; George Washington and Abraham Lincoln; a map of the United States or a reproduction of the Declaration of Independence or the Constitution; and the colors red, white, and blue.

Path To Purchase Institute—Formerly known as the In Store Marketing Institute, this membership-based organization is dedicated to satisfying the needs of the in-store marketing professionals and point-of-purchase field in general, and provides them with a constant update of what is happening in the retail field. The Institute publishes the *Shopper Marketing Magazine* and sponsors bi-yearly leadership events—League of Leaders and Forum of Merchandising Executives. The Shopper Marketing Summit is held annually in New York along with the Effie Awards.

PAVE (Planning and Visual Education Partnership)—A trade organization whose objective is to encourage students to study retail design and planning and visual merchandising. Each year, PAVE sponsors a design competition for students in art schools and colleges. PAVE also seeks to encourage retail management, store planners, visual presenters, architects, and manufacturers to interact with and support design students through seminars, workshops, and PAVE's annual fund-raising gala.

pedestals—Also known as risers, pedestals are wood, plastic, or cardboard bases in assorted sizes used to elevate merchandise presentations.

people-centered—Refers to placemaking and the design of spaces that support activities, people, and the community.

perimeter lighting—A method for lighting stores using wall washers on the perimeter walls to make the space look larger and more appealing to the shopper.

permanent exhibit—The presentation of an item or items for an unlimited time period; a concept that should be abolished from the world of merchandise display and visual presentation, an area in which nothing should ever be considered unchanging and immutable.

permanent unit—A store fixture used when the product is not likely to change in design or in packaging very rapidly; it usually displays more costly items, such as watches, fountain pens, samples of wood flooring, tires, or vacuum cleaners. The displayer/fixture is more costly to produce but is made to stand up to wear and tear for a year or so. Included in this category are neon signs and acrylic etched signs, electrified clocks, and illuminated menu boards.

petite mannequin—This figure wears a size 4 or 6 and is smaller in all proportions.

photomurals—Long, enlarged photographs; they can serve as a bridge between groups of ideas, explain the passage of time or a change of locale, or supply a historical setting.

pier—A wide area of masonry that acts as a physical divider.

pinup techniques—Make use of a panel, a wall, or some other vertical surface onto which a garment can be pinned, shaped, and dimensionalized. Pads, tissue, and straight pins are used to fill out the garment where form is needed. Accessories are pinned on at appropriate locations, and shoes are placed in front of the "dressed" panel.

pipe rack—A utilitarian fixture with wheels, made of round tubing and resembling an inverted U; it may have a flat wooden base, to which the wheels are attached.

placemaking—A people-centered approach to designing physical space that promotes gathering and interaction.

planogram—A diagram containing images and information indicating the placement of fixtures, products, and mannequins within a retail space or window display. The planogram is a tool to communicate merchandising standards between stores.

planning—For a display person, mapping out, in advance, when a particular display will be installed, where it will be installed, and what will be shown and promoted; it is necessary for creating of the display calendar.

planters—Containers holding ornamental plants or flowers; planters can contribute to a store's general ambiance, add depth to a window presentation, or become part of a display scheme through changes in the varieties and colors of plants.

plants—Plants can create a greenbelt that separates a large window into smaller, separated areas. Foliage can also create a semi-barrier in an open-back window.

platforms—Elevations; risers; raised stages or walkways.

plywood—A building material made of layers, or sheets or "plies" of wood glued together. The thickness and type of wood used on the outer surface will determine the actual cost per sheet. Plywood is commonly available in a variety of surfaces such as birch, pine, and poplar. Plywood comes in many "grades" from rough to fine and standardized thicknesses of ¼, ⅜, ½, and ¾ inch.

point of purchase (POP)—Traditionally, signage for attracting customers to a store; today, an entire industry, encompassing display, fixturing, store design, and advertising.

polished chrome—A bright, shiny finish sometimes applied to fixtures made of brass or nickel; also known as **mirror chrome**.

polystyrene—A high-density foam used in the production of display elements.

pop-up shop—A retail space designed to last for a limited amount of time to gain public attention and activate products and brands. Online retailers use pop-ups as a strategy to gain buzz and social media attention.

portfolio—A collection of an individual's best and most creative work, including, for the visual merchandising and display professional, photographs of previous displays, sample sketches, copy design, floor plans, and fixture designs. When on the job, smart individuals will continue to build their portfolio in preparation for new job opportunities or possible promotions within the company. For freelance visual merchandisers, a quality portfolio is essential.

prefabrication—A preparation stage in the design process where components are completed in sections for the purpose of staging.

prep—To prepare and assemble design components before the installation of a display.

preproduction—Preliminary work on the production of a display installation.

presentation—A formal pitch of a design concept consisting of inspiration boards, sketches, CAD renderings, and samples to the client or store management team.

preteen, or "tween," mannequin—Designed to wear the young girl's dress, sizes 8 to 10, which is proportioned for the 10- to 12-year-old; the figure is relatively flat, uncurved, and childlike.

price point—The suggested retail price of a product; often the determining factor when making a purchase. Price points can also refer to the level of a product on a demand curve. A price point is the price shown on a hangtag, label or sign.

primary colors—The three basic pigment colors from which all other colors can be mixed: red, yellow, and blue.

primary colors of light—The three colors of light that that can be mixed to create new and different color effects: red, green, blue.

primary lighting—The allover level of illumination in an area; also known as **general lighting**.

priority—Areas of the selling floor that are premium. An area within a display that is elevated or most evident to the consumer's viewing point is also considered a priority zone.

procurement—Refers to the sourcing or purchasing of items needed to complete a project or job.

promotional display—Advances or emphasizes a particular concept, trend, or item; it can be a one-item, line-of-goods, related merchandise, or variety display.

promotional, or temporary, unit—The store fixture with the shortest life expectancy, designed to serve on the counter, on the floor, or on the shelf for a few weeks to a month or two. Often produced of cardboard, corrugated materials, or lightweight vacuum forming, it is usually a timely or seasonal piece that ties in with other media, such as ads or TV commercials.

proportion—The relationship between the size, scale, or "weight," of elements and between each element and the composition as a whole.

props—Articles used in a display or presentation; they can be bought, rented, borrowed, or improvised from whatever is on hand.

proscenia (proscenium, singular)—From the Greek, "before the scenery," the structural arch, usually ornate, often seen in a theater surrounding the curtain; in window display, proscenia consist of a top valance, which masks the lighting across the top of the window, and side valances, which separate one window or display grouping from the next and also hide any side-lighting devices.

prototype—A handmade model or sample of a design element made to evaluate its success before production. A rapid prototype is produced through the process of 3D printing.

PVC—Polyvinyl chloride is an extremely durable, rigid form of plastic available in lightweight plastic sheets that can be custom dyed. Known by the brand name Sintra, PVC is easily thermoformed to create display elements and fixtures.

Q

quad rack, or four-way face-out—A four-armed fixture with each arm extending out from a central core; usually, each arm is turned out at a right angle from the center or upright, like a pinwheel. Because it is designed with four separate views, the quad-rack unit is ideal for showing separates or coordinate fashions.

quick cuff—Excess fabric from a trouser leg that is turned back inside, simulating a finished pants leg.

R

radiating—A design method in which elements spread from a central point.

raised floor—An elevation that dramatizes an object by forcing the viewer to look up at it.

raked floor—A floor in which the back is several inches higher than the front, creating a ramp effect. Allows small objects, such as shoes, handbags, and cosmetics, to be more easily seen when placed in the back.

rapid prototype—A quick machine process used to create a replica of a CAD design that utilizes a 3D printing process.

realistic mannequin—A mannequin designed and styled to represent the human figure as it really is; today's realistic mannequins are designed to look like ordinary, everyday people.

realistic setting—The depiction or a room, area, or otherwise recognizable locale, reinterpreted in the allotted display area, either in the windows or inside the store; best controlled and most effective in a fully enclosed display window; see also **vignette setting**.

reflector bulb—A lower-wattage alternative to the PAR bulb; made of clear glass, with a metallic reflector surface behind the bulb.

rehabilitation—The remodeling, redecorating, and refixturing of an existing structure, often by the store planner; a "rehab" will retain the architectural details and flavor of the old structure, but with a fresh spin.

related merchandise display—The showing of separates, accessories, or other items that go together because they are meant to be used together, because they are the same color, or because they share an idea or theme.

rendering—The process of creating a 3D drawing or image using CAD (computer-aided design) to communicate a design concept.

repetition—In design, reiteration of color, line, shape, or form; results in dominance of an idea or motif.

resins—Commonly used for casting forms using a poured or rotational molding process. A strong material, resin is a liquid plastic that cures into a polymer and is used to make reproductions, mannequins, props, and sets.

résumé—The résumé is "you on paper." It acquaints the reader with your goals, qualifications, education, and experiences. For positions in visual merchandising or related areas, the résumé might be written in a very standard manner or in an individualized, more imaginative style.

retail calendar—A calendar of key dates and events that assists retailers in the planning of seasons, promotions, sales, and merchandising strategies.

Retail Design Institute (RDI)—Formerly the Institute of Store Planners; professional membership is open to persons 25 years of age or older who have been working a minimum of eight years as full-time store planners. RDI has an active education program, sponsoring scholarships for students in store planning programs in schools across the country. There are also newsletters and other publications and many regional and joint meetings that are often combined with presentations by trade members. There are several local chapters that plan special programs for their groups.

retrofits—In lighting, a way to update an older light fixtures for the purpose of saving energy and efficiency.

return on investment—Also known as ROI; a term used in retail as an indicator to calculate the performance of retail space based on the square footage.

revisions—Changes, iterations, or a new version of a design proposed following a presentation.

rhythm—In a design, the self-contained movement from element to element, background to foreground, and side to side.

risers—Devices used to elevate merchandise in a window, showcase or on a table to achieve variation in height. Risers are available in many sizes and materials to suit accessory displays; they may be a simple block wood, a saddle, or a U-bend of acrylic.

ROI—An acronym for return on investment, commonly used to reference profits. ROI is an indicator retailers use to calculate the performance of retail space.

rollout—Introduction to the public; or, the reproduction of a design concept, like a store design after the prototype has been tested. Display and merchandising configurations that are preplanned are often referred to as a rollout.

round rack—A display unit usually consisting of a circular hang-rod, 3 feet in diameter, raised anywhere from 45 inches to more than 6 feet off the ground; it is set on an adjustable upright that is securely attached to a wide, weighted base, which is stable and holds the floor, even when fully weighted down with merchandise.

rubber mâché—A technique for producing a three-dimensional object by pouring a rubber, latex-like compound into a specially made hollow mold and allowing it to dry or force drying it in an oven; it gives depth to point-of-purchase (POP) displays; the resulting piece can then be painted, gilded, textured, and made to resemble natural materials such as wood or stone.

run—Also known as production run; refers to a quantity of work turned out, such as a promotion being produced

run-on window—A long window of 20 more feet; often, the designer will add dividers inside this window to separate it, creating individual areas for display.

S

Saarinen womb chair—A chair designed by Eero Saarinen produced by Knoll Furniture in 1948 during the mid-century modern period that continues to inspires fixture and retail design today.

scale (in mechanical drawing)—A proportional representation, for example, 1 inch = 1 foot.

scale—In display, scale can be adjusted along with proportion to create abnormal

size relationships that serve as an attention-getting device.

secondary colors—The colors that result from mixing equal parts of two primary colors: orange, green, violet.

secondary colors of light—The colors of light that result from mixing the three primary colors of light: magenta, cyan, and amber.

secondary, or accent, lighting—Feature or display lighting that highlights products. Accent or focal lighting not only highlights the product or the group of merchandise but also makes it stand out from its surroundings.

selling sign—A promotional sign; it should be clear, concise, and comprehensive.

semi-abstract mannequin—Even more stylized and decorative than the semi-realistic mannequin, with features that may be painted on or merely suggested; this type of mannequin is doll-like and decorative and more popular-priced than elegant in appeal.

semicircular rack—See **C-rack**.

semipermanent unit—A store fixture that is usually expected to be in use for about six months to a year, and though it is constructed to be rigid and tough, the materials may not be as fine as those used in a permanent fixture/displayer.

semi-realistic mannequins—Proportioned and sculpted like a realistic mannequin, with makeup that is neither natural nor realistic, but more decorative or stylized; they may also possess a completely realistic face with sculpted features but without any makeup at all.

semi-realistic, or vignette, setting—Presents the essence, the heart of a setting, and leaves the rest to the viewer's imagination; it is useful when space and budget do not allow for a more realistic setting.

shade—A full-value color to which black has been added, creating a deeper, rich, more full-bodied version of the original.

shadow—An area of partial darkness; an important aspect of secondary lighting.

shadow box—A small, elevated window used for the presentation of special merchandise or accessories.

shell form—A half-round, lightweight partial torso form similar to a bra, blouse, or sweater form. The front is fully sculpted, but the back is scooped out.

shirt board—A flat board onto which a shirt can be folded, with only the shirt-front and perhaps a folded-over sleeve cuff visible.

shirt form—The male version of the bust form.

shock—In display, something jarring can be an attention-getting device.

SHOP! Association—This global non-profit trade association is dedicated to enhancing retail environments and experiences. It represents more than 2,000 member companies worldwide and provides value to the global retail marketplace through their leadership in research, design, building, marketing and evaluation. SHOP! is the new name for ARE and the POPAI Association. Formerly known the National Association of Store Fixture Manufacturers, the organization has served the industry since 1956. SHOP! SHOP! publishes and distributes a yearly buyers' guide, SHOP! *Retail Environments* magazine, and a *Members Connect* publication to its membership.

shop-in-shop—A small, specialized shop within a larger store such as a major department store, targeted at a specific market and age group. The shop-in-shop may represent a single brand.

shoulder-out hanging—A type of display in which merchandise is hung with only one side showing, from shoulder to bottom.

showcase—A unit that combines the storage capacities of a cabinet, the selling surface of a table, and the display potentials of a shadow box; it may be made entirely of glass or wood or combined with metal.

side walls—Walls that forms the side of a display window.

sight line—Refers to the line of sight or the unobstructed area of the store above the fixtures in a shop or department. In order for shoppers to navigate intuitively, the eye must be able to see the directional signage leading to the desired area of the store.

signs—Graphics on the outside of a store's building displaying the store name; they set the look and image of the store, through their lettering, materials, color, size and scale; or, any brief informative messages that are presented in printed form within the store.

signage—A system of signs; in display, text should be simple, and excessive signage is to be avoided.

single-rod hanging—A single rod or rail upon which dresses or coats or suits are hung. The rod is attached to a wall or partition, usually 5½ to 6 feet from the ground. In the case of formal wear, the rod may be set higher.

size—One of a series of graduated measures for manufactured items; often the determining factor when making a purchase.

sketch model—A quick foamcore model that allows the designer to evaluate the design. The sketch model may or may not be executed in the exact size; it may be relative to scale to show the placement of objects and the overall concept.

sketches—Freehand drawings, a phase in the ideation process. Sketches enable the designer to communicate his or her ideas to the client quickly to begin a discussion about a design.

Skilsaw—A portable, lightweight circular saw used for ripping and crosscutting.

SKUs or stock keeping units—Identification code for a store or product, often portrayed as a machine-readable bar code that helps track the item for inventory.

slotted joiners—Cubes or spheres that are precision slotted or drilled with holes. Some are designed to accommodate sheets of glass, plastic, or composition board to form shelves, bins, or rectangular structures. Others work with rods and tubes to make skeletal frames.

slotted uprights—Simple, adaptable building device for fixturing and store planning; usually steel or aluminum squared tubes that are precision slotted on one, two, or four faces.

smart lighting—Energy efficient lighting combined with technology to adjust color, quality, or push digital messaging at retail.

Smooth-On—A recognized supplier in the industry that sells products online and provides comprehensive tutorials on the casting process (https://www.smooth-on.com).

soft-sculpted figure—A life-size doll covered in black, dark brown, or off-white jersey-like fabric, with little or no facial detail. The skeleton of this abstract figure is a bendable wire armature that is embedded in soft, spongy foam filler.

soft wigs—One of the two major types of wigs used for mannequins; soft wigs emulate the softness and texture of natural hair and usually can be combed.

sonic seal—A machine that electronically fuses and melds together finished pieces created from injection molding, as for the top, bottom, and sides of a box.

Sonotube—An inexpensive, rigid cardboard tube used in construction that is available in various diameters. It is commonly used for platforms and displays when a curved form is desired.

sourcing—The process of finding the necessary materials or props, fixtures, or design elements to create a display or store design.

spiral costumer—A corkscrewing waterfall extended out from a central upright or post. The merchandise is visible from all around, but the presentation is essentially shoulders out, with an occasional glimpse of the front of some of the merchandise.

spring—Spring is best represented by these symbols: early-blooming flowers, baby animals, garden equipment, vegetable patches, flower pots, latticework, butterflies, a flying kite, spring music, or a forest fantasy.

S-rack—Made by placing two C-racks end to opposing end, the S-rack has a greater potential for variety of merchandise presentation.

staging—Preparing design elements in advance to ensure an efficient installation; to set up in advance.

stand—A very widely used, basic fixture that comes with an assortment of tops that may be slipped interchangeably into an adjustable rod set on a weighted base; the base sits securely on the floor, and the rod

may be adjusted to the desired height for presenting the merchandise.

steamer trunk—An antique or replica of a large suitcase or trunk used as a fixture to showcase merchandise.

stock—The standard sizes to which boards or cards are cut down to create signage; or, the material (paper or cardboard) to be imprinted.

stock holders—"Bread-and-butter" fixtures, the workhorses that actually hold the selling stock. They may display, but primarily they are stockers. Two examples are the quad rack and the round rack.

stocking, or leg, form—A form in the shape of a leg, used for merchandising hosiery. It has a hollow top into which the waistband of the hose can be inserted. The form is available in assorted lengths, depending on the merchandise to be displayed, such as thigh-high, knee-high, or calf-high.

store image—How the store is perceived by shoppers. The image is determined by the store's look—the architecture, design, displays, color, lighting, and so on.

store planners—Today's store planners are designers, architects, space "surgeons," lighting experts, colorists, and visual merchandisers. Most of these individuals we now call store planners have a background in architecture or interior design, but more and more visual merchandisers are bringing their special talents into the field.

store promotion—A store event, such as a sale or holiday.

store's lighting plan—Includes the general, overall illumination of the retail space and the accents; it can also include atmospheric touches, like chandelier, wall, or column sconces or wall and ceiling washers.

straight front—A type of storefront in which the windows run parallel to the street; the entrance may be between a pair or a run of windows or to one side of a single window.

striking—A method used to stand a mannequin without a rod or foot flange using wires that tension to the floor. This method is reserved for a closed back window to ensure customer safety.

struck mannequin—A mannequin that is held in a standing position by means of invisible wires attached to the figure, then is pulled taut and nailed into the floor of the display.

styrene—A thermoplastic material used to manufacture small fixtures. Styrene is also used for prototyping and to create curved structures in window displays.

Styrofoam—Also known as floral foam; a green or white craft material available in sheets, blocks, and other shapes. It is easily cut, glued, and sculpted into shapes with a knife or cutting tool as a foundation for dry floral arrangements or as a substrate to glue objects onto.

substrate—Any material used beneath another for support. Substrate board is typically made of composite materials or particles of wood glued together; it is less expensive than wood.

surprise—In display, the unexpected, whether pleasant and amusing or a bit of fantasy, can be an attention-getting device.

Surrealism—An artistic and cultural movement that employed the use of abstract ideas, art and writing; it is favored by visual designers for it's use of mannequin parts, and playful iconography.

symmetrical, or formal, balance—The distribution of design elements in which one side is the mirror image of the other.

T

tables—In display, tables can be used as both a prop and a fixture. These everyday pieces of furniture can create a sense of time and can show off or hold merchandise in an interesting, personal, and intimate manner. Tables can also be used as elevations in window displays.

tall window—A window higher than the usual 9- or 10-foot window; in order to reduce the size of the window, the display person may add a valance or top proscenium; he or she may also take advantage of the height by placing mannequins on pedestals, piers, or columns or by making them "fly."

tambour—A wood or composite board with precision-machined slots that run across the length or width of the panel, providing a smooth curved surface. Tambour can bend to produce a 10-inch radius and can be easily painted or laminated. Tambour is also a term used to describe other woods with bending capability such as maple or cherry wood, so local research is recommended.

task lighting—The spotlighting and highlighting of an exhibit; it puts the light where it really counts and makes items stand out and show up at their very best.

taste—An individual preference; the visual merchandiser must rely on knowledge of the customer's tastes, lifestyle, and attitudes as well as the store's fashion image in determining what is right for the store, the product, the customer, and the location.

tavern chairs—Small chairs, usually with a curved spindle or slatted back, that were used in eighteenth-century New England taverns or inns.

teasers—A theatrical term for panels of fabric or screen that cut off the viewer's eye from what is behind, thereby tempting the viewer to peek at the remainder.

temporary exhibit—The presentation of an item or items that are on loan for a limited time.

terra-cotta—A hard, fired, brownish-orange clay used for pottery and architectural purposes; in food display, terra-cotta lends an earthy quality.

tertiary colors—The colors that result from mixing two secondary colors, in varying degrees.

texture—The surface treatment or "feel." Texture can affect the color of merchandise; it can also suggest familiar symbols by which the display person attempts to explain the merchandise in terms of surrounding materials.

Texture Plus—A supplier of faux surfaces, they use high-density molded polymer to create the look of real brick, stone, wood, bamboo, and metal, without the cost and complicated installation of traditional building materials (https://www.textureplus.com).

theme—A unifying element; for example, "100 Years of Men's Fashions."

thermoplastics—Resins or plastics that can be repeatedly softened by the application of heat. This material is very important in the vacuum forming processes.

thermosetting plastics—Resins or plastics that, once cured and set, either by the application of heat or the addition of chemicals, become infusible and insoluble.

three-part rack—A round rack composed of three separate but equal arcs; usually, the height of each arc is individually adjustable. It is effective for showing separates, coordinates, or assorted colors and styles of a particular item.

three-quarter form—A form that has a body extending to the knees or just below. It can have an adjustable rod and a weighted base. Usually, it has a head, and the legs are parted. It may or may not have arms.

tie-in—A promotional element related to a particular sale event.

tint—A full-value color to which white has been added, creating a lighter, gentler variation of the original; see also **pastel**.

T-joints—T-shaped connectors joining three pieces of tube in one plane to form a long line with a line bisecting it; two extensions at right angles to each other, with a third finger extending up or down.

tone—The mood conveyed by a presentation.

torso form—A headless three-quarter form that comes just to the knees.

trademark—A word, design, or device that identifies a single product or a line of products made by one manufacturer or sold by one company; it is used on goods, packaging, business documents, advertising, promotion, and display.

trade organizations—Industry trade groups that generally focus on advertising, education, and research; most sponsor trade shows once or twice a year. Associations for the visual merchandising and display professionals include NRF, SHOP Association, PAVE, and RDI.

trade shows—Commercial ventures wherein a manufacturer or distributor shows a line of merchandise, introduces a new product or an improvement on an existing one, or exhibits for the sake of goodwill or company image. Often, trade shows are produced in large exhibition halls in which several hundred exhibitors battle for attention in open and exposed areas.

traveling exhibit—A movable display. A traveling exhibit is conceived and designed to be moved from one location to another and to be assembled quickly, with few changes and a minimum of professional assistance.

trays—Small extensions or shaped dishes; they may be shaped compartments that can be added to a shelf or floor unit to separate and hold different items apart but still together on the same unit.

T square—A calibrated ruler with perpendicular crosspiece at one end, forming a T. It is used for drawing straight lines.

T-stand—A display specialty unit: a highlighter or accent piece; small, light, carries a minimal amount of merchandise, and makes big fashion statements.

T-walls—In the store interior, two-sided walls or partitions. T-walls extend from the back or perimeter wall out to the aisle. The flat end of this unit, on the aisle, can be converted into a valuable display space. A panel to cover the end of the unit makes the top stroke of the T. The merchandising wall is the upright of the T.

U

Ultraboard—A brand of display board stronger than foamcore used by visual merchandisers to build displays, signage components, models, and prototypes of their designs. Ultraboard can be used to create a curved display wall unlike other boards.

Upson Board—A compressed paperboard used primarily to make jewelry pads and panels. It resembles a thick ¼-inch cardboard. A soft padding is applied before

velvet or suede fabric is glued neatly onto the surface.

V

vacuum forming process—An extreme form of embossing, using a lightweight, thermoplastic material. The all-important element in the vacuum forming process is the mold.

Valentine's Day—Familiar symbols of this holiday are hearts, Romeo and Juliet, Cupid, cherubs, a bow and arrow, heart-shaped targets, lovers' knots, playing cards showing the king and queen of hearts, and the colors red and pink.

valet—Similar to the costumer, the valet has a heavier and wider hanger, along with a slacks bar, which makes this fixture especially useful for menswear; the hanger and the slacks or skirt bar attachment are adjustable, riding up and down on the vertical rod.

value—The amount of light or dark in a color.

value engineering—A method to evaluate the production process of an object or fixture that ensures the job is produced for the best value, with the appropriate materials using the most affordable process.

variety, or assortment, display—The showing and display of a collection of unrelated items that happen to be in the same store.

vendor shop—A shop within the retail establishment that is a showplace for a particular vendor/manufacturer or brand name. Within the space allocated by the retailer, the vendor creates a distinctive selling environment that complements the product line and projects the product's image. The vendor provides the fixtures, the furnishings, and the signage.

veneers—Thin sheets of wood or laminates that are adhered to a less expensive material called a substrate. Veneers suggest the appearance of real wood or a decorative surface for a fraction of the cost.

vertical blinds—These blinds can be used to mask an open-back window.

vertical line—A line perpendicular to the ground; an upright line that suggests a strong, masculine, dignified, or elegant presentation.

vertical presentation—Parts of an outfit shown one part above the other on a double rod attached to a wall; often tops (jackets, blouses, or shirts) are shown on the top rail, and bottoms (skirts, pants, or slacks) are shown directly below; or, a merchandise presentation in which items are hung on a two- or three-tier floor merchandiser, with the smaller sizes on the top tier and the larger sizes directly below, on the bottom tier.

vignette setting—A suggestion, or partial view, of a realistic setting. Rather than showing a full room, a chair, a drape, and a table and lamp suggest what the complete room would look like.

vinyl—A medium used for a vinyl cut machine that is available in a variety of colors, textures, and translucencies. It is used to create signage and graphic elements in stores on windows and surfaces.

vinyl cut—A signage technique; machine cut lettering that is adhered to window glass and other surfaces to convey branding or information for the shopper.

visible light—The light we see; composed of the whole spectrum of colors, from violet to red.

visual follow-through—A method in the design of a display composition used to direct the viewer's eye by using line, color, repetition, contrast, or proportion.

visual merchandising—Showing merchandise and concepts at their very best, with the end purpose of making a sale.

visual presentation—Display; how the merchandise is arranged to attract the shopper.

visual standards—Criteria established by a brand or a store to ensure a distinctive style and quality for displays and merchandising.

vitrine—A glass-enclosed, shelved cabinet or showcase, often with glass shelves and partitions. A vitrine is usually a decorative piece, sometimes made to look antique; it is used to display small, precious items or accessories.

VMSD (Visual Merchandising and Store Design)—A monthly magazine containing articles relevant to merchandise presentation and store planning as well as dozens of ads for the many elements necessary for the successful installation of windows and interiors. By filling in the numbers on the request card that is inserted at the back of the magazine, the display person is assured a steady flow of brochures, booklets, and illustrative material on new products and designs.

W

wall-mounted signs—Single-face signs or panels that are attached directly to the wall.

wardrobe trunks—A vintage or antique trunk for transporting wardrobe commonly used as a prop or fixture in display. When stood on its side the trunk opens to reveal an area for hanging on one side and several drawers on the other. Wardrobe trunks have inspired many contemporary fixture design solutions.

warm colors—Aggressive, spirited, advancing colors: red, orange, yellow, pink, rust, brown, peach.

waterfalled—Merchandise presentation in which items are placed on hangers in descending order, on a sloping arm, off of a wall or freestanding floor fixture. The evenly spaced hooks, knobs, or notches keep the hangers from sliding down.

wayfinding—A directional signage system used to assist shoppers in finding their way around the store.

website—An internet platform. In this book it is referred to as an online portfolio or place for designers to represent themselves. It has replaced the need for a physical portfolio.

weeding—In the vinyl cut, the process of weeding refers to peeling and removing the unwanted part of the design, around letters such as the inside of the O, R, P, and B for example.

wiggle board—Bendable plywood made from hardwood with the layers all running in one direction; this gives bendability to the panel and can be applied on a curved radius.

wings—In fixture design, wings are vertical panels that protrude off a fixture to introduce additional brand or product information. They are commonly positioned in the middle of a gondola or an endcap fixture.

wood fixtures—Fixtures or merchandisers constructed mainly of wood.

X

X-joints—Joints formed by four lengths of pipe made into a cross or X shape.

Y

yacht chairs—A type of director's chair; wood-framed chairs with a changeable canvas seat and back, and legs that scissor front and rear. They are usually available in a wide range of colored canvas accessories and can provide the desired ambiance for active sportswear.

young man mannequin—A size 16, 18, or 20—"preppie sizes."

Z

zones—Zones differentiate areas of priority or those parts of the selling floor that are premium. An area within a display that is elevated or most evident to the consumer's viewing point is also considered a priority zone.

Index